Harper College Library

3 2158 00466 4046

P9-BZT-895

AUG 2008

DATE DUE

GAYLORD   PRINTED IN U.S.A.

Software Evolution

Tom Mens · Serge Demeyer

Editors

Software Evolution

 Springer

HARPER COLLEGE LIBRARY
PALATINE, ILLINOIS 60067

QA
76.76
.D47
S658
2008

Tom Mens
Université de Mons-Hainaut
Institut d'Informatique
Avenue du champ de Mars 6
7000 Mons
Belgium
tom.mens@umh.ac.be

Serge Demeyer
Universiteit Antwerpen
Dept. Mathematics and Computer Science
Middelheimlaan 1
2020 Antwerpen
Belgium
serge.demeyer@ua.ac.be

ISBN 978-3-540-76439-7   e-ISBN 978-3-540-76440-3

DOI 10.1007/978-3-540-76440-3

ACM Computing Classification (1998): D.2.7, D.2.9, K.6.3

Library of Congress Control Number: 2007938804

© Springer-Verlag Berlin Heidelberg 2008

This work is subject to copyright. All rights are reserved, whether the whole or part of the material is concerned, specifically the rights of translation, reprinting, reuse of illustrations, recitation, broadcasting, reproduction on microfilm or in any other way, and storage in data banks. Duplication of this publication or parts thereof is permitted only under the provisions of the German Copyright Law of September 9, 1965, in its current version, and permission for use must always be obtained from Springer. Violations are liable for prosecution under the German Copyright Law.

The use of general descriptive names, registered names, trademarks, etc. in this publication does not imply, even in the absence of a specific statement, that such names are exempt from the relevant protective laws and regulations and therefore free for general use.

Typesetting and Production: LE-TEX Jelonek, Schmidt & Vöckler GbR, Leipzig, Germany
Cover Design: KünkelLopka, Heidelberg

Printed on acid-free paper

9 8 7 6 5 4 3 2 1

springer.com

HARPER COLLEGE LIBRARY
PALATINE, ILLINOIS 60067

To Inge, Sara and Paulien,
for being there – Tom Mens

To Ann, Sara, Niels and Jens,
for illustrating the value of life – Serge Demeyer

Foreword

by Mehdi Jazayeri

Faculty of Informatics, University of Lugano, Switzerland
Distributed Systems Group, Technical University of Vienna

The phenomenon of software evolution was observed back in the 1970s when the first large software systems were being developed, and it attracted renewed attention in the 1990s. Software evolution is now a common phrase and an accepted research area in software engineering. There are conferences and workshops devoted to the topic, and evolution papers appear frequently in the traditional software engineering conferences and journals. The 2004 ACM/IEEE Software Engineering Curriculum Guidelines list software evolution as one of ten key areas of software engineering education. And there are several research groups and international networks working on software evolution. As perhaps may be expected, there are diverging research efforts in sub-areas of software evolution, spanning theoretical studies, empirical studies, tools, visualization, and so on.

Since the classic and insightful work of Lehman and Belady [320], "software evolution" has been accepted as a phenomenon worth studying and one that we acknowledge poses serious problems to software projects. The problems are complex because they involve many dimensions, affecting, among others, all phases of the software process, managerial and economic aspects, and programming languages and environments. Further, as software engineering advances and new technologies (e.g., Web applications) and processes (e.g., open source) are introduced, software evolution faces different problems and challenges. At the same time, some new advances (e.g. agile and model-driven processes) enable novel solutions to software evolution.

Evolution in general parlance implies that something has changed for the better. The Merriam-Webster Dictionary defines evolution as "a process of continuous change from a lower, simpler, or worse to a higher, more complex, or better state," which captures our intuitive notion of something improving. With software, evolution is multi-faceted because certainly according to some metric the software gets better, for example it acquires a new feature or its performance improves or it is ported to a new platform. Unfortunately, most improvements come with some deterioration in some other dimension, for example, size of software or its performance or its structure.

In biology, the traditional area of evolution, evolution deals with species. Is there something analogous to "species" when we talk about software? The answer is definitely yes. The species are the high-level models that we use to describe (aspects of) software. An architectural description, in fact, describes a whole species of software systems. The family architecture (or product line) approach to software development makes this explicit by capturing a whole family (species) of systems in terms of their commonalities and differences. If evolution does take place in software, we can hope that it occurs at these meta-levels, where new architectures are created as improvements to previous architectures, leading to evolved species. Individual elements in the family certainly change over time but this change is hardly evolutionary in the sense that it leads to long-term improvement. What we do know about software and even Lehman's laws of evolution is that any individual software system will eventually reach an old age when it is no longer cost-effective to modify it and it is better to retire it. But even when we retire a software product, the associated knowledge about that product, captured in higher level models such as requirements and specifications lives on and influences the evolution of the species. Thus, understanding and capturing the way software evolves offers a fascinating and rich area of study.

With this wide range of issues involved in software evolution, where would a researcher new to the field turn to for an introduction and comprehensive overview of the state of the art? This book attempts to be that source. For example, this book is a good starting point for a PhD student looking for a research topic. It can also form the basis for a seminar course on software evolution. The book covers most areas of software evolution and many current problems and representative research approaches. I recommend the book to any researcher interested in software evolution.

The book, however, has value beyond the world of research. Because of the key role that evolution plays in software engineering, knowledge of the problems, approaches and solutions in software evolution is useful to anyone involved in software engineering. Thus, if you are a software engineer, or software engineering researcher, interested or just curious about what happens to software once it is developed, or how to develop software that is evolvable, this book offers you plenty of insights.

September 2007   *Mehdi Jazayeri*

Preface

In October 2002, on a cold wintery Monday in Antwerp, we kicked off the RELEASE network, a research network aiming to establish "Research Links to Explore and Advance Software Evolution". This research network (funded by the European Science Foundation) was an attempt to intensify the collaboration between a number of European research groups active in the field of software evolution. At that time, software evolution was steadily becoming a subject of serious academic study, because more and more researchers started to recognise that building software that lasts is one of the key challenges for our society in general and for the software engineering community in particular. The RELEASE network succeeded in fostering a community of European researchers who continue to meet on a regular basis, despite ceasing of funding in 2005. The book you are holding right now is one of the products of this continued activity and we sincerely hope that it will inspire you to become part of the active software evolution community as well.

What Is this Book About?

This book is a collection of chapters written and peer reviewed by renowned experts in the field of software evolution. The book does not cover all research topics in software evolution—given the wealth of information in this field that would be an impossible task. Instead, we focus on novel trends in software evolution research and its relation with other emerging disciplines such as model-driven software engineering, service-oriented software development, aspect-oriented software development. Also, we do not restrict ourselves to the evolution of source code only, but address evolution of other equally important software artefacts such as databases and database schemas, design models, software architectures, and so on. As such, this book provides a representative selection of the research topics under study in this field. Even better, it also demonstrates the diverse ways on how to conduct research in this field, so you will see various examples of tools, case studies (mainly open-source systems), empirical validation and formal models. All contributing authors did their very best to provide a broad overview of the related work, contribute to a comprehensive glossary and a list of acronyms used within the community, and—last but not least—collect a list of books, journals, web-sites, standards and conferences that together represent the community. So reading this book should give you a head start when diving into the field of software evolution.

As such, we hope that this book will become a key reference in the field, providing a basis for the next generation of software evolution researchers.

Who Should Read this Book?

This book is of interest to everyone working in the field of software engineering and wishing to acquire more knowledge on the state-of-the-art in software evolution, software maintenance and re-engineering. In particular, we target this book to researchers, teachers, students and practitioners that need up-to-date information on this very important research field.

So, whether you are a PhD researcher exploring a research topic, a student writing a master's thesis, a teacher in need of an overview, a practitioner looking for the state-of-the-art, or if you are simply curious about what the field of software evolution has to offer, this should be the book for you.

Why this Book?

Software has become omnipresent and indispensable in our information-based society. Almost all devices, machines and artefacts surrounding us incorporate software to some extent. The numerous organisations, businesses and enterprises we face on a daily basis could not function without software. As such, software is vital to our society and consequently we—the software engineering community—should take up our responsibility to produce reliable software. For a long, long time, reliable software was seen as software "without bugs". As a result, most of the software engineering research effort has concentrated on preventing, detecting and repairing mistakes in various stages of software development. However, more and more, reliable software has come to mean "easy to adapt". Indeed today's global society, with its extreme complexity and diversity imposes constant pressure to change ... to adapt. Hence all the software that surrounds us is forced to keep pace or is bound to be replaced by something else ... something new.

Software evolution is the subdomain of the software engineering discipline that investigates ways to adapt software to the ever-changing user requirements and operating environment (i.e., it addresses the *How?* question). However, software evolution also studies the change process itself, analysing remnants of the software (for instance in version repositories) to extract trends, make predictions or understand the very nature of the software evolution phenomenon itself (i.e., it explores the *What* and *Why?* questions). With the recent interest in agile software development, finding good answers for the *How?* question is necessary. On the other hand, the emergence of open-source software development with its sheer unlimited access to a wealth of data has provided an extra opportunity to address the *What and Why?* questions in a scientific way. Consequently, research in software evolution has seen a recent boost, and this book provides an up-to-date view on the ideas emerging from our research labs.

Acknowledgements

We would like to thank all persons that have contributed to this book, either directly or indirectly. There are many people that we are indebted to:

- The contributors of the chapters of this book;
- The Springer staff (in particular, Ralf Gerstner and Ulrike Stricker);
- Mehdi Jazayeri, who was so kind to write a very nice foreword for this book;
- David Notkin, Michael Godfrey, Václav Rajlich and Anne Keller, who spent their precious time to review this book in its entirety, and provided numerous suggestions for improvement;
- Joris Van Geet, Pieter Van Gorp, Filip Van Rysselberghe, Bart Van Rompaey, Bart Du Bois, Matthias Rieger and Hans Schippers, who provided valuable feedback on several chapters of this book;
- Last but not least, we would like to thank you, reader of this book.

Many of the results that are published in this book have been achieved in the context of research projects or research collaborations. In particular we would like to mention:

- The Scientific Network "Research Links to Explore and Advance Software Evolution" (RELEASE), financed by the *European Science Foundation* (ESF) from July 2002 to December 2005.
- The ongoing ERCIM Working Group on Software Evolution, a network of research institutes from all over the world working on the topic of software evolution, supported by the *European Research Consortium on Informatics and Mathematics* (ERCIM) since December 2004.
- The Interuniversity Attraction Poles Programme (IUAP) on "Modelling, Verification and Evolution of Software" (MOVES), financed by the *Belgian State - Belgian Science Policy* from January 2007 to December 2011.
- The Belgian FRFC project "Research Centre on Structural Software Improvement", financed by the *Fondation Nationale de Recherche Scientifique* (FNRS - Belgium) from January 2005 to December 2008.
- The Swiss joint research project "Controlling Software Evolution" (COSE), financed by the *Swiss National Science Foundation* from July 2005 to September 2007
- The Swiss joint research project "Multi-dimensional Navigation Spaces for Software Evolution" (EvoSpaces), financed by the *Hasler Foundation* from January 2006 to December 2007.

- The German "Bauhaus" Project on Software Architecture, Software Reengineering, and Program Understanding (see www.bauhaus-stuttgart.de)
- The European Leg2Net project: "From Legacy Systems to Services in the Net", supported by Marie Curie Fellowships for the Transfer of Knowledge - Industry Academia Partnership (MTK1-CT-2004-003169).
- The European SENSORIA project: "Software Engineering for Service-Oriented Overlay Computers", supported by the Information Society Technologies programme - Future Emerging Technologies (IST-2005-16004).
- The Dutch "Reconstructor" project sponsored by the NWO Jacquard programme, project number 638.001.408.

We hope you enjoy reading, and we welcome any comments you may have on the contents, structure or quality of this book.

Mons and Antwerp,   *Tom Mens*
September 2007   *Serge Demeyer*

Contents

List of Contributors

Luis Andrade
ATX Software
Rua Saraiva de Carvalho 207C
1350-300 Lisboa
Portugal
luis.andrade@atxsoftware.com

Olivier Barais
Université de Rennes 1
IRIA/INRIA Triskell project
Campus de Beaulieu
35042 Rennes Cédex
France
barais@irisa.fr

Magiel Bruntink
CWI
P.O. Box 94079
1090 GB, Amsterdam
   and
Software Engineering Research Group
Technische Universiteit Delft
Mekelweg 4, 2628 CD, Delft
The Netherlands
Magiel.Bruntink@cwi.nl

Andrea Capiluppi
Department of Computing
and Informatics
Faculty of Technology
University of Lincoln
Brayford Pool, Lincoln LN6 7TS
United Kingdom
acapiluppi@lincoln.ac.uk

Anthony Cleve
PReCISE Research Centre
Laboratory of Database Engineering
University of Namur
Rue Grandgagnage 21, 5000 Namur
Belgium
acl@info.fundp.ac.be

Rui Correia
Department of Computer Science
University of Leicester
University Road LE1 7RH
Leicester
United Kingdom
   and
ATX Software
Rua Saraiva de Carvalho 207C
1350-300 Lisboa
Portugal
rmc20@mcs.le.ac.uk

Marco D'Ambros
Faculty of Informatics
University of Lugano
Via G. Buffi 13, 6904 Lugano
Switzerland
marco.dambros@lu.unisi.ch

Serge Demeyer
Lab on Re-Engineering (LORE)
Department of Mathematics
and Computer Science
Universiteit Antwerpen
Middelheimlaan 1, 2020 Antwerpen
Belgium
serge.demeyer@ua.ac.be

Laurence Duchien
Université de Lille 1
LIFL/INRIA ADAM project
Cité Scientifique
59655 Villeneuve d'Ascq Cedex
France
duchien@lifl.fr

Mohammad El-Ramly
Computer Science Department
Cairo University
Egypt
m.elramly@fci-cu.edu.eg

Juan Fernandez-Ramil
Computing Department
and Centre for Research in Computing
The Open University
Walton Hall, Milton Keynes MK7 6AA
United Kingdom
j.f.ramil@open.ac.uk

Harald Gall
Software Engineering Group
Universität Zürich
Binzmühlestrasse 14
8050 Zürich
Switzerland
gall@ifi.unizh.ch

Jean-Luc Hainaut
PReCISE Research Centre
Laboratory of Database Engineering
University of Namur
Rue Grandgagnage 21, 5000 Namur
Belgium
jlh@info.fundp.ac.be

Reiko Heckel
Department of Computer Science
University of Leicester
University Road LE1 7RH, Leicester
United Kingdom
reiko@mcs.le.ac.uk

Jean Henrard
REVER s.a.
Boulevard Tirou 130, 6000 Charleroi
Belgium
jean.henrard@rever.eu

Jean-Marc Hick
REVER s.a.
Boulevard Tirou 130, 6000 Charleroi
Belgium
jean-marc.hick@rever.eu

Rainer Koschke
Fachbereich 03
Universität Bremen
Postfach 33 04 40, 28334 Bremen
Germany
koschke@informatik.uni-bremen.de

Georgios Koutsoukos
Department of Computer Science
University of Leicester
University Road LE1 7RH, Leicester
United Kingdom
georgios.koutsoukos@atxsoftware.com

Michele Lanza
Faculty of Informatics
University of Lugano
Via G. Buffi 13, 6904 Lugano
Switzerland
michele.lanza@unisi.ch

Julia Lawall
DIKU
University of Copenhagen
2100 Copenhagen
Denmark
julia@diku.dk

Anne Françoise Le Meur
Université de Lille 1
LIFL/INRIA ADAM project
Cité Scientifique
59655 Villeneuve d'Ascq Cedex
France
lemeur@lifl.fr

Angela Lozano
Computing Department
and Centre for Research in Computing
The Open University
Walton Hall, Milton Keynes MK7 6AA
United Kingdom
a.lozano-rodriguez@open.ac.uk

Carlos Matos
Department of Computer Science
University of Leicester
University Road LE1 7RH, Leicester
United Kingdom
    and
ATX Software
Rua Saraiva de Carvalho 207C
1350-300 Lisboa
Portugal
cmm22@mcs.le.ac.uk

Kim Mens
Département d'Ingénierie Informatique
Université catholique de Louvain
Place Sainte Barbe 2
1348 Louvain-la-Neuve
Belgium
kim.mens@uclouvain.be

Tom Mens
Institut d'Informatique
Université de Mons-Hainaut
Av. du Champ de Mars 6, 7000 Mons
Belgium
tom.mens@umh.ac.be

Leon Moonen
Software Engineering Research Group
Technische Universiteit Delft
Mekelweg 4, 2628 CD, Delft
The Netherlands
leon.moonen@computer.org

Nachiappan Nagappan
Microsoft Research
Redmond, Washington
USA
nachin@microsoft.com

Martin Pinzger
Department of Informatics
Universität Zürich
Winterthurerstrasse 190, 8057 Zürich
Switzerland
pinzger@ifi.unizh.ch

Tom Tourwé
Department of Software Engineering
and Technology
Eindhoven University of Technology
P.O. Box 513, 5600 MB Eindhoven
The Netherlands
t.tourwe@tue.nl

Arie van Deursen
Software Engineering Research Group
Technische Universiteit Delft
Mekelweg 4, 2628 CD, Delft
    and
CWI
P.O. Box 94079, 1090 GB, Amsterdam
The Netherlands
Arie.van.Deursen@cwi.nl

Michel Wermelinger
Computing Department
and Centre for Research in Computing
The Open University
Walton Hall, Milton Keynes MK7 6AA
United Kingdom
m.a.wermelinger@open.ac.uk

Andy Zaidman
Software Engineering Research Group
Technische Universiteit Delft
Mekelweg 4, 2628 CD, Delft
The Netherlands
A.E.Zaidman@tudelft.nl

Andreas Zeller
Dept. of Informatics
Saarland University
Postfach 15 11 50, 66041 Saarbrücken
Germany
zeller@cs.uni-sb.de

Thomas Zimmermann
Department of Computer Science
University of Calgary
2500 University Drive NW Calgary
Alberta, T2N 1N4 Canada
tz@acm.org

1

Introduction and Roadmap:
History and Challenges of Software Evolution

Tom Mens

University of Mons-Hainaut, Belgium

Summary. The ability to evolve software rapidly and reliably is a major challenge for software engineering. In this introductory chapter we start with a historic overview of the research domain of software evolution. Next, we briefly introduce the important research themes in software evolution, and identify research challenges for the years to come. Finally, we provide a roadmap of the topics treated in this book, and explain how the various chapters are related.

1.1 The History of Software Evolution

In early 1967, there was an awareness of the rapidly increasing importance and impact of software systems in many activities of society. In addition, as a result of the many problems faced in software manufacturing, there was a general belief that available techniques should become less ad hoc, and instead based on theoretical foundations and practical disciplines that are established in traditional branches of engineering. These became the main driving factors for organising the first conference on Software Engineering in 1968 [391]. The goal of this conference, organised by the NATO Science Committee, was "the establishment and use of sound engineering principles in order to obtain reliable, efficient and economically viable software". Among the many activities of software engineering, *maintenance* was considered as a post-production activity, i.e., after the delivery and deployment of the software product.

This view was shared by Royce, who proposed in 1970 the well-known *waterfall life-cycle* process for software development [446]. In this process model, that was inspired by established engineering principles, the *maintenance* phase is the final phase of the life-cycle of a software system, after its deployment. Only bug fixes and minor adjustments to the software are supposed to take place during that phase. This classical view on software engineering has long governed the industrial practice in software development and is still in use today by several companies. It even became a part of the IEEE 1219 Standard for Software Maintenance [239], which defines software maintenance as "the modification of a software product *after delivery* to

T. Mens, S. Demeyer (eds.), *Software Evolution.*
DOI 10.1007/978-3-540-76440-3, © Springer 2008

correct faults, to improve performance or other attributes, or to adapt the product to a modified environment."

It took a while before software engineers became aware of the inherent limitations of this software process model, namely the fact that the separation in phases was too strict and inflexible, and that it is often unrealistic to assume that the requirements are known before starting the software design phase. In many cases, the requirements continue to change during the entire lifetime of the software project. In addition, knowledge gained during the later phases may need to be fed back to the earlier phases.

Therefore, in the late seventies, a first attempt towards a more evolutionary process model was proposed by Yau with the so-called *change mini-cycle* [559] (see Fig. 1.1). In this process, important new activities, such as change impact analysis and change propagation were identified to accommodate the fact that software changes are rarely isolated.

Also in the seventies, Manny Lehman started to formulate his, now famous, *laws of software evolution*. The postulated laws were based on earlier work carried out by Lehman to understand the change process being applied to IBM's OS 360 operating system [317, 318]. His original findings were confirmed in later studies involving other software systems [320].

This was probably the first time that the term *software evolution* (or program evolution) was deliberately used the stress the difference with the post-deployment activity of software maintenance. To stress this difference even more, Lehman coined the term *E-type software* to denote programs that must be evolved because they "operate in or address a problem or activity of the real world". As such, changes in the real world will affect the software and require adaptations to it.

Nevertheless, it took until the nineties until the term software evolution gained widespread acceptance, and the research on software evolution started to become popular [24, 403]. This also lead to the acceptance of so-called *evolutionary processes* such as Gilb's *evolutionary development* [200], Boehm's *spiral model* [71] and Bennett and Rajlich's *staged model* [57].

The staged process model, visualised in Fig. 1.2, is interesting in that it explicitly takes into account the inevitable problem of *software aging* [410]. After the initial stage of development of a first running version, the evolution stage allows for any kind of modification to the software, as long as the architectural integrity remains

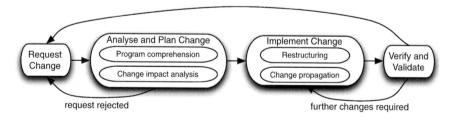

Fig. 1.1. The staged process model for evolution (adapted from [559] ©[1978] IEEE)

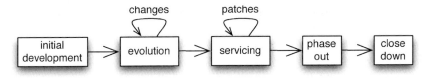

Fig. 1.2. The staged process model for evolution (adapted from [57] ©[2000] ACM)

preserved. If this is no longer the case, there is a loss of evolvability (also referred to as *decay*) and the servicing stage starts. During this stage, only small patches can be applied to keep the software up and running. If even such small patches become too costly to carry out, the phase-out stage starts, leading to ultimate close down of the system. If the system, despite of its degraded quality, is still valuable to its various stakeholders, it is called a *legacy system*. In that case, it may be wise to *migrate* to a new system that offers the similar or extended functionality, without exhibiting the poor quality of the legacy system. The planning to migrate to such a new system should be done as soon as possible, preferably during the servicing stage.

Software evolution is also a crucial ingredient of so-called *agile software development* [119, 351] processes, of which *extreme programming (XP)* [50] is probably the most famous proponent. In brief, agile software development is a lightweight iterative and incremental (evolutionary) approach to software development that is performed in a highly collaborative manner and explicitly accommodates the changing needs of its stakeholders, even late in the development cycle, because this offers a considerable competitive advantage for the customer. In many ways, agile methods constitute a return to iterative and incremental development as practiced early in the history of software development, before the widespread use of the waterfall model [312].

Nowadays, software evolution has become a very active and well-respected field of research in software engineering, and the terms *software evolution* and *software maintenance* are often used as synonyms. For example, the international ISO/IEC 14764 standard for software maintenance [242], acknowledges the importance of pre-delivery aspects of maintenance such as planning. Similarly, the Software Engineering Body of Knowledge (SWEBOK) [2] acknowledges the need for supporting maintenance in the pre-delivery as well as the post-delivery stages, and considers the following evolution-related research themes as being crucial activities in software maintenance: software comprehension, reverse engineering, testing, impact analysis, cost estimation, software quality, software measurement, process models, software configuration management, and re-engineering. These activities will be discussed in more detail in Section 1.2.

In this book, we will continue to use the term software evolution as opposed to maintenance, because of the negative connotation of the latter term. Maintenance seems to indicate that the software itself is deteriorating, which is not the case. It is changes in the environment or user needs that make it necessary to adapt the software.

1.2 Research Themes in Software Evolution

In this Section we provide an overview of some of the important research themes in software evolution. The various chapters of this book will explore some of these themes in more depth. Of course, it is not the aim of the book to provide complete and detailed coverage of all these themes. Instead, we have tried to offer a selection of important issues that are actively pursued by the research community. They have been identified, among others in the visionary articles by Bennett and Rajlich [57] and Mens et al. [371]. Therefore, in this section, we summarise some of the most important challenges and future research directions in software evolution, as reported in these articles.

1.2.1 Dimensions of Software Evolution

There are two prevalent views on software evolution, often referred to as the *what and why* versus the *how* perspectives [322].

The *what and why* view focuses on software evolution as a scientific discipline. It studies the *nature* of the software evolution phenomenon, and seeks to understand its driving factor, its impact, and so on. This is the view that is primarily taken in [338]. An important insight that has been gained in this line of research is that the evolution process is a multi-loop, multi-level, multi-agent feedback system that cannot be treated in isolation. It requires interdisciplinary research involving non-technical aspects such as human psychology, social interaction, complexity theory, organisational aspects, legislation and many more.

The *how* view focuses on software evolution as an engineering discipline. It studies the more pragmatic aspects that aid the software developer or project manager in his day-to-day tasks. Hence, this view primarily focuses on technology, methods, tools and activities that provide the *means* to direct, implement and control software evolution.

It is the latter view that is followed throughout most of the chapters in this book. Nevertheless, it remains necessary to develop new theories and mathematical models, and to carry out empirical research to increase understanding of software evolution, and to invest in research that tries to bridge the gap between the what and the how of software evolution.

As another "dimension" of software evolution, we can consider the types of changes that are being performed. Based on earlier studies by Lientz and Swanson [329], the ISO/IEC standard for software maintenance [242] proposes four categories of maintenance:

- *Perfective maintenance* is any modification of a software product after delivery to improve performance or maintainability.
- *Corrective maintenance* is the reactive modification of a software product performed after delivery to correct discovered faults.
- *Adaptive maintenance* is the modification of a software product performed after delivery to keep a computer program usable in a changed or changing environment.

- *Preventive maintenance* refers to software modifications performed for the purpose of preventing problems before they occur.

For completeness, we also mention the work of Chapin et al. [109], who further extended this classification, based on objective evidence of maintainers' activities ascertainable from observation, and including non-technical issues such as documentation, consulting, training and so on. A related article that is worthwhile mentioning is the work by Buckley et al. [94], in which a taxonomy of software change is presented based on various dimensions that characterise or influence the mechanisms of change.

1.2.2 Reverse and Re-Engineering

An important theme within the research domain of software evolution is *reverse engineering* [112]. This activity is needed when trying to understand the architecture or behaviour of a large software system, while the only reliable information is the source code. This may be the case because documentation and design documents are unavailable, or have become inconsistent with respect to the code because they have not been updated. Reverse engineering aims at building higher-level, more abstract, software models from the source code. *Program comprehension* or *program understanding* are activities that try to make sense of the wealth of information that reverse engineering produces, by building mental models of the overall software architecture, structure and behaviour. Program comprehension also includes activities such as task modelling, user interface issues, and many others.

Reverse engineering can also be regarded as the initial phase in the process of *software reengineering* [23]. Reengineering is necessary when we are confronted with *legacy systems*. These are systems that are still valuable, but are notoriously difficult to maintain [149]. Following the terminology used in the staged life cycle model of Fig. 1.2, we consider these systems to be in the servicing stage.

The goal of reengineering is thus to come to a new software system that is more evolvable, and possibly has more functionality, than the original software system. The reeengineering process is typically composed of three activities, as captured by the so-called *horseshoe model* visualised in Fig. 1.3 [271]. First, reverse engineering may be necessary when the technological platform of the software system (language, tools, machines, operating system) is outdated, or when the original developers are no longer available. This activity is typically followed by a phase of *software restructuring* [22] in which we try to improve crucial aspects of the system. Finally, in a *forward engineering* phase we build a new running system based on the new, restructured, model.

The topic of reengineering is very important and relevant to industry, and therefore the second part of this book will be entirely devoted to it. Chapter 5 will focus on the reengineering of object-oriented software systems. Chapter 6 will address the need for, and means to, migrate data when reengineering large information systems. Chapter 7 discusses how to reengineer legacy systems into service-oriented systems.

Another very important research topic in reengineering research is the quest for new and better visualisation techniques that aid in a better program comprehension,

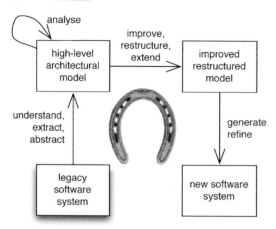

analyse

improve,
restructure,
extend

high-level
architectural
model

improved
restructured
model

understand,
extract,
abstract

generate
refine

legacy
software
system

new software
system

Fig. 1.3. The horseshoe process model for reengineering

as well as a better understanding of the evolution of software. Such visualisation techniques are explored in Chapter 3.

1.2.3 Incremental Change Techniques

In the change mini-cycle proposed by Yau et al. [559], and visualised in Fig. 1.1, a number of important activities related to the change process become apparent.

During the planning phase, program comprehension is of course essential to understand what parts of the software will be affected by a requested change. In addition, the extent or impact of the change needs to be assessed by resorting to *change impact analysis* techniques [74]. By predicting all parts of the system that are likely to be affected by a change, they give an estimation of how costly the change will be, as well as the potential risk involved in making the change. This analysis is then used to decide whether or not it is worthwhile to carry out the change.

Because of the fact that a change may have a non-local impact, support is needed for what is referred to as *change propagation* [424, 425]. It is necessary when a change to one part of a software system requires other system parts that depend on it to be changed as well. These dependent system parts can on their turn require changes in other system parts. In this way, a single change to one system part may lead to a propagation of changes to be made throughout the entire software system.

During the implementation phase, it may turn out that the change cannot be implemented directly, and that a *restructuring* or *refactoring* of the software is required first in order to accommodate the requested change. The goal is thus to improve the software structure or architecture without changing the behaviour [21, 183].

During the validation and verification phase, techniques to revalidate the software after having performed changes are crucial in order to ensure that the system integrity has not been compromised. *Regression testing* is one of those techniques [66]. Rather than repeating all tests for each new software release (which would be too costly, take too much time, and consume too many resources), a carefully selected subset of the tests is executed to verify that the changes did not have inadvertent effects. Chapter 8 of this book provides an excellent overview of software testing, and its interplay with software evolution.

1.2.4 Managerial Issues

Managerial issues are equally crucial to software evolution. Despite this fact, it remains a challenge to increase awareness among executives and project managers about the importance and inevitability of software evolution. Indeed, various studies and surveys indicate that over 80% of the total maintenance effort is used for non-corrective actions [1, 416]. In addition, other studies indicate that software maintenance accounts for at least 50% of the total software production cost, and sometimes even exceeds 90% [329, 457, 296].

According to Lehman, software evolution problems start to appear when there are at least two management levels involved in the software production process. This is confirmed by Brooks [85], who calls this the *large program problem*. A very important managerial issue has to do with the *economics of software evolution* [72]. It turns out that, in many cases, the reason for evolving software is non-technical. More specifically, it is an economic decision, driven by marketing or other reasons.

The main challenge is therefore to develop better predictive models, based on empirical studies, for measuring and estimating the cost and effort of software maintenance and evolution activities with a higher accuracy [261, 466, 427, 177]. Similar techniques may also be useful to measure the cost-effectiveness of regression testing [444].

Another point of attention for managers is the need for *software quality assurance*. If proper support for measuring quality is available, this can provide crucial information to determine whether the software quality is degrading, and to take corrective actions if this turns out to be the case. Numerous software metrics have been proposed, studied and validated as measures of software quality characteristics such as complexity, cohesion, coupling, size and many others [83, 39, 171, 231].

Besides metrics, other more heuristic approaches may be used to detect "bad smells" or other indicators of poor-quality software. For example, Chapter 2 of this book studies techniques to detect and remove software redundancies and code clones, which are generally considered to be an indication of poor quality. Chapter 4 analyses software failures stored in a bug repository to predict and improve the software quality over time.

1.2.5 The Software Process

An important area of research is to find the software process model that is most appropriate to facilitate software evolution. In Section 1.1 we already introduced a number of such process models. The IEEE standard for software maintenance [239] and the ISO/IEC standard for software maintenance [242] also propose such a maintenance process model.

It is important to observe that, due to the fact that the activity of software evolution is a continuous feedback process [338], the chosen software process model itself is likely to be subject to evolution. The research area of *software process improvement* aims to reduce cost, effort and time-to-market, to increase productivity and reliability, or to affect any other relevant properties. Software process improvement can be based on theory or empirical industrial case studies [208].

As software systems become larger and more complex, and are being developed in a collaborative and distributed way, it becomes inevitable to resort to dedicated *software configuration management* tools. Among others, they provide automated support for the change process, they allow for software *versioning* and *merging*, and they offer procedures (verification, validation, certification) for ensuring the quality of each software release. Even today, research in this area is continuing in order to advance the state-of-the-art.

Another aspect of software process improvement is the exploration and introduction of novel development paradigms such as agile software development [119, 351], aspect-oriented software development [247], model-driven software development [474], service-oriented architectures [393], and many more. All of these development paradigms claim to improve software development and to lead to higher productivity, higher quality, and more adaptable and maintainable software. Some of these claims are investigated in Chapter 9 for aspect-oriented development.

Of particular interest is the open source movement, which has provided a novel, strongly collaborative way of developing and evolving software. The question arises whether this style of software development is subject to the same laws that govern the evolution of traditional software development approaches [318]. This topic is under active study [206, 481, 461] and will be addressed in Chapter 11 of this book.

1.2.6 Model Evolution

One of the main difficulties of software evolution is that all artefacts produced and used during the entire software life-cycle are subject to changes, ranging from early requirements over analysis and design documents, to source code and executable code. This fact automatically spawns many subdisciplines in the research domain of software evolution, some of which are listed below:

Requirements evolution. The main objectives of *requirements engineering* are defining the purpose of a software system that needs to be implemented. Requirements evolve because requirements engineers and users cannot predict all possible uses of a system, because not all needs and (often mutually conflicting) goals of the various stakeholders can be taken into account, and because the environment in which the software is deployed frequently changes as well. Because the topic of requirements evolution is not covered in this book, we direct the reader to [571, 570, 191] for more information.

Architecture evolution. Based on an (initial) description of the software requirements, the overall software architecture (or high-level design) and the corresponding (low-level) technical design of the system can be specified. These are inevitably subject to evolution as well. The topic of architectural evolution is explored in detail in Chapter 10. The related problem of evolving software product families is not covered in this book, but we refer to [253, 252] for an in-depth treatment of this topic.

Data evolution. In information systems and other data-intensive software systems it is essential to have a clear and precise description of the database schema. Chapter 6 explores in detail how to evolve and migrate such schemas.

Runtime evolution. Many commercial software systems that are deployed by large companies need to be constantly available. Halting the software system to make changes cannot be afforded. Therefore, techniques are needed to change the software while it keeps on running. This very challenging problem is known under a variety of terms, including *runtime evolution, runtime reconfiguration, dynamic adaptation* and *dynamic upgrading* [297, 284].

Service-oriented architectures (SOA) provide a new paradigm in which a user-oriented approach to software is taken [162]. The software is developed in terms of which services are needed by particular users, and these users should be able to easily add, remove or adapt services to their needs. While this approach has many similarities with the component-oriented approach [486], services are only bound together at runtime, whereas components are statically (i.e., at design time) composed together. A service-oriented approach thus promises to be inherently more flexible than what is available today. This is crucial, especially in e-commerce applications, where rapid and frequent change is a necessity in order to respond to, and survive in, a highly competitive market. Chapter 7 of this book will be devoted to the migration towards service-oriented architectures.

Language evolution. When looking at languages (whether it be programming, modelling of formal specification languages), a number of research directions come to mind. The first one is the issue of co-evolution between software and the language that is used to represent it. Both are subject to evolution, albeit at different speed [167]. The second challenge is to provide more and better support for evolution in the context of multi-language software systems. A third challenge is to improve the design of languages to make them more robust to evolution (e.g., traits [451]). This challenge has always been the main driver of research in design of new computer languages. Unfortunately, every new programming paradigm promises to improve the software development process but introduces its own maintenance problems. This was the case for object-oriented programming (where the inheritance hierarchy needs to be mastered and kept under control when evolving software), aspect-oriented programming (where aspects need to be evolved next to the base code, see Chapter 9 for more details), component-oriented programming, and so on. In general, every new language or technology should always be evaluated in the light of its potential impact on the software's ability to evolve.

Interestingly, when starting to study evolution of software artefacts different from source code, new challenges arise that need to be dealt with, regardless of the type of software artefact under consideration. For example, we need techniques that ensure a *traceability* link between software artefacts at all different levels of abstraction, ranging from very high-level requirements documents to low-level source code [16].

In presence of many different types of software artefacts that co exist, we also need *inconsistency management* and *consistency maintenance* techniques to control the overall consistency of the software system [471], as well as techniques for *co-evolution* and *incremental synchronisation* of all related software artefacts [363].

1.3 Roadmap

The remainder of the book is structured into three parts, each containing at least three chapters. All chapters provide a detailed overview of relevant research literature.

Part I of the book, called *Understanding and Improving Software Evolution* is about understanding software evolution by analysing version repositories and release histories, and improving software evolution by removing software redundancies and fixing bugs:

- In Chapter 2, Koschke discusses and compares various state-of-the-art techniques that can be used to detect and remove software clones. In addition, he describes techniques to remove clones through refactoring and summarises studies on the evolution of clones.
- In Chapter 3, D'Ambros et al. report on how information stored in version repositories and bug archives can be exploited to derive useful information about the evolution of software systems.
- In Chapter 4, Zimmermann et al. explore how information about software failures contained in a bug database can be mined to predict software properties and to improve the software quality. Their results are validated on a number of industrial case studies.

Part II of the book, called *Reengineering of Legacy Systems* contains three chapters devoted to the topic of legacy software systems, and how one may migrate to, or reengineer these systems into a system that is no longer outdated and more easy to maintain and adapt:

- In Chapter 5, Demeyer discusses the state-of-the-art in object-oriented software reengineering. In particular, he focuses on the techniques of *refactoring* and *reengineering patterns*, and shows how these techniques can be used to capture and document expert knowledge about reengineering.
- In Chapter 6, Hainaut et al. address the problem of platform migration of large business applications and information systems. More specifically, they study the substitution of a modern data management technology for a legacy one. They develop a reference framework for migration strategies, and they focus on some migration strategies that minimize program understanding effort.
- In Chapter 7, Heckel et al. discuss an important research trend, namely the migration of legacy software systems to web services and service-oriented architectures by introducing architectural styles. In particular, they report on experience with an industrial case study in the context of a European research project, relying on the technique of graph transformation.

Part III of the book, called *Novel Trends in Software Evolution* addresses the relation between software evolution and other essential areas of software engineering such as software testing, software architectures, aspect-oriented software development, and open source software.

- In Chapter 8, van Deursen et al. discuss the current state of research and practice on the interplay between software evolution and software testing. In particular, they discuss and compare approaches for regression testing, unit testing (and the impact of refactoring on unit tests), test smells, and many more. They also consider tool support for test comprehension.
- In Chapter 9, Mens and Tourwé highlight some evolution-related issues and challenges that adopters of aspect-oriented software development approaches encounter. They discuss state-of-the-art techniques addressing the issues of aspect mining, extraction and evolution, and point out some issues for which no adequate solutions exist yet. This chapter can serve as a guideline for adopters of aspect technology to get a better idea of the evolution issues they may confront sooner or later, of the risks involved, and of the state-of-the-art in the techniques currently available to help them in addressing these issues.
- In Chapter 10, Barais et al. provide a detailed treatment of state-of-the-art approaches to evolving software architectures. In addition, they discuss in more detail *TranSAT*, one particular framework for software architecture evolution. The proposed solution combines ideas from aspect-oriented software development with architectural description languages.
- In Chapter 11, Fernandez-Ramil et al. discuss state-of-the-art techniques to study characteristics of evolving open source systems and their processes based on empirical studies. Results of the application of these techniques are given, including growth patterns, productivity, complexity patterns, social networks, cloning, processes and quality in open source systems, and so on.

## Part I

Understanding and Analysing Software Evolution

2

Identifying and Removing Software Clones

Rainer Koschke

Universität Bremen, Germany

Summary. Ad-hoc reuse through copy-and-paste occurs frequently in practice affecting the evolvability of software. Researchers have investigated ways to locate and remove duplicated code. Empirical studies have explored the root causes and effects of duplicated code and the evolution of duplicated code. This chapter summarizes the state of the art in detecting, managing, and removing software redundancy. It describes consequences, pros and cons of copying and pasting code.

2.1 Introduction

A venerable and long-standing goal and ideal in software development is to avoid duplication and redundancy. Yet, in reality code duplication is a common habit. Several authors report on 7–23% code duplication [29, 291, 303]; in one extreme case even 59% [156].

Duplication and redundancy can increase the size of the code, make it hard to understand the many code variants, and cause maintenance headaches. The goal of avoiding redundancy has provided the impetus to investigations on software reuse, software refactoring, modularization, and parameterization. Even in the face of the ethic of avoiding redundancy, in practice software frequently contains many redundancies and duplications. For instance the technique of "code scavenging" is frequently used, and works by copying and then pasting code fragments, thereby creating so-called "clones" of duplicated or highly similar code. Redundancies can also occur in various other ways, including because of missed reuse opportunities, purposeful duplication because of efficiency concerns, and duplication through parallel or forked development threads.

Because redundancies frequently exist in code, methods for detecting and removing them from software are needed in many contexts. Over the past few decades, research on clone detection have contributed towards addressing the issue. Techniques for finding similar code and on removing duplication have been investigated in several specific areas such as software reverse engineering, plagiarism in student programs, copyright infringement investigation, software evolution analysis, code

T. Mens, S. Demeyer (eds.), *Software Evolution.*
DOI 10.1007/978-3-540-76440-3, © Springer 2008

compaction (e.g., for mobile devices), and design pattern discovery and extraction. Common to all these research areas are the problems involved in understanding the redundancies and finding similar code, either within a software system, between versions of a system, or between different systems.

Although this research has progressed over decades, only recently has the pace of activity in this area picked up such that significant research momentum could be established. This chapter summarizes the state of the art in detecting, managing, and removing software redundancy. It describes consequences, pros and cons of copying and pasting code.

Software clones are important aspects in software evolution. If a systems is to be evolved, its clones should be known in order to make consistent changes. Cloning is often a strategic means for evolution. For instance, copies can be made to create a playground for experimental feature evolution, where modifications are made in cloned code of a mature feature reducing the risk to break stable code. Once stable, the clone can replace its original. Often, cloning is the start of a new branch of evolution if the changes in the cloned code are not merged back to the main development branch. Clone detection techniques play an important role in software evolution research where attributes of the same code entity are observed over multiple versions. Here, we need to identify for an entity in one version the corresponding entity in the next version (known as *origin analysis* [568]). If refactoring (as for instance *renaming*) is applied between versions, the relation between entities of different versions is not always obvious. And last but not least, the evolution of clones can be studied to better understand the nature of cloning in practice.

2.2 Software Redundancy, Code Cloning, and Code Duplication

There are different forms of redundancy in software. Software comprises both programs and data. In the data base community, there is a clear notion of redundancy that has lead to various levels of normal forms. A similar theory does not yet exist for computer programs.

In computer programs, we can also have different types of redundancy. We should note that not every type of redundancy is harmful. For instance, programming languages use redundant declarations so that a compiler is able to check consistency between declarations and their uses. Also, at the architectural level, n-version programming is a strategy in which redundancy is purposefully and consciously used to implement reliable systems.

Sometimes *redundant* is used also in the sense of *superfluous* in the software engineering literature. For instance, Xie and Engler show that superfluous (they call them redundant) operations such as idempotent operations, assignments that are never read, dead code, conditional branches that are never taken, and redundant NULL-checks can pinpoint potential errors [550, 551].

Redundant code is also often misleadingly called *cloned* code in the literature—although that implies that one piece of code is derived from the other one in the original sense of this word. According to the Merriam-Webster dictionary, a *clone* is one that appears to be a copy of an original form. It is a synonym to *duplicate*. Although cloning leads to redundant code, not every redundant code is a clone. There may be cases in which two code segments that are no copy of each other just happen to be similar or even identical by accident. Also, there may be redundant code that is semantically equivalent but has a completely different implementation.

There is no agreement in the research community on the exact notion of redundancy and cloning. Ira Baxter's definition of clones expresses this vagueness:

> Clones are segments of code that are similar according to some definition of similarity.   —Ira Baxter, 2002

According to this definition, there can be different notions of similarity. They can be based on text, lexical or syntactic structure, or semantics. They can even be similar if they follow the same pattern, that is, the same building plan. Instances of design patterns and idioms are similar in that they follow a similar structure to implement a solution to a similar problem.

Semantic similarity relates to the observable behavior. A piece of code, *A*, is semantically similar to another piece of code, *B*, if *B* subsumes the functionality of *A*, in other words, they have "similar" pre and post conditions.

Unfortunately, detecting such semantic similarity is undecidable in general although it would be worthwhile as you can often estimate the number of developers of a large software system by the number of hash table or list implementations you find.

Another definition of cloning considers the program text: Two code fragments form a clone if their program text is similar. The two code fragments may or may not be equivalent semantically. These pieces are redundant because one fragment may need to be adjusted if the other one is changed. If the code fragments are executable code, their behavior is not necessarily equivalent or subsumed at the concrete level, but only at a more abstract level. For instance, two code pieces may be identical at the textual level including all variable names that occur within but the variable names are bound to different declarations in the different contexts. Then, the execution of the code changes different variables. Figure 2.1 shows two textually identical segments in the line range of 4–6 and 10–12, respectively. The semantic difference is that the first segment sets a global variable whereas the second one a local variable. The common abstract behavior of the two code segments is to iterate over a data structure and to increase a variable in each step.

Program-text similarity is most often the result of *copy&paste*; that is, the programmer selects a code fragment and copies it to another location. Sometimes, these programmers are forced to copy because of limitations of the programming language. In other cases, they intend to reuse code. Sometimes these clones are modified slightly to adapt them to their new environment or purpose.

Clearly, the definition of redundancy, similarity, and cloning in software is still an open issue. There is little consensus in this matter. A study by Walenstein et al. [532], for instance, reports on differences among different human raters for clone candidates. In this study, clones were to be identified that ought to be removed and Walenstein et al. gave guidelines towards clones worthwhile being removed. The

```
1   int sum = 0;
2
3   void foo(Iterator iter){
4     for (item = first(iter); has_more(iter); item = next(iter)){
5       sum = sum + value (item);
6     }
7   }
8   int bar(Iterator iter){
9     int sum = 0;
10    for (item = first(iter); has_more(iter); item = next(iter)){
11      sum = sum + value (item);
12    }
13  }
```

Fig. 2.1. Example of code clones

human raters of the clones proposed by automated tools did rarely agree upon what constitutes a clone worth to be removed. While the sources of inter-rater difference could be the insufficient similarity among clones or the appraisal of the need for removal, the study still highlights that there is no clear consensus yet, even for task-specific definitions of clones.

Another small study was performed at the Dagstuhl seminar 06301 "Duplication, Redundancy, and Similarity in Software" 2007. Cory Kapser elicited judgments and discussions from world experts regarding what characteristics define a code clone. Less than half of the clone candidates he presented to these experts had 80% agreement amongst the judges. Judges appeared to differ primarily in their criteria for judgment rather than their interpretation of the clone candidates.

2.3 Types of Clones

Program-text clones can be compared on the basis of the program text that has been copied. We can distinguish the following types of clones accordingly:

- **Type 1** is an exact copy without modifications (except for whitespace and comments).
- **Type 2** is a syntactically identical copy; only variable, type, or function identifiers have been changed.
- **Type 3** is a copy with further modifications; statements have been changed, added, or removed.

Baker further distinguishes so called parameterized clones [28], which are a subset of type-2 clones. Two code fragments A and B are a parameterized clone pair if there is a bijective mapping from A's identifiers onto B's identifiers that allows an identifier substitution in A resulting in A' and A' is a type-1 clone to B (and vice versa).

While type-1 and type-2 clones are precisely defined and form an equivalence relation, the definition of type-3 clones is inherently vague. Some researchers consider

Table 2.1. Classification by Balazinska et al. [33] ©[1999] IEEE

- difference in method attributes (static, private, throws, etc.)
- single-token difference in function body
  - further distinction into type of token:
  - called method
  - parameter type
  - literal
  - ...
- token-sequence difference in function body
  - one unit (expression or statement) differs in token sequence
  - two units
  - more than two units

two consecutive type-1 or type-2 clones together forming a type-3 clone if the gap in between is below a certain threshold of lines [29, 328]. Another precise definition could be based on a threshold for the Levenshtein Distance, that is, the number of deletions, insertions, or substitutions required to transform one string into another. There is no consensus on a suitable similarity measure for type-3 clones yet.

The above simple classification is still very rough. Balazinska et al. introduced a more refined classification for function clones [33] as described in Table 2.1. This classification makes sense for selecting a suitable strategy for clone removal. For instance, the design pattern *TemplateMethod* may be used to factor out differences in the types used in different code fragments or the design pattern *Strategy* can be used to factor out algorithmic differences [31, 32]. Furthermore Balazinska et al. argue that each class is associated with a different risk in clone removal.

Kapser et al.'s classification is the most elaborated classification to date [267, 265, 264] (cf. Table 2.2). The first level is a hint about the distance of clones. An argument can be made (although there is no empirical study on this hypothesis) that it is likely that clones between files are more problematic than within the same file as that it is more likely to overlook the former clones when it comes to consistent changes. The second decision distinguishes which syntactic units are copied. The third gives the degree of similarity and the fourth may be used to filter irrelevant or spurious clones.

2.4 The Root Causes for Code Clones

A recent ethnographic study by Kim and Notkin [277] has shed some light on why programmers copy and paste code. By observing programmers in their daily practice they identified the following reasons.

Sometimes programmers are simply forced to duplicate code because of limitations of the programming language being used. Analyzing these root causes in more detail could help to improve the language design.

Furthermore, programmers often delay code restructuring until they have copied and pasted several times. Only then, they are able to identify the variabilities of their

Table 2.2. Classification by Kapser et al. [265, 264] ©[2003] IEEE

1. At first level, distinguish clones within the same or across different files
2. then, according to type of region:
   - functions
   - declarations
   - macros
   - hybrids (in more than one of the above)
   - otherwise (among typedefs, variable declarations, function signatures)
3. then, degree of overlap or containment
4. then, according to type of code sequence:
   - initialization clones (first five lines)
   - finalization clones (last five lines)
   - loop clones (60% overlap of bodies)
   - switch and if (60% overlap of branches)
   - multiple conditions: several switch and if statements
   - partial conditions: branches of switch/if are similar

code to be factored out. Creating abstract generic solutions in advance often leads to unnecessarily flexible and hence needlessly complicated solutions. Moreover, the exact variabilities may be difficult to foresee. Hence, programmers tend to follow the idea of extreme programming in the small by not investing too much effort in speculative planning and anticipation.

Systems are modularized based on principles such as information hiding, minimizing coupling, and maximizing cohesion. In the end—at least for systems written in ordinary programming languages—the system is composed of a fixed set of modules. Ideally, if the system needs to be changed, only a very small number of modules must be adjusted. Yet, there are very different change scenarios and it is not unlikely that the chosen modularization forces a change to be repeated for many modules. The triggers for such changes are called *cross-cutting concerns* (see also Chapter 9). For instance, logging is typically a feature that must be implemented by most modules. Another example is parameter checking in defensive programming where every function must check its parameters before it fulfills its purpose [92]. Then copy&paste dependencies reflect important underlying design decisions, namely, cross-cutting concerns.

Another important root cause is that programmers often reuse the copied text as a template and then customize the template in the pasted context.

Kapser et al. have investigated clones in large systems [266]. They found what they call *patterns of cloning* where cloning is consciously used as an implementation strategy. In their case study, they found the following cloning patterns:

Forking is cloning used to bootstrap development of similar solutions, with the expectation that evolution of the code will occur somewhat independently, at least in the short term. The assumption is that the copied code takes a separate evolution path independent of the original. In such a case, changes in the copy may be made that have no side effect on the original code.

Templating is used as a method to directly copy behavior of existing code but appropriate abstraction mechanisms are unavailable. It was also identified as a main driver for cloning in Kim and Notkin's case study [277]. Templating is often found when a reused library has a relatively fixed protocol (that is, a required order of using its interface items) which manifests as laying out the control flow of the interface items as a fixed pattern. For instance, the code in Fig. 2.1 uses a fixed iteration scheme for variable `iter`.

Customization occurs when currently existing code does not adequately meet a new set of requirements. The existing code is cloned and tailored to solve this new problem.

Very likely other more organizational aspects play a role, too. Time pressure, for instance, does not leave much time to search for the best long-term solution. Unavailable information on the impact of code changes leads programmers to create copies in which they make the required enhancement; such changes then are less likely to affect the original code negatively. Inadequate performance measures of programmers' productivity in the number of lines of code they produce neither invite programmers to avoid duplicates.

2.5 Consequences of Cloning

There are plausible arguments that code cloning increases maintenance effort. Changes must be made consistently multiple times if the code is redundant. Often it is not documented where code has been copied. Manual search for copied code is infeasible for large systems and automated clone detection is not perfect when changes are made to the copies (see Section 2.8). Furthermore during analysis, the same code must be read over and over again, then compared to the other code just to find out that this code has already been analyzed. Only if you make a detailed comparison, which can be difficult if there are subtle differences in the code or its environment, you can be sure that the code is indeed the same. This comparison can be fairly expensive. If the code would have been implemented only once in a function, this effort could have been avoided completely.

For these reasons, code cloning is number one on the stink parade of bad smells by Beck and Fowler [183]. But there are also counter arguments. In Kapser and Godfrey's study [266], code cloning is a purposeful implementation strategy which may make sense under certain circumstances (see Section 2.4).

Cordy makes a similar statement [128]. He argues that in the financial domain, cloning is the way in which designs are reused. Data processing programs and records across an organization often have very similar purposes, and, consequently, the data structures and programs to carry out these tasks are therefore very similar. Cloning becomes then a standard practice when authoring a new program. Opponents would argue that a better means would be to pursue systematic and organized reuse through software product lines.

Cordy also argues that the attempt to avoid cloning may lead to higher risks. Making changes to central data structures bears the risk to break existing applications and requires to run expensive regression tests. Instead programmers tend to copy the data structure if they want to restructure or add a different view and make the necessary changes in the copy. Even the argument that errors must be fixed in every copy does not count, he states. Errors would not necessarily be fixed in the original data structure because the many running applications may already rely on these errors, Cordy argues. On the other hand, repeated work, need for data migration, and risk of inconsistency of data are the price that needs to be paid following this strategy. The Y2K problem has shown how expensive and difficult it is to remedy systems that have suffered from massive decentralized use of data structures and algorithms.

While it is difficult to find arguments for type-1 and type-2 clones, one can more easily argue in favor of type-3 clones. It is not clear when you have type-3 clones whether the unifying solution would be easier to maintain than several copies with small changes. Generic solutions can become overly complicated. Maintainability can only be defined in a certain context with controlled parameters. That is, a less sophisticated programmer may be better off maintaining copied code than a highly parameterized piece of code. Moreover, there is a risk associated with removing code clones [128]. The removal requires deep semantic analyses and it is difficult to make any guarantees that the removal does not introduce errors. There may be even organizational reasons to copy code. Code cloning could, for instance, be used to disentangle development units [128].

The current debate lacks empirical studies on the costs and benefits of code cloning. There are very few empirical studies that explore the interrelationship of code cloning and maintainability. All of them focus on code cloning and errors as one (out of many) maintainability aspect.

Monden et al. [374] analyzed a large system consisting of about 2,000 modules written in 1 MLOC lines of Cobol code over a period of 20 years. They used a token-based clone detector (cf. Section 2.8.2) to find clones that were at least 30 lines long. They searched for correlations of maximal clone length with change frequency and number of errors. They found that most errors were reported for modules with clones of at least 200 lines. They also found many errors—although less than in those with longer clones—in modules with shorter clones up to 50 lines. Yet, interestingly enough, they found the lowest error rate for modules with clones of 50 to 100 lines. Monden et al. have not further analyzed why these maintainability factors correlate in such a way with code cloning.

Chou et al. [113] investigated the hypothesis that if a function, file, or directory has one error, it is more likely that is has others. They found in their analysis of the Linux and OpenBSD kernels that this phenomenon can be observed most often where programmer ignorance of interface or system rules combines with copy-and-paste. They explain the correlation of bugs and copy-and-paste primarily by programmer ignorance, but they also note that—in addition to ignorance—the prevalence of copy-and-paste error clustering among different device drivers and versions suggests that programmers believe that "working" code is correct code. They note that if the copied code is incorrect, or it is placed into a context it was not intended for, the assumption of goodness is violated.

Li et al. [328] use clone detection to find bugs when programmers copy code but rename identifiers in the pasted code inconsistently. On average, 13% of the clones flagged as copy-and-paste bugs by their technique turned out to be real errors for the systems *Linux kernel*, *FreeBSD*, *Apache*, and *PostgreSQL*. The false positive rate of their technique is 73% on average, where on average 14% of the potential problems are still under analysis by the developers of the analyzed systems.

2.6 Clone Evolution

There are a few empirical studies on the evolution of clones, which describe some interesting observations. Antoniol et al. propose time series derived from clones over several releases of a system to monitor and predict the evolution of clones [14]. Their study for the data base system *mSQL* showed that their prediction of the average number of clones per function is fairly reliable. In another case study for the Linux kernel, they found that the scope of cloning is limited [15]. Only few clones can be found across subsystems; most clones are completely contained within a subsystem. In the subsystem *arch*, constituting the hardware architecture abstraction layer, newer hardware architectures tend to exhibit slightly higher clone rates. The explanation for this phenomenon is that newer modules are often derived from existing similar ones. The relative number of clones seems to be rather stable, that is, cloning does not occur in peaks. This last result was also reported by Godfrey and Tu who noticed that cloning is common and steady practice in the Linux kernel [205]. However, the cloning rate does increase steadily over time. Li et al. [328] observed for the Linux kernel in the period of 1994 to 2004 that the redundancy rate has increased from about 17% to about 22%. They observed a similar behavior for FreeBSD. Most of the growth of redundancy rate comes from a few modules, including *drivers* and *arch* in Linux and *sys* in FreeBSD. The percentage of copy-paste code increases more rapidly in those modules than in the entire software suite. They explain this observation by the fact that Linux supports more and more similar device drivers during this period.

Kim et al. analyzed the clone genealogy for two open-source Java systems using historical data from a version control system [278]. A clone genealogy forms a tree that shows how clones derive in time over multiple versions of a program from common ancestors. Beyond that, the genealogy contains information about the differences among siblings. Their study showed that many code clones exist in the system for only a short time. Kim et al. conclude that extensive refactoring of such short-lived clones may not be worthwhile if they likely diverge from one another very soon. Moreover, many clones, in particular those with a long lifetime that have changed consistently with other elements in the same group cannot easily be avoided because of limitations of the programming language.

One subproblem in clone evolution research is to track clones between versions. Duala-Ekoko and Robillard use a clone region descriptor [155] to discover a clone of version n in version $n + 1$. A clone region descriptor is an approximate location that is independent from specifications based on lines of source code, annotations, or other similarly fragile markers. Clone region descriptors capture the syntactic block nesting of code fragments. A block therein is characterized by its type (e.g., for or while), a string describing a distinguishing identifier for the block (the anchor), and a corroboration metric. The anchor of a loop, for instance, is the condition as string. If two fragments are syntactic siblings, their nesting and anchor are not sufficient to distinguish them. In such cases, the corroboration metric is used. It measures characteristics of the block such as cyclomatic complexity and fan-out of the block.

2.7 Clone Management

Clone management aims at identifying and organizing existing clones, controlling growth and dispersal of clones, and avoiding clones altogether. Lague et al. [303] and Giesecke [199] distinguish three main lines of clone management:

- *preventive* clone management (also known as *preventive control* [303]) comprises activities to avoid new clones
- *compensative* clone management (also known as *problem mining* [303]) encompasses activities aimed at limiting the negative impact of existing clones that are to be left in the system
- *corrective* clone management covers activities to remove clones from a system

This section describes research in these three areas.

2.7.1 Corrective Clone Management: Clone Removal

If you do want to remove clones, there are several way to do so. There are even commercial tools such as *CloneDr*[1] by *Semantic Designs* to automatically detect and remove clones. Cloning and automatic abstraction and removal could even be a suitable implementation approach as hinted by Ira Baxter:

> Cloning can be a good strategy if you have the right tools in place. Let programmers copy and adjust, and then let tools factor out the differences with appropriate mechanisms.   —Ira Baxter, 2002

In simple cases, you can use functional abstraction to replace equivalent copied code by a function call to a newly created function that encapsulates the copied code [166, 287]. In more difficult cases, when the difference is not just in the variable names that occur in the copied code, one may be able to replace by macros if the programming languages comes with a preprocessor. A preprocessor offers textual transformations to handle more complicated replacements. If a preprocessor is available, one can also use conditional compilation. As the excessive use of macros and

---

[1] Trademark of Semantic Designs, Inc.

conditional compilation may introduce many new problems, the solution to the redundancy problem may be found at the design level. The use of design patterns is an option to avoid clones by better design [31, 32]. Yet, this approach requires much more human expertise and, hence, can be less automated. Last but not least, one can develop code generators for highly repetitive code.

In all approaches, it is a challenge to cut out the right abstractions and to come up with meaningful names of generated functions or macros. Moreover, it is usually difficult to check the preconditions for these proposed transformations—be they manual or automated–in order to assure that the transformation is semantic preserving.

2.7.2 Preventive and Compensative Clone Management

Rather than removing clones after the offense, it may be better to avoid them right from the beginning by integrating clone detection in the normal development process. Lague et al. identify two ways to integrate clone detection in normal development [303].

It can be used as *preventive control* where the code is checked continuously—for instance, at each check-in in the version control system or even on the fly while the code is edited—and the addition of a clone is reported for confirmation.

A complementary integration is *problem mining* where the code currently under modification is searched in the rest of the system. The found segments of code can then be checked whether the change must be repeated in this segment for consistency.

Preventive control aims at avoiding code clones when they occur first whereas problem mining addresses circumstances in which cloning has been used for a while.

Lague et al. assessed the benefits of integrating clone detection in normal development by analyzing the three-year version history of a very large procedural telecommunication system [303]. In total, 89 millions of non-blank lines (including comments) were analyzed, for an average size of 14.83 million lines per version. The average number of functions per release was 187,000.

Problem mining is assessed by the number of functions changed that have clones that were not changed; that is, how often a modification was missed potentially. Preventive control is assessed by the number of functions added that were similar to existing functions; that is, the code that could have been saved.

It is interesting to note, that—contrary to their expectations—they observed a low rate of growth in the number of overall clones in the system, due to the fact that many clones were actually removed from the system.

They conclude from their data that preventive control would help to lower the number of clones. Many clones disappeared only long after the day they came into existence. Early detection of clones could lead to taking this measure earlier.

They also found that problem mining could have provided programmers with a significant number of opportunities for correcting problems before end-user experienced them. The study indicates a potential for improving the software quality and customer satisfaction through an effective clone management strategy.

An alternative to clone removal is to live with clones consciously. Clones can be managed, linked, and changed simultaneously using linked editing as proposed by Toomim et al. [504]. Linked editing is also used by Duala-Ekoko and Robillard. Linked editing allows one to link two or more code clones persistently. The differences and similarities are then analyzed, visualized, and recorded. If a change needs to be made, linked editing allows programmers to modify all linked elements simultaneously, or particular elements individually. That is, linked editing allows the programmer to edit all instances of a given clone at once, as if they were a single block of code. It overcomes some of the problems of duplicated code, namely, verbosity, tedious editing, lost clones, and unobservable consistency without requiring extra work from the programmer.

2.8 Clone Detection

While there is an ongoing debate as to whether remove clones, there is a consensus about the importance to at least detect them. Clone avoidance during normal development, as described in the previous section, as well as making sure that a change can be made consistently in the presence of clones requires to know where the clones are. Manual clone detection is infeasible for large systems, hence, automatic support is necessary.

Automated software clone detection is an active field of research. This section summarizes the research in this area. The techniques can be distinguished at the first level in the type of information their analysis is based on and at the second level in the used algorithm.

2.8.1 Textual Comparison

The approach by Rieger et al. compares whole lines to each other textually [156]. To increase performance, lines are partitioned using a hash function for strings. Only lines in the same partition are compared. The result is visualized as a dotplot, where each dot indicates a pair of cloned lines. Clones may be found as certain patterns in those dotplots visually. Consecutive lines can be summarized to larger cloned sequences automatically as uninterrupted diagonals or displaced diagonals in the dotplot.

Johnson [258, 259] uses the efficient string matching by Karp and Rabin [268, 269] based on fingerprints, that is, a hash code characterizing a string is used in the search.

Marcus et al. [345] compare only certain pieces of text, namely, identifiers using latent semantic indexing, a technique from information retrieval. Latent semantic analysis is a technique in natural language processing analyzing relationships between a set of documents and the terms they contain by producing a set of concepts related to the documents and terms. The idea here is to identify fragments in which similar names occur as potential clones.

2.8.2 Token Comparison

Baker's technique is also a line-based comparison. Instead of a string comparison, the token sequences of lines are compared efficiently through a suffix tree. A suffix tree for a string S is a tree whose edges are labeled with substrings of S such that each suffix of S corresponds to exactly one path from the tree's root to a leaf.

First, Baker's technique summarizes each token sequence for a whole line by a so called *functor* that abstracts of concrete values of identifiers and literals [29]. The functor characterizes this token sequence uniquely. Assigning functors can be viewed as a perfect hash function. Concrete values of identifiers and literals are captured as parameters to this functor. An encoding of these parameters abstracts from their concrete values but not from their order so that code fragments may be detected that differ only in systematic renaming of parameters. Two lines are clones if they match in their functors and parameter encoding.

The functors and their parameters are summarized in a suffix tree, a tree that represents all suffixes of the program in a compact fashion. A suffix tree can be built in time and space linear to the input length [356, 30]. Every branch in the suffix tree represents program suffixes with common beginnings, hence, cloned sequences.

Kamiya et al. increase recall for superficially different, yet equivalent sequences by normalizing the token sequences [263]. For instance, each single statement after the lexical patterns `if(...)`, `for(...)`, `while(...)`, and `do` and `else` in C++ is transformed to a compound block; e.g., `if (a) b = 2;` is transformed to `if (a) {b = 2;}`. Using this normalization, the if statement can be matched with the equivalent (with parameter replacement) code `if (x) {y = 2;}`.

Because syntax is not taken into account, the found clones may overlap different syntactic units, which cannot be replaced through functional abstraction. Either in a preprocessing [485, 127, 204] or post-processing [234] step, clones that completely fall in syntactic blocks can be found if block delimiters are known. Preprocessing and postprocessing both require some syntactic information—gathered either lightweight by counting tokens opening and closing syntactic scopes or island grammars [377] or a full-fledged syntax analysis [204].

2.8.3 Metric Comparison

Merlo et al. gather different metrics for code fragments and compare these metric vectors instead of comparing code directly [303, 291, 353, 289]. An allowable distance (for instance, Euclidean distance) for these metric vectors can be used as a hint for similar code. Specific metric-based techniques were also proposed for clones in web sites [151, 307].

2.8.4 Comparison of Abstract Syntax Trees

Baxter et al. partition subtrees of the abstract syntax tree (AST) of a program based on a hash function and then compare subtrees in the same partition through tree matching (allowing for some divergences) [47]. A similar approach was proposed earlier by Yang [557] using dynamic programming to find differences between two versions of the same file.

Suffix trees—central to token-based techniques following Baker's idea—can also be used to detect sequences of identical AST nodes. In the approach by Koschke et al. [294], the AST nodes are serialized in preorder traversal, a suffix tree is created for these serialized AST nodes, and the resulting maximally long AST node sequences are then cut according to their syntactic region so that only syntactically closed sequences remain.

The idea of metrics to characterize code and to use these metrics to decide which code segments to compare can be adopted for ASTs as well. Jian et al. [257] characterize subtrees with numerical vectors in the Euclidean space $\Re$ and an efficient algorithm to cluster these vectors with respect to the Euclidean distance metric. Subtrees with vectors in one cluster are potential clones.

2.8.5 Comparison of Program Dependency Graphs

Textual as well as token-based techniques and syntax-based techniques depend upon the textual order of the program. If the textual order is changed, the copied code will not be found. Programmers modify the order of the statements in copied code, for instance, to camouflage plagiarism. Or they use code cloning as in the templating implementation strategy (see Section 2.4), where the basic skeleton of an algorithm is reused and then certain pieces are adjusted to the new context.

Yet, the order cannot be changed arbitrarily without changing the meaning of the program. All control and data dependencies must be maintained. A program dependency graph [175] is a representation of a program that represents only the control and data dependency among statements. This way program dependency graph abstract from the textual order. Clones may then be identified as isomorphic subgraphs in a program dependency graph [298, 286]. Because this problem is NP hard, the algorithms use approximative solutions.

2.8.6 Other Techniques

Leitao [324] combines syntactic and semantic techniques through a combination of specialized comparison functions that compare various aspects (similar call subgraphs, commutative operators, user-defined equivalences, transformations into canonical syntactic forms). Each comparison function yields an evidence that is summarized in an evidence-factor model yielding a clone likelihood. Walter et al. [531] and Li et al. [327] cast the search for similar fragments as a data mining problem. Statement sequences are summarized to item sets. An adapted data mining algorithm searches for frequent item sets.

2.9 Comparison of Clone Detection Algorithms

The abundance of clone detection techniques calls for a thorough comparison so that we know the strength and weaknesses of these techniques in order to make an informed decision if we need to select a clone detection technique for a particular purpose.

Clone detectors can be compared in terms of recall and precision of their findings as well as suitability for a particular purpose. There are several evaluations along these lines based on qualitative and quantitative data.

Bailey and Burd compared three clone and two plagiarism detectors [27]. Among the clone detectors were three of the techniques later evaluated by a subsequent study by Bellon and Koschke [55], namely, the techniques by Kamiya [263], Baxter [47], and Merlo [353]. For the latter technique, Bailey used an own re-implementation; the other tools were original. The plagiarism detectors were JPlag [420] and Moss [452].

The clone candidates of the techniques were validated by Bailey, and the accepted clone pairs formed an oracle against which the clone candidates were compared. Several metrics were proposed to measure various aspects of the found clones, such as scope (i.e., within the same file or across file boundaries), and the findings in terms of recall and precision.

The syntax-based technique by Baxter had the highest precision (100%) and the lowest recall (9%) in this experiment. Kamiya's technique had the highest recall and a precision comparable to the other techniques (72%). The re-implementation of Merlo's metric-based technique showed the least precision (63%).

Although the case study by Bailey and Burd showed interesting initial results, it was conducted on only one relatively small system (16 KLOC). However, because the size was limited, Bailey was able to validate all clone candidates.

A subsequent larger study was conducted by Bellon and Koschke [54, 55]. Their likewise quantitative comparison of clone detectors was conducted for 4 Java and 4 C systems in the range of totaling almost 850 KLOC. The participants and their clone detectors evaluated are listed in Table 2.3.

Table 2.4 summarizes the findings of Bellon and Koschke's study. Row *clone type* lists the type of clones the respective clone detector finds (for clone types, see Section 2.3). The next two rows qualify the tools in terms of their time and space consumption. The data is reported at an ordinal scale $--, -, +, ++$ where $--$ is worst (the exact measures can be found in the paper to this study [54, 55]). Recall and precision are determined as in Bailey and Burd's study by comparing the clone

Table 2.3. Participating scientists

Participant	Tool	Comparison
Brenda S. Baker [29]	*Dup*	Token
Ira D. Baxter [47]	*CloneDr*	AST
Toshihiro Kamiya [263]	*CCFinder*	Token
Jens Krinke [298]	*Duplix*	PDG
Ettore Merlo [353]	*CLAN*	Function Metrics
Matthias Rieger [156]	*Duploc*	Text

Table 2.4. Results from the Bellon and Koschke study. Adapted from [54, 55] ©[2007] IEEE

	Baker	Baxter	Kamiya	Krinke	Merlo	Rieger
Clone type	1, 2	1, 2	1, 2, 3	3	1, 2, 3	1, 2, 3
Speed	+ +	−	+	− −	+ +	?
RAM	+	−	+	+	+ +	?
Recall	+	−	+	−	−	+
Precision	−	+	−	−	+	−

detectors' findings to a human oracle. The same ordinal scale is used to qualify the results; exact data are reported in the paper [54, 55].

Interestingly, Merlo's tool performed much better in this experiment than in the experiment by Bailey and Burd. However, the difference in precision of Merlo's approach in this comparison to the study by Bailey and Burd can be explained by the fact that Merlo compared not only metrics but also the tokens and their textual images to identify type-1 and type-2 clones in the study by Bellon and Koschke.

While the Bailey/Burd and Bellon/Koschke studies focus on quantitative evaluation of clone detectors, other authors have evaluated clone detectors for the fitness for a particular maintenance task. Rysselberghe and Demeyer [525] compared text-based [156, 438], token-based [29], and metric-based [353] clone detectors for refactoring. They compare these techniques in terms of suitability (can a candidate be manipulated by a refactoring tool?), relevance (is there a priority which of the matches should be refactored first?), confidence (can one solely rely on the results of the code cloning tool, or is manual inspection necessary?), and focus (does one have to concentrate on a single class or is it also possible to assess an entire project?). They assess these criteria qualitatively based on the clone candidates produced by the tools. Figure 2.2 summarizes their conclusions.

Bruntink et al. use clone detection to find cross-cutting concerns in C programs with homogeneous implementations [93]. In their case study, they used *CCFinder*—Kamiya's [263] tool evaluated in other case studies, too—one of the Bauhaus[2] clone detectors, namely *ccdiml*, which is a variation of Baxter's technique [47], and the PDG-based detector *PDG-DUP* by Komondoor [286]. The cross-cutting concerns they looked for were error handling, tracing, pre and post condition checking, and memory error handling. The study showed that the clone classes obtained by Bauhaus' *ccdiml* can provide the best match with the range checking, null-pointer

criterion	most suitable technique
suitability	metric-based
relevance	no difference
confidence	text-based
focus	no difference

Fig. 2.2. Assessment by Rysselberghe and Demeyer. Adapted from [525] ©[2004] IEEE

---

[2] http://www.axivion.com.

checking, and error handling concerns. Null-pointer checking and error handling can be found by *CCFinder* almost equally well. Tracing and memory error handling can best be found by *PDG-DUP*.

2.10 Clone Presentation

Because there is typically a huge amount of clones in large systems and these clones differ in various attributes (type, degree of similarity, length, etc.), presentation issues of clone information are critical. This huge information space must be made accessible to a human analyst. The analyst needs a holistic view that combines source code views and architectural views.

There have been several proposals for clone visualization. Scatter plots—also known as dot plots—are two-dimensional charts where all software units are listed on both axes [114, 156, 512] (cf. Fig. 2.3). There is a dot if two software units are similar. The granularity of software units may differ. It can range from single lines to functions to classes and files to packages and subsystems. Visual patterns of cloning may be observed by a human analyst. A problem with this approach is scalability for many software units and the order of the listed software units as this has an impact on the visual patterns. While there is a "natural" order for lines (i.e., lexical order) within a file, it is not clear how to order more coarse-grained units such as functions, files, and packages. Lexical order of their names is in most cases as arbitrary as random order.

Johnson [260] proposes Hasse diagrams for clone representation between sets of files so that one can better see whether code has been copied between files, which is possibly more critical than cloning within a file (cf. Fig. 2.4). A Hasse diagram (named after a German mathematician) is used to draw a partial order among sets as an acyclic graph. Directed arcs connect nodes that are related by the order relation and for which no other directed path exists.

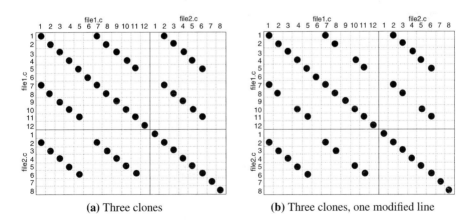

(a) Three clones   (b) Three clones, one modified line

Fig. 2.3. Dot plots [114, 156, 512]

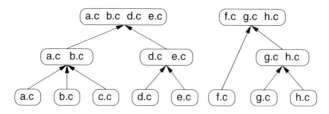

Fig. 2.4. Hasse diagram adapted from [260]

In Johnson's context, each match of a block of text identifies a range of characters (or lines) from two (or more) files. For each subset of files, one can total the number of characters that the matching process has discovered to match between the given set of files. A subset of files forms a node, if the files have non-zero matches. The inclusion between subsets of files yields the edges.

Rieger et al. [437] propose to use Michele Lanza's polymetric views[309] to visualize various aspects of clones in one view (cf. Fig. 2.5). A polymetric view is again based on the graph metaphor and representation where a node represents a software unit and an edge a cloning relation. Visually, additional information can be attached to the graph by the degrees of freedom for the position (X/Y in the two-dimensional space), color of nodes and edges, thickness of edges, breadth and width of nodes. Rieger et al. propose a fixed set of metric combinations to be mapped onto graphical aspects to present the clone information from different perspective for different tasks.

Beyond polymetric views, Rieger et al. [437] propose a variation of tree maps to show the degree of cloning along with the system decomposition (cf. Fig. 2.6). Tree maps display information about entities with a hierarchical relationship in a fixed space (for instance, the whole system on one screen) where the leaves of the hierarchy contain a metric to be visualized. Each inner node aggregates the metric values of its descendants. Each node is represented through a piece of the available space. The space of a descendent node is completely contained in the space of its ancestor.

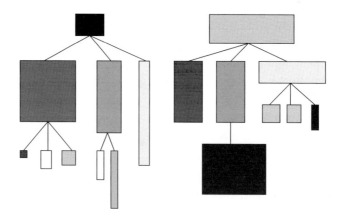

Fig. 2.5. Polymetric view adapted from [437]

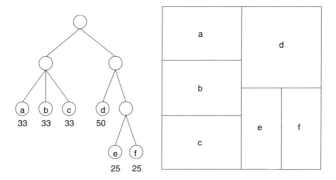

Fig. 2.6. A system decomposition whose leaves are annotated with the number of cloned lines of code and its corresponding tree map

There is no overlap in space for nodes that are not in an ancestor/descendant relation. This is how the hierarchy is presented. Essentially the hierarchy is projected onto the two dimensional space seen from the root of the hierarchy. In order to show the hierarchy clearly, the space of each node appears as rectangle where the direction of subdivision of nested nodes is alternated horizontally and vertically at each level. The space of each rectangle is proportional to the metric.

This visualization was originally proposed by Ben Shneiderman in the early 1990s to show space consumption of a hard disk with a hierarchical file system. While space is used very efficiently, problems arise when the hierarchy is deeply nested.

Another visualization was proposed by Wattenberg to highlight similar substrings in a string. The arc diagram has an arc connecting two equal substrings in a string where the breadth of the arc line covers all characters of the identical substrings. The diagram shows the overlapping of strings but becomes quickly unreadable if many arcs exist. Another disadvantage is that it shows only pairs but not classes of equal strings.

Tairas et al. [489] have created an Eclipse plugin to present clone information. One of their visualizations is the clone visualizer view, a window showing the distribution of clone classes among files (cf. Fig. 2.8). A bar in this view represents a source file, a stripe within a bar a cloned code segment, and its colors the set of clone classes the segment is member of.

hklABCDEFqwertjtaABCDEFzuiopopgABCDEFasdf   **Fig. 2.7.** Arc diagram adapted from [537]

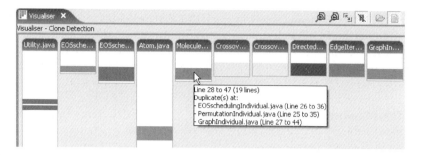

Fig. 2.8. Clones visualizer view in Eclipse adapted from [489]

2.11 Related Fields

Clone detection has applications in other fields and—vice versa—ideas from related fields can be reused for clone detection.

Bruntink et al. for instance, use clone detectors to search for code that could be factored out as aspects using an aspect-oriented language [92, 93]. They identify error handling, tracing, pre and post condition checking, and memory error handling. Although they used classic clone detectors that were not designed for this particular purpose, the clone detectors appeared to be helpful. Classic clone detectors try to find similar code—similar in terms of their program text. The implementations of an aspect, on the other hand, are often very heterogeneous and are similar only at a more semantic level. For instance, precondition checking tests each parameter of a function for certain criteria. At the implementation level, functions differ in the order and type of parameters so that checks are generally different in the program text.

The code compaction community tries to minimize the memory footprint of programs for small devices. They use very similar algorithms to identify redundant code that could be compressed [124].

The detection of plagiarism faces similar but even worse problems as clone detection [452, 420, 180, 343, 251, 337, 210]. In plagiarism cases, people try to camouflage their copy in order to make it more difficult to detect the plagiarism. In order to reuse classic clone detectors for plagiarism, we would need to reduce programs to a normal form for comparison. This normalization, on the other hand, could lead to false positives. Also in virus detection, code patterns significant for a particular hostile code need to be quickly identified in large code bases, where virus programmers try to vary the patterns.

Another application of clone detection is the comparison of versions or variants of software systems. While versions derive from each other, variants have a common ancestor. In both cases, they are very similar. In software evolution research, where information on software units is observed over time or versions, respectively, it is necessary to map the software entities of one version to those of the other version in order to carry over the information. This problem is called the *origin analysis* [508]. The same problem needs to be solved when two software variants are to be compared or merged [237]. Relaying solely on names of these units for this analysis may be misleading if a refactoring like *renaming* has taken place [183]. Also, the refactoring *extract method* moves statements from one function to create a new function. Clone detection can help to establish a mapping between two versions or variants of a program. Several authors have used clone detection techniques or at least a code similarity measure to determine this mapping [509, 568, 206, 205, 524, 552, 553].

The difference of comparing versions or variants to detecting clones is that the task here is to map a code entity onto only one or at least a small set of candidates in the other system, the comparison is only between systems (clones within the same version or variant are irrelevant), cloning is the rule rather than the exception as the two versions or variants overlap to a very high degree, the focus is on the differences rather than the similarities, and the comparison should tolerate renaming and all refactorings that move entities around such as pull-up field, move method, etc.

2.12 Conclusions

This section summarizes the open issues of the subareas in software cloning presented in this chapter.

One fundamental issue is that there is no clear consensus on what is a software clone. We should develop a general notion of redundancy, similarity, and cloning, and then identify more task-oriented categorizations of clones. Other research areas have similar difficulties in defining their fundamental terms. For instance, the architecture community debates the notion of *architecture* and the community of object-oriented programming the notion of *object*. To some extent, these fundamental terms define the field. So it is important to clarify them. It is difficult, for instance, to create benchmarks to evaluate automatic clone detectors if it is unclear what we consider a clone. It were very helpful if we could establish a theory of redundancy similar to normal forms in databases.

Concerning types of clones, we should look at alternative categorizations of clones that make sense (e.g., semantics, origins, risks, etc.). On the empirical side of clone categorizations, we should gather the statistical distribution of clone types in practice and investigate whether there are correlations among apparently orthogonal categories. Studying which strategies of removal and avoidance, risks of removal, potential damages, root causes, and other factors are associated with these categories would be worthwhile, too.

Although the two empirical studies by Kim and Notkin as well as Kapser and Godfrey on the root causes and main drivers for code cloning are important first contributions, this area certainly requires more similar studies. Other potential reasons should be investigated, such as insufficient information on global change impact, badly organized reuse and development processes, questionable productivity measures (e.g., LOCs per day), time pressure, educational deficiencies, ignorance, or shortsightedness, intellectual challenges (e.g., generics), lack of professionalism/end-user programming by non experts, and organizational issues, e.g., distributed development and organizations.

Identifying the root causes would help us to fight the reasons, not just the symptoms, for instance, by giving feedback for programming language design.

Clearly, more empirical studies are required. These studies should take industrial systems into account, too, as it is unclear to which extent these current observations can be attributed to the nature of open-source development. It would also be interesting to investigate what the degree of cloning tells about the organization or development process. For instance, a study by Nickell and Smith reports that the extreme programming projects in their organization produce significantly fewer clones [394, 533].

In particular, empirical investigations of costs and benefits of clone removal are needed so that informed refactoring decisions can be made. We currently do not have a clear picture of the relation of clone types to quality attributes. Most of what we report on the consequences of cloning is folklore rather than fact. We should expect that there is a relevance ranking of clone types for removal, that is, some clones should be removed, others are better left in certain circumstances. Moreover, we can expect that different types of clones are associated with different removal techniques in turn associated with different benefits, costs, and risks.

Unwanted clones should be avoided right from the start. But it is not yet clear what is the best integration of clone detection in the normal development process. In particular, what are the benefits and costs of such possible integrations and what are reliable cloning indicators to trigger refactoring actions?

If it is too late to avoid cloning and if existing clones cannot be removed, we should come up with methods and tools to manage these clones. This clone management must stop further spread of clones and help to make changes consistently.

The most elaborated field in software cloning is the automatic detection of clones. Yet, there is still room for improvement as identified in the quantitative and qualitative comparisons. Most helpful would be a ranking function that allows to present clone candidates in an order of relevance. This ranking function can be based on measures such as type, frequency, and length of clones but should also take into account the task driving the clone detection.

Although various types of visualization to present clones have been proposed we have not fully explored all opportunities. There is a large body of research on information visualization in general and software visualization in particular that we have not yet explored for clone visualization. In order to understand which visualization works best for which purpose, we need more systematic empirical research. Clone representation is difficult due to the large and complex information space. We have various aspects that we need to master: the large amount of data, clone class membership, overlap and inclusion of clones, commonalities and differences among clones in the same class, degree of similarity, and other attributes such as length, type, frequency, and severity.

Clone detection overlaps with related fields, such as code compression or virus detection. The interesting questions here are "What can clone detection learn from other fields?" and "What can other fields learn from clone detection?"

3

Analysing Software Repositories
to Understand Software Evolution

Marco D'Ambros[1], Harald C. Gall[2], Michele Lanza[1], and Martin Pinzger[2]

[1] Faculty of Informatics, University of Lugano, Switzerland
[2] Department of Informatics, University of Zurich, Switzerland

Summary. Software repositories such as versioning systems, defect tracking systems, and archived communication between project personnel are used to help manage the progress of software projects. Software practitioners and researchers increasingly recognize the potential benefit of mining this information to support the maintenance of software systems, improve software design or reuse, and empirically validate novel ideas and techniques. Research is now proceeding to uncover ways in which mining these repositories can help to understand software development, to support predictions about software development, and to plan various evolutionary aspects of software projects.

This chapter presents several analysis and visualization techniques to understand software evolution by exploiting the rich sources of artifacts that are available. Based on the data models that need to be developed to cover sources such as modification and bug reports we describe how to use a Release History Database for evolution analysis. For that we present approaches to analyse developer effort for particular software entities. Further we present change coupling analyses that can reveal hidden change dependencies among software entities. Finally, we show how to investigate architectural shortcomings over many releases and to identify trends in the evolution. Kiviat graphs can be effectively used to visualize such analysis results.

3.1 Introduction

Software evolution analysis is concerned with software changes, their causes, and their effects. It uses all sources of a software system to perform a retrospective analysis. Such data comprises the release history with all the source code and the change information, bug report data, and data that can be extracted from the running system. In particular the analysis of release and bug reporting data has gained importance because they store valuable information for analysing the evolution of software. While the recovery of the data residing in versioning systems such as CVS or Subversion has become a well explored topic, the ultimate challenge lies in the recovered data and its interpretation.

Some recent topics addressed in the field of analysing software repositories include the following:

T. Mens, S. Demeyer (eds.), *Software Evolution.*
DOI 10.1007/978-3-540-76440-3, © Springer 2008

- *Developer effort and social network analysis.* One of the goals in this topic is to find out the effort that team members are spending on maintaining and evolving software modules and how they communicate with each other. This allows a project manager to plan resources and reason about shortcomings in development processes and the team structure.
- *Change impact and propagation.* The main focus of this topic is to assess the impact of a change, such as the addition of a new or change of an existing feature, on the architecture, design and implementation of a software system. Being able to assess the impact of changes allows one to estimate the effort for maintenance and evolution tasks, to determine the impact of a change on the existing architecture and design of a system. Results are also used to provide guidelines for programmers such as if changing method a the programmer should also change method b and c.
- *Trend and hotspot analysis.* In this topic the trend of software entities is observed to find out shortcomings in the current architecture, design and implementation of software systems. Hotspots are the entities that frequently change and therefore are critical for the evolution of a system. One of the goals is to find heuristics and warning mechanisms that alarm project managers and architects of negative trends of software entities (and in particular of system hotspots) and provide suggestions to return the system into a stable state.
- *Fault and defect prediction.* A wealth of information is provided by software repositories that can be input to data mining and machine learning algorithms to characterize current and predict future properties of software entities. One property of software entities that is addressed by many approaches is the prediction of the location and number of defects in software entities such as source files. The result is a list of entities that will likely to be affected by defects which allows the development team to plan preventive actions such as refactoring.

In this chapter we address the first three topics and present techniques such as our Fractal Figures to analyse development effort, the Evolution Radar to analyse the change impact on source files, and Kiviat diagrams to analyse metric trends and to detect system hotspots. In the next section we present a general approach for analysing software repositories to understand software evolution. Examples of how to model and retrieve the data is presented in Section 3.3. The modeled data is the input for the different software evolution analysis techniques we present in Section 3.4.

3.2 An Overview of Software Repository Analysis

When mining software repositories one can consider many software artifacts: Source code from versioning systems, bugs from bug tracking systems, communication from e-mail lists or any further software artifacts such as documentation. This diversity of information is the foundation for many kinds of evolution analyses.

3.2.1 A General Approach

Figure 3.1a shows a sketch of how to analyse software repositories for studying software evolution. In the schema we identify three fundamental steps necessary for the final analysis of the data:

1. *Data modeling*. The first step of mining consists of creating a data model of an evolving software system. Various aspects of the system and its evolution can be modeled: The last version of the source code, the history of files as recorded by the versioning system, several versions of the source code (e.g., one per release), documentation, bug reports, developers mailing list archives, etc.

   While aspects such as source code or file histories have a direct mapping to the system, for others like bug reports or mailing list archives the useful information has to be filtered and linked to software artifacts. When designing the model it is important to consider the tradeoff between the amount of data to deal with (in the analysis phase) and the potential benefit this data can have, i.e., not all aspects of a system's evolution have to be considered, but only the ones which can address a specific software evolution problem or set of problems.

2. *Data retrieval and processing*. Once the model is defined, a concrete instance of it has to be created. For this, we need to retrieve and process the information from the various data sources. The processing can include the parsing of the data (e.g., source code, log files, bug report etc.), the application of matching

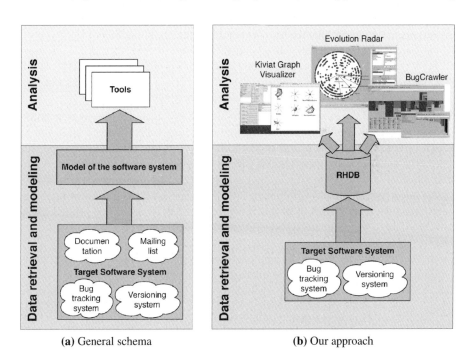

(a) General schema   (b) Our approach

Fig. 3.1. The general approach and our customization to mining software repositories

techniques to link different data sources (e.g., versioning system artifacts with bug reports [179, 136]), the reconstruction of information not recorded (e.g., reconstruct commit information from CVS log files [566]) and the application of other techniques such as data mining.

3. *Data analysis.* The analysis consists of using the modeled and retrieved data to tackle a software evolution problem or set of problems by means of different techniques and approaches.

3.2.2 Our Approach

Figure 3.1b sketches how we approach software evolution analysis through mining software repositories. As data sources we consider versioning system log files together with bug report data. We define a data model describing an evolving software system based on these two data sources (data modeling). Given a system to analyse, versioning system log files and bug report data are parsed and a concrete instance of the model is created (data retrieval). All the models are then stored in a Release History Database (RHDB), which is the starting point for all the subsequent analyses. For the analysis part we use different techniques and tools, aimed at addressing specific software evolution problems.

In the remainder of this chapter we first introduce the RHDB, the data model behind it and the way the database is populated. Then we present different types of software evolution analyses built on top of the RHDB: Developers effort distribution, change coupling, trend analysis and hot-spot detection. For the RHDB and each evolution analysis technique we also present related work in the field.

3.3 Release History

When we refer to the history of a software artifact, we mean the way it was developed, how it grew or shrank over time, how many developers worked on it and to which extent. These kinds of information are recorded by versioning systems and can be reconstructed by parsing their log files. However, when we analyse evolution our goal is to understand a system's architecture, the dependencies among its components and to detect evolutionary hot-spots. To support this kind of analysis, additional information such as problem bug reports can be used. The problem is to link this data to the software artifacts to answer specific questions, e.g., which files were affected by a given bug?

In this section we present our approach for integrating versioning system information and bug report data and populating a RHDB [179, 136]. We first introduce the versioning system and the bug tracking system from which we retrieve the data. Then we describe the model behind the RHDB, i.e., the model of an evolving software system and we finally explain how we populate the database.

CVS and Bugzilla. CVS [135] has been the most used version control system by the open source community over the last years. Currently it is being replaced by Subversion [480] (SVN).

Our approach for populating the RHDB is based on the versioning system log files, thus it can be applied to both CVS and SVN. For each versioned file, the log file contains the information recorded by the versioning system at commit-time: The version number (or revision), the timestamp of the commit, the author who performed the commit, the state (whether the file is still under development or removed), the number of lines added and removed with respect to the previous commit, the branches having the current version as root and the comments written by the author during the commit. Listing 3.1 shows a chunk of a CVS log file.

```
RCS file: /cvsroot/mozilla/js/src/xpconnect/codelib/Attic/mozJSCodeLib.cpp,v
Working file: codelib/mozJSCodeLib.cpp
head: 1.1
branch:
locks: strict
access list:
symbolic names:
        FORMS_20040722_XTF_MERGE: 1.1.4.1
        XTF_20040312_BRANCH: 1.1.0.2
keyword substitution: kv
total revisions: 6;     selected revisions: 6
description:
----------------------------
revision 1.1
date: 2004/04/19 10:53:08;  author: alex.fritze%crocodile-clips.com;  state: dead;
branches:  1.1.2;  1.1.4;
file mozJSCodeLib.cpp was initially added on branch XTF_20040312_BRANCH.
----------------------------
revision 1.1.4.2
date: 2004/07/28 09:12:21;  author: bryner%brianryner.com;  state: Exp;  lines: +1 -0
Sync with current XTF branch work.
----------------------------
...
----------------------------
revision 1.1.2.1
date: 2004/04/19 10:53:08;  author: alex.fritze%crocodile-clips.com;  state: Exp;  lines: +430 -0
Fixed bug 238324 (XTF javascript utilities).
============================================================================================
```

Listing 3.1. A CVS log file chunk of `mozJSCodeLib.cpp`

Bugzilla [95] is a bug tracking system that is used heavily in the open source community. Its core is a customizable database with a web interface which allows developers, testers as well as normal users to report and keep track of issues detected in the software system.

A typical bug report contains the following pieces of information: An *id* which unequivocally identifies the bug, the bug status composed of *status* (new, assigned, reopened, resolved, verified, closed) and *resolution* (fixed, invalid, wontfix, notyet, remind, duplicate, worksforme), the location in the system identified by the *product* and the *component*, the *operating system* and the *platform* on which the bug was detected, a *short description* of the problem and a list of comments about it (*long description*). Moreover, each bug refers to several people: The *reporter* who reported the bug, a person who is in charge to fix it (*assigned to*), quality assurance people who are responsible for ensuring that the software meets certain quality standards (*qa*), and a list of people interested in being notified of the bug fixing progress (*CC*).

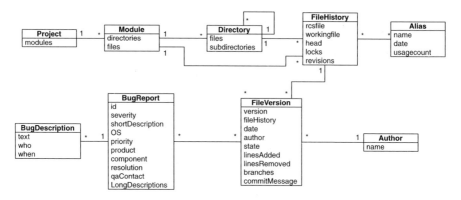

Fig. 3.2. The RHDB data model

3.3.1 The RHDB Model

Figure 3.2 shows the core of the RHDB model.

In the model a CVS commit corresponds to a file version, having all the commit-related information: Version associated to the commit, date, author, state (exp or dead), lines added and removed with respect to the previous commit, branches associated with the version and the comment written by the author. A file history, which corresponds to the actual file in the file system, is composed of a sequence of file versions, one per commit. It has a filename with (rcsfile) and without (workingfile) the entire path name. A file history can be associated to many aliases, used for tagging system releases. A project is composed of modules which contain directories and file histories. A directory can contain sub-directories and file histories. Finally, a file version can be associated to one or more bug reports. The relationship between bug reports and file versions is "many to many", meaning that a file version (and therefore a file history) can be affected by many bugs and a bug can affect different file versions and file histories.

3.3.2 Populating the RHDB

Figure 3.3 sketches the RHDB populating process. The user needs to enter the url of the CVS repository and of the Bugzilla database, and then the populating task (which depending on the size of the system can take several hours) is executed in batch mode. The main steps of the process are:

1. The latest version of the system is retrieved by means of a CVS checkout command. Then, for each directory, the log file describing the history of the contained files is retrieved and parsed.
2. For each file, the data about all its commits (its history) is stored in the database as well as a link to the actual file.
3. Every time a reference to a bug is found in the commit message (the comment written by the author at commit time), the corresponding bug report is retrieved

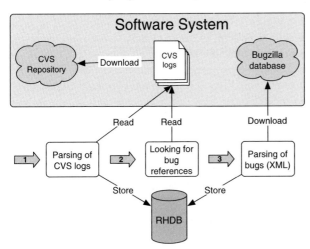

Fig. 3.3. The RHDB populating process

from the Bugzilla database, parsed and stored in the database, together with the link to the affected file. Since the link between CVS artifacts and Bugzilla problem report is not formally defined, we use regular expressions to detect bug references.

3.3.3 Related Work

Several approaches were proposed to create and populate an underlying model of an evolving software system. These approaches vary according to which information they consider (e.g., only source code repository or also bug tracking system and mail archives), which data sources they support (e.g., only CVS or also SVN, ClearCase etc.) and how these sources are linked to each other.

The previously presented RHDB is based on the CVS versioning system and the Bugzilla bug tracking system, where the links between the two sources are built as presented in Section 3.3.2. The main contribution of the RHDB is that it was the first to link CVS artifacts and Bugzilla problem reports.

Two other approaches similar to the RHDB, also based on CVS and Bugzilla, but which also use other sources of information are Hipikat [133, 511, 510] by D. Čubranić et al. and softChange [196, 195] by D. German. Both techniques use information from mail archives and, in addition, Hipikat also considers data from documentation on the analysed project website (if available).

In both approaches the links between different information sources are inferred based either on conventions (e.g., in some projects there is a convention to include in the commit comment a reference to the bug tracking system entry) or heuristics (e.g., it is likely that the author of a bug fix has committed a source code revision close to the time that the problem report was closed in the bug tracking system).

A common problem encountered while linking mail archives with CVS repository is that people tend to have multiple e-mail addresses, which might not be the same as the ones recorded in the CVS log files [197].

In the Hipikat model (see Figure 3.4), a message is a mail in the mail archive, a file version corresponds to a CVS commit in the repository (a revision), a change task is a Bugzilla problem report and a document is a design document retrieved, for example, from the project web site.

In the softChange architecture (see Figure 3.5), we see two main components: The Trail Extractor and the Fact Enhancer. The Trail Extractor retrieves the following software trails: CVS logs, Bugzilla problem report, ChangeLogs and releases of the system (tar files distributed by the software team). The Fact Enhancer uses the retrieved software trails to generate/infer new facts. For example it reconstructs the commit-set, since the commit operation in CVS is not atomic, it links CVS artifacts with Bugzilla problem report or messages from the mail archives, etc.

The information stored by Hipikat forms an "implicit group memory" (where group stands for group of developers) which is then used to facilitate the insertion of newcomers in the group, by recommending relevant artifacts for specific tasks. The data retrieved and processed by softChange is used for two types of software evolution analysis and visualization: (i) Statistics of the overall evolution of the project, using histograms where the x axis usually represents the time dimension and (ii) analysis of the relationships among files and authors, using graphs where authors and/or files are represented as nodes and their relationships as edges.

Another approach similar to the RHDB is the Kenyon framework [58] by J. Bevan et al. Kenyon provides an extensible infrastructure to retrieve the history of a software project from a SCM repository or a set of releases and to process the retrieved information. It also provides a common interface based on ORM (Object-Relational Mapping) to access to processed data stored in a database.

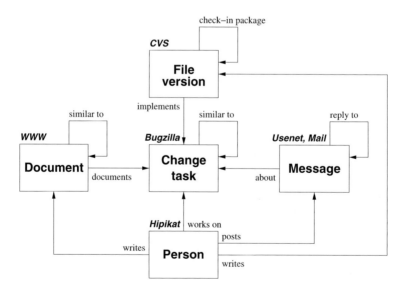

Fig. 3.4. The Hipikat model [511] ©[2005] IEEE

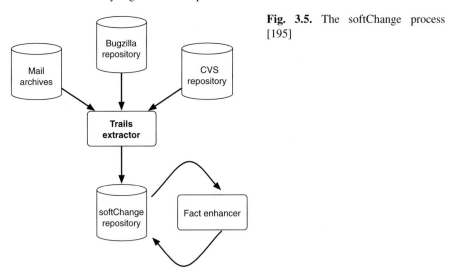

Fig. 3.5. The softChange process [195]

Figure 3.6 shows the high-level data flow architecture of Kenyon. The DataMan-ager class is the execution entry point: It reads a configuration file and invokes the other components, i.e., the Configuration Retrieval, the Fact Extractor and the Object Data Storage. The SCMInterface class isolates Kenyon from the concrete implementation of different SCM systems. The FactExtractor and MetricLoader abstract classes are the API points for specific tool invocation extensions. This means that users of Kenyon are free to attach their own external Fact Extractor and Metric Loader tools (typically analysis-specific). Besides this extension, Kenyon offers predefined fact extractor and metric loader tools. Kenyon saves the results from each

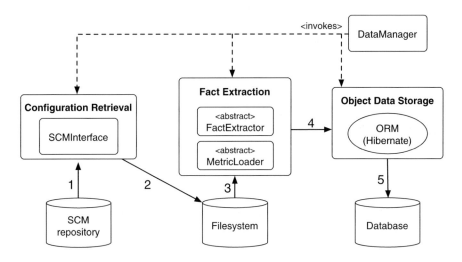

Fig. 3.6. The high-level data flow architecture of Kenyon [58], ©ACM, 2005

processed configuration to a database. An ORM mechanism is provided to help automate the storage to and retrieval of Java object from the database.

As depicted in Figure 3.6 Kenyon retrieves information from SCM only (or filesystem, i.e., set of releases), without considering other sources, such as bug tracking system or mail archives. On the other hand Kenyon supports several SCMs, namely: CVS, SVN, ClearCase and sets of releases in the filesystem.

A common aspect of Kenyon and the RDHB is that both store the data for later evolution analyses, while for softChange and Hipikat the task for using the data is already defined.

3.4 Software Evolution Analysis

The RHDB contains a concrete instance of our model of an evolving software system. This is the starting point from which, with the support of tools and techniques, we can do several types of analyses. Each technique we designed and each tool we implemented considers a particular perspective on software evolution, and addresses a particular goal. In the following, we present some software evolution analysis problems and describe our techniques to tackle them.

3.4.1 Analysing Developer Effort

The first software evolution problem we address concerns development effort. We want to answer questions such as: How many developers worked on an entity? How was the effort distributed among them? Is there an owner of the entity, based on the code-ownership principle? Moreover, we also want to be able to categorize entities in terms of "effort distribution". For an analyst or a project manager, the answers to these questions provide valuable information for a possible restructuring of the development teams.

Version control systems record the information necessary to answer these questions, as each ach artifact has a list of versions corresponding to commits, and the list of authors who performed the commits[3]. The problem is how to represent and aggregate this large amount of low-level information[4] to get an insight into the team structure and to understand who are the responsible/s of a software entity, scaling from a module down to the individual file.

Our approach is based on the *"Fractal Figure"* [139, 136] visualization, which encapsulates all the author-related information of a given software artifact. It gives an immediate view of how, in terms of development effort and distribution among authors, an artifact has been developed. We can easily figure out whether the development was done mainly by one author or many people contributed to it and to

---

[3] We only know who performed the commit, i.e., if a commit includes changes done by several people, those are all mapped to a single developer.

[4] As an example: The Mozilla system, on the first of September 2005, had 4656 source code files with a total number of 326,000 file versions, corresponding to hundreds of thousands of commit-related data to analyse.

which extent. A fractal figure is composed of a set of rectangles with different sizes and colors. Each rectangle, and thus each color, represents an author who worked on the file. The area of the rectangle is proportional to the percentage of commits performed by the author over the whole set of commits. For more details on the layout algorithm and the expressive power of Fractal Figures see [139].

Fractal Figures allow software entities to be categorized in terms of effort distribution among developers following the *gestalt principle*. We defined four visual patterns representing four development models, depicted in Figure 3.7: (a) One developer, (b) few balanced developers, (c) one major developer and (d) many balanced developers.

Development patterns allow us to categorize entities according to the way they were developed from an authors' perspective. However, the visual nature of both the patterns and the Fractal Figures themselves, is useful to get a qualitative impression only of the development model. To provide also a quantitative measure, we introduced the *Fractal Value*, which for a given software artifact is defined as:

$$\text{Fractal Value} = 1 - \sum_{a_i \in A} \left(\frac{nc(a_i)}{NC} \right)^2, \quad \text{with} \quad NC = \sum_{a_i \in A} nc(a_i) \qquad (3.1)$$

where $A = \{a_1, a_2, \ldots, a_n\}$ is the set of authors and $nc(a_i)$ is the number of commits performed by the author a_i with respect to the given software artifact. The Fractal Value measures how fragmented a Fractal Figure is, that is how much the work spent on the corresponding entity is distributed among different developers. (3.1) is defined such that the smaller the quantity $\frac{nc(a_i)}{NC}$ is (always less than 1), the more it is reduced by the square power, since the square equation is sub-linear between 0 and 1. Therefore, the smaller a rectangle is, the less its negative contribution to the Fractal Value is. The Fractal Value ranges from 0 to 1 (not reachable). It is 0 for entities developed by one author only, while it tends to 1 for entities developed by a large number of authors.

To exploit the expressive power of Fractal Figures we applied them in context of polymetric views [309]. Figures represent RHDB entities, namely files, directories, and modules. To apply them on a directory or a module, we sum up the commit information of all the files belonging to the given directory or module. We map a metric measurement of the size of the figure. The metric can be structural such as LOC

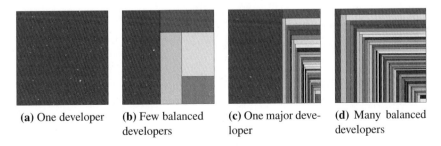

(a) One developer   (b) Few balanced developers   (c) One major developer   (d) Many balanced developers

Fig. 3.7. Development patterns based on the *gestalt* of Fractal Figures [139] ©[2005] IEEE

or evolutionary such as number of commits, number of bugs, number of lines added etc.

In the following we present different example scenarios which show how to use Fractal Figures to address the problem of understanding development effort distribution.

Detecting a Major Developer

Figure 3.8 shows the webshell directory hierarchy of Mozilla. Fractal Figures represent directories containing at least one file, while grey figures represent container directories, i.e., directories containing only subdirectories. The size metric maps the directory size in terms of number of contained files. We see that the webshell hierarchy of Mozilla includes all the four development patterns. The sub-hierarchy marked as 1 has a major developer pattern (the blue author did most of the commits). The reverse engineer knows whom to ask questions about the design and the code contained in this sub-hierarchy. On the contrary, the directory marked as 2 shows that many developers worked on it, and there is no main developer. Modifying code in these directories will be more effort since there is not a single person to ask questions about the code. The reverse engineer will need support of other tools such as Code-Crawler [310] or BugCrawler [138]. This information is not complex or hard to get, but the value of the Fractal Figure visualization is that it conveys this information in a context (the hierarchy in this case), easy and fast to read, and with the same visual principle for all the software entities to which it is applied.

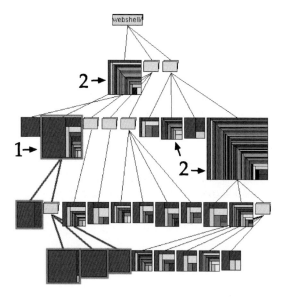

Fig. 3.8. Fractal Figures applied to the webshell hierarchy of Mozilla [139] ©[2005] IEEE. The size metric maps the directory size in terms of number of contained files

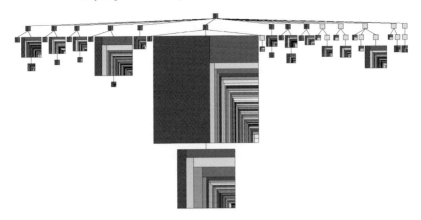

Fig. 3.9. Fractal Figures applied to the `network/protocol` hierarchy of Mozilla. The size metric maps the number of bug reports

Re-Assessing Development Team Formation

Figure 3.9 shows an example with the network protocol implementation of Mozilla. Most of the directories which introduced bugs have a many balanced developer patterns, but one which has a one major developer pattern: `network/protocol/http/src`. This directory is responsible for most of the bugs generated in the `network/protocol` hierarchy. Such a view can be valuable for a project manager or an analyst. It shows that a re-assessment of the formation of the development team is needed, given the high number of bugs and one major developer pattern of the `network/protocol/http/src` directory.

Related Work

Many software evolution analysis techniques focus more on the developers and their interaction with software artifacts than on software artifacts themselves. Liu et al [330] applied the CVSChecker tool to analyse CVS log files with the aim of understanding author contributions and identifying patterns. They wanted to study the open source development process and to understand what activities are carried out in open source project and by whom. The CVSChecker tool supports the analysis of the performance of an individual developer and the effort distribution patterns of teams.

CVSChecker has a set of parsers which extract information from the CVS source code repository and store them in a relational database. The tool then uses this information to produce four kinds of visualizations:

1. Temporal distribution of CVS activity, for each developer (see Figure 3.10a);
2. Distribution of CVS operation types, for each developer;
3. Distribution of CVS operation types, for each file;
4. Added and removed lines of code (LOC) by each developer, on each file (see an example in Figure 3.10b).

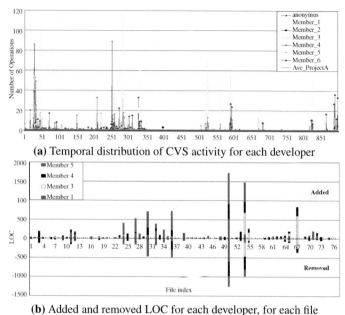

(a) Temporal distribution of CVS activity for each developer

(b) Added and removed LOC for each developer, for each file

Fig. 3.10. CVSChecker example visualizations [330]

The visualizations are used in [330] to extract development patterns to characterize the open source development process.

Gîrba et al. [203] defined a measurement for the notion of code ownership in CVS repositories. They defined that a developer is the owner of a file if he/she owns the major part of it in terms of lines. He/she owns a line of code if he/she was the last one that committed a change to that line in the repository. Based on that principle, they introduced the Ownership Map visualization, which shows the evolution of a software project, according to the following rules (summarized in Figure 3.11):

- Each file is represented as a colored line;
- The x axis represents the time dimension, from left to right;
- Each commit of a file in the repository is represented as a colored circle on the corresponding line;
- Each developer is represented by a color;
- Commits (circles) are colored according to the developer who did them, while pieces of histories of files (corresponding to pieces of lines) are colored according to the owner of the file, during the considered time interval.

In [203] the authors used the Ownership Map visualization to define development patterns such as *monologue* (a period where all the changes and most files belong to the same author), *takeover* (a developer takes over a large amount of code in a short amount of time), *team work* (two or more developers commit a quick succession of

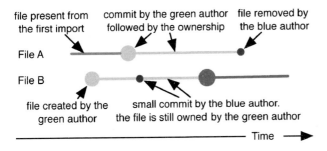

file present from · commit by the green author · file removed by
the first import · followed by the ownership · the blue author

File A

File B

file created by the · small commit by the blue author.
green author · the file is still owned by the green author

Time →

Fig. 3.11. The principles of the Ownership Map visualization [203] ©[2005] IEEE

changes to multiple files) etc. The patterns were defined with the aim of characterizing different developer behaviors.

In [528], Voinea and Telea presented a similar visualization, in which CVS files are represented as colored lines and the color represents the developer. The visualization is implemented in CVSgrab, a tool which also supports the visualization and analysis of activities in the repository. In [528] the authors applied a cluster algorithm on the visualizations to put files (lines) with similar development (with respect to either the authors or the activity) close to each other. The aim of their work was to allow developers and project managers to visually explore the evolution of a software project in a way that facilitates the system and process understanding.

Voinea et al. also presented the CVSscan tool [529], based on CVSgrab for extracting the data from the CVS repository. The tool can visualize the evolution of CVS files by visualizing the evolution of individual lines. CVSscan provides three types of color encoding to associate the color of each code line to its author. This visualization is used in [529] to understand who performed modifications on the code and where, thus facilitating the development process understanding.

Author information stored in CVS repositories was also used in the context of social networks. In [68] Bird et al. created social networks or email correspondents from OSS email archives. They linked emails with CVS accounts to analyse the relationship of email activity and commit activity and the relationship of social status with commit activity. The case study they conducted on the Apache HTTP server project indicated a strong relationship between the level of activity in the source code, and a less strong relationship with document change activity. They also found out that developers (people with email *and* CVS accounts) play a much more significant social role than other participants in the mail archives.

3.4.2 Change Coupling Analysis

Change coupling is the implicit dependency between two or more software artifacts that have been observed to frequently change together during the evolution of a system. This co-change information can either be present in the versioning system, or must be inferred by analysis. For example SVN marks co-changing files at commit time as belonging to the same *change set* while in CVS the files which are change (i.e., logically) coupled must be inferred from the modification time of each individual file.

The Evolution Radar [137, 140] is an interactive visualization technique for analysing change couplings to detect architecture decay and coupled components in a given software system. It addresses the following questions: What are the components (e.g., modules) with the strongest coupling? Which low level entities (e.g., files) are responsible for these couplings?

Figure 3.12 shows the structural principles of the Evolution Radar. It visualizes dependencies between groups of entities, in this specific case dependencies between modules (groups) as group of files (entities). The module in focus is visualized as a circle and placed in the center of a pie chart. All the other system modules are represented as sectors. The size of the sectors is proportional to the number of files contained in the corresponding module. The sectors are sorted according to this size metric, i.e., the smallest is placed at 0 radian and all others clockwise (see Figure 3.12). Within each sector files are represented as colored circles and positioned using polar coordinates where the angle and the radius are computed according to the following rules:

- *Radius d* (or distance from the center). It is inversely proportional to the change coupling the file has with the module in focus, i.e., the more they are coupled, the closer the circle (representing the file) is to the center circle (representing the module in focus).
- *Angle θ*. The files of each module are alphabetically sorted considering the entire directory path, and the circles representing them are then uniformly distributed in the sectors with respect to the angle coordinates.

Arbitrary metrics can be mapped on the color and the size of the circle figures. In the Evolution Radar files are placed according to the change coupling they have with the module in focus. To compute this metric value we use the following formula:

$$CC(M, f) = \max_{f_i \in M} CC(f_i, f) \qquad (3.2)$$

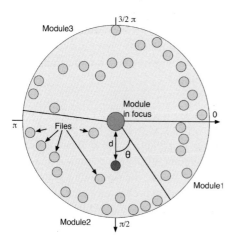

Fig. 3.12. The structural principles of the Evolution Radar [137] ©[2006] IEEE

$CC(M,f)$ is the change coupling between the module M in focus and a given file f and $CC(f_i,f)$ is the change coupling between the files f_i and f. It is also possible to use other group operators instead of the maximum such as the average or the median. We use the maximum because it points us to the files with the strongest coupling, i.e., the main responsible for the change dependencies.

The value of the coupling between two files is equal to the number of transactions which include both files. Since change transactions are not recorded by CVS we reconstruct them using the sliding time window approach proposed by Zimmermann and Weißgerber in [566], which is an improvement of the simpler fixed time window approach. For further details about the sliding and the fixed time window approach we refer the readers to [137, 566].

The Evolution Radar is implemented as an interactive visualization. It is possible to inspect all the entities visualized, i.e., files and modules, to see commit-related information like author, timestamp lines added and removed etc. Moreover, it is also possible to see the source code of selected files. Three important features for performing analyses with the Evolution Radar are (1) moving through time, (2) tracking and (3) spawning.

(1) **Moving through Time.** The change coupling measure is time dependent. If we compute it for the whole history of the system we would obtain misleading results. Figure 3.13 shows an example of such a situation.

Figure 3.13 shows the history, in terms of commit, of two files, where the time is on the horizontal axis from left to right and commits are represented as circles. If we compute the change coupling measure according to the entire history we obtain 9 shared commits on a total of 17, which is an high value because it means that the files changed together more than fifty percent of the time. Although this result is correct, it is misleading because it brings us to the conclusion that file1 and file2 are strongly coupled, but they were so only in the past and they are not coupled at all during the last year of the system. Since we analyse change coupling information for detecting architecture decay and design issues in the current version of the system, recent change couplings are more important than old ones [202]. In other words, if two files were strongly coupled at the early phases of a system, but they are not coupled in recent times (perhaps because the coupling was removed during a reengineering phase), we do not consider them as a potential problem.

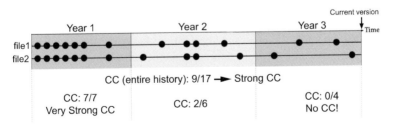

Fig. 3.13. An example of misleading results obtained by considering the entire history of artifacts to compute the change coupling value: We obtain a strong change coupling, while file1 and file2 are not coupled at all during the last year

For these reasons the Evolution Radar is time dependent, i.e., it can be computed either considering the entire history of files or with respect to a given time window. When creating the radar the user can divide the lifetime of the system into time intervals. For each interval a different radar is created, and the change coupling is computed with respect to the given time interval. The radius coordinate has the same scale in all the radars, i.e., the same distance in different radars represents the same value of the coupling. This makes it possible to compare radars and to analyse the evolution of the coupling over time. In our tool implementation the user "moves through time" by using a slider, which causes the corresponding radar to be displayed. This feature introduced also a problem: How do we keep track of the same entity over time, i.e., on different radars? To answer this question we introduced a second feature called tracking.

(2) Tracking. It allows the user to keep track of files over time. When a file is selected for tracking in a visualization related to a particular time interval, it is highlighted in all the radars (with respect to all the other time intervals) in which the file exists. The highlighting consists in using a yellow border for the tracked files and in showing a text label with the name of the file. Like this it is possible to detect files with a strong change coupling with respect to the latest period of time and then move backward in time and analyse the coupling in the past. This allows the distinction between persistent change coupling, i.e., always present, and recent change coupling, i.e., present during the last time intervals only.

(3) Spawning. The spawn feature is aimed at inspecting the change coupling details. Outliers indicate that the corresponding files have a strong coupling with certain files of the module in focus, but we ignore which ones. To uncover this dependency between files we spawn a secondary Evolution Radar as follows: The outliers are grouped to form a temporary module M_t represented by a circle figure. The module in focus (M) is then expanded, i.e., a circle figure is created for each file composing it. Finally, a new Evolution Radar is created. The temporary module M_t is placed in the center of the new radar. The files belonging to the module previously in focus (M) are placed around the center. The radius coordinate, i.e., the distance from the center, is inversely proportional to the change coupling they have with the module in the center M_t. For the angle coordinate alphabetical sorting is used. Since all the files belong to the same module there is only one sector.

We use the Evolution Radar to answer the questions mentioned at the beginning of this section: Which are the modules with the strongest coupling in a given software system? Which files are responsible for these evolutionary dependencies? In the following we apply the radar on ArgoUML, a large and long-lived open source software system. We first present example scenarios of how to study change coupling at different levels of abstraction, detecting architecture decay and design problems and performing impact analysis. We finally use the radar to analyse the evolution of couplings and to identify phases in the history of the system.

Detecting Design Issues and Architecture Decay

From the documentation of ArgoUML we know the system decomposition in modules[5] We focused our analysis on the three largest modules Model, Explorer and Diagram. From the documentation we know that Model is the central module that all the others rely and depend on. Explorer and Diagram do not depend on each other.

We created a radar for every six months of the system's history. We started the study from the most recent one, since we are interested in problems in the current version of the system. Using a relatively short time interval (six months) ensures that the coupling is due to recent changes and is not "polluted" by commits far in the past. As metrics we used the change coupling for both the position and the color of the figures. The size (the area) is proportional to the total number of lines modified in all the commits performed during the considered time interval.

Figure 3.14b shows the Evolution Radar for the last six months of history of the Explorer module. From the visualization we see that the coupling with Diagram is much stronger than the one with Model, although the documentation states that the dependency is with Model and not with Diagram. The most coupled files in Diagram are FigActionState.java, FigAssociationEnd.java, FigAssociation.java. Using the tracking feature, we found out that these files have only been recently coupled with the Explorer module. In Figure 3.14a showing the previous six months, they are not close to the center. This implies that the dependency is due to recent changes only.

To inspect the change coupling details, we used the spawning feature: We grouped the three files and generated another radar, shown in Figure 3.15 having this group as the center. We now see that the dependency is mainly due to ExplorerTree.java. The high-level dependency between two modules is thus reduced to a dependency between four files. These four files represent a problem in the system, because modifying one of them may break the others. The fact that they belong to different modules buries this hidden dependency.

The visualization in Figure 3.14b shows that the file GeneratorJava.java is an outlier, since its coupling is much stronger with respect to all the other files in the same module (CodeGeneration). By spawning the group composed of GeneratorJava.java we obtained a visualization very similar to Figure 3.15, in which the main responsible for the dependency is again ExplorerTree.java. Reading the code revealed that the ExplorerTree class is responsible for managing mouse listeners and generating names for figures. This explains the dependencies with FigActionState, FigAssociationEnd and FigAssociation in the Diagram module, but not the dependency with GeneratorJava.

The past (see Figure 3.14a and Figure 3.16a) reveals that GeneratorJava.java is an outlier since January 2003. This long-lasting dependency indicates design problems.

---

[5] We did not consider some modules for which the documentation says "They are all insignificant enough not to be mentioned when listing dependencies." [19].

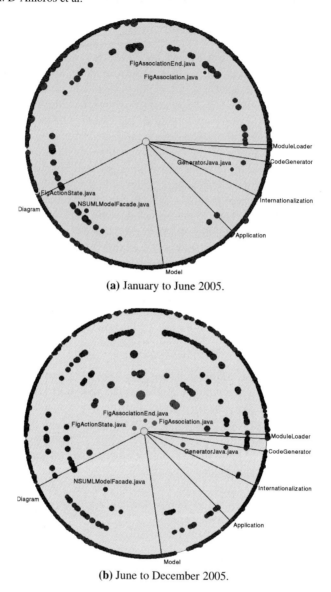

(a) January to June 2005.

(b) June to December 2005.

Fig. 3.14. Evolution Radars for the Explorer module of ArgoUML in 2005 [137] ©[2006] IEEE

A further inspection is required for the ExplorerTree.java file in the Explorer module, since it is the main responsible for the coupling with the modules Diagram and CodeGeneration.

The radars in Figure 3.14b and Figure 3.14a show that during 2005 the file NSUMLModelFacade.java in the Model module had the strongest coupling with

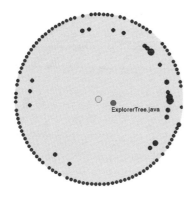

Fig. 3.15. Details of the change coupling between the `Explorer` module and the files `FigActionState.java`, `FigAssociationEnd.java` and `FigAssociation.java` [137] ©[2006] IEEE

`Explorer` (module in the center). Going six months back in time, from June to December 2004 (see Figure 3.16a), we see that the coupling with `NSUMLModelFacade` `.java` was weak, while there was a very strong dependency with `ModelFacade.` `java`. This file was also heavily modified during that time interval, given its dimension with respect to the other figures (the area is proportional to the total number of lines modified). `ModelFacade.java` was also strongly coupled with the `Diagram` module (see Figure 3.16b). By looking at its source code we found out that this was a God class [439] with thousands of lines of code, 444 public and 9 private methods, all static. The `ModelFacade` class is not present in the other radars (Figure 3.14b and Figure 3.14a) because it was removed from the system in January 2005. By reading the source code of the most coupled files in these two radars, i.e.,`NSUMLModelFacade.java`, we discovered that it is also a very large class with 317 public methods. Moreover, we found out that 292 of these methods have the same signature of methods in the `ModelFacade` class[6], with more that 75% of the code duplicated. `ModelFacade` represented a problem in the system and thus was removed. Since many methods were copied to `NSUMLModelFacade`, the problem has just been relocated.

This example shows how historical information can reveal problems, which are difficult to detect with only one version of the system. Knowing the evolution of `ModelFacade` helped us in understanding the role of `NSUMLModelFacade` in the current version of the system.

We showed examples of how to use the Evolution Radar to detect problematic parts of the ArgoUML system, which represent good candidates for reengineering. The main findings of the discussed example scenario are:

- The `Diagram` and `Explorer` modules are the most coupled. Since this dependency is not mentioned in the module relationships page in the documentation,

---

[6] With the difference that in `NSUMLModelFacade` the methods are not static and that it contains only two attributes, while `ModelFacade` has 114 attributes.

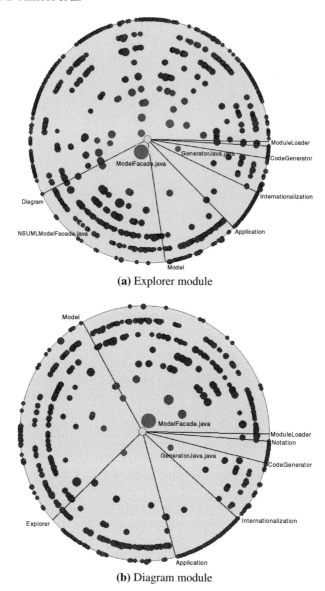

(a) Explorer module

(b) Diagram module

Fig. 3.16. Evolution Radars of the `Explorer` and `Diagram` modules of ArgoUML from June to December 2004 [137] ©[2006] IEEE

either the modules should be restructured to decrease the coupling or at least the documentation should be updated. We identified the four files mainly responsible for this hidden dependency.

- The files GeneratorJava.java in the CodeGeneration module and ExplorerTree.java in the Explorer module should be further analysed and, if possible, refactored. GeneratorJava.java has a persistent coupling with the Explorer module, while ExplorerTree.java is coupled with both CodeGeneration and Diagram.
- Two problematic classes were detected: ModelFacade and NSUMLModelFacade. Most of the methods of the first class were copied to the second one, and then ModelFacade was removed from the system.

Related Work

The concept of change (i.e., logical) coupling was first introduced by Gall et al. [185] to detect implicit relationships between modules. They used logical coupling to analyse the dependencies between the different modules of a large telecommunications software system and showed that the approach can be used to derive useful insights on the architecture of the system. Later the same authors revisited the technique to work at a lower abstraction level. They detected logical couplings at the class level [187] and validated it on 28 releases of an industrial software system. The authors showed through a case study that architectural weaknesses such as poorly designed interfaces and inheritance hierarchies could be detected based on logical coupling information.

Ratzinger et al. [433] used the same technique to analyse the logical coupling at the class level with the aim of learning about, and improving the quality of the system. To accomplish this, they defined *code smells* based on the logical coupling between classes of the system.

Other work has been performed at finer granularity levels. Zimmermann et al. [567] used the information about changes that are occurring together to predict entities (classes, methods, fields etc.) that are likely to be modified when one is being modified. Breu and Zimmermann [80] applied data mining techniques on co-changed entities to identify and rank cross-cutting concerns in software systems. Ying et al. applied data mining techniques to the change history of the code base to identify change patterns to recommend potentially relevant source code for a particular modification task [561] Bouktif et al. [77] improved precision and recall of co-chancing files detection with respect to previous approaches. They introduced the concept of change patterns in general and the particular Synchrony change-pattern for co-changing files. They proposed an approach to detect such change-patterns in CVS repositories based on dynamic time warping.

Similar to the Evolution Radar the EvoLens visualization technique can be used to analyse the change coupling relationships between source files and software modules. Instead of radar views it uses a graph-based visualization that allows the user to navigate the change coupling information from the level of modules down to the source files. It allows the user to reveal detailed change couplings to the cost of always having a radar view of the whole system. The basic ideas and underlying concepts of the EvoLens Views have been developed by Ratzinger et al. [432].

Beyer and Hassan in [59] presented the Evolution Storyboards, a visualization technique for software evolution that offers dynamic views. The storyboards emphasizes the history of a project using a sequence of panels, each representing a particular time period in the life of the project. To create each panel they compute a co-change graph and use a layout in which the stronger the coupling between two files is, the closer they are placed, thus revealing clusters of frequently co-changed files. They showed two main applications of the tool: First they analysed how the structure of a software system decayed or remained stable over time, by comparing the clusters of co-changed files with the authoritative system decomposition. In the second application, they detected files which implement cross-cutting concerns, by detecting the files which are always moving from panel to panel, meaning that these files are coupled (close in the layout) with many others during the life of the project.

In [178] Fischer and Gall presented EvoGraph, a lightweight approach based on the RHDB data to evolutionary and structural analysis of software systems. They compounded change history and source code information spaces in a single approach, to support the comprehension about the interaction between evolving requirements and system development. The EvoGraph technique is composed of five phases: (1) File selection: Source files which exhibit an extraordinary logical coupling with respect to cross-cutting change transactions are selected. (2) Co-change visualization. (3) Fact extraction: For the selected files in the preceding step, the detailed change transaction information is collected from the RHDB and as result change vectors are created for every file within a transaction. (4) Mining: The change vectors are the input to mining of change transaction data step; The output is a description of the longitudinal evolution of structural dependencies of selected files. (5) Visualization: The structural dependencies are visualized in an electrocardiogram style diagram.

3.4.3 Trend Analysis and Hot-Spots Detection

In this section we present the ArchView approach used to create different higher-level views on the source code. Views visualize the software modules which stem from the decomposition of a system into manageable implementation units. Such units, for example, are packages, source code directories, classes, or source files. The objective of ArchView is to point out implementation specific aspects of *one* and *multiple* source code releases. For instance, highlighting modules that are exceptionally large, complex, and exhibit strong dependency relationships to other modules. They are the so called *hot-spots* in the system. Furthermore, modules with a strong increase in size and complexity, or modules that have become unstable are highlighted. Such views can be used by software engineers, for instance to (1) get a clue of the implemented design and its evolution; (2) to spot the important modules implementing the key-functionality of a software system; (3) to spot the heavily coupled modules; (4) to identify critical evolution trends. The basic ideas and underlying concepts of ArchView have been developed in the work of Pinzger et.al [417].

ArchView obtains metric values of each module and dependency relationship from the RHDB and assigns them to a feature vector m. Feature vectors are tracked

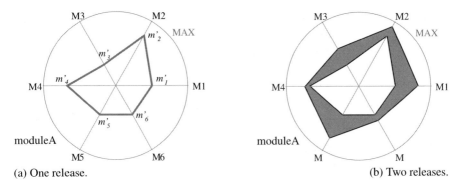

(a) One release.   (b) Two releases.

Fig. 3.17. Kiviat diagram of moduleA representing measures of six source code metrics $M_1, M_2, ..., M_6$ of one release

over the selected n releases and composed to the evolution matrix E. The values in the matrix quantify the evolution of a software module:

$$E_{i \times n} = \begin{pmatrix} m'_1 & m''_1 & .. & m^n_1 \\ m'_2 & m''_2 & .. & m^n_2 \\ . & . & ... & . \\ . & . & ... & . \\ m'_i & m''_i & .. & m^n_i \end{pmatrix}$$

The matrix contains n feature vectors with measures of i metrics. Evolution matrices are computed for each module. They form the basic input to our ArchView visualization approach that we will present next.

The ArchView approach uses the Polymetric Views visualization technique presented by Lanza et al. [309]. Instead of using rectangles to present modules and metric values ArchView uses *Kiviat* diagrams which are also known as *Radar* diagrams. These diagrams are suited to present multiple metric values available for a module as described next.

Figure 3.17 (a) shows an example of a Kiviat diagram representing measures of six metrics $M_1, M_2, ..., M_6$ of one release of the module moduleA. The underlying data is from the following evolution matrix E:

$$E_{6 \times 1} = \begin{pmatrix} m'_1 \\ . \\ . \\ m'_6 \end{pmatrix}$$

In a Kiviat diagram the metric values are arranged in a circle. For each metric there is a straight line originating in the center of the diagram. The length of this line is fixed for all metrics and each metric value is normalized according to it. In the examples presented in this section we use the following normalization:

$$l\left(m'_i\right) = \frac{m'_i * cl}{max(m'_i)} \qquad (3.3)$$

where cl denotes the constant length of the straight line, and $max(m_i')$ the maximum value for a metric m_i' across all modules to be visualized. With the normalized value and the angle of the straight line denoting the metric the drawing position of the point on the line is computed. To make the metric values visible in the diagram adjacent metric values are connected forming a polygon such as the one shown in Figure 3.17.

When visualizing the metric values for a number of subsequent releases our main focus is on highlighting the change between metric values. Typically, increases in metric values indicate the addition and decreases the removal of functionality. The addition of functionality is a usual sign of evolving software systems so it represents no particular problem. In contrast, the removal of functionality often indicates changes in the design. For instance, methods are moved to a different class to resolve a (bidirectional) dependency relationship and improve separation of concerns or methods are deleted because of removal of dead code (i.e., code that is not used anymore).

To highlight the changes in metric values we use the Kiviat diagrams as described before. The n values of each metric obtained from the multiple releases are drawn on the same line. Again the adjacent metric values of the same release are connected by a line forming a polygon for each release. Then the emerging area between two polygons of two subsequent releases are filled with different colors. Each color indicates and highlights the change between the metric values of two releases. The larger the change the larger the polygon.

Figure 3.17 (b) depicts the same set of measure for moduleA but this time of two releases. By filling the area between the releases the change of metric values are highlighted. To distinguish the changes between different source code releases we use gray tones. This allows the user to spot trends in metric values as we will show in the following two analysis scenarios.

Analysing the Size and Complexity of Software Modules

The first scenario concerns an analysis of the growth in size and program complexity of software modules. We demonstrate this by visualizing typical size and program complexity metrics taken from three releases 0.92, 1.3a, and 1.7 of Mozilla content and layout modules. We configure ArchView with the following set of metrics: Halstead intelligent content (HALCONT), Halstead mental effort (HALEFF), Halstead program difficulty (HALDIFF), McCabe Cyclomatic Complexity (CYCL), and lines of code (LOC). The resulting view is depicted in Figure 3.18.

The interesting modules are represented by Kiviat diagrams with large, filled, gray polygons. They indicate strong increase and decrease in the size and program complexity of software modules whereas small polygons represent more stable modules. Following this guideline we can easily see that NewLayoutEngine and DOM (Document Object Model) are the two largest and most complex modules in the Mozilla content and layout implementation. For instance, in release 1.7 DOM comprises 197.498 and NewLayoutEngine 156.438 lines of C/C++ code. In contrast, the XML module comprises 23.471 lines of code.

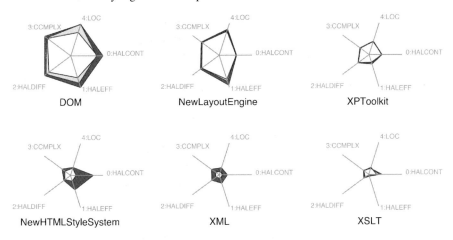

Fig. 3.18. Kiviat graph of six Mozilla content and layout modules showing the growth in program size and complexity. Light gray polygons indicate changes between releases 0.92 and 1.3a. Dark gray polygons show changes between 1.3a and 1.7

Large gray polygons are contained by the Kiviat diagrams of the modules DOM, NewHTMLStyleSystem, and XML indicating that the implementation of these three modules changed the most. Looking at the selected size and program complexity metric values we found out that the values of the three modules first increased from release 0.92 to 1.3a and then decreased from release 1.3a to 1.7. For instance, the HALCONT metric of the DOM module from release 0.92 to release 1.3a increased from 15.167 to 18.228 followed by a decrease to 14.714 in release 1.7. Apparently, from release 0.92 to 1.3a functionality was added to these three modules which during the implementation of the last release then was refactored or removed. In comparison to these three modules the metric values of the other modules indicate only minor changes in size and program complexity hence they are stable. Based on the assumption that modules that changed in a past release will be likely to change in future releases the three modules DOM, NewHTMLStyleSystem, and XML are the candidates who are critical for the evolution of the content and layout implementation of Mozilla.

Detecting System Hot-Spots

System hot-spots are modules with high activity indicated by different measures such as the number of problems affecting a module or the number of changes in a module. In this scenario of analysing system hot-spots we focus on providing answers to the following three questions: Which are the modules with frequent bugs? Which are the most critical modules? Which modules became stable? The answers to these questions can be found in the RHDB in particular in the Bugzilla data. We quantify the criticality and stability of a software module by the number of source code modifications (i.e., CVS log entries) performed for fixing bugs that were reported

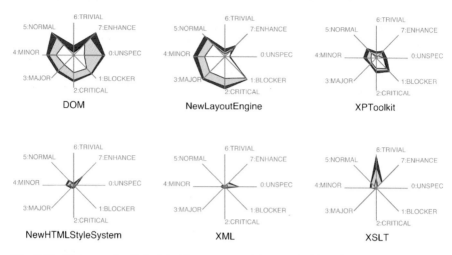

Fig. 3.19. Kiviat graph of six Mozilla content and layout modules showing criticality and stability. Light gray polygons indicate changes between releases 0.92 and 1.3a. Dark gray polygons show changes between 1.3a and 1.7

during a given observation period such as the time between two releases. To further detail criticality and stability we take the different severity levels of bugs ranging from blockers, to minor and trivial bugs into account (severity levels are taken from the Bugzilla repository). This leads to the following set of measures: number of modifications for bugs with unspecified severity (UNSPEC), number of modifications for blocker bugs (BLOCKER), number of modifications for critical bugs (CRITICAL), number of modifications for major bugs (MAJOR), number of modifications for minor bugs (MINOR), number of modifications for normal bugs (NORMAL), number of modifications for trivial bugs (TRIVIAL), and number of modifications for suggested enhancements (ENHANCE). We configured ArchView with these measures and selected six Mozilla content and layout modules from release 0.92, 1.3a, and 1.7. The resulting system hot-spot view is depicted by Figure 3.19.

The large gray polygons of the DOM and NewLayoutEngine indicate that these two modules got the highest number of CVS log entries for fixing bugs. For instance, up to release 1.7 DOM got 254 modifications from 130 bugs rated as blocker and 904 modifications from 487 bugs rated as critical. NewLayoutEngine got 309 CVS log entries from 121 blocker and 1.097 log entries from critical bug reports. Interestingly, most of the modifications in the implementation of these two modules were due to bugs of high severity and only few due to trivial bugs. This fact is indicated by the cut of the TRIVIAL measure occurring in both Kiviat diagrams. Compared with these two modules the other content and layout modules needed less modifications to fix bugs. For instance, XSLT got 7 modifications due to 3 blocker bugs and 48 modifications due to 12 critical bugs. Interestingly, the Kiviat of XSLT shows a peak in the number of trivial bugs (TRIVIAL). 123 modifications due to 3 trivial bugs were performed which is more than twice as much as the values of the other five modules (e.g., DOM got 55 and NewLayoutEngine 43 modifications). Apparently, a large number of files had to be touched to fix the three trivial bugs. For instance, 56 files were modified to fix bug #88623. This raises the question about how "trivial" this bug was when modifications had to be done in 56 source files.

Concerning the criticality and stability of software modules we investigated the trend of these measures. More specifically, stable modules are indicated by small dark gray polygons meaning less bugs and modifications during the development of release 1.7. According to Figure 3.19 the modules NewHTMLStyleSystem and XML were affected by almost zero changes. They represent the most stable content and layout modules. The other four modules seem to be more critical as indicated by larger light and dark gray polygons whereas the light gray polygons dominate the diagrams. This means that a large amount of bug fixing took place in the time period from release 0.92 to 1.3a which then decreased in the time of developing release 1.7. For instance, the number of modifications for fixing blocker bugs decreased from 65 between the releases 0.92 and 1.3a to 8 modifications between 1.3a and 1.7. That is a clear indicator that the other four modules were critical in previous releases but became stable in release 1.7.

Related Work

A number of approaches have been developed that address the visualization of data of several software releases. For instance, Riva et al. use 2D and 3D graphs to visualize and navigate the release history of a software system [188]. Time is visualized on the z coordinate expressed in release sequence numbers (RSN). The structure of each software release is visualized using 3D graphs with a tree layout. Each graph is spatially positioned along the z-coordinate showing the sequence of releases. A cube denotes a subsystem or a software module. Edges indicate the decomposition of each release into subsystems and modules. One measure can be mapped to the 3D-graphs using the color attribute. For instance, they mapped the version number of a module such that a module that is not present in a release is represented by a black cube, a module in version 1 is represented by a red cube, in version 2 by a blue cube, etc.

An approach similar to the approach of Riva et al. is presented by Collberg et al. in [121]. They developed GEVOL, a graph-based system for visualizing the evolution of software systems. Each state of a system is represented by a graph. Colors are applied to indicate change over time such as when particular parts of the program were first created and modified, which programmer modified which parts, or which parts have grown in complexity. All nodes start out being red, then grow paler for every time they have remained unchanged. When a node changes again it return to red. When a user notices an interesting event, such as a code segment changes frequently, he can click on a node to examine the set of authors who have affected these changes.

Lanza developed an approach called the Evolution Matrix [308]. Instead of using a tree layout Lanza uses a matrix layout. The Evolution Matrix displays the evolution of the classes of a software system. Each column of the matrix represents a version of the software, while each row represents the different versions of a class. Figure 3.20

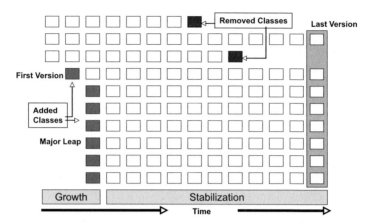

Fig. 3.20. Evolution Matrix with four typical characteristics of an evolving software system [308], ©ACM, 2001

shows an example of an Evolution Matrix with typical characteristics of a system such as the classes of the first version, removed classes, a major leap in the evolution, and the last version of the system.

Following the Polymetric View principle a number of measures can be mapped to the width, height, and color of rectangles that represent classes. Recurring patterns in the matrix arise that led to a categorization of the evolution of classes. For instance, a class that is alternately growing and shrinking in size is called Pulsar. Pulsar classes can be seen as hot-spots in the system: for every new version of the system changes on a pulsar class must be performed. Other categories of classes, for instance, are Supernova (class suddenly explodes in size) or Dayfly (class with a short life-time).

In [548] Wu et al. present Evolution Spectographs, a visualization technique that combines metrics and gradient colors to portray the evolution of software systems. A spectograph is shown as a matrix similar to the Evolution Matrix in which time is presented on the X axis and the dimension of files is presented on the Y axis. A row in the matrix represents the change history of a file and a column stores change metrics for all the files during a particular time period. Each cell represents a file in a particular period. After a file is changed its color becomes lighter and lighter as long as there is no change made to that file. In other words, the file starts to cool down if no future change occurs to it. Using this color function Evolution Spectographs can be used to highlight system growth and dependency change in one chart.

3.5 Conclusion

Mining software repositories is a fairly recent research topic that has been embraced by both the software evolution and the empirical software engineering community. As we have seen in this chapter there are two major challenges:

- *Technical challenge.* The challenge resides in modeling and handling various kinds of informations. The sheer amount of information available in source repositories also poses scalability problems that have however been tackled to a large extent. As we have seen, in most cases researchers have chosen to use relational databases to handle the data as they allow for easy querying.
- *Conceptual challenge.* Once the data is retrieved and modeled, a major challenge resides in doing something meaningful with the available data. As we have seen in the various approaches, at the beginning there is always a number of research questions that need to be answered, and subsequently researchers develop the necessary mechanisms to answer those questions. A heavily used technique in this case is visualization, as it allows (if well chosen) to detect patterns in the sea of data that one has to navigate.

As a major future challenge we see the current dichotomy between forward engineering and software evolution. We believe that software repositories, currently mostly used for retrospective analyses, need to become an integral part of any software project, and as such should not be separated from the most recent version, which is usually the focus of all maintenance efforts.

4

Predicting Bugs from History

Thomas Zimmermann[1], Nachiappan Nagappan[2], and Andreas Zeller[1]

[1] University of Calgary, Alberta, Canada
[2] Microsoft Research, Redmond, Washington, USA
[3] Saarland University, Saarbrücken, Germany

Summary. Version and bug databases contain a wealth of information about software failures—how the failure occurred, who was affected, and how it was fixed. Such defect information can be automatically mined from software archives; and it frequently turns out that some modules are far more defect-prone than others. How do these differences come to be? We research how code properties like (a) code complexity, (b) the problem domain, (c) past history, or (d) process quality affect software defects, and how their correlation with defects in the past can be used to predict future software properties—where the defects are, how to fix them, as well as the associated cost.

4.1 Introduction

Suppose you are the manager of a large software project. Your product is almost ready to be released—where "almost ready" means that you suspect that a number of defects remain. To find these defects, you can spend some resources for quality assurance. Since these resources are limited, you want to spend them in the most effective way, getting the best quality and the lowest risk of failure. Therefore, you want to spend the most quality assurance resources on those modules that need it most—those modules which have the highest risk of producing failures.

Allocating quality assurance resources wisely is a risky task. If some non-defective module is tested for months and months, this is a waste of resources. If a defective module is not tested enough, a defect might escape into the field, causing a failure and potential subsequent damage. Therefore, identifying defect-prone modules is a crucial task for management.

During the lifetime of a project, developers remember failures as well as successes, and this experience tells them which modules in a system are most frequently associated with problems. A good manager will exploit this expertise and allocate resources appropriately. Unfortunately, human memory is limited, selective, and sometimes inaccurate. Therefore, it may be useful to complement it with findings from actual facts—facts on software defects as found after release.

In most quality-aware teams, accessing these facts requires no more than a simple database query. This is so because *bug databases* collect every problem reported

T. Mens, S. Demeyer (eds.), *Software Evolution.*
DOI 10.1007/978-3-540-76440-3, © Springer 2008

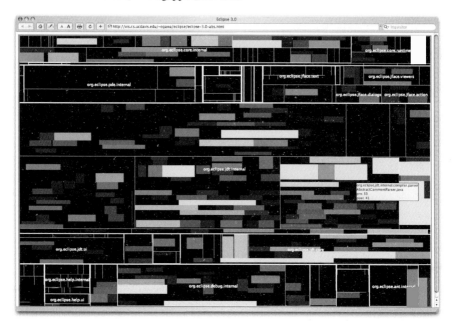

Fig. 4.1. Michael Ogawa's visualisation of the Eclipse Bug Data [401], inspired by Martin Wattenberg's "Map of the Market" [536]. Each rectangle stands for a package; the brighter the rectangle, the more post-release defects it has

about a software product. For a system that already has a large user community, bug databases are central to the development process: new bugs are entered into the system, unresolved issues are tracked, and tasks are assigned to individual developers. However, as a bug database grows, it can also be used to learn which modules are prone to defects and failures. This is so because as the problems are fixed, the fixes apply to individual modules—and therefore, one can actually compute how many defects (or reported failures) some module is associated with. (How to establish these mappings between bug reports, fixes, and locations is described in Chapter 3 of the present book.)

Figure 4.1 visualises defect data in the modules of the Eclipse programming environment. As the picture shows, the distribution of defects across modules is very uneven. For instance, compiler components in Eclipse have shown 4–5 times as many defects as user interface components [455]. Such an uneven distribution is not at all uncommon; Pareto's law [160, p. 132], for instance, already stated in 1975 that approximately 80 % of the defects are found in 20 % of the modules. Still, this uneven distribution calls for our first research question:

Why are some modules more defect-prone than others?

Answering this question helps in understanding the nature of defects—starting with the symptoms, and then following the cause-effect chain back to a root cause—and will help avoiding defects in the future.

Unfortunately, at the present time, we have no universal answer for this question. It appears that every project has its own individual factors that make specific modules prone to defects and others unlikely to fail. However, we can at least try to capture these *project-specific properties*—for instance, by examining and summarising the common symptoms of defect-prone modules. Coming back to our original setting, knowing these common properties will also help in allocating quality assurance resources. This will answer the second, more opportunistic, but no less important question:

Can we predict how defect-prone a component will be?

At first glance, this question may seem absurd. Did we not just discuss how to measure defect-proneness in the past? Unfortunately, the number of defects in the past may not be a good indicator of the future:

- Software *evolves,* with substantial refactorings and additions being made all the time. Over time, this invalidates earlier measurements about defects.
- The defects we measure from history can only be mapped to components because *they have been fixed.* Given that we consider defects that occur after release, by definition, any measurement of defect-prone components applies to an already obsolete revision.

For these reasons, we need to devise with predictive methods that can be applied to new as well as evolved components—predictions that rely on *invariants* in people, process, or structure that allow predicting defects although the code itself has changed. In the next section, we discuss how to find some of such invariants, and how they may impact the likelihood of defects.

4.2 What Makes a Module Defect-Prone?

If software needs to be fixed, it needs to be fixed because it does not satisfy a requirement. This means that between the initial requirement and the actual deployment of the software system, some mistake has been made. This mistake manifests itself as an error in some development artefact, be it requirements, specification, or a design document. Ultimately, it is the source code that matters most, since it is the realisation of the software system; errors in source code are called *defects.* If an error in some earlier stage does not become a defect, we are lucky; if it becomes a defect, it may cause a failure and needs to be fixed.

The defect likelihood of some module thus depends on its history—not only its code history, but the entire history of activities that led to its creation and maintenance. As the code evolves, this earlier history still stays unchanged, and the history may well apply to other modules as well. Therefore, when trying to predict the error-proneness of modules, we must look for *invariants* in their history, and how these invariants might manifest themselves in modules. In this chapter, we discuss the following invariants:

Complexity. In general, we assume that the likelihood of making mistakes in some artefact increases with

1. the number of details, and
2. the extent of how these details interact and interfere with each other.

This is generally known as *complexity,* and there are many ways complexity manifests itself in code. More specifically, *complexity metrics* attempt to measure the complexity of code, and therefore, it may be useful to check whether it is possible to predict defect-proneness based on complexity metrics. This is discussed in Section 4.3.

Problem domain. As stated initially, software fixes come to be because requirements are unsatisfied. This implies that the more likely it is to violate a requirement, the higher the chances of making a mistake. Of course, a large number of interfering requirements results in a higher problem complexity—and should thus manifest itself in complex code, as described above. However, we assume that specific *problem domains* imply their own set of requirements. Therefore, one should be able to predict defect-proneness based on the domain alone. How does one determine the problem domain? By examining the modules another module interacts with, as shown in Section 4.4.

Evolution. Requirements can be unsatisfied for a simple reason: They may be changing frequently. Modified requirements result in changed code—and therefore, *code that is frequently changed* indicates frequently changing requirements. The same applies for imprecise requirements or requirements that are not well understood, where trial-and-error approaches may also cause frequent fixes. Finally, since changes may introduce new defects [160], a high change rate implies a higher defect likelihood. Relying on the change rate to predict defects is discussed in Section 4.5.

Process. Every defect that escapes into the field implies a failure of quality assurance—the defect simply should have been caught during checking, testing, or reviewing. A good software process can compensate many of the risks described above; and therefore, the *quality of the development process* should also be considered when it comes to predicting defects. We discuss these open issues in Section 4.6.

The role of these invariants in software development has been analysed before, and a large body of knowledge is available that relates complexity, the problem domain, or evolution data to defects. What we see today, however, is the *automation* of these approaches. By having bug and change databases available for automated analysis, we can build tools that automatically relate defects to possible causes. Such tools allow for product- and project-specific approaches, which may be far more valuable than general (and therefore vague) recommendations found in software engineering textbooks. Our results, discussed in the following sections, all highlight the necessity of such goal-oriented approaches.

Related to this is the notion of *software reliability*. Software reliability is defined as the probability that the software will work without failure under specified conditions and for a specified period of time [388]. A number of software reliability models are available. They range from the simple Nelson model [392] to more sophisticated models using hyper-geometric coverage [248] and Markov chains [540].

4.3 Metrics

A common belief is that the more complex code is, the more defects it has. But is this really true? In order to investigate this hypothesis, we first must come up with a measure of complexity—or, in other words, a *complexity metric*. A metric is defined as *quantitative measure of the degree to which a system, component or process possesses a given attribute* [238]; the name stems from the Greek work *metron* ($\mu\acute{\epsilon}\tau\rho o\nu$), meaning "measure". Applied to software, a metric becomes a *software metric*.

Software metrics play an essential part in understanding and controlling the overall software engineering process. Unfortunately, metrics can be easily misinterpreted leading to making poor decisions. In this section, we investigate the relationships between metrics and quality, in particular defects:

Do complexity metrics correlate with defect density?

4.3.1 Background

We begin this section by quickly summarising some of the more commonly used complexity metrics in software engineering in Table 4.1. These metrics can be extracted from the source code information of projects.

Software engineering research on metrics has examined a wide variety of topics related to quality, productivity, communication, social aspects, etc. We briefly survey studies investigating the relationship between metrics and software quality.

Studies have been performed on the distribution of faults during development and their relationship with metrics like size, complexity metrics, etc. [172].

From a design metrics perspective, there have been studies involving the Chidamber/Kemerer (CK) metric suite [111]. These metrics can be a useful early internal indicator of externally-visible product quality [39, 479]. The CK metric suite consist of six metrics (designed primarily as object oriented design measures):

- weighted methods per class (WMC),
- coupling between objects (CBO),
- depth of inheritance (DIT),
- number of children (NOC),
- response for a class (RFC), and
- lack of cohesion among methods (LCOM).

The CK metrics have also been investigated in the context of fault-proneness. Basili et al. [39] studied the fault-proneness in software programs using eight student projects. They observed that the WMC, CBO, DIT, NOC and RFC metrics were

Table 4.1. Commonly used complexity metrics

Metric	Description
Lines of code	The number of non-commented lines of code
Global variables	The number of global variables in a module
Cyclomatic complexity	The Cyclomatic complexity metric [479] measures the number of linearly-independent paths through a program unit
Read coupling	The number of global variables read by a function. (The function is thus coupled to the global variable through the read operation)
Write coupling	The number of global variables written by a function. (The function is thus coupled to the global variable through the write operation)
Address coupling	The number of global variables whose address is taken by a function and is not read/write coupling. (The function is coupled to the global variable as it takes the address of the variable)
Fan-in	The number of other functions calling a given function in a module
Fan-out	The number of other functions being called from a given function in a module
Weighted methods per class	The number of methods in a class including public, private and protected methods
Depth of inheritance	For a given class the maximum class inheritance depth
Class coupling	Coupling to other classes through (a) class member variables, (b) function parameters, (c) classes defined locally in class member function bodies. (d) Coupling through immediate base classes. (e) Coupling through return type
Number of subclasses	The number of classes directly inheriting from a given parent class in a module

correlated with defects while the LCOM metric was not correlated with defects. Further, Briand et al. [82] performed an industrial case study and observed the CBO, RFC, and LCOM metrics to be associated with the fault-proneness of a class.

Structure metrics take into account the interactions between modules in a product or system and quantify such interactions. The information-flow metric defined by Henry and Kafura [230], uses *fan-in* (the number of modules that call a given module) and *fan-out* (the number of modules that are called by a given module) to calculate a complexity metric, $C_p = (fan\text{-}in \times fan\text{-}out)^2$. Components with a large fan-in and large fan-out may indicate poor design. Such modules have to be decomposed correctly.

4.3.2 Case Study: Five Microsoft Projects

Together with Thomas Ball we performed a large scale study at Microsoft to investigate the relation between complexity metrics and defects [390]. We addressed the following questions:

1. Do metrics correlate with defect density?
2. Do metrics correlate *universally* with defect density, i.e., across projects?
3. Can we predict defect density with regression models?
4. Can we transfer (i.e., reuse) regression models across projects?

For our study, we collected code complexity metrics and post-release defect data for five components in the Windows operating system:

- the HTML rendering module of *Internet Explorer 6 (IE6)*
- the application loader for *Internet Information Services (IIS)*
- *Process Messaging Component*—a Microsoft technology that enables applications running at different times to communicate across heterogeneous networks and systems that may be temporarily offline.
- *Microsoft DirectX*—a Windows technology that enables higher performance in graphics and sound when users are playing games or watching video on their PC.
- *Microsoft NetMeeting*—a component for voice and messaging between different locations.

To protect proprietary information, we have anonymised the components and refer to them as projects A, B, C, D, and E.

In our study, we observed *significant correlations* between complexity metrics (both object oriented (OO) and non-OO metrics) and post-release defects. The metrics that had the highest correlations are listed in Table 4.2. The interesting part of this result is that across projects, different complexity metrics correlated significantly with post-release defects. This indicates that none of the metrics we researched would qualify as universal predictor, even in our closed context of only Windows operating system components.

When there is no universal metric, can we build one by combining existing metrics? We tried by building *regression models* [282] using complexity metrics. In order to avoid inter-correlations between the metrics, we applied *principal component*

Table 4.2. Metrics with high correlations

Project	Correlated Metrics
A	Number of classes and five derivations
B	Almost all metrics
C	All except depth of inheritance
D	Only lines of code
E	Number of functions, number of arcs, McCabe complexity

Table 4.3. Transferring predictors across projects

Project learned from	Project predicted for				
	A	B	C	D	E
A	–	no	no	no	no
B	no	–	yes	no	no
C	no	yes	–	no	yes
D	no	no	no	–	no
E	no	no	yes	no	–

analysis [246] first. For our regression models, we used the principal components as independent variables. As a result of this experiment, we obtained for every project a predictor that was capable of accurately predicting defect-prone components of the project [390].

Next, we applied these predictors across projects. The results in Table 4.3 show that in most cases, predictors could not be transferred. The only exceptions are between projects B and C and between C and E, where predictors are interchangeable. When comparing these projects, we observed that they had similar development processes.

A central consequence of this result would be to reuse only predictors that were generated in similar environments. Put another way: *Always evaluate with history before you use a metric to make decisions.* Or even shorter: *Never blindly trust a metric.*

Key Points

- ✎ Complexity metrics indeed correlate with defects.
- ✎ There is no universal metric and no universal prediction model.
- ✎ Before relying on a metric to make predictions, evaluate it with a true defect history.

4.4 Problem Domain

The chances of making mistakes depend strongly on the number and complexity of the *requirements* that some piece of code has to satisfy. As discussed in the Section 4.3, a large number of interfering requirements can result in a higher code complexity. However, this may not necessarily be so: an algorithm may have a very simple structure, but still may be difficult to get right. Therefore, we expect that specific requirements, or more generally, specific *problem domains,* to impact how defect-prone program code is going to be:

How does the problem domain impact defect likelihood?

Table 4.4. Good and bad imports (packages) in Eclipse 2.0 (taken from [455], ©ACM, 2006)

Packages imported into a component C	Defects	Total	p(Defect | C)
org.eclipse.jdt.internal.compiler.lookup.*	170	197	0.8629
org.eclipse.jdt.internal.compiler.*	119	138	0.8623
org.eclipse.jdt.internal.compiler.ast.*	111	132	0.8409
org.eclipse.jdt.internal.compiler.util.*	121	148	0.8175
org.eclipse.jdt.internal.ui.preferences.*	48	63	0.7619
org.eclipse.jdt.core.compiler.*	76	106	0.7169
org.eclipse.jdt.internal.ui.actions.*	37	55	0.6727
org.eclipse.jdt.internal.ui.viewsupport.*	28	42	0.6666
org.eclipse.swt.internal.photon.*	33	50	0.6600
...			
org.eclipse.ui.model.*	23	128	0.1797
org.eclipse.swt.custom.*	41	233	0.1760
org.eclipse.pde.internal.ui.*	35	211	0.1659
org.eclipse.jface.resource.*	64	387	0.1654
org.eclipse.pde.core.*	18	112	0.1608
org.eclipse.jface.wizard.*	36	230	0.1566
org.eclipse.ui.*	141	948	0.1488

4.4.1 Imports and Defects

To demonstrate the impact of the problem domain on defect likelihood, let us come back to the distribution of defects in Eclipse, as shown in Figure 4.1. Let us assume we want to extend the existing code by two new components from different problem domains: *user interfaces* and *compiler internals*. Which component is more likely to be defect-prone?

Adding a new dialog box to a GUI has rather simple requirements, in most cases you only have to extend a certain class. However, assembling the elements of the dialog box takes lots of additional complicated code. In contrast, using a parser to build an abstract syntax tree requires only a few lines of code, but has many rather complicated requirements such as picking the correct parameters. So which domain more likely leads to defects?

In the context of Eclipse, this question has been answered. Together with Adrian Schröter, we examined *the components that are used* as an implicit expression of the component's domain [455]. When building an Eclipse plug-in that works on Java files, one has to *import* JDT classes; if the plug-in comes with a user interface, GUI classes are mandatory. Therefore, what a component imports determines its problem domain.

Once one knows what is imported, one can again relate this data to measured defect densities. Table 4.4 shows how the usage of specific packages in Eclipse impacts defect probability. A component which uses compiler internals has a 86% chance to have a defect that needs to be fixed in the first six months after release. However, a component using user interface packages has only a 15% defect chance.

This observation raises the question whether we can predict defect-proneness by just using the names of imported components? In other words: "Tell me what you import, and I'll tell you how many defects you will have."

4.4.2 Case Study: Eclipse Imports

Can one actually predict defect likelihood by considering imports alone? We built statistical models with linear regression, ridge regression, regression trees, and support vector machines. In particular, we addressed the following questions:

Classification. Can we predict whether a component will have defects?
Ranking. Can we predict which components will have the most defects?

For our experiments, we used *random splits*: we randomly chose one third of the 52 plug-ins of Eclipse version 2.0 as our training set, which we used to build our models. We validated our models in versions 2.0 and 2.1 of Eclipse. Both times we used the complement of the training set as the validation set. We generated a total of 40 random splits and averaged the results for computing three values:

- The *precision* measures how many of the components predicted as defect-prone actually have been shown to have defects. A high precision means a low number of false positives.
- The *recall* measures how many of the defect-prone components are actually predicted as such. A high recall means a low number of false negatives.
- The *Spearman correlation* measures the strength and direction of the relationship between predicted and observed ranking. A high correlation means a high predictive power.

In this section, we discuss our results for support vector machines [132] (which performed best in our evaluation).

Precision and Recall

For the validation sets in version 2.0 of Eclipse, the support vector machines obtained a *precision* of 0.67 (see Table 4.5). That is, two out of three components predicted as defect-prone were observed to have defects. For a random guess instead, the precision would be the percentage of defect-prone packages, which is only 0.37. The *recall* of 0.69 for the validation sets in version 2.0 indicates that two third of the observed defect-prone components were actually predicted as defect-prone. Again, a random guess yields only a recall of 0.37.

In practice, this means that import relationships provide a good predictor for defect-prone components. This is an important result since relationships between components are typically defined in the design phase. Thus, defect-prone components can be identified early, and designers can easily explore and assess design alternatives in terms of predicted defect risk.

Table 4.5. Predicting defect-proneness of Eclipse packages with Support Vector Machines and import relations (taken from [455], ©ACM, 2006)

	Precision	Recall	Spearman Correlation
training in Eclipse v2.0	0.8770	0.8933	0.5961
validation in Eclipse v2.0	0.6671	0.6940	0.3002
—top 5%	0.7861		
—top 10%	0.7875		
—top 15%	0.7957		
—top 20%	0.8000		
validation in Eclipse v2.1	0.5917	0.7205	0.2842
—top 5%	0.8958		
—top 10%	0.8399		
—top 15%	0.7784		
—top 20%	0.7668		

Ranking vs. Classification

The low values for the Spearman rank *correlation* coefficient in Table 4.5 indicate that the predicted rankings correlate only little with the observed rankings. However, the precision values for the top 5% are higher than the overall values. This means that the chances of finding defect-prone components increase for highly ranked components.

In practice, this means that quality assurance is best spent on those components ranked as the most defect-prone. It is therefore a good idea to analyse imports and bug history to establish appropriate rankings.

Applying Models Across Versions

The results for the validation sets of Eclipse version 2.1 are comparable to the ones of version 2.0; for the top 5% and 10% of the rankings, the precision values are even higher. This indicates that our models are robust over time.

For our dataset, this means that one can learn a model for one version and apply it to a later version without losing predictive power. In other words, the imports actually act as *invariants,* as discussed in Section 4.2.

4.4.3 Case Study: Windows Server 2003

At Microsoft, we repeated the study by Schröter et al. [455] on the defect data of Windows Server 2003. Instead of import relationships, we used *dependencies* to describe the problem domain between the 2252 binaries. A dependency is a directed relationship between two pieces of code such as expressions or methods. For our experiments, we use the MaX tool [473] that tracks dependency information at the function level and looks for calls, imports, exports, RPC, and Registry accesses. Again, the problem domain was a suitable predictor for defects and performed substantially better than random (precision 0.67, recall 0.69, Spearman correlations between 0.50 and 0.60).

In addition to the replication of the earlier study (and its results), we also observed a *domino effect* in Windows Server 2003. The *domino effect* was stated in 1975 by Randell [430]:

> *Given an arbitrary set of interacting processes, each with its own private recovery structure, a single error on the part of just one process could cause all the processes to use up many or even all of their recovery points, through a sort of uncontrolled domino effect.*

Applying the domino effect on dependencies, this would mean that defects in one component can increase the likelihood of defects in dependent components. Figure 4.2 illustrates this phenomenon on a defect-prone binary B. Out of the three binaries that directly depend on B (distance $d = 1$), two have defects, resulting in a *defect likelihood* of 0.67. When we increase the distance, say to $d = 2$, out of the four binaries depending on B (indirectly), only two have defects, thus the likelihood decreases to 0.50. In other words, the extent of the domino effect decreases with distance—just like with real domino pieces.

In Figure 4.3 we show the distribution of the defect likelihood, as introduced above, when the target of the dependency is defect-prone ($d = 1$). We also report results for indirect dependencies ($d = 2, d = 3$). The higher the likelihood, the more dependent binaries are defect-prone.

To protect proprietary information, we anonymised the y-axis which reports the frequencies; the x-axis is relative to the highest observed defect likelihood which was

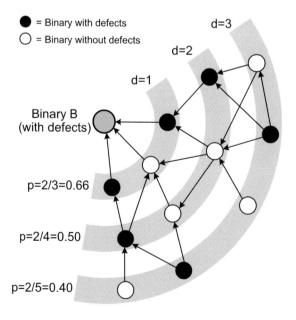

Fig. 4.2. Example of a domino effect for a binary B

Binaries with Defects

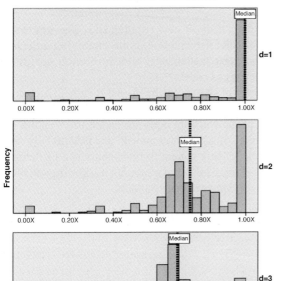

Fig. 4.3. The domino effect in Windows Server 2003

greater than 0.50 and is reported as X. The likelihood X and the scale of the x-axis are constant for all bar charts. Having the highest bar on the left (at 0.00), means that for most binaries the dependent binaries had no defects; the highest bar on the right (at X), shows that for most binaries, their dependent binaries had defects, too.

As Figure 4.3 shows, directly depending on binaries with defects, causes most binaries to have defects, too ($d = 1$). This effect decreases when the distance d increases (trend towards the left). In other words, the domino effect is present for most defect-prone binaries in Windows Server 2003. As the distance d increases, the impact of the domino effect decreases. This trend is demonstrated by the shifting of the median from right to left with respect to the defect likelihood.

Key Points

- ✎ The set of used components is a good predictor for defect proneness.
- ✎ The problem domain is a suitable predictor for future defects.
- ✎ Defect proneness is likely to propagate through software in a domino effect.

4.5 Code Churn

Code is not static; it evolves over time to meet new requirements. The way code evolved in the past can be used to predict its evolution in the future. In particular, there is an often accepted notion that code that changes a lot is of lower quality— and thus more defect-prone than unchanged code.

How does one measure the amount of change? Lehman and Belady [320] introduced the concept of *code churn* as the rate of growth of the size of the software. But measuring the changes in the size of the software does not necessarily capture all changes that have occurred during the software development, this is especially true if the software has been re-architected. More generally, code churn can be defined as a measure of the *amount of code change taking place within a software unit over time.* [389]. The primary question we address in this section is:

Does code churn correlate with defects?

4.5.1 Background

Several researchers have investigated how evolution relates to defects. Ostrand et al. [408] use information of file status such as new, changed, unchanged files along with other explanatory variables such as lines of code, age, prior faults etc. to predict the number of faults in multiple releases of an industrial software system. The predictions made using binomial regression model were of a high accuracy for faults found in both early and later stages of development.

Munson et al. [384] studied a 300 KLOC (thousand lines of code) embedded real time system with 3700 modules programmed in C. Code churn metrics were found to be among the most highly correlated with problem reports.

Graves et al. [209] predicted fault incidences using software change history. The most successful model they built computed the fault potential by summing contributions from changes to the module, where large and/or recent changes contribute the most to fault potential.

4.5.2 Case Study: Windows Server 2003

In addition to the above research results, we now summarise in detail the results of a case study performed on Windows Server 2003 [389]. We analysed the code churn between the release of Windows Server 2003 and the release of the Windows Server 2003 Service Pack 1 (Windows Server 2003-SP1) to predict the defect density in Windows Server 2003-SP1.

As discussed in Section 4.5.1, there are several measures that can be used to explain code churn. In our study, we used the following churn measures [389]:

- *Total LOC* is the number of lines of non-commented executable lines in the files comprising the new version of a binary.

- *Churned LOC* is the sum of the added and changed lines of code between a base-line version and a new version of the files comprising a binary.
- *Deleted LOC* is the number of lines of code deleted between the baseline version and the new version of a binary.
- *File count* is the number of files compiled to create a binary.
- *Weeks of churn* is the cumulative time that a file was opened for editing from the version control system.
- *Churn count* is the number of changes made to the files comprising a binary between the two versions (Windows Server 2003 and Windows Server 2003-SP1).
- *Files churned* is the number of files within the binary that churned.

The overall size of the analysed code base was around 40 million lines of code from more than 2000 binaries. Using the above extracted metrics from the version control system, we use a *relative approach* (as shown in Figure 4.4) to build our statistical regression models to predict system defect density. Our rationale for relative metrics is that in an evolving system, it is highly beneficial to use a relative approach to quantify the change in a system. A more detailed discussion of the experiment is available in [389].

Using random splitting techniques we used the above "relative" code churn measures as predictor variables in our statistical models. We selected two-thirds of the binaries to build our statistical prediction models (multiple regression, logistic regression) to predict overall system defect density/fault-proneness. Based on our sta-

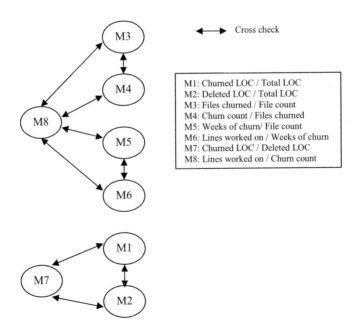

Fig. 4.4. Relative churn measures (taken from [389], ©ACM, 2005)

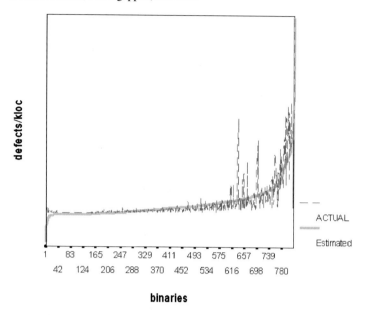

Fig. 4.5. Plot of actual versus estimated defect density (taken from [389], ©ACM, 2005)

tistical analysis we were able to predict system defect density/fault-proneness at high levels of statistical significance. Figure 4.5, for example, shows the results of the one of the random split experiments to predict the actual system defect density.

Key Points

☞ The more a component has changed (churned), the more likely it is to have defects.
☞ Code churn measures can be used to predict defect-prone components.

4.6 Open Issues

We have seen how complexity, the problem domain, or the change rate can be used to learn from history and to predict the defect density of new and evolved components. We can thus indeed predict bugs from history, and even do so in a fully automatic way. This is a clear benefit of having a well-kept track of earlier defects: avoiding future defects by directing quality assurance efforts.

The examples in this chapter all rely on *code features* to predict defects. By no means have we analysed all possible code features that might turn out to be good defect predictors. We expect future research to come up with much better predictors; Table 4.6 lists several data sets that are publicly available such that anyone can test her or his favourite idea.

Table 4.6. Datasets for empirical studies

Promise Data Repository	The *Promise Data Repository* contains data sets for effort estimation, defect prediction, and text mining. Currently, it comprises 23 datasets, but this number is constantly growing (*free*). `http://promisedata.org/`
NASA Metrics Data	The repository of the *NASA IV&V Facility Metrics Data Program* contains software metrics (such as McCabe and Halstead) and the associated error data at the function/method level for 13 projects (*free*). `http://mdp.ivv.nasa.gov/`
Eclipse Bug Data	This data contains the pre-release and post-release defects for three versions of the Eclipse IDE (*free*). `http://www.st.cs.uni-sb.de/softevo/`
ISBSG	The repository of ISBSG contains empirical data for software estimation, productivity, risk analysis, and cost information (*commercial*). `http://www.isbsg.org/`
Finnish Data Set	This dataset is collected by STTF to support benchmarks of software costs, development productivity, and software processes (*commercial*). `http://www.sttf.fi/`
FLOSSmole	FLOSSmole is a "collaborative collection and analysis of free/libre/open source project data." `http://ossmole.sourceforge.net/`

Another common feature of the approaches discussed so far is that they all predict the number of defects. In general, though, managers not only want to minimise the number of defects, but minimise the overall *damage,* which involves the impact of each defect—that is, the number of actual *failures,* and the damage caused by each failure.

Finally, all the predictions discussed in this chapter require a *history of defects* to learn from. Over history, we can learn which features of the code or the development process are most likely to correlate with defects—and these very features can thus be used to predict defect-prone components. Of course, the more detailed this history of failures is, the more accurate our predictions will be. However, having a long history of failures is something we would like to avoid altogether. At least, we would like to learn enough from one project history to avoid repeating it in the next project:

- Is there a way to make predictions for new products with no known history yet?
- How can we leverage and abstract our knowledge about defects from one project to another one?
- Are there any *universal* properties of programs and processes that invariably result in a higher defect density?

We believe that such universal properties indeed do exist. However, it is very unlikely that these properties are code properties alone. Remember that we focus on defects that occur *after* release, that is, at a time where people already have taken care of quality assurance. It is reasonable to assume that the more (and better) quality assurance is applied, the fewer defects will remain. However, none of our predictor models takes the extent or effectiveness of quality assurance into account—simply because code does not tell how it has been tested, checked, reviewed, or verified.

The effectiveness of quality assurance is a feature of the software process, not the software itself. There are ways to characterise and evaluate quality assurance techniques—for instance, one can check the coverage of a test suite or its effectiveness in uncovering mutations. These are important features of the software process that may help predicting defects.

Besides quality assurance, there are further process features to look into. The qualification of the programmer, combined with the time taken to write a component; the quality of the specification; the quality of the design; the competence of management; continuity of work flow—all these, and many more, are factors which contribute to people making mistakes (or avoiding them). In some way, looking for universal properties that cause defects is like looking for a universal way to write software. As an intermediate goal, it may already be helpful to choose between multiple "good" ways.

Whatever features future predictors will be based upon—there is one invariant that remains: Any predictor will eventually turn out to be wrong. This is because if a predictor predicts a higher number of defects (or failures, or damage, for that matter), the component will be checked more carefully—which will, of course, reduce density. Any defect predictor will thus produce self-defeating prophecies—and this is a good thing.

Key Points

✏ So far, all defect predictors require a history of earlier defects.
✏ Automated predictors do not yet directly leverage process data.
✏ The quest for universal (e.g. history-less) defect predictors is still open.

4.7 Threats to Validity

As with all empirical studies drawing general conclusions from case studies in software engineering is difficult because any process depends to a large degree on a potentially large number of relevant context variables. For this reason, we cannot assume a priori that the results of a study generalise beyond the specific environment in which it was conducted [40]. Some of the threats to validity of our studies are discussed below.

- There could have been errors in measurement. In general, all the measurement of software data in our studies was done using automated tools. This alleviates to a certain degree errors in measurement. But it is possible that these tools could have had design errors that could have led to errors in measurement

- Our case studies were performed for two large systems namely Windows Server 2003 and Eclipse. It is possible that these results may not be observed for smaller or other systems. Further these systems have possibly several million users. Hence it is possible that other systems which do not have such an active usage profile may not have most of its field defects found equally.
- At least one of the three authors were part of each case study described in this chapter. Unknowingly it would have been possible to introduce experimenter bias into the case studies.
- All the analysis in our studies was done after-the-fact, i.e., all the field defects had been reported back and we had used it for our prediction models. It is difficult for us to gauge how our prediction made before hand would have influenced the development team behaviour effectively benefiting them to identify problem-prone components early.
- The statistical models built for the software systems may apply only for the particular family of systems for which they are built for [61]. For example it may not be useful to use a model built on Eclipse to predict bugs in small toy programs.
- Though our case studies predict defects significantly other information such as severity, impact of failure information etc. are missing from our predictions. This type of predictions would be part of future investigations in this research area.

Basili et al. state that researchers become more confident in a theory when similar findings emerge in different contexts [40]. Towards this end we hope that our case study contributes towards building the already existing empirical body of knowledge in this field [275, 274, 384, 402, 172, 209, 408, 326].

4.8 Conclusion and Consequences

Learning from history means learning from successes and failures—and how to make the right decisions in the future. In our case, the history of successes and failures is provided by the bug database: systematic mining uncovers which modules are most prone to defects and failures. Correlating defects with complexity metrics or the problem domain is useful in predicting problems for new or evolved components. Likewise, code that changes a lot is more prone to failures than code that is unchanged.

Learning from history has one big advantage: one can focus on the aspect of history that is most relevant for the current situation. In our case, this means that predictions will always be best if history is taken from the product or project at hand. But while we can come up with accurate predictors, we need more work in understanding the root causes for software defects—and this work should take into account the roles of quality assurance and the general software process.

In this light, we feel that our work has just scratched the surface of what is possible, and of what is needed. Our future work will concentrate on the following topics:

More process data. As stated above, code features are just one factor in producing software defects; process features may be helpful in finding out why defects are not caught. We plan to tap and mine further data sources, notably quality assurance information, to cover more process data.

Better metrics and models. Right now, the metrics we use as input for predictors are still very simple. We plan to leverage the failure data from several projects to evaluate more sophisticated metrics and models that again result in better predictors.

Combined approaches. So far, the approaches described in this chapter all have examined specific features in isolation. Combining them, as in "I have a complex module importing internal.compiler, which has had no defects so far" should yield even better predictions.

Increased granularity. Rather than just examining features at the component level, one may go for more fine-grained approaches, such as caller-callee relationships. Such fine-grained relationships may also allow predictions of defect density for individual classes or even individual methods or functions.

Overall, these steps should help us not only to predict where defects will be, but also to understand their causes, such that we can avoid them in the future. Version archives play a key role in telling which hypotheses apply, and which do not—for the project at hand, or universally.

Acknowledgement. Christian Lindig, Rahul Premraj, and Andrzej Wasylkowski provided helpful comments on earlier revisions of this chapter. The work of Andreas Zeller and Thomas Zimmmermann on mining software archives was supported by Deutsche Forschungs-gemeinschaft, grant Ze 509/1-1. Thomas Zimmermann is additionally supported by the DFG Graduiertenkolleg "Leistungsgarantien für Rechnersysteme". We would like to acknowledge the Eclipse developers as well as the product groups at Microsoft for their cooperation in these studies.

## Part II

Reengineering of Legacy Systems

5

Object-Oriented Reengineering

Serge Demeyer

University of Antwerp, Belgium

Summary. Reengineering has long been considered a loathsome activity, commonly associated with "legacy" software technology and programming languages. The simplistic way to avoid reengineering switches to "modern" software technology (objects, models, aspects, ...) and assumes that the legacy problem will soon disappear. Unfortunately, practice shows that this "modern" technology is just as vulnerable to ageing symptoms and—due to rapid turnaround cycles—becomes legacy even faster. This chapter examines two recent approaches (namely refactoring and reengineering patterns) that provide a possible way out. This way, we want to help future researchers, practitioners and educators to build upon existing knowledge and make progress in our field.

5.1 Introduction

legacy: A sum of money, or a specified article, given to another by will; anything handed down by an ancestor or predecessor.

[Oxford English Dictionary]

If you consider the traditional meaning of the word "legacy", you see that it has a positive connotation. Legacy is something handed down by an ancestor; hence it is deemed worth passing on to the next generation. True, it is old and because of that may be a bit awkward for daily use, but still people would rarely throw it away—it has value after all. In software engineering however, the word "legacy" has received quite a negative undertone. In our field a legacy system is defined as "a system which significantly resists modification and evolution" [84]. "Legacy" in software is typically associated with systems developed using long forgotten methods, running on outdated platforms and written in archaic programming languages. Because of that, there is a strong urge to get rid of this legacy as soon as possible and start with something shiny and new. Unfortunately, practice shows that once in the field, this shiny and new system will soon resist modification and evolution as well, and probably faster than the legacy system it was bound to replace.

Why is it that these newer systems become legacy much faster? Was the 40 years of software engineering research a waste of time? Is all this new technology not

T. Mens, S. Demeyer (eds.), *Software Evolution.*
DOI 10.1007/978-3-540-76440-3, © Springer 2008

capable to deal with change? On the contrary: software engineering research has been very successful in making software more flexible. On the one hand, requirements engineering has improved a lot so that today we have the techniques in place into separate requirements in stable and volatile parts (consider techniques like use-cases, CRC-Cards, feature modelling, . . .). This way we can design systems to anticipate likely changes. On the other hand, today's development technology allows to deploy changes much later in the life-cycle (database schema-updates are performed on-the fly, system components get installed over the internet at run-time, . . .). This way, it becomes way easier to modify systems in the field.

Unfortunately, our users have learned to exploit this flexibility and today the demand for changes far exceeds our capacity to deploy them. Indeed, in the 70's we were building monolithic systems where the context adapts itself to make optimal use of the software system. Today this situation is reversed: users expect that software adapts itself to match the context it is being used in. Thus, newer systems will be changed more often and consequently they will erode much faster. Put in other words: "*it is not age that turns a piece of software into a legacy system, but the rate at which it has been developed and adapted without being reengineered*" [149].

In the same vein, object-oriented programming (and follow-up technology like components and aspects) have made it easier to design software that anticipates certain changes. Software objects use the metaphor of lego-blocks; i.e., changing a software system should be as simple as replacing one object (= lego-block) with another. However, objects are not as robust as there plastic counterparts: while lego-blocks can be assembled and disassembled forever, objects are more brittle. That is, replacing one object with another typically involves patching a bit of code in another object. In the beginning, this is not so bad, but after a few replacements objects rely so much on each other that they appear to be glued together.

Therefore, to ensure the flexibility of a software system, one should not only invest in a good initial design, but—more importantly—one should continue that investment to sustain the quality of that design. Luckily, this issue has been addressed and the community has developed techniques to maintain the quality of a software design. This chapter will investigate two recent approaches (namely refactoring and reengineering patterns) that help software engineers sustain the long term maintainability of their system. Note that while these approaches were developed with object-oriented systems in mind, many principles apply to other systems as well. We will provide an overview of the research topics that have been investigated in the past and afterwards define an agenda of research issues that need to be tackled in the future. The list of research topics and research agendas are necessarily incomplete, yet do provide a good starting point for any researcher starting in the field.

5.2 Refactoring

Refactoring (the verb) is defined as "the process of changing a software system in such a way that it does not alter the external behaviour of the code, yet improves its internal structure" [183]. The refactoring process supposedly consists of several smaller steps, where each of these steps is also called "refactoring" (a noun); now defined as "a behaviour preserving source-to-source program transformation" [440]. Refactoring is widely recognised as one of the principal techniques applied when evolving object-oriented software systems. The key idea is to redistribute instance variables and methods across the class hierarchy in order to prepare the software for future extensions [404, 405]. If applied well, refactoring is said to improve the design of software, make software easier to understand, help to find bugs, and help to program faster [183]. As such, refactoring has received widespread attention within both academic [502] and industrial circles [50], and is mentioned as a recommended practice in the software engineering body of knowledge (SWEBOK) [2].

Although it is possible to refactor manually, tool support is considered crucial. Tools such as the *Refactoring Browser* support a semi-automatic approach [440], which has also been adopted by industrial strength software development environ- ments (see http://www.refactoring.com/ for an overview of refactoring tools). Other researchers demonstrated the feasibility of fully automated tools [107], studied ways to make refactoring tools less dependent on the implementation language being used [499, 305] and investigated refactoring in the context of UML [73, 184].

Already from its inception, refactoring research focussed on defining a list of so-called *primitive* refactorings which can be combined to form arbitrary chains of *composite* refactorings [404]. The initial list of primitive refactorings contained transformations on object-oriented code, such as (i) adding a class, method or at- tribute (verifying that the new name does not exist); (ii) renaming a class, method or attribute (patching all references to the old name); (iii) moving an attribute or method up and down the hierarchy (and removing duplicates in case the inheritance hierar- chy allows); (iv) removing a class, method or attribute (verifying that nobody uses it anymore); (v) extracting chunks of code in separate methods (again sometimes removing duplicates by inserting appropriate method calls). These primitive refac- torings are then combined into a larger composite refactorings. Note that it is only in rare cases that the sequence contains purely primitive refactorings. In practice, most complex refactoring scenarios require some small code massaging in order for the refactoring to work smoothly. As an example, consider a "split class" refactoring, which consists out of the following steps:

1. Create new superclass with a name that did not occur before, and which is a su- perclass of the class to be split.
2. Extract pieces of code that should be moved onto the new class into separate methods. This will most likely entail some real code editing.
3. Move the attributes that logically belong to the superclass up in the hierarchy.
4. Move the methods that logically belong to the superclass up in the hierarchy.
5. Rename the methods and attributes in the new superclass to create a consistent interface.
6. Add abstract methods to the new superclass to suggest which ones should be overridden in the subclass.
7. Declare items in the new and old class public/private/protected/...

The success of refactoring implies that the topic has been approached from various angles. This has as the unfortunate consequence that refactoring research is scattered over different software engineering fields, among others object-orientation, language engineering, modelling, formal methods, software evolution and reengineering (see [369] for a thorough overview of refactoring research). Therefore, it has been very difficult to assess current research and see where more work is necessary. In the following paragraphs we give an overview of research issues which have been dealt with and those that need further work. The overview takes a pragmatic stance, trying to see which research may actually influence how practitioners use refactoring in the field.

5.2.1 Current Research Issues

Behaviour Preserving. A crucial aspect of the definition of refactoring is the fact that refactoring must preserve the "external behaviour". In principle, this is a sufficiently precise criterion as the external behaviour is known and regression testing can be used to verify that the system did not regress during refactoring. However, for theoretical purposes it is not precise enough as one needs precise formal specifications in order to guarantee that the refactored system still meets it specification.

Consequently, researchers have looked for formal models which can be used to express preservation of behaviour. The most natural candidate is algebraic models with pre- and postconditions, first expressed in natural language [404, 499], later via assertions on the abstract syntax tree of Smalltalk programs [441] or constraints on the type graph [501]. A more operational formalism is graph rewriting, where refactorings then correspond with graph rewriting rules [365, 519, 76] (see also Chapter 7). Among others, the use of such rules could prove that a refactoring preserves certain structural properties, such as the access to attributes, or the calling of methods [370].

While such formalisms are helpful to improve our understanding of how refactorings affect the behaviour of programs, all of them fall short compared to actual language semantics. Indeed, all industrial-strength programming languages have special mechanisms in place that escape formal models. Features such as procedure-pointers, reflection, dynamic load-libraries are necessary to build full-fledged systems, yet make it unfeasible to predict the precise effect of a refactoring transformation. As such, regression tests will remain the pragmatic approach to ensure that the refactored program still functions as it used to. Researchers seeking for ways to help practitioners should consider coverage of (regression) tests as a viable research topic.

Language Independence. An important implication of formal verification of preserving behaviour is that all formalisms restrict themselves to a language-independent meta-model typically consisting of classes, methods, attributes and the relationships between them (inheritance, invocation, access). Sometimes, explicit extensions are made to deal with language specific issues [499].

Classes, methods and attributes are arguably a representative subset of the majority of class-based object-oriented languages in use today. However, they do not include other language constructs (most notably exceptions) which play an important role in the semantics of languages and which are heavily used in practice. More importantly, they do not cover language specific idioms which are little details from a theoretical point of view, but which are crucially important to make a refactoring tool fit seamlessly into the rest of the toolchain. Consider for instance the "rename class" refactoring in Java; this should not only patch all old instances of the class name in the source code, but also rename the file the class resides in (Java has the convention of a 1-on-1 mapping between classes and files), all the makefiles referring to that file, and all the javadoc references referring to that classname. Researchers worrying whether practicioners will adopt their results, should be aware of these issues.

Composite Refactorings. The combination of primitive refactorings into more complex refactorings spawned at least two research topics. First, several researchers used logic reasoning on the pre- and postcondition to verify properties of complex refactorings. Roberts showed that some of the pre-conditions of a primitive refactoring automatically follow from the post-condition of another refactoring [441]. Kniesel could logically deduce which refactoring sequences were valid chains of pre- and postconditions [285]. Second, it made it easier to "transpose" the refactorings outside of the traditional programming language medium. For instance, when defining refactorings for UML class models Sunyé started with the basic categories for refactoring primitives, namely add-rename-move-remove [184]. These basic categories more or less worked for state-charts and activity diagrams as well, where both Sunyé and Boger also defined operations that correspond to the same add-rename-move-remove classification [73, 184].

Metaphorically speaking, the primitive refactorings resemble the twelve musical notes which can be combined to form an infinite number of melodies. However, one shouldn't forget that these twelve notes represent certain well-defined tone frequencies which are known to form pleasant combinations for the human ear. Similarly, one should not forget that the original list of primitive refactorings was chosen because the authors knew from experience that these were used time and time again in various refactoring scenarios. Rather than specifying all possible behaviour preserving program transformations, the original list of primitive refactorings focussed on the 20% transformations that occurred in 80% of the cases, and that is the main reason why refactoring is well received in practice. So to find new refactorings, researchers should not only look for primitive transformations with nice pre- and postconditions that seem to combine well. Much more importantly they should demonstrate that these primitive refactorings indeed support a wide variety of realistic refactoring scenarios.

Learn from the past. Several researchers have tried to mine version repositories to learn which refactorings are applied in practice (see among others [148, 207, 523, 522]; see also Chapter 3 to learn more about mining software repositories). These resulted in some nice observations. For instance, in a comparison of three pairs of major releases of a large open source software system (Eclipse), Xing and Stroulia [554] found that as much as 70% of the detected structural modifications (excluding extensions of functionality) are refactorings similar to those proposed by

Fowler [183]. These findings confirm previous research by Dig and Johnson [152], noting that as much as 80% of the changes applied in the context of Application Programmer Interface (API) evolution are refactorings. In an attempt to identify those refactorings that were most commonly used across the development of seven open source Java systems, Counsell et al. [130] found that six of the 15 preselected refactorings were used most often. Classified according to Fowler's refactoring categories [183], the objective of two of these is *Move Features between Objects*, of two others is *Making Method Calls Simpler*, and of one is *Dealing with Generalisation*. In a refinement of this work, Advani et al. [3] noticed a tendency towards the frequent application of simple refactorings (i.e., rename and move operations).

These papers illustrate that refactoring is indeed used in practice. But much more importantly, they show *how* it is used. That is, not only does it help us to identify which refactorings are heavily used (the 80%-20% rule mentioned above) and how they are combined with others (the composite refactorings). But much more importantly it can help us to reverse engineer *refactoring strategies*: when are which refactorings used and how did it help to solve certain quality problems. Such information is very valuable to demonstrate to practicioners how refactorings can be used to solve the problems they are facing in their systems.

5.2.2 Future Research Issues

Model Refactoring. Due to the success of refactoring for programming languages, several authors studied how to apply refactorings in a model-driven engineering context as well [184, 73, 26]. However, this raises a number of questions which are far from resolved [367]. First of all, there is the question of behaviour preservation: how can you specify the behaviour of a UML model? And once you done that: how can you guarantee that it is preserved? We might find some answers in the model testing community as testing is the usual means to demonstrate that the system (model) did not regress. Secondly, there is the question of synchronisation. In a model-driven reengineering context, one model is typically built up from different views, using different types of diagrams that all need to be kept consistent. Moreover, these models are used to generate code which is afterwards changed to include manual additions. Thus one "refactoring" applied in a single view (say "rename class") should ripple through all related views and code. To some degree this is similar to programs which must be kept synchronised with related software artefacts (databases, user interfaces, test suites), however the problem is typically much bigger because there are more views in place and some of them are necessarily incomplete. Fortunately, many tools offer some kind of traceability links which specify which model elements rely upon another.

Given the interest in both refactoring and model-driven engineering one may expect lots of work in this area in the near future. For the moment it remains unclear which avenues will be able to answer the questions of behaviour preservation and model synchronisation, which makes it a fruitful area for future research.

Refactoring in the Large. Refactoring is by definition performed on a local level. However, the intent of refactoring is to influence quality characteristics of a software system, thus to have global effect. In that sense, one could imagine refactoring at architectural level as this is the abstraction level that is expected to deal with non-functional requirements such as maintainability or performance.

Much of the refactoring vocabulary could be transferred to the architectural level. A *code smell* would become a *design smell*, the elements moved around would become components and connectors, ... What will become much more difficult though is (again) the notion of preserving behaviour. After all, it is the very idea of architectural refactoring to change the non-functional behaviour.

Refactoring Economics. Refactoring is applied to improve the internal structure of a software system, which is believed to increase its long-term maintainability. However, this belief is based mainly on anecdotal evidence and has yet to be validated empirically. The few experiments conducted on that subject so far were inconclusive at best. Indeed, both Arisholm [20] and Du Bois [154] reported that the maintainability of an object-oriented system depends much less on the programming style (delegated versus centralised control style) and much more on the expertise of the maintainer.

In that sense more empirical work is needed to demonstrate that refactoring—if applied well—truly improves the maintainability. Controlled experiments like the ones mentioned above may certainly help, however an economic perspective may be worthwhile as well. Indeed, given the many software organisations that are at CM-MMI level three our higher, obtaining data about the cost per new feature shouldn't be too difficult. If we then project how the cost per feature changes over time, we expect to see an increasing cost growth, while after a refactoring period the cost growth should decrease again. If this expectation proves realistic, what then remains to be done is verifying whether the refactoring investment pays off. Thus, whether the effort spent on refactoring plus the effort spent on adding new features to the refactored system is less than the effort that would be spent when adding features to the base system.

Education. Refactoring has received widespread attention, and is listed as a recommended practice in the software engineering body of knowledge [2]. Unfortunately, the diversity in the field implies a lack of standardisation which goes against the very idea of a *standard* body of knowledge. This problem has been recognised by a number of European Universities and research institutes which have founded a network—named RELEASE—addressing this problem. During four years they have exchanged tools and cases in order to identify a typical refactoring scenario to be used for both teaching and research. In the end this resulted in a small but realistic software system (a simulation of a Local Area Network; the so-called LAN-simulation) which suffers from some typical code smells that could be refactored away. To demonstrate that the refactoring indeed preserves behaviour, the system includes a few unit tests which serve as regression tests. A paper reporting about the use of this demonstrator as a research vehicle has been presented at the International Workshop on Principles of Software Evolution (IW-PSE) [150] and during the first refactoring tools workshop [147]. The code—both in C++ and Java— and accompanying teacher and student instructions can be found at http://www.lore.ua.ac.be/Research/Artefacts/.

The LAN-simulation is but one example of concrete teaching material freely available on the web that can be used both in class room settings as well as on self-learning basis. It demonstrates that reengineering skills in general and refactoring skills in particular can be taught. However, to raise awareness and to train the current and future generation of software engineers, more such material will be needed.

5.3 Reengineering Patterns

Patterns have emerged in recent years as a literary form used to document expert knowledge in solving certain kinds of software problems, most notably design [190], but also analysis [182], architecture [97] and testing [66]. First of all, they address *recurring problems* which are very similar, yet never exactly alike. That is why most patterns explicitly describe the context in which the problem occurs and a solution which might be applicable. Secondly, these problems entail a number of conflicting *forces* and the solution entails a number of trade-offs. Good patterns therefore help to convey the complex decision process that experts use to determine whether a solution really applies to a given problem. Thirdly, patterns are solutions that have proven their value in real problem situations. That is why patterns are not invented but discovered; that is also why typical patterns list *known uses* of that solution. Fourthly, patterns teach the essence of a solution to a complex problem in a form which is accessible to an apprentice. A critical section of a pattern is therefore the choice of a good *example*, as examples are one of the best teaching vehicles available to mankind. Fifthly, complex problems cannot be solved in a single shot. That is why most patterns refer to one another, and are often organised in *pattern systems* as a way to convey the different viewpoints one may take to tackle a complex problem. Last but not least, patterns carry a *name*, thus introducing a certain vocabulary. Such a vocabulary is important since it enables experts to discuss alternative solutions at a higher level of abstraction where technical approaches and their tradeoffs are implicitly captured by their names.

Patterns are a form of documentation, so they are naturally presented using written text. Yet, to avoid forcing readers to wade through pages and pages of text to identify the essence of a pattern, patterns typically follow some kind of template (the so-called *pattern form*) which provides quick access to key information. Most pattern templates therefore include separate sections for the problem (in context), the solution, the forces and trade-offs, an example, the known uses and any related patterns. Figure 5.1 shows an example of such a template for reengineering patterns, adapted from [149].

Since reengineering is an important but very complex endeavour—entailing both technical and personal skills—designers need help. Patterns have proven to be a form that is very well adapted to describe best practices in reengineering. Stevens was one of the first to advocate the development of reengineering patterns [475]. However, at that time several authors were already documenting reengineering expertise in patterns form; among others Foote about the lack of architecture [181] and Brown

Name	Speculate About Design
Intent	Progressively refine your model of the system by checking hypotheses about the design against the source code.
Problem	How do you recover the way design concepts are represented in the source code?
Solution	Use your development expertise to conceive a hypothetical class diagram representing the design. Refine that model by verifying whether the names in the class diagram occur in the source code and by adapting the model accordingly. Repeat the process until your class diagram stabilises.
Hints	True learning occurs when the hypothetical class diagram does not match the source code, because then you have to come-up with alternatives and you will better understand the thought process involved by the original designers.
Tradeoffs	*Pro:* (a) Scales well; (b) quite cheap in terms of resources and tools. *Con:* (a) requires expertise; (b) consumes much time. *Difficulties:* You should plan to keep the class diagram up to date.
Example	*(Description of a typical trial-and-error process ...)*
Rationale	In order to gain a true understanding of the legacy problem, you must go through a learning process. Speculate about Design is intended to stimulate such a learning process.
Known Uses	The reflection model [386, 385], the concept assignment problem [64, 63] or the DALI tool [41, 270] are all examples of this pattern in action.
What Next	After this pattern, you will have a class diagram representing a part of the design. You may want to Study the Exceptional Entities to get an impression of the design quality.

Fig. 5.1. A condensed representation of the reengineering pattern "Speculate About Design" (adapted from [149] ©Morgan Kaufmann)

on anti-patterns [86]. It was Demeyer et al. who then assembled the first catalogue with reengineering patterns [149].

In what follows, we give an overview of the various patterns, pattern catalogues and pattern systems that document expert knowledge about reengineering in general and object-oriented reengineering in particular. We organise the overview by showing how reengineering patterns are similar to other patterns, by showing how they differ, and finally by pointing out some difficulties. Again, we hope to stimulate researchers to build upon existing knowledge.

5.3.1 Reengineering Patterns Are Just Like Patterns

Since reengineering patterns are patterns they have some obvious resemblances, for instance the use of a template, the forces and trade-offs. However, there are deeper parallels which illustrate quite well the kind of skills required for reengineering large software projects, be it object-oriented ones are not.

Keep it Simple. Patterns address complex problems, hence one might expect the solutions to be complex too. However, most patterns adhere to the "keep it stupidly simple" principle and reengineering patterns are no exception.

HARPER COLLEGE LIBRARY
PALATINE, ILLINOIS 60067

To see an example of a lightweight approach in patterns, have a look at Specu-late About Design [149] summarised in Figure 5.1. The pattern explains a top-down approach for extracting a coarse-grained design view (we hesitate to use the term "Architecture") from the source code. Basically, the pattern argues to design an ini-tial model and afterwards verify that model against the source code. When the model matches the code, that's fine because then you have found a valid design view. When it doesn't, it is even better, because then the reverse engineering is forced to consider alternatives, which enhances the inevitable learning experience that every reverse engineer must go through when taxing a new system.

Pattern System. Obviously, the "keep it stupidly simple" principle cannot solve everything. When dealing with real problems we must somehow divide the problem into manageable chunks and devise an overall solution out of several smaller solu-tions. That is why most pattern catalogues (and here as well reengineering patterns are no exception) are organised as a so-called "Pattern System". They help experts to divide a complex problem into pieces, show how each of these pieces can be solved, and afterwards explain how these solutions may be combined into a greater whole.

A good example of a pattern system is the catalogue written by Michael Feath-ers [169]. There he argues that legacy systems resist change because they lack (unit) tests or regression tests. He then explains how to gradually develop a regression test suite, first by doing the quick and dirty work (Sprout Method), then by introducing mock objects (The Case of the Irritating Parameter) and gradually moving towards refac-toring a system so that it becomes easier to write the unit tests (Varieties of Monsters).

Pattern Language. Pattern languages assemble a tightly-knit group of patterns, going beyond a simple catalogue of patterns. The ultimate goal for a pattern lan-guage is to create a collection whose whole becomes more than the sum of its parts. Thus, each individual pattern makes sense when applied on its own, yet the different patterns work together to fulfil a shared objective.

An initial attempt at a pattern language tackling the program comprehension problem can be found in Temporal Details [387]. The authors have observed that most humans understand program code via a multitude of intermediate representations which are refined and revised as the understanding improves. This implies that the order in which humans create those representations affects their understanding, or, in the authors' words, *"[. . .] you create representations over time, and your dynamic interactions contain meaning"*. They go on and explain how several Snapshots can be combined over time into a Long View and how it is necessary to rearrange this network to Retain Meaning. The authors include numerous examples of program tools that partly support these program understanding patterns. As such, this pattern lan-guage is a nice example of a vocabulary for discussing features of reverse engineering tools.

The Human in the Loop. While there exists quite a lot of tools to support various reengineering tasks, in the end the people must do the job. Patterns will mention tools and refer to code in the examples and known uses, however the bulk of the content is technology neutral. In contrast, patterns will include various tips and tricks that directly address the human in the loop.

To see an example of how patterns put people in the centre, consider the refactoring catalogue by Fowler [183]. Today, various refactoring tools automatically perform certain tedious tasks, such as renaming all occurrences of a method or checking whether a method may be removed. However, the descriptions in the refactoring catalogue emphasise that it is possible to refactor without a tool; in fact they contain various tips on how to relax preconditions that are required to ensure that the refactoring preserves behaviour. For instance, the Pull Up Method explains how you can move methods with similar behaviour (duplicated code) into a common superclass. One of the hairy issues for any refactoring tool is how to determine whether two method bodies are indeed similar, and most tools take a very strict view to ensure that the refactoring does not break anything. The refactoring catalogue however, takes a much more liberal view and even explains how to transform the bodies of methods when "they look like they do the same thing but are not identical" [183]—p.323.

5.3.2 Reengineering Patterns Are Quite Different from Patterns

Despite their similarities, reengineering patterns differ from patterns in general and design patterns in particular. Below we list the most striking differences and again document them with examples drawn from the literature.

Process Oriented. Reengineering patterns are mainly process-oriented, explaining something you should do rather than something that you should produce. Therefore, reengineering patterns typically describe the situation before and after, and the steps needed to make the transition. To emphasise the necessity to act, reengineering patterns are often named with verb phrases instead of noun phrases.

There are splendid examples of such transformation steps in the "Refactoring to Patterns" book [273]. The patterns in this book illustrate how to recognise certain code smells as symptoms for design problems which can be solved by applying a design pattern. Thus rather than explaining the end result (the design pattern), the book explains you how to recognise where you could apply a design pattern (the situation before), gives a stepwise instruction on how to refactor the code (the transition) and provides a concrete example of the resulting design (the situation after). For instance, the authors nicely explain subtle differences of the Adapter by explaining two different motivations and ways to introduce them. An Unify Interface with Adapter is used to create a unified interface for two similar classes that you can't change for some reason (e.g., they are part of a 3rd party library). The goal is to simplify client code which accesses both of these classes by routing calls through an adapter. Extract Adapter, however is used to factor out conditional logic or state-variables used to switch between different versions of a component, library or API. In that case, we have an adapter class which is taking too many responsibilities (i.e., adapting between too many parties) and which is resolved by creating different adapters for each version.

Intermediate Solutions. Reengineering patterns must address what may happen long after the solution has been applied. This is partly because reengineering projects take considerable time, hence must introduce temporary solutions. From a "Design the Perfect System" perspective such temporary steps are of course suboptimal, but from a pragmatic point of view they are a necessary evil.

A good example of dealing with time is Deprecation [475]; which explains how to deal with clients depending on interfaces that have been refactored. Rather than forcing all clients to adapt to the new interface immediately, the old interface is kept along as well. But the interface is documented as "Deprecated", which implies that it might removed in the near future. This gives clients time to implement the necessary changes.

Bad Examples. Reengineering patterns must distinguish the good from the bad and motivate that distinction. From an aesthetic point of view, showing the negative example might have its disadvantages. However, for learning purposes, negative examples have proven to be valuable.

The pattern system Big Ball of Mud is an example of concentrating on poor design since it explains why the de-facto standard software architecture is in fact the total lack of structure [181]. The authors argue that in order to clean up the mess in such systems, one should understand why—despite obvious disadvantages—these haphazardly structured systems remain so popular. Using the metaphor of urbanism, they show that such systems are a consequence of organic growth; the lack of structure then just reflects a poorly understood problem domain.

However, the most extreme case of negative examples are the so-called anti-patterns. Anti-patterns describe a solution which—on the surface—looks appealing, but once applied have very negative consequences. Some anti-patterns stop after explaining why the naive solution does not work, but the good anti-patterns also recommend ways to remedy the situation, or even prevent it from reoccurring.

The most visible collection of anti-patterns is written by Brown at. al. [86]. Among others, these authors listed a number of anti-patterns commonly applied by programmers not experienced with object-oriented thinking. The Blob (also known as a "God Class" [439, 149]) is an example of a design where one class monopolises control and the other classes primarily encapsulate data. However, good object-oriented designs try to distribute the responsibilities evenly. Blobs can be refactored by moving behaviour from the blob (the god class) to the surrounding classes. The Functional Decomposition on the other hand is procedural thinking disguised as objects and classes. Instead of writing subroutines that call subroutines, such functional decompositions involve classes calling other classes ignoring the concept of inheritance and polymorphism altogether. The refactored solution basically involves redesigning the class hierarchy from scratch based on the functionality provided in the original set of classes. Finally, the Poltergeists are controller classes with limited responsibilities and roles to play in the system, which have quite a short life-cycle and appear only to invoke methods of other classes and then disappear again. The refactored solution involves moving behaviour from the poltergeists to the related classes and then get rid the poltergeists.

Politics. Reengineering is not only about the technical solutions applicable when redesigning a system. It is also about convincing others of the viability of a given solution and the social interaction surrounding a project. You risk offending colleagues when pointing out problematic areas in a given system, so special care must be taken when criticizing the work of others. Therefore, many reengineering patterns also address "political" issues.

This is illustrated in the forces of First Contact *[. . .] Typically, your new colleagues will fall into three categories. The first category are the faithful, the people who believe that reengineering is necessary and who trust that you are able to (help them) do it. The second is the category of the sceptical, who believe this whole reengineering business is just a waste of time either because they want to protect their jobs or either because they think the whole project should start again from scratch. The third category is the category of the fence sitters, who do not have a strong opinion on whether this reengineering will pay off, so they just wait and see what happens. Consequently, in order to make the project a success, you must keep convincing the faithful, gain credit with the fence sitters and be wary of the sceptics.* [149]—p. 29.

5.3.3 Difficulties

Reengineering patterns also have some particular characteristics which makes them difficult to write. In this section we show a number of successful reengineering patterns to demonstrate how to overcome these difficulties.

Lack of Experience Reports. Software designers don't advertise that they once wrote poor code that needed to be reengineered. And even if they want to publish their stories, they are often bound by non-disclosure agreements which forbid them from divulging details of the design (be they good or bad). The fact that so few stories from the trenches make it into press is quite unfortunate, since the pattern community agrees that a pattern needs three *known uses* before we can consider it to be a *recurring* solution. However, when pattern writers get hold on a known use, they provide an amount of credibility to the solution that cannot be obtained otherwise.

As an example, consider the Design disharmonies listed in [311]. A design disharmony explains how to detect certain code smells using metrics and visualisation. Nevertheless, most software designers are very sceptical about using metrics to assess the quality of a design, because they rightfully claim that one cannot capture the beauty of a design in a mere number. However, through the use of many examples of ArgoUML (an open source system), the authors demonstrate that it is feasible to identify potential design problems. They proceed how to confirm this suspicion through manual inspection of the code.

Lack of Experts. Reengineering is all too often considered second class work, akin to cleaning up someone else's trash. It bears repeating that there are few systems that start off with bad code; most of the time bad code is the unfortunate result of making extensive changes and patches without allotting the time needed to clean up. Hence, we should identify the expert reengineers and convince them that they should be proud of the knowledge and skills they possess. Indeed, reengineering is more difficult than forward engineering, as reengineering requires all the skills of the latter plus a number of additional ones.

An example to illustrate that industrial sponsorship may provide the necessary reengineering expertise can be found in Gold Mining [313]. This pattern deals with the reconstruction and re-documentation of the requirements captured in the code of a legacy system. In there, the authors argue that according to their experience, most of the knowledge about a system is tacit, hidden in the heads of the people using the system. The authors describe a workshop approach, involving intensive code-inspections alongside the maintainers of the legacy system as a way to make this tacit knowledge explicit.

Lack of Forces. Purists might argue that some of the patterns referenced here are not really patterns because they do not list the forces and tradeoffs explicitly. Fowler [183], Feathers [169] and Lanza [311] certainly did not claim they wrote (reengineering) patterns. We included them in this overview anyway, because these texts resemble patterns both in spirit and in form. That is, they convey expert knowledge about a complex subject, and they do so by following some kind of template. Most importantly, they give designers the vocabulary they need to discuss how to tackle their redesign. In our own experience, we have found the vocabulary provided by patterns to be the most important, hence our pragmatic stance.

5.4 Conclusion

During the last two decades, the software engineering field saw an enormous amount of new methods, tools and languages. Most of these are aimed at making software easier to change; it is *soft*ware after all. Unfortunately, we have become victims of our success. Software systems today live longer, are changed more frequently, and as such erode much faster. As a consequence, the ability to change software in fact nullifies itself over time—the more we change a software system, the more difficult it becomes to apply changes in the future, thus the faster it becomes a legacy system.

Legacy systems have a bad reputation in the software engineering field, because of the many problems associated with operating them. Instead, we argue that legacy systems represent an opportunity: you have loyal customers who firmly believe in the value of the system and who are willing to invest time and money to continue operation. This is good, but means that reengineering becomes more important. It also means that we as software engineers should change our attitude. Rather than seeing design as an upfront phase in the development life-cycle, we should see it as a continuous learning activity where we redesign and reengineer to reflect a better understanding of the problem domain.

The bad news is that such continuous reengineering is very difficult and requires skilled software engineers; skills which are rarely taught at our universities and colleges. The good news is that these skills can be learned and that there is a growing body of material available to aid software engineers willing to learn. In this chapter, we provide an overview of the refactoring techniques and reengineering patterns that document expert knowledge about reengineering. This way, we invite researchers to test potential solutions in practice and expand the material; we invite practicioners to consult that material and apply it in their projects and—last but not least— we invite educators to refer to that material and teach it to the future generation.

6

Migration of Legacy Information Systems

Jean-Luc Hainaut[1], Anthony Cleve[1], Jean Henrard[2], and Jean-Marc Hick[2]

[1] PReCISE Research Centre, University of Namur, Belgium
[2] REVER s.a., Charleroi, Belgium

Summary. This chapter addresses the problem of platform migration of large business applications, that is, complex software systems built around a database and comprising thousands of programs. More specifically, it studies the substitution of a modern data management technology for a legacy one. Platform migration raises two major issues. The first one is the conversion of the database to a new data management paradigm. Recent results have shown that automated lossless database migration can be achieved, both at the schema and data levels. The second problem concerns the adaptation of the application programs to the migrated database schema and to the target data management system. This chapter first poses the problem and describes the State of the Art in information system migration. Then, it develops a two-dimensional reference framework that identifies six representative migration strategies. The latter are further analysed in order to identify methodological requirements. In particular, it appears that transformational techniques are particularly suited to drive the whole migration process. We describe the database migration process, which is a variant of database reengineering. Then, the problem of program conversion is studied. Some migration strategies appear to minimise the program understanding effort, and therefore are sound candidates to develop practical methodologies. Finally, the chapter describes a tool that supports such methodologies and discusses some real-size case studies.

6.1 Introduction

Business applications are designed as informational and behavioural models of an organization, such as an enterprise or an administration, and are developed to efficiently support its main business processes. The term *information system* is often used to designate large-scale business applications. Though this term has been given several interpretations, we will limit its scope in this chapter to a complex software and information system comprising one or several databases and programs, whatever their technologies, that support the organization's business processes. In particular, we will ignore other important components such as user interfaces as well as distribution and cooperation frameworks. The information system relies on a technological platform, made up of such components as operating systems, programming languages and database management systems.

T. Mens, S. Demeyer (eds.), *Software Evolution.*
DOI 10.1007/978-3-540-76440-3, © Springer 2008

6.1.1 Information System Evolution

Since every organization naturally evolves over time, its information system has to change accordingly. This evolution is often driven by the business environment, that forces the organization to change its business processes, and, transitively, the information system that supports them. Practically, the integration of new concepts and new business rules generally translates into the introduction of new data structures and new program components, or into the updating of existing ones.

On the other hand, the rapid technological evolution also induces a strong pressure to modify the information system in order to make it apt to support new requirements that the legacy technological platform was unable to meet. Two common motivations are worth being mentioned, namely flexibility and vanishing skills.

Flexibility. As summarised by Brodie and Stonebraker [84], *a legacy Information System is any Information System that significantly resists modifications and change.* One of the most challenging instances of this problem comes from the increasing requirement to answer, almost in real time, unplanned questions by extracting data from the database. COBOL file managers, as well as most legacy data management technologies, are efficient for batch and (to some extent) transaction processing. However, answering a new query requires either extending an existing program or writing a new one, an expensive task that may need several days. On the contrary, such a query can be formulated in SQL on a relational database in minutes, most often by non-expert users.

Skill shortage. Many core technologies enjoy a surprisingly long life, often encompassing several decades. Hiring experts that master them has become more and more difficult, so that companies may be forced to abandon otherwise satisfying technologies due to lack of available skills.

The business and technological dimensions of evolution can be, to a large extent, studied independently. In this chapter, we address the issue of adapting an information system to technological changes, a process generally called *migration*. More precisely we will study the substitution of a modern data management system for a legacy technology.

6.1.2 Information System Reengineering and Migration

As defined by Chikofsky and Cross [112], *reengineering, also known as [...] renovation [...], is the examination and alteration of a subject system to reconstitute it in a new form and the subsequent implementation of the new form. Reengineering generally includes some form of reverse engineering (to achieve a more abstract description) followed by some more form of forward engineering or restructuring.* Migration is a variant of reengineering in which the transformation is driven by a major technology change.

Replacing a DBMS with another one should, in an ideal world, only impact the database component of the information system. Unfortunately, the database most often has a deep influence on other components, such as the application programs.

Two reasons can be identified. First, the programs invoke data management services through an API that generally relies on complex and highly specific protocols. Changing the DBMS, and therefore its protocols, involves the rewriting of the invocation code sections. Second, the database schema is the technical translation of its conceptual schema through a set of rules that is dependent on the DBMS data model. Porting the database to another DBMS, and therefore to another data model, generally requires another set of rules, that produces a significantly different database schema. Consequently, the code of the programs often has to be adapted to this new schema. Clearly, the renovation of an information system by replacing an obsolete DBMS with a modern data management system leads to non trivial database (schemas and data) and programs modifications.

6.1.3 System Migration: State of the Art

Technically, a legacy information system is made up of large and ageing programs relying on legacy database systems (like IMS or CODASYL) or using primitive DMSs[3] (a.o., COBOL file system, ISAM). Legacy information systems often are isolated in that they do not easily interface with other applications. Moreover, they have proved critical to the business of organizations. To keep being competitive, organizations must improve their information system and invest in advanced technologies, specially through system evolution. In this context, the claimed 75% cost of legacy systems maintenance (w.r.t. total cost) is considered prohibitive [541].

Migration is an expensive and complex process, but it greatly increases the information system control and evolution to meet future business requirements. The scientific and technical literature ([69, 84]) mainly identifies two migration strategies, namely rewriting the legacy information system from scratch or migrating by small incremental steps. The incremental strategy allows the migration projects to be more controllable and predictable in terms of calendar and budget. The difficulty lies in the determination of the migration steps.

Legacy IS migration is a major research domain that has yielded some general migration methods. For example, Tilley and Smith [500] discuss current issues and trends in legacy system reengineering from several perspectives (engineering, system, software, managerial, evolutionary, and maintenance). They propose a framework to place reengineering in the context of evolutionary systems. The butterfly methodology proposed by Wu et al. [546] provides a migration methodology and a generic toolkit to aid engineers in the process of migrating legacy systems. This methodology, that does not rely on an incremental strategy, eliminates the need of interoperability between the legacy and target systems.

Below, we gather the major migration approaches proposed in the literature according to the various dimensions of the migration process as a whole.

---

[3] DMS: Data Management System.

Language Dimension

Language conversion consists in translating (parts of) an existing program from a source programming language to a target programming language. Ideally, the target program should show the same behaviour as the source program. Malton [342] identifies three kinds of language conversion scenarios, with their own difficulties and risks:

- **Dialect conversion** is the conversion of a program written in one dialect of a programming language to another dialect of the same programming language.
- **API migration** is the adaptation of a program due to the replacement of external APIs. In particular, API migration is required when changing the data management system.
- **Language migration** is the conversion from one programming language to a different one. It may include dialect conversion and API migration.

Two main language conversion approaches can be found in the literature. The first one [535], that might be called *abstraction-reimplementation*, is a two-step method. First, the source program is analysed in order to produce a high-level, language-independent description. Second, the reimplementation process transforms the abstract description obtained in the first step into a program in the target language. The second conversion approach [493, 342] does not include any abstraction step. It is a three-phase conversion process: (1) *normalization*, that prepares the source program to make the translation step easier; (2) *translation*, that produces an equivalent program that correctly runs in the target language; (3) *optimization*: that improves the maintainability of the target source code.

Terekhov and Verhoef [493] show that the language conversion process is far from trivial. This is especially true when the source and the target languages come from different paradigms. A lot of research has been carried out on specific cases of language conversion, among which PL/I to C++ [290], Smalltalk to C [558], C to Java [350] and Java to C# [158].

User Interface Dimension

Migrating user interfaces to modern platforms is another popular migration scenario. Such a process may often benefit from an initial reverse engineering phase, as the one suggested by Stroulia et al. [478]. This method starts from a recorded trace of the user interaction with the legacy interface, and produces a corresponding state-transition model. The states represent the unique legacy interface screens while the transitions correspond to the user action sequences enabling transitions from one screen to another. De Lucia et al. [333] propose a practical approach to migrating legacy systems to multi-tier, web-based architectures. They present an Eclipse-based plugin to support the migration of the graphical user interface and the restructuring and wrapping of the original legacy code.

Platform and Architecture Dimensions

Other researches, that we briefly discuss below, examine the problem of migrating legacy systems towards new architectural and technological platforms.

Towards distributed architectures. The Renaissance project [534] develops a systematic method for system evolution and re-engineering and provides technical guidelines for the migration of legacy systems (e.g., COBOL) to distributed client/server architectures. A generic approach to reengineering legacy code for distributed environments is presented by Serrano et al. [458]. The methodology combines techniques such as data mining, metrics, clustering, object identification and wrapping. Canfora et al. [101] propose a framework supporting the development of thin-client applications for limited mobile devices. This framework allows Java AWT applications to be executed on a server while the graphical interfaces are displayed on a remote client.

Towards object-oriented platforms. Migrating legacy systems towards object-oriented structures is another research domain that has led to a lot of mature results, especially on object identification approaches ([560, 99, 517, 201, 449]). Regarding the migration process itself, the approach suggested by De Lucia et al. [144] consists of several steps combining reverse engineering and reengineering techniques. More recently, Zou and Kontogiannis [569] have presented an incremental and iterative migration framework for reengineering legacy procedural source code into an object-oriented system.

Towards aspect-orientation. System migration towards aspect-oriented programming (AOP) still is at its infancy. Several authors have addressed the initial reverse engineering phase of the process, called *aspect mining*, which aims at identifying crosscutting concern code in existing systems. Among the various aspect mining techniques that have been proposed, we mention *fan-in analysis* [348], *formal concept analysis* [506], *dynamic analysis* [503] and *clone detection* [93]. Regarding clone detection, Chapter 2 provides an overview of techniques to identify and remove software redundancies. We also refer to Chapter 9 for a more complete discussion about current issues as well as future challenges in the area of aspect mining, extraction and evolution.

Towards service-oriented architectures. Migrating legacy systems towards service-oriented architectures (SOA) appears as one of the next challenges of the maintenance community. Sneed [465] presents a wrapping-based approach according to which legacy program functions are offered as web services to external users. O'Brien et al. [400] propose the use of architecture reconstruction to support migration to SOA. Chapter 7 presents a tool-supported methodology for migrating legacy systems towards three-tier and service-oriented architectures. This approach is based on graph transformation technology.

Database Dimension

Closer to our data-centred approach, the Varlet project [249] adopts a typical two phase reengineering process comprising a reverse engineering process phase followed by a standard database implementation. The approach of Jeusfeld [256] is divided into three parts: mapping of the original schema into a meta model, rearrangement of the intermediate representation and production of the target schema. Some works also address the migration between two specific systems. Among those, Menhoudj and Ou-Halima [361] present a method to migrate the data of COBOL legacy system into a relational database management system. The hierarchical to relational database migration is discussed in [360, 359]. General approaches to migrate relational database to object-oriented technology are proposed by Behm et al. [53] and Missaoui et al. [373]. More recently, Bianchi et al. [62] propose an iterative approach to database reengineering. This approach aims at eliminating the ageing symptoms of the legacy database [527] when incrementally migrating the latter towards a modern platform.

Related Work Limitations

Though the current literature on data-intensive systems migration sometimes recommend a semantics-based approach, relying on reverse engineering techniques, most technical solutions adopted in the industry are based on the so-called *one-to-one* migration of the data structures and contents, through a fully-automated process. As we will see below, these approaches lead to poor quality results. Secondly, while most papers provide ad hoc solutions for particular combinations of source/target DB platforms, there is still a lack of generic and systematic studies encompassing database migration strategies and techniques. Thirdly, the conversion of application programs in the context of database migration still remains an open problem. Although some work (e.g., [62]) suggests the use of wrapping techniques, very little attention is devoted to the way database wrappers are built or generated. In addition, the impact of the different conversion techniques on target source code maintainability has not been discussed.

6.1.4 About This Chapter

This chapter presents a practical approach to data-intensive application reengineering based on two independent dimensions, namely the data and the programs. We first propose a reference model that allows us to describe and compare the main migration approaches that are based on DBMS substitution (Section 6.2). This model identifies six representative strategies [228]. Section 6.3 develops a transformational framework that forms a sound basis to formalise database and program evolution, including migration. Then, the conversion of three main components of the information system, namely database schemas, database contents and programs, are described and discussed in Sections 6.4, 6.5 and 6.6 respectively. Section 6.7 describes a prototype CASE environment for information system migration while Section 6.8 discusses some experimental results. The six reference migration strategies are compared in Section 6.9. Finally, Section 6.10 draws some conclusions and suggests paths for future work.

   To make the discussion more concrete, we base it on one of the most popular problem patterns, that is, the conversion of a legacy COBOL program, using standard indexed files, into an equivalent COBOL program working on a relational database. The principles of the discussion are of course independent of the language and of the DMS.

6.2 Migration Reference Model

There is more than one way to migrate a data-intensive software system. Some approaches are quite straightforward and inexpensive, but lead to poorly structured results that are difficult to maintain. Others, on the contrary, produce good quality data structures and code, but at the expense of substantial intelligent (and therefore difficult to automate) code restructuring. We have built a reference model based on two dimensions, namely data and programs. Each of them defines a series of change strategies, ranging from the simplest to the most sophisticated. This model outlines a solution space in which we identify six typical strategies that will be described below and discussed in the remainder of the chapter. This model relies on a frequently used scenario, called *database-first* [545], according to which the database is transformed before program conversion. This approach allows developers to cleanly build new applications on the new database while incrementally migrating the legacy programs.

Information system migration consists in deriving a new database from a legacy database and in further adapting the software components accordingly [84]. Considering that a database is made up of two main components, namely its schema(s) and its contents (the *data*), the migration comprises three main steps: (1) *schema conversion*, (2) *data conversion* and (3) *program conversion*. Figure 6.1 depicts the organization of the database-first migration process, that is made up of subprocesses that implement these three steps. Schema conversion produces a formal description of the mapping between the objects of the legacy (S) and renovated (S') schemas. This mapping is then used to convert the data and the programs. Practical methodologies differ in the extent to which these processes are automated.

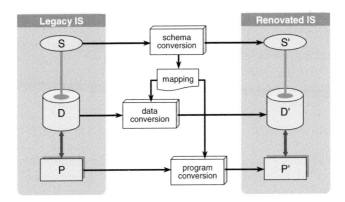

Fig. 6.1. Overall view of the *database-first* information system migration process

- **Schema conversion** is the translation of the legacy database structure, or schema, into an equivalent database structure expressed in the new technology. Both schemas must convey the same semantics, i.e., all the source data should be losslessly stored into the target database. Most generally, the conversion of a source schema into a target schema is made up of two processes. The first one, called database reverse engineering [215], aims at recovering the conceptual schema that expresses the semantics of the source data structure. The second process is standard and consists in deriving the target physical schema from this conceptual specification. Each of these processes can be modelled by a chain of semantics-preserving schema transformations.
- **Data conversion** is the migration of the data instance from the legacy database to the new one. This migration involves data transformations that derive from the schema transformations described above.
- **Program conversion**, in the context of database migration, is the modification of the program so that it now accesses the migrated database instead of the legacy data. The functionalities of the program are left unchanged, as well as its programming language and its user interface (they can migrate too, but this is another problem). Program conversion can be a complex process in that it relies on the rules used to transform the legacy schema into the target schema.

6.2.1 Strategies

We consider two dimensions, namely database conversion and program conversion, from which we will derive migration strategies.

The Database dimension (D)

We consider two extreme database conversion strategies leading to different levels of quality of the transformed database. The first strategy (*Physical conversion* or D1) consists in translating each construct of the source database into the closest constructs of the target DMS without attempting any semantic interpretation. The process is quite cheap, but it leads to poor quality databases with no added value. The second strategy (*Conceptual conversion* or D2) consists in recovering the precise semantic description (i.e., its conceptual schema) of the source database first, through reverse engineering techniques, then in developing the target database from this schema through a standard database methodology. The target database is of high quality according to the expressiveness of the new DMS model and is fully documented, but, as expected, the process is more expensive.

The program dimension (P)

Once the database has been converted, several approaches to application programs adaptation can be followed. We identify three reference strategies. The first one (*Wrappers* or P1) relies on wrappers that encapsulate the new database to provide the application programs with the legacy data access logic, so that these programs keep reading and writing records in (now fictive) indexed files or CODASYL/IMS

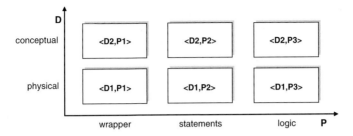

Fig. 6.2. The six reference IS migration strategies

databases, generally through program calls instead of through native I/O file state-ments. The second strategy (*Statement rewriting* or P2) consists in rewriting the ac-cess statements in order to make them process the new data through the new DMS-DML[4]. For instance, a READ COBOL statement is replaced with a select-from-where (SFW) or a fetch SQL statement. In these two first strategies, the program logic is neither elicited nor changed. According to the third strategy (*Logic rewriting* or P3), the program is rewritten in order to use the new DMS-DML at its full power. It requires a deep understanding of the program logic, since the latter will generally be changed due to, for instance, the change in database paradigm. These dimensions define six reference information system migration strategies (Figure 6.2).

6.2.2 Running Example

The strategies developed in this chapter will be illustrated by a small case study in which the legacy system comprises a standalone COBOL program and three files. Despite its small size, the files and the program exhibit representative instances of the most problematic patterns. This program records and displays information about customers that place orders. The objective of the case study is to convert the legacy files into a new relational database and to transform the application program into a new COBOL program, with the same business functions, but that accesses the new database.

6.3 The Transformational Approach

Any process that consists in deriving artefacts from other artefacts relies on such techniques as renaming, translating, restructuring, replacing, refining and abstract-ing, which basically are *transformations*. Most database engineering processes can be formalised as chains of elementary schema and data transformations that preserve some of their aspects, such as its information contents [217]. Information system evolution, and more particularly system migration as defined in this chapter, consists

---

[4] DML: Data Manipulation Language.

of the transformation of the legacy database and of its programs into a new system comprising the renovated database and the renovated programs. As far as programs are concerned, the transformations must preserve the behaviour of the interface with the database management system, though the syntax of this interface may undergo some changes. Due to the specific scope of the concept of migration developed here, only simple program transformations will be needed.

6.3.1 Schema Transformation

Roughly speaking, an elementary schema transformation consists in deriving a target schema S' from a source schema S by replacing construct C (possibly empty) in S with a new construct C' (possibly empty). Adding an attribute to an entity type, replacing a relationship type by an equivalent entity type or by a foreign key and replacing an attribute by an entity type (Figure 6.3) are some examples of schema transformations.

More formally, a transformation Σ is defined as a couple of mappings $<T,t>$ such that, $C' = T(C)$ and $c' = t(c)$, where c is any instance of C and c' the corresponding instance of C'. *Structural mapping* T is a rewriting rule that specifies how to modify the schema while *instance mapping* t states how to compute the instance set of C' from the instances of C.

There are several ways to express mapping T. For example, T can be defined (1) as a couple of predicates defining the minimal source precondition and the maximal target postcondition, (2) as a couple of source and target patterns or (3) through a procedure made up of removing, adding, and renaming operators acting on elementary schema objects. Mapping t will be specified by an algebraic formula, a calculus expression or even through an explicit procedure.

Any transformation Σ can be given an inverse transformation $\Sigma' = <T',t'>$ such that $T'(T(C)) = C$. If, in addition, we also have: $t'(t(c)) = c$, then Σ (and Σ') are called semantics-preserving[5]. Figure 6.3 shows a popular way to convert an attribute into an entity type (structural mapping T), and back (structural mapping T'). The instance mapping, that is not shown, would describe how each instance of source attribute A2 is converted into an EA2 entity and an R relationship.

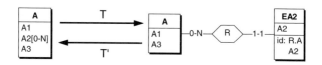

Fig. 6.3. Pattern-based representation of the structural mapping of ATTRIBUTE-to-ET transformation that replaces a multivalued attribute (A2) by an entity type (EA2) and a relationship type (R)

---

[5] The concept of semantics (or information contents) preservation is more complex, but this definition is sufficient in this context. A more comprehensive definition can be found in [217].

Practically, the application of a transformation will be specified by its signature, that identifies the source objects and provides the names of the new target objects. For example, the signatures of the transformations of Figure 6.3 are:

T : (EA2,R) ← ATTRIBUTE-to-ET(A,A2)

T' : (A2)   ← ET-to-ATTRIBUTE(EA2)

Transformations such as those in Figure 6.3 include names (A, A1, R, EA2, etc.) that actually are variable names. Substituting names of objects of an actual schema for these abstract names provides fully or partially instantiated transformations. For example, ('PHONE','has') ← ATTRIBUTE-to-ET('CUSTOMER','Phone') specifies the transformation of attribute Phone of entity type CUSTOMER, while (EA2,R) ← ATTRIBUTE-to-ET('CUSTOMER',A2) specifies the family of transformations of any attribute of CUSTOMER entity type.

The concept of transformation is valid whatever the granularity of the object it applies to. For instance, transforming conceptual schema CS into equivalent physical schema PS can be modelled as a (complex) semantics-preserving transformation CS-to-PS = <CS-to-PS, cs-to-ps> in such a way that PS = CS-to-PS(CS). This transformation has an inverse, PS-to-CS = <PS-to-CS, ps-to-cs> so that CS = PS-to-CS(PS).

6.3.2 Compound Schema Transformation

A compound transformation $\Sigma = \Sigma_2 \circ \Sigma_1$ is obtained by applying Σ_2 on the database (schema and data) that results from the application of Σ_1 [216]. Most complex database engineering processes, particularly database design and reverse engineering, can be modelled as compound semantics-preserving transformations. For instance, transformation CS-to-PS referred to here above actually is a compound transformation, since it comprises logical design, that transforms a conceptual schema into a logical schema, followed by physical design, that transforms the logical schema into a physical schema [43]. So, the database design process can be modelled by transformation CS-to-PS = LS-to-PS ∘ CS-to-LS, while the reverse engineering process is modelled by PS-to-CS = LS-to-CS ∘ PS-to-LS.

6.3.3 Transformation History and Schema Mapping

The *history* of an engineering process is the formal trace of the transformations that were carried out during its execution. Each transformation is entirely specified by its signature. The sequence of these signatures reflects the order in which the transformations were carried out. The history of a process provides the basis for such operations as undoing and replaying parts of the process. It also supports the traceability of the source and target artefacts.

In particular, it formally and completely defines the mapping between a source schema and its target counterpart when the latter was produced by means of a transformational process. Indeed, the chain of transformations that originates from any definite source object precisely designates the resulting objects in the target schema, as well as the way they were produced. However, the history approach to mapping specification has proved complex, essentially for three reasons [218]. First, a history includes information that is useless for schema migration. In particular, the signatures often include additional information for undoing and inverting transformations. Second, making histories evolve consistently over time is far from trivial. Third, real histories are not linear, due to the exploratory nature of engineering processes. Therefore, simpler mappings are often preferred, even though they are less powerful. For instance, we proposed the use of the following lighweight technique based on stamp propagation [232]. Each source object receives a unique stamp that is propagated to all objects resulting from the successive transformations. When comparing the source and target schemas, the objects that have the same stamp exhibit a pattern that uniquely identifies the transformation that was applied on the source object. This approach is valid provided that (1) only a limited set of transformations is used and (2) the transformation chain from each source object is short (one or two operations). Fortunately, these conditions are almost always met in real database design.

6.3.4 Program Transformation

Program transformation is a modification or a sequence of modifications applied to a program. Converting a program generally involves basic transformation steps that can be specified by means of *rewrite rules*. Term rewriting is the exhaustive application of a set of rewrite rules to an input term (e.g., a program) until no rule can be applied anywhere in the term. Each rewrite rule uses pattern matching to recognise a subterm to be transformed and replaces it with a target pattern instance.

Program transformations form a sound basis for application program conversion in the context of database migration. Indeed, the legacy I/O statements have to be rewritten with two concerns in mind, namely making the program comply with the new DMS API, and, more important, adapting the program logic to the new schema. The latter adaptation obviously depends on the way the legacy database schema was transformed into the new schema. This issue has already been addressed in previous work [116]. We have proposed a general approach, based on *coupled transformations* [306], according to which program rewrite rules are associated to schema transformations in a DML-independent manner.

For instance, Figure 6.4 shows an abstract rewrite rule that propagates the schema transformation depicted in Figure 6.3 to primitives that create an instance of entity type A from the values of variables $a1$, $a2_1$, ..., $a2_N$, $a3$. Since attribute $A2$ has been converted into an entity type, the way instances of A are created has to be changed. Creating an instance of entity type A now involves the creation of N instances of entity type $EA2$ within an extra loop. Created instances of $EA2$ are connected to instance a of A through relationship type R.

6.4 Schema Conversion

The schema conversion strategies mainly differ in the way they cope with the explicit and implicit constructs (that is, the data structures and the integrity constraints) of the

$$
\begin{array}{l}
create\ a := A((:A1 = a1) \\
\qquad and\ (:A2[1] = a2_1) \\
\qquad and\ (:A2[2] = a2_2) \\
\qquad \cdots \\
\qquad and\ (:A2[N] = a2_N) \\
\qquad and\ (:A3 = a3))
\end{array}
\quad
\begin{array}{c} t_c \\ \rightarrow \end{array}
\quad
\begin{array}{l}
create\ a := A((:A1 = a1) \\
\qquad and\ (:A3 = a3)) \\
\qquad for\ i\ in\ 1..N\ do \\
\qquad\qquad create\ ea2 := EA2((:A2 = a2_i) \\
\qquad\qquad\qquad and\ (R:a)) \\
\qquad endfor
\end{array}
$$

Fig. 6.4. Create mapping t_c associated with structural mapping T of Fig. 6.3

source schema. An *explicit construct* is declared in the DDL code [6] of the schema and can be identified through examination or parsing of this code. An *implicit construct* has not been declared, but, rather, is controlled and managed by external means, such as decoding and validating code fragments scattered throughout the application code. Such construct can only be identified by sophisticated analysis methods exploring the application code, the data, the user interfaces, to mention the most important sources.

The schema conversion process analyses the legacy application to extract the source physical schema (SPS) of the underlying database and transforms it into a target physical schema (TPS) for the target DMS. The TPS is used to generate the DDL code of the new database. In this section, we present two transformation strategies. The first strategy, called the *physical* schema conversion, merely simulates the explicit constructs of the legacy database into the target DMS. According to the second one, the *conceptual* schema conversion, the complete semantics of the legacy database is retrieved and represented into the technology-neutral conceptual schema (CS), which is then used to develop the new database.

6.4.1 Physical Conversion Strategy (D1)

Principle

According to this strategy (Figure 6.5) each explicit construct of the legacy database is directly translated into its closest equivalent in the target DMS. For instance, considering a standard file to SQL conversion, each record type is translated into a table, each top-level field becomes a column and each record/alternate key is translated into a primary/secondary key. No conceptual schema is built, so that the semantics of the data is ignored.

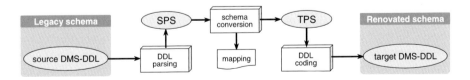

Fig. 6.5. Physical schema conversion strategy (D1)

---

[6] DDL: Data Description Language.

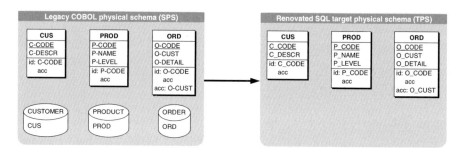

Fig. 6.6. Example of COBOL/SQL physical schema conversion

Methodology

The *DDL parsing* process analyses the DDL code to retrieve the physical schema of the source database (SPS). This schema includes explicit constructs only. It is then converted into its target DMS equivalent (TPS) through a straightforward *one-to-one* mapping and finally coded into the target DDL. The *schema conversion* process also produces the source to target schema mapping.

Illustration

The analysis of the file and record declarations produces the SPS (Figure 6.6/left). Each COBOL record type is translated into an SQL table, each field is converted into a column and object names are made compliant with the SQL syntax (Figure 6.6/right). In this schema, a box represents a physical entity type (record type, table, segment, etc.). The first compartment specifies its name, the second one gives its components (fields, columns, attributes) and the third one declares secondary constructs such as keys and constraints (*id* stands for primary identifier/key, *acc* stands for access key, or index, and *ref* stands for foreign key). A cylinder represents a data repository, commonly called a file.

6.4.2 Conceptual Conversion Strategy (D2)

Principle

This strategy aims at producing a target schema in which all the semantics of the source database are made explicit, even those conveyed by implicit source constructs. In most cases, there is no complete and up to date documentation of the information system, and in particular of the database. Therefore, its logical and conceptual schemas must be recovered before generating the target schema. The physical schema of the legacy database (SPS) is extracted and transformed into a conceptual schema (CS) through reverse engineering. The conceptual schema is then transformed into the physical schema of the target system (TPS) through standard database development techniques.

Methodology

The left part of Figure 6.7 depicts the three steps of a simplified database reverse engineering methodology used to recover the logical and conceptual schemas of the source database.

- As in the first strategy, the first step is the parsing of the DDL code to extract the physical schema (SPS), which only includes the explicit constructs.
- The *schema refinement* step consists in refining the SPS by adding the implicit constructs that are identified through the analysis of additional information sources, such as the source code of the application programs and the database contents, to mention the most common ones. Program code analysis performs an in-depth inspection of the way the programs use and manage the data. Data validation, data modification and data access programming *clichés* are searched for in particular, since they concentrate the procedural logic strongly linked with data properties. The existing data are also analysed through data mining techniques, either to detect constraints, or to confirm or discard hypotheses on the existence of constraints. This step results in the source logical schema (SLS), that includes the explicit representation of such constructs as record and field decomposition, uniqueness constraints, foreign keys or enumerated domains that were absent in SPS. The history SPS-to-SLS of the refinement process forms the first part of the source-to-target mapping.
- The final step is *schema conceptualisation* that semantically interprets the logical schema. The result is expressed by the conceptual schema (CS). This schema is technology independent, and therefore independent of both the legacy and new DMSs. The history SLS-to-CS of this process is appended to the source-to-target mapping.

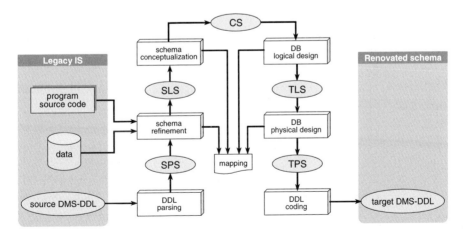

Fig. 6.7. Conceptual schema conversion strategy (D2)

A complete presentation of this reverse engineering methodology can be found in [215] and [214], together with a fairly comprehensive bibliography on database reverse engineering.

The conceptual schema is then transformed into an equivalent logical schema (TLS), which in turn is transformed into the physical schema (TPS). TPS is then used to generate the DDL code of the target database. These processes are quite standard and are represented in the right part of Figure 6.7. The histories CS-to-TLS and TLS-to-TPS are added to the source-to-target mapping. The mapping SPS-to-TPS is now complete, and is defined as SPS-to-SLS ∘ SLS-to-CS ∘ CS-to-TLS ∘ TLS-to-TPS.

Illustration

The details of this reverse engineering case study have been described in [219]. We sketch its main steps in the following. The legacy physical schema SPS is extracted as in the first approach (Figure 6.8/top-left).

The *Refinement* process enriches this schema with the following implicit constructs:

(1) Field O-DETAIL appears to be compound and multivalued, thanks to program analysis techniques based on variable dependency graphs and program slicing.

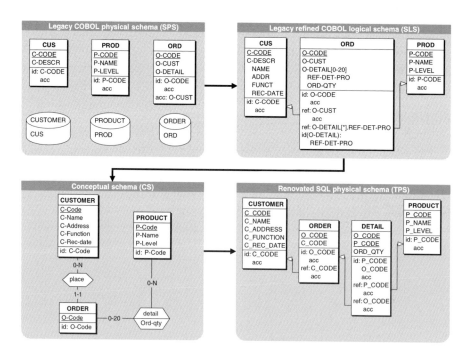

Fig. 6.8. Example of COBOL/SQL conceptual schema conversion

(2) The implicit foreign keys O-CUST and REF-DET-PRO are identified by schema names and structure patterns analysis, program code analysis and data analysis.
(3) The multivalued identifier (uniqueness constraint) REF-DET-PRO of O-DETAIL can be recovered through the same techniques.

The resulting logical schema SLS is depicted in Figure 6.8/top-right.

During the *data structure conceptualisation*, the implementation objects (record types, fields, foreign keys, arrays,...) are transformed into their conceptual equivalent to produce the conceptual schema CS (Figure 6.8/bottom-left).

Then, the database design process transforms the entity types, the attributes and the relationship types into relational constructs such as tables, columns, keys and constraints. Finally physical constructs (indexes and storage spaces) are defined (Figure 6.8.bottom-right) and the code of the new database is generated.

6.5 Data Conversion

6.5.1 Principle

Data conversion is handled by a so-called Extract-Transform-Load (ETL) processor (Figure 6.9), which transforms the data from the data source to the format defined by the target schema. Data conversion requires three steps. First, it performs the extraction of the data from the legacy database. Then, it transforms these data in such a way that their structures match the target format. Finally, it writes these data in the target database.

Data conversion relies on the mapping that holds between the source and target physical schemas. This mapping is derived from the instance mappings (t) of the source-to-target transformations stored in the history.

Deriving data conversion from the physical schema conversion (D1) is straightforward. Indeed, both physical schemas are as similar as their DMS models permit, so that the transformation step most often consists in data format conversion.

The conceptual schema conversion strategy (D2) recovers the conceptual schema (CS) and the target physical schema (TPS) implements all the constraints of this schema. Generally, both CS and TPS include constraints that are missing in SPS, and that the source data may violate. Thus data migration must include a preliminary data cleaning step that fixes or discards the data that cannot be loaded in the target database [423]. This step cannot always be automated. However, the schema refinement step identifies all the implicit constraints and produces a formal specification

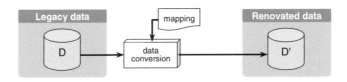

Fig. 6.9. Data migration architecture: converter and schema transformation

for the data cleaning process. It must be noted that the physical schema conversion strategy (D1) makes such data cleaning useless. Indeed, both SPS and TPS express the same constraints that the source data are guaranteed to satisfy.

6.5.2 Methodology

Data conversion involves three main tasks. Firstly, the target physical schema (TPS) must be implemented in the new DMS. Secondly, the mapping between the source and target physical schemas must be defined as sequences of schema transformations according to one of the two strategies described in Section 3. Finally, these mappings must be implemented in the converter for translating the legacy data according to the format defined in TPS.

Since each transformation is formally defined by $<T,t>$, the instance mapping sps-to-tps is automatically derived from the compound transformation SPS-to-TPS built in the schema conversion process. The converter is based on the structural mappings SPS-to-TPS to write the extraction and insertion requests and on the corresponding instance mappings sps-to-tps for data transformation.

6.6 Program Conversion

The program conversion process aims at re-establishing the consistency that holds between application programs and the migrated database. The nature of this consistency is twofold. First, the programs have to comply with the API of the DMS, by using the right data manipulation language and interaction protocols. Second, the programs have to manipulate the data in their correct format, i.e., the format declared in the database schema.

This section analyses the three program modification strategies specified in Figure 6.2. The first one relies on *wrapper technology* (P1) to map the access primitives onto the new database through wrapper invocations that replace the DML statements of the legacy DMS. The second strategy (P2) replaces each statement with its equivalent in the new DMS-DML. According to the P3 strategy, the access logic is rewritten to comply with the DML of the new DMS. In strategies P2 and P3, access statements are expressed in the DML of the new DMS.

In order to compare the three program conversion strategies, we will apply them successively on the same legacy COBOL fragment, given in Figure 6.10. This code fragment deletes all the orders placed by a given customer.

6.6.1 Wrapper Strategy (P1)

Principle

In migration and interoperability architectures, wrappers are popular components that convert legacy interfaces into modern ones. Such wrappers allow the reuse of legacy components [464] (e.g., allow Java programs to access COBOL files). The

```
DELETE-CUS-ORD.
   MOVE C-CODE TO O-CUST.
   MOVE 0 TO END-FILE.
   READ ORDERS KEY IS O-CUST
      INVALID KEY MOVE 1 TO END-FILE.
   PERFORM DELETE-ORDER UNTIL END-FILE = 1.

DELETE-ORDER.
   DELETE ORDERS.
   READ ORDERS NEXT
      AT END MOVE 1 TO END-FILE
      NOT AT END
         IF O-CUST NOT = C-CODE
            MOVE 1 TO END-FILE.
```

Fig. 6.10. A legacy COBOL code fragment that deletes the orders corresponding to a given customer

wrappers discussed in this chapter are of a different nature, in that they simulate the legacy data interface on top of the new database. For instance, they allow COBOL programs to *read*, *write*, *rewrite* records that are built from rows extracted from a relational database. In a certain sense, they could be called *backward* wrappers. An in-depth analysis of both kinds of wrappers can be found in [497].

The wrapper conversion strategy attempts to preserve the logic of the legacy programs and to map it on the new DMS technology [84]. A *data wrapper* is a *data model conversion* component that is called by the application program to carry out operations on the database. In this way, the application program invokes the wrapper instead of the legacy DMS. If the wrapper simulates the modelling paradigm of the legacy DMS and its interface, the alteration of the legacy code is minimal. It mainly consists in replacing DML statements with wrapper invocations.

The wrapper converts all legacy DMS requests from legacy applications into requests against the new DMS that now manages the data. Conversely, it captures results from the new DMS, converts them to the appropriate legacy format [409] (Figure 6.11) and delivers them to the application program.

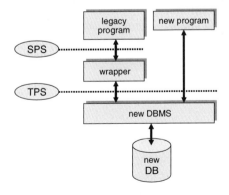

Fig. 6.11. Wrapper-based migration architecture: a wrapper allows the data managed by a new DMS to be accessed by the legacy programs

Methodology

Schemas SPS and TPS, as well as the mapping between them (SPS-to-TPS) provide the necessary information to derive the procedural code of the wrappers. For each COBOL source record type, a wrapper is built that simulates the COBOL file handling statements. The simulated behaviour must also include the management of currency indicators (internal dynamic pointers to current records) as well as error handling.

Once the wrappers have been built, they have to be interfaced with the legacy programs. This can be done by replacing, in the latter, original data access operations with wrapper invocations. Such a transformation is straightforward, each instruction being replaced with a call to the corresponding wrapper and, in some cases, an additional test. In the case of COBOL file handling, the test checks the value of the wrapper status in order to simulate *invalid key* and *at end* clauses.

Legacy code adaptation also requires other minor reorganizations like modifying the *environment division* and the *data division* of the programs. The declaration of files in the *environment division* can be discarded. The declaration of record types has to be moved from the *input-output section* to the *working storage section*. The declarations of new variables used to call the wrapper (action, option and status) are added to the *working storage section*. Finally, new code sections are introduced into the program (e.g., database connection code).

Some legacy DMS, such as MicroFocus COBOL, provide an elegant way to interface wrappers with legacy programs. They allow programmers to replace the standard file management library with a customised library (the *wrapper*). In this case, the legacy code does not need to be modified at all.

The <D1,P1> and <D2,P1> strategies only differ in the complexity of the wrappers that have to be generated. The program transformation is the same in both strategies since each legacy DML instruction is replaced with a wrapper invocation. The code of the wrappers for the <D1,P1> strategy is trivial because each explicit data structure of the legacy database is directly translated into a similar structure of the target database. In the <D2,P1> strategy the conceptual schema is recovered and the new physical schema can be very different from the legacy one. For instance, a record can be split into two or more tables, a table may contain data from more than one record, new constraints might be implemented into the new DMS, etc. In this strategy, translating a READ command may require to access more than one table and to perform additional tests and loops.

Illustration

To illustrate the way data wrappers are used, let us consider the legacy COBOL fragment of Figure 6.10, which comprises READ and DELETE primitives. As shown in Figure 6.12, each primitive is simply replaced with a corresponding wrapper invocation. From the program side, the wrapper is a black box that simulates the behaviour of the COBOL file handling primitives on top of the SQL database. Note that the P1 program adaptation strategy does not depend on the schema conversion strategy.

```
DELETE-CUS-ORD.
    MOVE C-CODE TO O-CUST.
    MOVE 0 TO END-FILE.
    SET WR-ACTION-READ TO TRUE.
    MOVE "KEY IS O-CUST" TO WR-OPTION.
    CALL WR-ORDERS USING WR-ACTION, ORD, WR-OPTION, WR-STATUS
    IF WR-STATUS-INVALID-KEY MOVE 1 TO END-FILE.
    PERFORM DELETE-ORDER UNTIL END-FILE = 1.

DELETE-ORDER.
    SET WR-ACTION-DELETE TO TRUE.
    CALL WR-ORDERS USING WR-ACTION, ORD, WR-OPTION, WR-STATUS.
    SET WR-ACTION-READ TO TRUE.
    MOVE "NEXT" TO WR-OPTION.
    CALL WR-ORDERS USING WR-ACTION, ORD, WR-OPTION, WR-STATUS.
    IF WR-STATUS-AT-END
        MOVE 1 TO END-FILE
    ELSE
        IF O-CUST NOT = C-CODE
            MOVE 1 TO END-FILE.
```

Fig. 6.12. Code fragment of Fig. 6.10 converted using the *Wrapper* strategy (P1)

This choice only affects the complexity of the wrapper code, since the latter is directly derived from the mapping that holds between the legacy and new database schemas.

6.6.2 Statement Rewriting (P2)

Principle

This program modification technique depends on the schema conversion strategy. It consists in replacing legacy DMS-DML statements with native DML statements of the new DMS. For example, every file access statement in a COBOL program has to be replaced with an equivalent sequence of relational statements. As for the wrapper strategy, program data structures are left unchanged. Consequently, the relational data must be stored into the legacy COBOL variables.

In the case of the physical schema conversion strategy (D1), the conversion process can be easily automated, thanks to the simple SPS-to-TPS mapping. The conceptual schema conversion strategy (D2) typically flattens complex COBOL structures in the target relational schema. This makes the use of additional loops necessary when retrieving the value of a compound multivalued COBOL variable. Although the substitution process is more complex than in the D1 strategy, it can also be fully automated.

Methodology

The program modification process may be technically complex, but does not need sophisticated methodology. Each DML statement has to be located, its parameters have to be identified and the new sequence of DML statements has to be defined and inserted in the code. The main point is how to translate iterative accesses in a systematic way. For instance, in the most popular COBOL-to-SQL conversion, there exist several techniques to express the typical START/READ NEXT loop with SQL statements. The task may be complex due to loosely structured programs and the use of dynamic DML statements. For instance, a COBOL READ NEXT statement can follow a statically unidentified START or READ KEY IS initial statement, making it impossible to identify the record key used. A description of a specific technique that solves this problem is provided below.

Illustration

The change of paradigm when moving from standard files to relational database raises such problems as the identification of the sequence scan. COBOL allows the programmer to start a sequence based on an indexed key (START/READ KEY IS), then to go on in this sequence through READ NEXT primitives. The most obvious SQL translation is performed with a cursor-based loop. However, since READ NEXT statements may be scattered throughout the program, the identification of the initiating START or READ KEY IS statement may require complex static analysis of the program data and control flows.

The technique illustrated in Figure 6.13 solves this problem. This technique is based on state registers, such as ORD-SEQ, that specify the current key of each record type, and consequently the matching SQL cursor. A cursor is declared for each kind of record key usage (*equal*, *greater*, *not less*) in the program. For instance, the table ORD gives at most six cursors (combination of two record keys and three key usages).

The example of Figure 6.13 shows the <D2,P2> conversion the COBOL code fragment of Figure 6.10. During the schema conversion process, the O-DETAIL compound multivalued field has been converted into the DETAIL SQL table. So, rebuilding the value of O-DETAIL requires the execution of a loop and a new FILL-ORD-DETAIL procedure. This new loop retrieves the details corresponding to the current ORD record, using a dedicated SQL cursor.

6.6.3 Logic Rewriting (P3)

Principle

The program is rewritten to explicitly access the new data structures and take advantage of the new data system features. This rewriting task is a complex conversion process that requires an in-depth understanding of the program logic. For example, the processing code of a COBOL record type may be replaced with a code section that copes with several SQL tables or a COBOL loop may be replaced with a single SQL join.

The complexity of the problem prevents the complete automation of the conversion process. Tools can be developed to find the statements that *should* be modified by the programmer and to give hints on how to rewrite them. However, modifying the code is still up to the programmer.

```
EXEC SQL DECLARE CURSOR ORD_GE_K1 FOR
  SELECT CODE, CUS_CODE
  FROM ORDERS WHERE CUS_CODE >= :O-CUST
  ORDER BY CUS_CODE
END-EXEC.
...
EXEC SQL DECLARE CURSOR ORD_DETAIL FOR
  SELECT PROD_CODE, QUANTITY
  FROM DETAIL WHERE ORD_CODE = :O-CODE
END-EXEC.
...
DELETE-CUS-ORD.
  MOVE C-CODE TO O-CUST.
  MOVE 0 TO END-FILE.
  EXEC SQL
    SELECT COUNT(*) INTO :COUNTER
    FROM ORDERS WHERE CUS_CODE = :O-CUST
  END-EXEC.
  IF COUNTER = 0
    MOVE 1 TO END-FILE
  ELSE
    EXEC SQL OPEN ORD_GE_K1 END-EXEC
    MOVE "ORD_GE_K1" TO ORD-SEQ
    EXEC SQL
      FETCH ORD_GE_K1
      INTO :O-CODE, :O-CUST
    END-EXEC
    IF SQLCODE NOT = 0
      MOVE 1 TO END-FILE
    ELSE
      EXEC SQL OPEN ORD_DETAIL END-EXEC
      SET IND-DET TO 1
      MOVE 0 TO END-DETAIL
      PERFORM FILL-ORD-DETAIL UNTIL END-DETAIL = 1
    END-IF
  END-IF.
  PERFORM DELETE-ORDER UNTIL END-FILE = 1.
DELETE-ORDER.
  EXEC SQL
    DELETE FROM ORDERS
    WHERE CODE = :O-CODE
  END-EXEC.
  IF ORD-SEQ = "ORD_GE_K1"
    EXEC SQL
      FETCH ORD_GE_K1 INTO :O-CODE,:O-CUST
    END-EXEC
  ELSE IF ...
    ...
  END-IF.
  IF SQLCODE NOT = 0
    MOVE 1 TO END-FILE
  ELSE
    IF O-CUST NOT = C-CODE
      MOVE 1 TO END-FILE.
...
FIlL-ORD-DETAIL SECTION.
  EXEC SQL
    FETCH ORD_DETAIL
    INTO :REF-DET-PRO(IND-DET),:ORD-QTY(IND-DET)
  END-EXEC.
  SET IND-DET UP BY 1.
  IF SQLCODE NOT = 0
    MOVE 1 TO END-DETAIL.
```

Fig. 6.13. Code fragment of Fig. 6.10 converted using the *Statement Rewriting* strategy (P2)

This strategy can be justified if the whole system, that is database and programs, has be renovated in the long term (strategy <D2,P3>). After the reengineering, the new database and the new programs take advantage of the expressiveness of the new technology. When the new database is just a *one-to-one* translation of the legacy database (<D1,P3>), this strategy can be very expensive for a poor result. The new database just simulates the old one and takes no advantage of the new DMS. Worse, it inherits all the flaws of the old database (bad design, design deteriorated by maintenance, poor expressiveness, etc.). Thus, we only address the <D2,P3> strategy in the remaining of this section.

Methodology

The P3 strategy is much more complex than the previous ones since every part of the program may be influenced by the schema transformation. The most obvious method consists in (1) identifying the file access statements, (2) identifying and understanding the statements and the data objects that depend on these access statements and (3) rewriting these statements as a whole and redefining these data objects.

Illustration

Figure 6.14 shows the code fragment of Figure 6.10 converted using the *Logic Rewriting* strategy. The resulting code benefits from the full power of SQL. The two-step *position then delete* pattern, which is typical of navigational DMS, can be replaced with a single predicate-based *delete* statement.

```
DELETE-CUS-ORD.
    EXEC SQL
        DELETE FROM ORDERS
        WHERE CUS_CODE = :C-CODE
    END-EXEC.
    IF SQLCODE NOT = 0 THEN GO TO ERR-DEL-ORD.
```

Fig. 6.14. Code fragment of Fig. 6.10 converted using the *Logic Rewriting* strategy (P3)

6.7 Tool Support

Some of the information system migration strategies we developed in this chapter have been implemented using two complementary transformational technologies, namely DB-MAIN and the ASF+SDF Meta-Environment.

6.7.1 The Tools

The DB-MAIN CASE Environment

DB-MAIN [143] is a data-oriented CASE environment developed by the Laboratory of Database Application Engineering (LIBD) of the University of Namur. Its purpose is to help the analyst in the design, reverse engineering, reengineering, maintenance and evolution of database applications.

DB-MAIN offers general functions and components that allow the development of sophisticated processors supporting data-centred application renovation:

- A generic model of schema representation based on the GER (Generic Entity/Relationship) model to describe data structures in all abstraction levels and according to all popular modelling paradigms.
- A graphical interface to view the repository and apply operations.
- A transformational toolbox rich enough to encompass most database engineering and reverse engineering processes.
- Customizable assistants (e.g., transformation, reverse engineering, conformity analysis) to help solve complex and repetitive problems.
- A history processor to record, replay, save or invert history.

DB-MAIN also includes several processors specific to the reverse engineering process [229], such as DDL parsers for most popular DMSs, a foreign key discovery assistant, and program analysis tools (pattern matching, variable dependency analysis and program slicing). Experience of actual reverse engineering taught us that there are no two reengineering projects are the same. Hence the need for programmable, extensible and customisable tools. DB-MAIN (and more specifically its meta functions) includes features to extend its repository and develop new functions. It includes in particular a 4GL (*Voyager2*) as well as a Java API that allow analysts to quickly develop their own customised processors [215].

The ASF+SDF Meta-Environment

The ASF+SDF Meta-Environment [515] is an interactive development environment for the automatic generation of interactive systems for manipulating programs, specifications, or other texts written in a formal language. It is developed by the SEN1 research group of the CWI in Amsterdam. In the context of system migration, the ASF+SDF Meta-Environment provides tool generators to support the program conversion step. It allows both defining the syntax of programming languages and specifying transformations of programs written in such programming languages [514].

The next sections describe the tool support in the different steps of the methodologies described in this chapter for schema, data and program conversion.

6.7.2 Schema Conversion

The physical schema conversion strategy uses simple tools only, such as a DDL parser to extract SPS, an elementary schema converter to transform SPS into TPS and a DDL generator. Complex analysers are not required.

In the conceptual schema conversion strategy, extracting SPS and storing it in the CASE tool repository is done through a DDL parser (SQL, COBOL, IMS, CODASYL, RPG, XML) from the parser library. Schema refinement requires schema, data and program analysers. Data structure conceptualization and database design are based on schema transformations. Code generators produce the DDL code of the new database according to the specifications of TPS.

6.7.3 Mapping Definition

We use the transformation toolkit of DB-MAIN to carry out the chain of schema transformations needed during the schema conversion phase. DB-MAIN automatically generates and maintains a history log of all the transformations that are applied to the legacy DB schema (SPS) to obtain the target DB schema (TPS). This history log is formalised in such a way that it can be analysed and transformed. Particularly, it can be used to derive both the mappings between SPS and TPS. A visual mapping assistant has been developed to support the definition, the visualization and the validation of inter-schema mappings. This tool is based on the stamping technique described in Section 6.3.3.

6.7.4 Data Conversion

Writing data converters manually is an expensive task, particularly for complex mappings (for simple mappings parametric ETL converters are quite sufficient). The DB-MAIN CASE tool includes specific history analysers and converter generators that have been described in [146].

6.7.5 Program Conversion

Wrapper Generation

So far, wrapper generators for COBOL-to-SQL and IDS/II[7]-to-SQL have been developed. These generators are implemented through Java plug-ins of DB-MAIN, and require the following inputs:

- the legacy database schema
- an optional intermediate schema
- the target database schema
- the mapping between these two (three) schemas

The generators produce the code that provides the application programs with a legacy interface to the new database. In practice, we generate one wrapper per legacy record type. Each generated wrapper is a COBOL program with embedded SQL primitives. The generated wrappers simulate the legacy DMS on top on the renovated database. Note that the same tools can be used for supporting both P1 and P2 program conversion strategies, which mainly differ from the target location of the generated code (wrapper or new program section).

---

[7] IDS/II is the BULL implementation of CODASYL.

Legacy Code Transformation

The adaptation of the legacy application programs relies on the ASF+SDF Meta-Environment. We use an SDF version of the IBM VS COBOL II grammar, which was obtained by Lämmel and Verhoef [304]. We specify a set of rewrite rules (ASF equations) on top of this grammar to obtain two similar program transformation tools. The first tool is used in the context of COBOL-to-SQL migration, while the second one supports IDS/II-to-SQL conversion.

The main input arguments of the program transformers are automatically generated. These parameters include:

- the list of the migrated record types
- additional variable declarations
- additional program code sections
- owner and members of each set (IDS/II)
- list of the declared record keys (IDS/II)

The program transformation tools are suitable in case of partial migration, i.e., when only some legacy record types actually are migrated to the new database platform. In that case, only the DML instructions manipulating migrated data are adapted. The other DML instructions, which still access the legacy data, are left unchanged.

6.8 Industrial Application

We have been involved in several industrial reverse engineering and reengineering projects during the last three years. In this section, we particularly report on an on-going IDS/II-to-SQL database migration project.

6.8.1 Project Overview

The project aims at migrating a large COBOL system towards a relational (DB2) database platform. The legacy system runs on a Bull mainframe and is made of nearly 2300 programs, totalling more than 2 million lines of COBOL code. The information system makes use of an IDS/II database. The source physical DB schema comprises 231 record types, 213 sets and 648 fields. The migration strategy chosen is based on the combination of a conceptual database conversion (D2) and a wrapper-based program conversion (P1).

6.8.2 Process Followed

The project started with a prototyping phase, during which a consistent subset of the data and programs has been fully migrated. This initial phase aims at verifying the correctness of the overall migration through a systematic testing process. The database subset includes 26 IDS/II record types and 31 sets. The legacy programs selected for conversion comprise 51 KLOC and make use of almost every possible

IDS/II statement (*find*, *get*, *erase*, *store*, *modify*, *connect*, *disconnect*, etc.). The tests, performed with the help of IDS/II experts from the customer side, have shown the correctness of the automated program conversion.

Below, we describe the main phases that we followed to migrate the complete legacy system.

Inventory

The purpose of the inventory process is twofold. First, it aims at checking that we have received a complete and consistent set of source code files from the customer. Second, it allows us to get a rapid overview of the application architecture in order to evaluate the complexity of the migration task, as well as the part of the work that cannot be automated. In this project, the inventory phase produced the following results :

- complete statistics about the IDS/II statements (number, type, location);
- the program call graph, specifying which program calls which program;
- the database usage graph, specifying which program uses which IDS/II record type;
- a classification of the legacy source code files based on their database usage (no access, indirect access or direct access).

Schema Conversion Through DBRE

During the database reverse engineering process, program analysis techniques have been used in order to retrieve different kinds of information about the legacy database. In particular, dataflow analysis allowed us to find which program variables are used to manipulate the records, in order to deduce a more precise record decomposition. Dataflow analysis was also used to elicit implicit data dependencies that exist between database fields, among which potential foreign keys. Our dataflow analysis approach is inspired by the interprocedural slicing algorithm proposed by Horwitz et al. [235], based on the system dependency graph (SDG). We refer to [117] for more details on the use of SDGs in database reverse engineering.

Among others, the DBRE process allowed us to:

- recover finer-grained structural decompositions for record types and attributes;
- retrieve implicit data dependencies, including 89 foreign keys, 37 computed foreign keys, and 60 other redundancies.

Table 6.1 gives a comparison of the successive versions of the database schema. The physical IDS/II schema is the initial schema extracted from the DDL code (here we consider the subset of the schema actually migrated). The refined IDS/II schema is the physical schema with a finer-grained structure. It was obtained by resolving numerous copybooks in which structural decompositions of physical attributes are declared. In the refined IDS schema, most attributes are declared several times through *redefines* clauses, hence the huge total number of attributes. The conceptual schema

Table 6.1. Comparison of successive versions of the complete database schema

	Physical IDS/II	Refined IDS/II	Conceptual	Relational DB2
# entity types	159	159	156	171
# relationship types	148	148	90	0
# attributes	458	9 027	2 176	2 118
max # att./entity type	8	104	61	94

is the result of the conceptualization phase. It comprises only one declaration per attribute. When a conflict occurs, the chosen attribute decomposition is the one the analyst considers to be the most expressive. In addition, the number of entity type is different since some technical record types were discarded while other ones were split (sub-types). Finally, the relational schema shows an increase in the number of entity types, due to the decomposition of arrays, as well as a reduction of the number of attributes due to the aggregation of compound fields.

Data Validation and Migration

During the schema conversion phase, the mapping of the various components is recorded between the successive schemas, such that we know precisely how each concept is represented in each schema. From such mappings we can generate two kinds of programs:

- Data validators, which check if the legacy data comply with all recovered implicit constraints;
- Data migrators, that actually migrate the legacy data to the relational database.

The data validation step revealed that many implicit referential constraints were actually violated by the legacy data. This is explained by the fact that most rules are simply encoding rules which are not always checked again when data are updated, and by the fact that users find tricks to bypass some rules.

Wrapper-Based Program Conversion

The wrapper generation phase produced 159 database wrappers. Each generated wrapper is a COBOL program containing embedded SQL primitives. The total wrapper code size is about 450 KLOC.

The results obtained during the legacy code adaptation are summarised in Table 6.2. A total of 669 programs and 3 917 copybooks were converted. We notice that about 92% of the IDS/II verbs were transformed automatically, while the manual work concerned 85 distinct source code files only.

Table 6.2. Program transformation results

	Migrated	Manually transformed
# programs	669	17
# copybooks	3 917	68
# IDS/II verbs	5 314	420

6.8.3 Lessons Learned

Methodology

As in previous projects, the initial inventory step proved to be critical. It required several iterations since we discovered missing copybooks and programs, as well as code fragments containing syntax errors. The prototyping phase also proved valuable, since it allowed us to detect problems early in the process and to better confront our results with the customer requirements. Another conclusion is that the database reverse engineering process may benefit from the data validation phase. Indeed, analysing database contents does not only allow to detect errors, it may also serve as a basis for formulating new hypotheses about potential implicit constraints.

Automation

Although large-scale system conversion needs to be supported by scalable tools, the full automation of the process is clearly unrealistic. Indeed, such a project typically requires several iterations as well as multiple human decisions. In particular, while previous smaller projects allowed us to automate the schema design process with minor manual corrections, assisted manual conversion becomes necessary when dealing with larger schemas. For instance, translating a compound attribute into SQL columns can be done either by disaggregation, by extraction or by aggregation. In this project, the chosen technique depended on the nature of the compound attribute (e.g., each compound attribute representing a date has been translated as a single column). The database design must respect various other constraints like the type and naming conventions of the customer.

Wrapper development

Writing correct wrapper generators requires a very good knowledge of the legacy DMS. In this project, the difficulties of wrapper generation were due to the paradigm mismatch between network and relational database systems. Simulating IDS/II verbs on top of a native relational database appeared much more complicated than expected. The generated wrappers must precisely simulate the IDS/II primitives behaviour, which includes the synchronised management of multiple currency indicators, reading sequence orders and returning status codes. Another challenge, as for the data extractors, was to correctly manage IDS/II records that have been split into several SQL tables.

6.9 Strategies Comparison

Six representative strategies of information system migration have been identified. In this section, we compare them according to each dimension and we suggest possible applications for each system migration strategy.

6.9.1 Database Conversion Strategies

The *physical schema conversion* (D1) does not recover the semantics of the database but blindly translates in the target technology the design flaws as well as the technical structures peculiar to the source technology. This strategy can be fully automated, and can be performed manually, at least for small to medium size databases. Further attempts to modify the structure of the database (e.g., adding some fields or changing constraints) will force the analyst to think in terms of the legacy data structures, and therefore to recover their semantics. The source database was optimised for the legacy DMS, and translating it in the new technology most often leads to poor performance and limited capabilities. For example, a COBOL record that includes an array will be transformed into a table in which the array is translated into an unstructured column, making it impossible to query its contents. Doing so would require writing specific programs that recover the implicit structure of the column. Clearly, this strategy is very cheap (and therefore very popular), but leads to poor results that will make future maintenance expensive and unsafe. In particular, developing new applications is almost impossible.

Nevertheless, we must mention an infrequent situation for which this strategy can be valuable, that is, when the legacy database has been designed and implemented in a disciplined way according to the database theory. For instance, a database made up of a collection of 3NF [8] record types can be migrated in a straightforward way to an equivalent relational database of good quality.

The *conceptual schema conversion* (D2) produces a high quality conceptual schema that explicitly represents all the semantics of the data, but from which technology and performance dependent constructs have been discarded. It has also been cleaned from the design flaws introduced by inexperienced designers and by decades of incremental maintenance. This conceptual schema is used to produce the TPS that can use all the expressiveness of the new DMS model and can be optimised for this DMS. Since the new database schema is normalised and fully documented, its maintenance and evolution is particularly easy and safe. In addition, making implicit constraints explicit automatically induces drastic data validation during data migration, and increases the quality of these data. However, this strategy requires a complex reverse engineering process that can prove expensive. For example, the complete reverse engineering of a medium size database typically costs two to four man-months.

---

[8] 3NF stands for *third normal form*.

6.9.2 Program Conversion Strategies

The *wrapper strategy* (P1) does not alter the logic of the legacy application program. When working on the external data, the transformed program simply invokes the wrapper instead of the legacy DMS primitives. The transformation of the program is quite straightforward: each legacy DMS-DML is replaced with a call to the wrapper. So, this transformation can easily be automated. The resulting program has almost the same code as the source program, so a programmer who has mastered the latter can still maintain the new version without any additional effort or documentation. When the structure of the database evolves, only the wrapper need be modified, while the application program can be left unchanged. The complexity of the wrapper depends on the strategy used to migrate the database. In the D1 strategy, the wrapper is quite simple: it reads one line of the table, converts the column values and produces a record. In the D2 strategy, the wrapper can be very complex, since reading one record may require complex joins and loops to retrieve all the data. Despite the potentially complex mapping between SPS and TPS, which is completely encapsulated into the wrapper, the latter can be produced automatically, as shown in [16]. A wrapper may induce computing and I/O overhead compared to P2 and P3 strategies.

The *statement rewriting* strategy (P2) also preserves the logic of the legacy program but it replaces each legacy DMS-DML primitive statement with its equivalent in the target DMS-DML. Each legacy DMS-DML instruction is replaced with several lines of code that may comprise tests, loops and procedure calls. In our case study the number of lines increased from 390 to almost 1000 when we applied the <D1,P2> strategy. The transformed program becomes difficult to read and to maintain because the legacy code is obscured by the newly added code. If the code must be modified, the programmer must understand how the program was transformed to write correct code to access the database. When the structure of the database is modified, the entire program must be walked through to change the database manipulation statements. In summary, this technique is inexpensive but degrades the quality of the code. In addition, it is fairly easy to automate. As expected, this migration technique is widely used, most often in the <D1,P2> combination.

The *logic rewriting* strategy (P3) changes the logic of the legacy program to explicitly access the new database and to use the expressiveness of the new DMS-DML. This rewriting task is complex and cannot be automated easily. The programmer that performs it must have an in-depth understanding of the legacy database, of the new database and of the legacy program. This strategy produces a completely renovated program that will be easy to maintain at least as far as database logic is concerned.

6.9.3 System Migration Strategies

By combining both dimensions, we describe below typical applications for each of the strategies that have been described.

- **<D1,P1>**: This approach produces a (generally) badly structured database that will suffer from poor performance but preserves the program logic, notably because the database interface is encapsulated in the wrapper. It can be recommended when the migration must be completed in a very short time, e.g., when the legacy environment is no longer available. Developing new applications should be delayed until the correct database is available. This approach can be a nice first step to a better architecture such as that produced by <D2,P1>. However, if the legacy database already is in 3NF, the result is close to that of strategy <D2,P1>.

- **<D2,P1>**: This strategy produces a good quality database while preserving the program logic. New quality applications can be developed on this database. The legacy programs can be renovated later on, step by step. Depending on the impedance mismatch between the legacy and target technologies, performance penalty can be experienced. For instance, wrappers that simulate CODASYL DML on top of a relational database have to synchronise two different data manipulation paradigms, a process that may lead to significant data access overhead.
- **<D1,P2>**: Despite its popularity, due to its low cost, this approach clearly is the worst one. It produces a database structure that is more obscure than the source one, and that provides poorer performance. The programs are inflated with obscure data management code that makes them complex and more difficult to read, understand and maintain. Such a renovated system cannot evolve at sustainable cost, and therefore has no future. If the legacy database already is in 3NF, the result may be similar to that of strategy <D2,P2>.
- **<D2,P2>**: Produces a good quality database, but the programs can be unreadable and difficult to maintain. It can be considered if no maintenance of the application is planned and the programs are to be rewritten in the near future. If the wrapper overhead is acceptable, the<D2,P1> strategy should be preferred.
- **<D1,P3>**: Data migration produces a very poor quality database that simulates the legacy database. Adapting, at high cost, the program to these awkward structures is meaningless, so that we can consider this strategy not pertinent
- **<D2,P3>**: This strategy provides both a database and a set of renovated programs of high quality, at least as far as database logic is concerned. Its cost also is the highest. This is a good solution if the legacy program language is kept and if the programs have a clean and clear structure.

6.10 Conclusions

The variety in corporate requirements, as far as system reengineering is concerned, naturally leads to a wide spectrum of migration strategies. This chapter has identified two main independent lines of decision, the first one related to the precision of database conversion (schema and contents) and the second one related to program conversion. From them, we were able to identify and analyse six reference system migration strategies. The thorough development of these technical aspects is the major contribution of this chapter since most of these aspects have only been sketched in the literature [84].

Despite the fact that a supporting technology has been developed, and therefore makes some sophisticated strategies realistic at an industrial level, we still lack sufficient experience to suggest application rules according to the global corporate strategy and to intrinsic properties of the legacy system. As is now widely accepted in maintenance, specific metrics must be identified to score the system against typical reference patterns. Such criteria as the complexity of the database schema, the proportion of implicit constructs, the underlying technology, the normalisation level or the redundancy rate, to mention only a few, should certainly affect the feasibility of each migration strategy. Corporate requirements like performance, early availability of components of the renovated system, program independence against the database structure, evolvability, skill of the development team, or availability of human resources are all aspects that could make some strategies more valuable than others.

Though some conclusions could seem obvious at first glance, such as, strategy <D2,P3> yields better quality results than strategy <D1,P2>, we have resisted providing any kind of decision table that would have been scientifically questionable. Indeed, each strategy has its privileged application domains, the identification of which would require much more analysis than we have provided in this chapter. One important lesson we learned in this study is that the quality of the target database is central in a renovated system, and is a major factor in the quality of the programs, whatever the program transformation strategy adopted. For instance, renovated program performance, maintenance costs and the readability of the programs to be developed are strongly dependent on the quality of the database schema.

So far, we have developed a solid methodology and a sophisticated CASE environment for database reverse engineering, wrapper development and automated program conversion (according to P1 and P2 strategies). We have also built a toolset of code analysers, such as a pattern matching engine, a dependency and data flow diagram analyser and a program slicer. They allow us to find code sections that meet structural criteria such as data access sections or the statement streams that influence the state of objects at some point of a program aka program slice).

At present time, we are exploring the automation of the P3 program conversion strategy (*Logic Rewriting*). This strategy aims at adapting the logic of the legacy program to explicitly access the new database and to use the expressiveness of the new DMS-DML. This rewriting task is complex and could not be fully automated. Only the identification of the file access statements and the statements and data objects that depend on them can be automated. These identification tasks relate to the program understanding realm, where such techniques as searching for *clichés*, variable dependency analysis and program slicing (see [538, 229]) are often favourite weapons.

Acknowledgement. Anthony Cleve received support from the Belgian *Région Wallonne* and the European Social Fund via the RISTART project.

7

Architectural Transformations:
From Legacy to Three-Tier and Services

Reiko Heckel[1], Rui Correia[1,2], Carlos Matos[1,2], Mohammad El-Ramly[3], Georgios Koutsoukos[1], and Luís Andrade[2]

[1] Department of Computer Science, University of Leicester, United Kingdom
[2] ATX Software, Lisboa, Portugal
[3] Computer Science Department, Cairo University, Egypt

Summary. With frequent advances in technology, the need to evolve software arises. Given that in most cases it is not desirable to develop everything from scratch, existing software systems end up being reengineered. New software architectures and paradigms are responsible for major changes in the way software is built.

The importance of Service Oriented Architectures (SOAs) has been widely growing over the last years. These present difficult challenges to the reengineering of legacy applications. In this chapter, we present a new methodology to address these challenges. Additionally, we discuss issues of the implementation of the approach based on existing program and model transformation tools and report on an example, the migration of an application from two-tier to three-tier architecture.

7.1 Introduction

As business and technology evolve and software becomes more complex, researchers and tool vendors in reengineering are constantly challenged to come up with new techniques, methods, and solutions to effectively support the transition of legacy systems to modern architectural and technological paradigms. Such pressure has been witnessed repeatedly over the past decades. Examples include the adoption of object-oriented programming languages [380, 149] and more recently the advent of Web technologies [463] and in particular Service-Oriented Architectures (SOAs).

The adoption of SOAs, as well as their enabling technology of Web Services [7], has been steadily growing over the last years. According to Gartner [194], a leading technology market research and analysis firm, "mainstream status for SOA is not far off" and "by 2008, SOA will be a prevailing software engineering practice" [355]. However, practice indicates that Service-Oriented Architecture initiatives rarely start from scratch. Gartner projects that "through 2008, at least 65 percent of custom-developed services for new SOA projects will be implemented via wrapping or reengineering of established applications (0.8 probability)". In other words, most SOA projects are being implemented on top of existing legacy systems. That being the

T. Mens, S. Demeyer (eds.), *Software Evolution.*
DOI 10.1007/978-3-540-76440-3, © Springer 2008

context, the goal of this work is to present a methodology for reengineering legacy systems towards new architectural styles in general and SOA in particular.

We will argue that, starting from a (monolithic) legacy application, such a transition involves several steps of decomposition, along both technological and functional dimensions. The technological decomposition will lead, for example, to a 3-tiered architecture, separating application logic, data, and user interface (UI). The functional decomposition separates components providing different functions which, when removing their UI tiers, represent candidate services.

The technical contribution of this chapter concentrates on the iterated decomposition, regarding each cycle as an instance of the reengineering Horseshoe Model [271]. This is a conceptual model that distinguishes different levels of reengineering while providing a foundation for transformations at each level, with a focus on transformations to the architectural level. We support it by providing automation through graph-based architectural transformation. This allows us to

- abstract (in large parts of the process) from the specific languages involved, as long as they are based on similar underlying concepts
- describe transformations in a more intuitive and "semantic" way (compared to code level transformations), making them easier to adapt to different architectural styles and technological paradigms

With this in mind the remainder of this chapter is organised as follows: Section 7.2 discusses the impact of service-oriented computing on legacy systems, as well as the issues for reengineering. Section 7.3 presents our methodology for architectural transformation including a formalisation based on typed graph transformation system. The implementation of our approach and an example are discussed in Section 7.4. We review related work in Section 7.5 and discuss conclusions and further work in Section 7.6.

7.2 From Legacy Systems to Three-Tier Applications and Services

The authors' experience with customers from the finance, telecommunications, and public administration sectors as well as IT partners indicates that adoption of SOA in industry is inevitable and that such adoption is typically gradual, evolving through various stages in which different organisational and technical goals and challenges are addressed. A typical first stage, the transition from legacy to web-based systems, consists in the technological separation of GUI from logic and database code, and subsequent replacement of the GUI code by HTML forms. Even if the details are highly dependent on the languages and platforms involved, the perception that organisations have of the overall aim, the transition towards SOA, is largely congruent, and in line with what has also been described by several authors [349, 393, 162] and major technology providers [407, 472, 543, 483].

In Table 7.1 we outline six of the basic SOA principles that constitute important properties of SOA from an industry perspective. It should be noted that our goal is

Table 7.1. Industry View of SOA

SOA Property	Definition
Well-defined interfaces	A well specified description of the service that permits consumers to invoke it in a standard way
Loose coupling	Service consumer is independent of the implementation specifics of service provider
Logical and physical separation of business logic from presentation logic	Service functionality is independent of user interface aspects
Highly reusable services	Services are designed in such a way that they are consumable by multiple applications
Coarse-grained granularity	Services are business-centric, i.e., reflect a meaningful business service not implementation internals
Multi-party & business process orientation	Service orientation involves more than one party (at least one provider and one consumer), each with varying roles, and must provide the capacity to support seamless end-to-end business processes, that may span long periods of time, between such parties

not to provide a comprehensive analysis of how industry views SOA, but, instead, to provide a basis that will help us to explain the impact of service-orientation to legacy systems.

The first two properties in Table 7.1 (Well-defined interfaces, Loose coupling) are typically, at least at the technology level, provided by the underlying SOA implementation infrastructures such as Web Services. The last four properties however, have considerable impact on legacy systems and their reengineering. Such impact is analysed in the next three subsections. The first addresses the "Logical and physical separation of business logic from presentation logic" property, the second analyses the "Highly reusable services" property and the last addresses both "Coarse-grained granularity" and "Multi-party & business process orientation" properties.

7.2.1 Technological Decomposition

It is a common practice in legacy applications to mix together, in a kind of "architectural spaghetti", code that is concerned with database access, business logic, interaction with the user, presentation aspects, presentation flow, validations and exception handling, among others. For example, consider interactive COBOL programs: Typically these are state-machine programs that interleave the dialog with the user (menus, options, etc.) with the logic of the transactions triggered by their inputs. Similar coding practices are found in client-server applications like Oracle Forms, Java-Swing, VB applications, etc. The code listing in Figure 7.1 presents a simple Java example that partially illustrates this issue. In this code fragment, if data access and data processing code fails or no data is found, a message dialog appears to the user prompting for subsequent actions. The PL/SQL code of Figure 7.2 refers

```
public void Transaction () {
  try {
    //Data access-processing code
    fis = new FileInputStream ("Bank.dat");
    ... //fetch some data from file
  }
  catch (Exception ex) {
    total = rows;
    //Validations and respective UI actions
    if (total == 0) {
      JOptionPane.showMessageDialog (null, "Records File is Empty.\nEnter
        Records First to Display.", "BankSystem - EmptyFile",
        JOptionPane.PLAIN_MESSAGE);
      btnEnable ();
    }
    else {
      try {
        //Data access-processing code
        fis.close();
      }
      catch (Exception exp) {
        ...
      }
    }
  }
}
```

Fig. 7.1. A simple "spaghetti" code example in Java. (We use spaghetti here in the sense of tangling different concerns, not in the sense of having many goto statements)

```
PROCEDURE Confirm()

DECLARE

alert_button NUMBER;

BEGIN

alert_button := SHOW_ALERT('alert_name'); IF alert_button =
ALERT_BUTTON1 THEN
    program statements after clicking first button (OK button);
ELSE
    program statements after clicking second button (Cancel button);
END IF;

END;
```

(a) Alert dialog code mixed with business processing

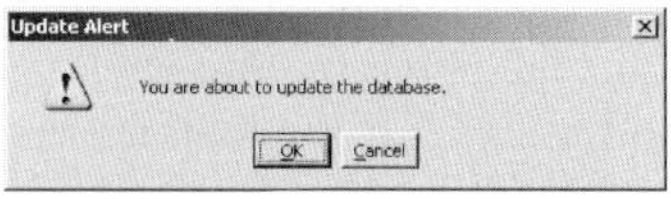

(b) Oracle Forms Alert dialog for confirmation

Fig. 7.2. PL/SQL example

to a similar scenario in Oracle Forms: The whole business processing code (in bold in Figure 7.2a), which may concern complex calculations and updates of database tables, is placed together with the code that manages the interaction with the user via a simple alert dialog (Figure 7.2b) prompting for confirmation for performing such a transaction. In such cases, since the business logic is tightly coupled with the presentation logic, it is impossible to derive services directly. Therefore, what is required is an appropriate decoupling of the code, such that "pure" business processes are isolated as candidate services or service constituents. This technological dimension of reengineering towards SOA amounts to an architectural transformation towards a multi-tiered architecture.

7.2.2 Reusable Services

For an SOA initiative to realise its full potential a significant number of implemented and deployed services should be actually invoked by more than one application. Service repositories facilitate such reuse, but only *a posteriori*, i.e., after the reusable services have been identified. From a reengineering perspective what is needed is support for the *a priori* identification of reusable services across multiple functional domains. Unfortunately, many legacy systems can be characterised as "silos", i.e., consisting of independent applications where lots of functionality is redundant or duplicated (cf. Chapter 2). Even worse, in many cases such redundancy and duplication also exists within the same application. Take, for instance, the example of financial systems, where the interest calculation functionality is very often implemented multiple times in different applications only to accommodate the needs of the various departments that those applications are designed to serve. But even within single applications such redundancy is a common practice, for instance between interactive and batch parts. The ability to identify such redundant functionality and its appropriate refactoring to reusable services is vital for the success of service-oriented computing initiatives.

7.2.3 Functional Decomposition

Most legacy applications were developed with different architectural paradigms in mind and typically consist of elements that are of a fine-grained nature, for instance components with operations that represent logical units of work, like reading individual items of data. OO class methods are an example of such fine-grained operations. The notion of service, however, is of a different, more coarse-grained nature. Services represent logical groupings of, possibly fine-grained, operations, work on top of larger data sets, and in general expose a greater range of functionality. In particular, services that are deployed and consumed over a network must exhibit such a property in order to limit the number of remote consumer-to-provider roundtrips and the corresponding processing cycles. In general, finding the right balance of service granularity is a challenging design task that is also related with the service reusability issue above. A good discussion on the granularity of services in systems that follow the SOA paradigm can be found in [543], from where Figure 7.3 has been

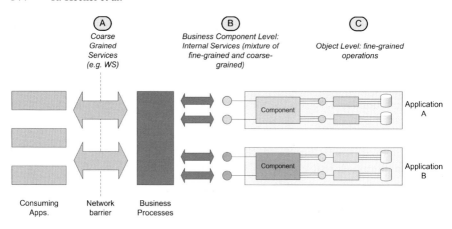

Fig. 7.3. Service granularity across application tiers

adapted to show the various levels of service granularity. In general, it is clear that the granularity of services has major implications for what concerns legacy reengineering. As already mentioned at the beginning of the paragraph, most of the systems currently in use were not built with service orientation in mind. Hence, existing services at levels B and C of Figure 7.3 are not at the level of granularity required for SOA.

The granularity problem is also associated with the fact that service-orientation involves more than one party (at least one provider and one consumer), each with varying roles and, if designed properly, must provide the capacity to support seamless end-to-end business processes (spanning long periods of time) between such parties. This is a fundamental shift from previous architectural paradigms in which the business processes workflow and rules are typically defined by one party only and executed entirely on the IT system of this same party (e.g., a customer self-service system). Legacy systems are not prepared for such a shift in paradigm: For example, a legacy function that returns information from a single transaction was not intended to be called several times in succession in order to obtain the larger set of data that a service consumer may require. Even more recent systems, built on top of web services technologies that expose services at level A in Figure 7.3 suffer from poor granularity decisions and are unable to support the desired end-to-end multi-party business processes. Hence, software reengineering solutions with respect to service orientation are concerned with all 3 levels (A,B,C) of services depicted in Figure 7.3. In particular, we are convinced that methods and tools are needed that allow service designers to discover the allocation of domain functionalities into the code structure so that legacy logical units of work can be appropriately composed and reengineered in order to form services of desired granularity and of adequate support for multi-party business processes.

In the following sections we are going to concentrate on the technical aspect of the decomposition, rather than on questions of granularity and reusability. While the techniques described below are applicable to both technological and functional decomposition we will use an example of technological decomposition to illustrate them.

7.3 The Approach to Architectural Transformation

In this section we discuss methodological as well as formal aspects of the approach to architectural redesign. Methodologically we are following the Horseshoe Model, refining it to support automation and traceability. Formally our models are represented as graphs conforming to a metamodel with constraints while transformations are specified by graph transformation rules.

7.3.1 Methodology

Our methodology consists of the three steps of *reverse engineering, redesign*, and *forward engineering*, preceded by a preparatory step of *code annotation*. The separation between code annotation and reverse engineering is made in order to distinguish the three fully automated steps of the methodology from the first one, which involves input from the developer, making it semi-automatic. The steps are illustrated in Figure 7.4.

1. Code Annotation

The source code is annotated by *code categories*, distinguishing its constituents (packages, classes, methods, or fragments thereof) with respect to their foreseen association to architectural elements of the target system, e.g., as GUI, Application Logic, or Data.

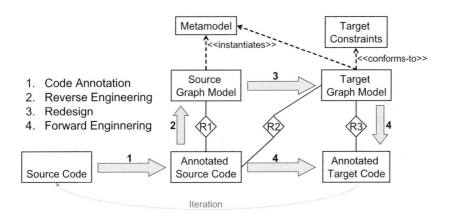

Fig. 7.4. Methodology for transformation-based reengineering

The annotation is based on input by the developer, propagated through the code by *categorisation rules* defined at the level of abstract syntax trees, and taking into account information obtained through control and data flow analysis. The results may have to be revised and the propagation repeated in several iterations, leading to an interleaving of automatic and manual annotations.

The code categories to be used depend on the target architecture, which depends on the technology paradigm but also on the intended functional decomposition of the target system. Thus, depending on the type of decomposition to be performed, we consider either technological categories, like user interface, application logic, and data management, or functional ones, like the contribution to particular services for managing accounts, customers, employees, etc.

2. Reverse Engineering

From the annotated source code, a *graph model* is created, whose level of detail depends on the annotation. For example, a method wholly annotated with the same code category is represented as a single node, but if the method is fragmented into several categories, each of these fragments has to have a separate representation in the model. The relation *R1* between the original (annotated) source code and the graph model is kept to support traceability. This step is a straightforward translation of the relevant part of the abstract syntax tree representation of the code into its graph-based representation.

The AST representation is more adequate, both from a performance point of view and because of the amount of information present, to the annotation process. However, for the redesign step, the graph representation allows us to abstract from the specific programming languages involved and to describe transformations in a more intuitive way. Additionally, given that we only represent in graphs the elements that we need according to the annotation, as explained in the previous paragraph, the model to be transformed is simpler and the performance needs are not so demanding.

The graph model is based on a *metamodel* which is general enough to accommodate both the source and the target system, but also all intermediate stages of the redesign transformation. Additionally, this metamodel contains the code categories that were available in the code annotation step. An example of graph model and metamodel (type graph) is presented in Figure 7.5.

3. Redesign

The source graph model is restructured to reflect the association between code fragments and target architectural elements. The intended result is expressed by an extra set of constraints over the metamodel, which are satisfied when the transformation is complete. During the transformation, the relation with the original source code is kept as *R2* in order to support the code generation in the next step.

This *code category-driven transformation* is specified by graph transformation rules, conceptually extending those suggested by Mens et al. [365] to formalise refactoring by graph transformation. Indeed, in our approach, code categories provide the

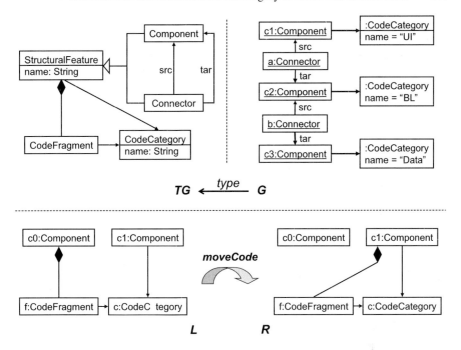

Fig. 7.5. Type and instance graph (top) and transformation rule (*bottom*)

control required to automate the transformation process, focussing user input on the annotation phase. An example of graph transformation rule can be seen in Figure 7.5.

Rules as well as source, target and intermediate graphs are instances of the meta-model. Additional *target constraints* are given to specify the success criteria of the transformation.

4. Forward Engineering

The target code is either generated from the target graph model and the original source code or obtained through the use of refactorings at code level. The result of this step, the annotated code in relation with a graph model, has the same structure as the input to Step 1. Hence the process can be iterated.

This is particularly relevant if the reengineering is directed towards service-oriented systems. In this case the transformation has to address both the technological and functional dimensions, e.g., transformation into a three-tier architecture should be followed up by a decomposition into functional components (cf. Section 7.2). For example, if the first iteration separates application logic and data from user interface code, the latter can be removed (and substituted with the appropriate service infrastructure) in a second round of transformation, thus exposing basic functionality as a service.

7.3.2 Redesign by Graph Transformation

Next we detail the formalism used to specify redesign transformations and discuss potential proof obligations for well-definedness of transformations in terms of their relevance, consequences, and support for verification.

Metamodelling with Typed Graphs

Graphs are often used as abstract representations of models. For example in the UML specification [398] a collection of object graphs is defined by means of a metamodel as abstract syntax of UML models.

Formally, a *graph* consists of a set of vertices V and a set of edges E such that each edge e in E has a source and a target vertex $s(e)$ and $t(e)$ in V, respectively. Advanced graph models use attributed graphs [332] whose vertices and edges are decorated with textual or numerical information, as well as inheritance between node types [157, 365, 370].

In metamodelling, graphs occur at two levels: the type level (representing the metamodel) and the instance level (given by all valid object graphs). This concept can be described more generally by the concept of *typed graphs* [129], where a fixed *type graph* TG serves as abstract representation of the metamodel. Its instances are graphs equipped with a structure-preserving mapping to the type graph, formally expressed as a *graph homomorphism*. For example, the graph in the top right of Figure 7.5 is an instance of the type graph in the top left, with the mapping defined by $type(o) = C$ for each instance node $o : C$.

In order to define more precisely the class of instance graphs, constraints can be added to the type graph expressing, for example, cardinalities for in- or outgoing edges, acyclicity, etc. Formalising this in a generic way, we assume for each type graph TG a class of constraints $Constr(TG)$ that could be imposed on its instances. A metamodel is thus represented by a type graph TG plus a set $C \subseteq Constr(TG)$ of constraints over TG. The class of instance graphs over TG is denoted by $Inst(TG)$ while we write $Inst(TG,C)$ for the subclass satisfying the constraints C. Thus, if (TG,C) represents a metamodel with constraints, an instance is an element of $Inst(TG,C)$.

The transformations described in this paper implement a mapping from a general class of (potentially unstructured) systems into a more specific one of three-tier applications. This restriction is captured by two levels of constraints, global constraints C_g interpreted as requirements for the larger class of all input graphs, also serving as invariants throughout the transformation, and target constraints C_t that are required to hold for the output graphs only. Global constraints express basic well-formedness properties, like that *every code fragment is labelled by exactly one code category and part of exactly one component*. The corresponding target constraint would require that *the component containing the fragment is consistent with the code category*.

Rule-Based Model Transformations

After having defined the objects of our transformation as instances of type graphs satisfying constraints, model transformations can be specified in terms of graph transformation. A *graph transformation rule* $p : L \rightarrow R$ consists of a pair of TG-typed instance graphs L, R such that the union $L \cup R$ is defined. (This means that, e.g., edges which appear in both L and R are connected to the same vertices in both graphs, or that vertices with the same name have to have the same type, etc.) The left-hand side L represents the pre-conditions of the rule while the right-hand side R describes the post-conditions. Their intersection $L \cap R$ represents the elements that are needed for the transformation to take place, but are not deleted or modified.

A *graph transformation* from a pre-state G to a post-state H, denoted by $G \stackrel{p(o)}{\Longrightarrow} H$, is given by a graph homomorphism $o : L \cup R \rightarrow G \cup H$, called *occurrence*, such that

- $o(L) \subseteq G$ and $o(R) \subseteq H$, i.e., the left-hand side of the rule is embedded into the pre-state and the right-hand side into the post-state, and
- $o(L \setminus R) = G \setminus H$ and $o(R \setminus L) = H \setminus G$, i.e., precisely that part of G is deleted which is matched by elements of L not belonging to R and, symmetrically, that part of H is added which is matched by elements new in R.

Rule *moveCode* in the lower part of Figure 7.5 specifies the relocation of a code fragment (package, class, method, etc.) from one component to another one based on its code category. Operationally, the application of a graph transformation rule is performed in three steps. First, find an occurrence of the left-hand side L in the current object graph. Second, remove all the vertices and edges which are matched by $L \setminus R$. In our example this applies to the composition edge from *c0:Component* to *f:CodeFragment*. Third, extend the resulting graph with $R \setminus L$ to obtain the derived graph, in our case adding a composition edge from *c1:Component* to *f:CodeFragment*.

Altogether, a transformation system is specified by a four-tuple

$$\mathcal{T} = (TG, C_g, C_t, P)$$

consisting of a type graph with global and target constraints, and a set of rules P.

A sequence like s is *consistent* if all graphs G_i satisfy the global constraints C_g. We write $G \stackrel{\checkmark}{\Longrightarrow} H$ for a complete and consistent transformation sequence from G to H in $\mathcal{T}$.

Well-Definedness and Correctness of Transformations

Besides offering a high level of abstraction and a visual notation for model transformations, one advantage of graph transformations is their mathematical theory, which can be used to formulate and verify properties of specifications. Given a transformation system $\mathcal{T} = (TG, C_g, C_t, P)$ the following properties provide the ingredients for the familiar notions of partial and total correctness.

Global Consistency. All rule applications preserve the global invariants C_g, i.e., for every graph $G \in Inst(TG, C_g)$ and rule $p \in P$, $G \stackrel{p(o)}{\Longrightarrow} H$ implies that $H \in Inst(TG, C_g)$.

Typical examples of global consistency conditions are cardinalities like *each Code Fragment is part of exactly one Structural Feature*. While such basic conditions can be verified statically [227], more complex ones like the (non-)existence of certain paths or cycles may have to be checked at runtime. This is only realistic if, like in the graph transformation language PROGRES [456], database technology can be employed to monitor the validity of constraints in an incremental fashion. Otherwise runtime monitoring can be used during testing and debugging to identify the causes of failures.

Partial Correctness. Terminating transformation sequences starting out from graphs satisfying the global constraints should end in graphs satisfying the target constraints. A transformation sequence $s = (G_0 \overset{p_1(o_1)}{\Longrightarrow} \cdots \overset{p_n(o_n)}{\Longrightarrow} G_n)$ in $\mathcal{T}$ is terminating if there is no transformation $G_n \overset{p(o)}{\Longrightarrow} X$ extending it any further. The system is *partially correct* if, for all $G_s \in Inst(TG, C_g)$, $G_s \overset{*}{\Longrightarrow} G_t$ terminating implies that $G_t \in Inst(TG, C_t)$.

To verify partial correctness we have to show that the target constraints are satisfied when none of the rules is applicable anymore. In other words, the conjunction of the negated preconditions of all rules in P and the global constraints imply the target constraints C_t. The obvious target constraint with respect to our single rule in Figure 7.5 should state that *every Code Fragment is part of a Component of the same Code Category as the Fragment*, which is obviously true if the rule is no longer applicable.

To verify such a requirement, theorem proving techniques are required which are hard to automate and computationally expensive. On the other hand, since it is only required on the target graphs of transformations, the condition can be checked on a case-by-case basis.

Total Correctness. Assuming partial correctness, it remains to show termination, i.e., that that there are no infinite sequences $G_0 \overset{p_1(o_1)}{\Longrightarrow} G_1 \overset{p_2(o_2)}{\Longrightarrow} G_2) \cdots$ starting out from graphs $G_0 \in Inst(TG, C_g)$ satisfying the global constraints.

Verifying termination typically requires to define a mapping of graphs into some well-founded ordered set (like the natural numbers), so that the mapping can be shown to be monotonously decreasing with the application of rules. Such a progress measure is difficult to determine automatically. In our simple example, it could be *the number of Code Fragments in the graph not being part of Components with the same Code Category*. This number is obviously decreasing with the application of rule *moveCode*, so that it would eventually reach a minimum (zero in our case) where the rule is not applicable anymore.

Uniqueness. Terminating and globally consistent transformation sequences starting from the same graph produce the same result, that is, for all $G \in Inst(TG, C_g)$, $G \overset{\checkmark}{\Longrightarrow} H_1$ and $G_s \overset{\checkmark}{\Longrightarrow} H_2$ implies that H_1 and H_2 are equal up to renaming of elements.

This is a property known by the name of confluence, which has been extensively studied in term rewriting [60]. It is decidable under the condition that the transformation systems is terminating. The algorithm has been transferred to graph transformation systems [419] and prototypical tool support is available for part of this verification problem [487].

It is worth noting that, like with all verification problems, a major part of the effort is in the complete formal specification of the desirable properties, in our case the set of global constraints C_g and the target constraints C_t. Relying on existing editors or parsers it may not always be necessary (for the execution of transformations) to check such conditions on input and output graphs, so the full specification of such constraints may represent an additional burden on the developer. On the other hand they provide an important and more declarative specification of the requirements for model transformations, which need to be understood (if not formalised) in order to implement them correctly and can play a role in testing model transformations.

7.4 Implementation and Example

In this section we describe an implementation of our methodology, demonstrating it on an example. This implementation addresses the technological decomposition (cf. Section 7.2) that is one of the steps to achieve SOA. The four-step methodology presented and formalised in Section 7.3 is instantiated for transforming Java 2-tier applications to comply with a 3-tier architecture.

We present the metamodel definition and the four steps as applied to a simple example, a Java client-server application composed of twenty one classes and over three thousand lines of code (LOC). The example was chosen to illustrate the kind of entanglement between different concerns that is typically found in the source code of legacy applications. For presentation purposes, in this chapter we will focus on a couple of methods of one of the classes only. Both categorisation and transformation are based on a metamodel describing the source and target architectural paradigms.

7.4.1 Metamodel

The metamodel is composed of two parts, detailing code categories and the architectural and technology paradigms used. Its definition is a metalevel activity, preceding the actual reengineering process. The same metamodel (or after slight changes) can be used in different projects where the source and target architectural and technology paradigms are similar.

Code Categories

As stated in Section 7.3, code categories are derived from the target architectural and technology paradigm. Different models can be used for the categories. We have opted for the one presented in Figure 7.6 and explained next, together with our instantiation.

In the chosen model, code categories can be divided in two types:

- components consisting of a concern
- connectors representing links between components

Concerns are conceptual classifications of code fragments that derive from their purpose, i.e., the tiers found in 3-tier architectures:

- User Interface (UI)

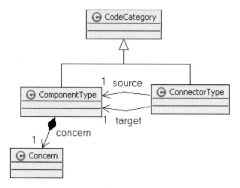

Fig. 7.6. Code categories model for 3-tier

- Business Logic (BL)
- Data

The connectors are one-way (non-commutative) links between different concerns and include:

- Control: UI to BL
- Control: BL to UI
- Control: BL to Data
- Control: Data to BL

This model is detailed enough to capture the distinctions required by the target architecture; other architectural paradigms might require different categories and more complex ways to represent them. It may be even desirable in some situations to allow multiple categories for the same element. In Figure 7.6, components and connectors are represented by "ComponentType" and "ConnectorType", respectively, in order not to use the names attributed to architectural concepts. We have both "ComponentType" and "Concern" for reusability issues given that the first is likely to be extended for certain types of target architectures. For instance, if our goal was to achieve a rich-client 2-tier architecture, then "ComponentType" would contain also a "Role" concept whose values would be "Definition", "Action" and "Validation".

Architectural and Technology Paradigm

The next metalevel activity consists in the definition of a model for program representation which, like the categories, may be shared with other instantiations of the methodology, either as source or target. As we are going to take advantage of graph transformation rules in the transformation specification, we developed the model in the form of a type graph.

The model shown in Figure 7.7 has the goal of being flexible enough so it can be instantiated by any OO application regardless of the specific technology. This way there is a better chance that it can be reused for different instantiations of our methodology. The type graph is an extension of the one presented by Mens et al. in [368] in order to introduce classification attributes and the notion of code blocks, needed because the code categorisation requires a granularity lower than that of methods.

CodeFragment elements are physical pieces of code which implies that they belong only to one *StructuralElement* (component or connector). Additionally, we have included the concepts of *Component* and *Connector* that allow us to represent the mapping between the programming language elements and the architecture level. Note that the names for nodes *ClassType* and *PackageType* were defined as such, instead of *Class* and *Package*, to avoid collisions with Java reserved keywords, since we generate Java code from the model in this implementation.

During a transformation, we may have components and connectors that belong either to the source or the target architecture. For instance, after some transformation rules have been applied components of the source and target architectures may coexist in the model. The concept of *Stage* was added to cope with those intermediate phases.

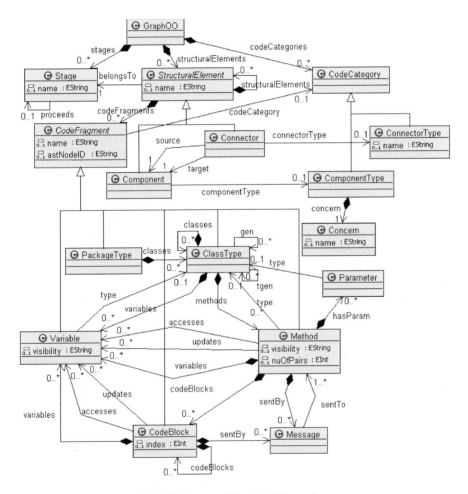

Fig. 7.7. Type graph for the OO paradigm

Since it is necessary to keep traceability to the code in order to facilitate the transformation/generation process, a way to associate it to the type graph had to be considered. Given that we want to be as language-independent as possible we did not link the type graph directly to the source code. Instead, we used an attribute (ASTNodeID) to associate some of its elements to the Abstract Syntax Tree (AST) of the program. ASTs are very common representations of source code and, in our case, allow for a loose integration between the model and the programming language.

7.4.2 Code Annotation

The annotated source code is obtained through an iteration of manual input and the application of categorisation rules, based on the categories defined in the metamodel.

Categorisation Rules

The rules used in the categorisation process are applied over the AST rather than based on the graph-based presentation. The following examples are presented informally.

1. Statements that consist of variable/attribute declarations for a type that is known to belong to a certain concern, will be categorised as belonging to the same concern.
   Example: the Java statement 'private JLabel lbNo;' is categorised as UI Definition because it is known that *JLabel* belongs to the UI concern;
2. Assignments to variables/attributes that are known to belong to a certain concern and whose right-hand side only includes the use of elements (e.g. variables or method invocations) that belong to the same concern, will have that concern.
   Example: the Java statement 'lbNo = new JLabel ("Account No:");' is categorised as UI Definition because it is known that the attribute *lbNo* and the *JLabel* method/constructor invocation belong to the UI concern;
3. Variables/attributes/parameters definition/assignment that are used to store values directly from Data Action methods/functions belong to the Data Action category.
   Example: the Java statement 'records[rows][i] = dis.readUTF();' belongs to the Data Action because the *readUTF* operation is known to belong to that category.

The same rule might have to be applied multiple times. The reason for this is that the application of a rule can enable the application of another. An example for this can be given using rule number 2: if a method invocation that exists in the right-hand side of the assignment is not yet categorised, the rule will not be applied. However, after some other rule categorises the method, rule number 2 can be applied. The transformation stops if no more rules are applicable or the code is completely categorised. Given that our rules do not delete previous categorisations nor change them, the transformation is guaranteed to terminate. For pattern matching and rule application over ASTs we can use the L-CARE tool, which provides a scalable solution to program transformation problems.

Example

As mentioned above, the original source code is categorised considering the intended target architecture. In Figure 7.8 we present the code that has been previously used to explain the implementation of our methodology. The code is annotated using simple comments.

In this paragraph we explain how the categorisation was achieved for some of the statements of this example. The first three attribute declarations are categorised as UI Definition based on the first categorisation rule previously presented, since it is known that *JLabel*, *JTextField* and *JButton* belong to the UI concern in Java. The assignment to array *records* is categorised as Data Action based on rule number 3 which states that variables assignments used to store values from Data Action functions belong to the same category, and the *readUTF()* operation belongs to this category. This enables the categorisation of the assignment of *dis* as Data Definition through rule 2 since this variable is used next in Data Action code.

The need of several iterations of the categorisation process is now clear. In the first iteration the assignment of *dis* could not be categorised, but after categorising some of the following statements as Data Action, a second iteration is able to identify this statement as Data Definition.

7.4.3 Reverse Engineering

After having annotated the code, the process of transforming it into a graph model is straightforward. Its level of granularity is controlled by the results of the categorisation and the needs of the transformation process.

Program Representation

The graph model together with its traceability relation to the original code constitutes the *program representation*. This is an instance of the type graph previously defined and shown in Figure 7.7, where the code is categorised and its dependencies are defined. An example can be seen in Figure 7.10. The value "*" for the attribute "name" of the "concern" means that the element contains more than one concern. For example, the "populateArray" method contains three code blocks that include the concerns "UI" and "Data". This graph is obtained from the AST presented in Figure 7.9b. The corresponding source code can be seen in Figure 7.9a.

In this section only some of the elements of the Class "DepositMoney" are being presented, namely the attribute "lbNo" and the methods "txtClear" and "populateArray". The attribute "lbNo" corresponds to a label that exists in the UI—it is the label that states 'Account No:' before the text box that prompts for the customer account number to which the deposit money operation is being done. The method "txtClear" has the goal of clearing all the input fields for the deposit money window. The "populateArray" method is called each time it is necessary to refresh the data in the window.

```
\\concern = *
package General;

import java.awt.*;
import java.awt.event.*;
import javax.swing.*;

public class Deposit Money extends JInternalFrame implements ActionListener {
\\concern = UI
private JLabel lbNo, lbName, lbDate, lbDeposit;
private JTextField txtNo, txtName, txtDeposit;
private JButton btnSave, btnCancel;
\\concern = *
void populateArray () {
\\connectorType = Control UI -> BL
    try {
\\concern = Data
        fis = new FileInputStream ("Bank.dat");
        dis = new DataInputStream (fis);
\\concern = Data
        while (true) {
            for (int i = 0; i < 6; i++) {
                records[rows][i] = dis.readUTF();
            }
            rows++;
        }
\\connectorType = Control UI -> BL
    }
    catch (Exception ex) {
        total = rows;
        if (total == 0) {
\\concern = UI
            JOptionPane.showMessageDialog (null, "Records File is Empty.
                \nEnter Records First to Display.", "BankSystem
                - EmptyFile", JOptionPane.PLAIN_MESSAGE);
            btnEnable ();
\\connectorType = Control UI -> BL
        }
        else {
\\concern = Data
            try {
                dis.close();
                fis.close();
            }
            catch (Exception exp) { }
\\connectorType = Control UI -> BL
        }
    }
\\concern = *
}
\\concern = UI
void txtClear() {
    txtNo.setText("");
    txtName.setText("");
    txtDeposit.setText("");
    txtNo.requestFocus();
}
```

Fig. 7.8. Source code categorised

Example

The annotated source code previously presented is translated, in a straight-forward way, into the source graph model (cf. Figure 7.10). Naturally this graph has to conform to the type graph in Figure 7.7 in order for the transformation to be possible.

```
import java.awt.*;
import java.awt.event.*;
import javax.swing.*;
// ASTNode0001
public class DepositMoney
      extends JInternalFrame
      implements ActionListener {
 private JLabel lbNo /* ASTNode0002 */,
                lbName, lbDate,
                lbDeposit; // ASTNode0010
 private JTextField txtNo, txtName,
                    txtDeposit;
 private JButton btnSave, btnCancel;
 // (...)
 // ASTNode0003
 void populateArray () {
   // ASTNode0005
   try {
    fis = new FileInputStream ("Bank.dat");
    dis = new DataInputStream (fis);
    //Loop to Populate the Array.
    while (true) {
        for (int i = 0; i < 6; i++) {
            records[rows][i] = dis.readUTF();
        }
        rows++;
    }
   }
   catch (Exception ex) {
   // ASTNode0006
    total = rows;
    if (total == 0) {
        JOptionPane.showMessageDialog (null,
         "Records File is Empty.\nEnter
            Records First to Display.",
             "BankSystem - EmptyFile",
                JOptionPane.PLAIN_MESSAGE);
        btnEnable ();
    }
    // ASTNode0007
    else {
        try {
            dis.close();
            fis.close();
        }
        catch (Exception exp) { }
    }
   }
 }
//(...)
// ASTNode0004
void txtClear() {
  txtNo.setText("");
  txtName.setText("");
  txtDeposit.setText("");
  txtNo.requestFocus();
}
//(...)
public void editRec () {
  //(...)
}
//(...)
}
```

```
PACKAGE: null
IMPORTS(3)
TYPES(1)
 TypeDeclaration
 ASTNode0001
 type binding: DepositMoney
 BODY_DECLARATIONS(6)
  FieldDeclaration
  ASTNode0010
  TYPE
   SimpleType
   type binding:
   javax.swing.JLabel
  FRAGMENTS(4)
   VariableDeclarationFragment
   ASTNode0002
   variable binding:
   DepositMoney.lbNo
  (...)
 MethodDeclaration
 ASTNode0003
 method binding:
 DepositMoney.populateArray()
 BODY
   TryCatchStatement
   ASTNode0005
   TryStatement
    EXPRESSION
    EXPRESSION
    WhileStatement
   CatchStatement
   ASTNode0006
    EXPRESSION
    IfStatement
     THEN_STATEMENT
     ASTNode0007
     ELSE_STATEMENT
     TryCatchStatement
     (...)
 MethodDeclaration
 ASTNode0004
 method binding:
 DepositMoney.txtClear()
 (...)
```

(a) Example source code   (b) Example AST

Fig. 7.9. Source code and AST extracts from a Java sample application

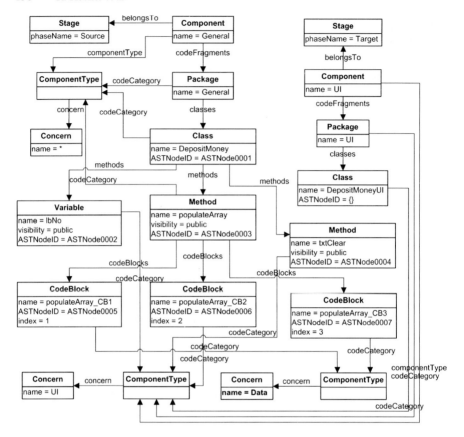

Fig. 7.10. Graph representing a subset of a Java sample application

For this translation one can parse the annotated AST and create the corresponding instance of the type graph, which will next be used as the start graph for the architectural redesign.

7.4.4 Redesign

For transforming the graph model we create transformation rules that, applied to the source model, yield a model complying to the target constraints.

Transformation Specification

A sample transformation rule is given in Figure 7.11.

Its specification, according to the graph transformation rules fundaments previously formalised and explained, is defined visually in Tiger EMF Transformation [488]. This is an Eclipse plugin for model transformation that allows to design rules and apply them to an instance graph.

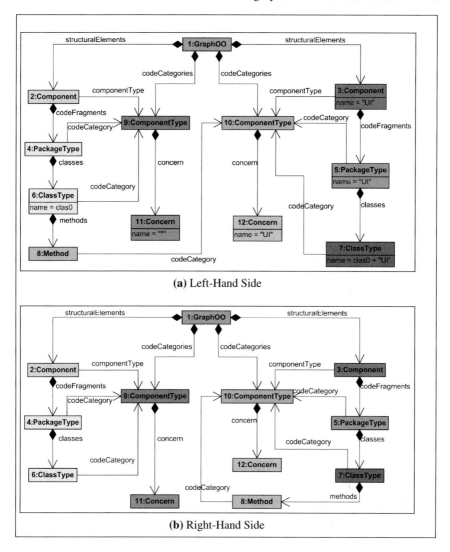

(a) Left-Hand Side

(b) Right-Hand Side

Fig. 7.11. Move Method UI transformation rule

The approach is similar to refactoring by graph transformation [370], except for the use of code categories for controlling the application. More generally, refactoring rules may not be enough for all redesign transformations because sometimes it is necessary to apply changes that are not behaviour preserving. An example is the transformation of a legacy client-server system into a web-based application. The UI has to be changed because of the differences in the user communication paradigm between these different architectural styles. For instance, in the legacy application we may have a feature that performs a database query and then asks a question to the user, waits synchronously for the answer and then, based on the user input, updates a row in the database. To transform this code into a web-based system, it is not enough to separate the UI from the data access layer. Due to the way that requests are processed on the web, we have to transform the UI in such a way that the communication will be asynchronous.

In order to ensure that the target model complies with the desired architecture, it is possible to define constraints over the metamodel that correctly reflect the architectural paradigm. For instance, in 3-tier applications:

- there should be no UI and Business Logic methods in the same class
- no direct links from UI to Data allowed
- ...

Transformation Execution

The example graph for the BankSystem application seen previously (Figure 7.10) is a candidate for the application of the Move Method UI transformation. This transformation is an example of a rule that contributes to the technological layering of the application.

As we can see from the transformation rule, this graph has an occurrence of the LHS. As a result, we can apply the rule, obtaining the graph shown in Figure 7.12.

The method "txtClear" was moved from the class "DepositMoney" to "DepositMoneyUI", a class belonging to the UI concern.

The execution of transformation rules can either be based on a tool that interprets the transformation specification, or a manually developed transformation program using the set of rules as requirement specification. We are presently using the code generation facility of the Tiger tool.

Example

At this stage we have a graphical representation of the categorised source code conforming to the type graph. Having designed the transformation rules in Tiger EMF we can generate the transformation code automatically.

As an example, when we apply the transformation rule Move Method UI illustrated in Figure 7.11 to the start graph of Figure 7.10, we obtain the representation shown in Figure 7.12.

If we keep applying appropriate transformation rules, this graph will be transformed until the representation achieved complies to the intended target model. The rule Move Variable UI can transfer variable *lbNo* to the class *DepositMoneyUI*. Applying the rules Move Code Block Data, followed by Move Code Block UI and finally Move Code Block Data again, we can completely transform the source graph into one that conforms to the constraints defined for the target model. This graph is presented in Figures 7.13 and 7.14. The size of this graph made us divide it into two figures to render it readable. The ellipses show the connections between the two Figures. The first shows the architecture level and includes packages. The second includes all the information from the code block level until class level. For transforming the whole application from 2-Tier to 3-Tier, 26 transformation rules are needed.

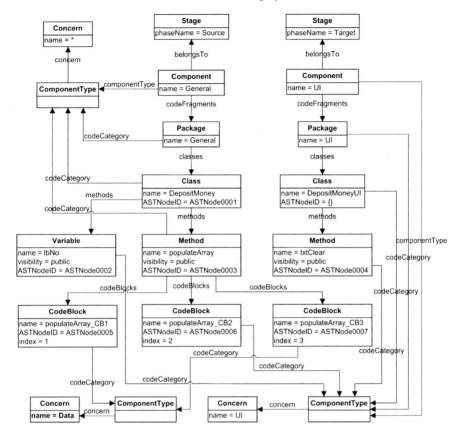

Fig. 7.12. Graph representing a subset of the BankSystem sample application after the execution of rule Move Method UI. {} represents new AST nodes identifiers created during the transformation process

Some of these rules, namely the ones that move code blocks, are quite more complex than Move Method UI, which was selected to be presented for readability purposes.

7.4.5 Forward Engineering

The target code can be achieved using two alternative strategies discussed below. However, we are still exploring both of them to see their practicality, challenges and limitations.

1. During transformation execution, a log of the applied rules is kept, to be replicated at the code level using a standard refactoring tool. This requires to associate each graph transformation rule to one or more standard code refactorings. Depending on the complexity of the rules or the specificities of the situation, traditional refactorings may not be enough, in which case it is necessary to develop more complex code level transformations.

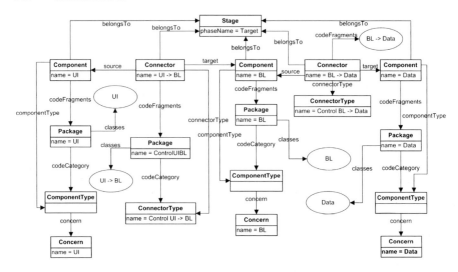

Fig. 7.13. Graph representing a subset of the BankSystem sample application after being transformed (Architecture and packages). The ellipses show the connections with Figure 7.14

2. Alternatively we can generate the code directly, using the target program representation and the links to the original AST. The code can be generated top-down, copying most of it from the original source code to the new structure and generating the necessary "extra code". This "extra code" can be, for example, the code that changes method invocations when the called method has moved to a new class.

Example

Finally the code complying to the desired architecture can be generated. For this purpose, we use the target model previously generated as well as the traceability relation with the original source code. In this process the code is refactored to be coherent with the model and *glue* code vital for the preservation of the application's functionality is created.

A sample of the code transformed is presented in Figures 7.15, 7.16, 7.17 and 7.18. The code is not integrally presented for simplicity reasons.

7.5 Related Work

Three areas of research constitute relevant work related to the approach presented in this chapter: program representation/reverse engineering, program transformation and code generation. However, the work in these areas is evolving mostly independently, i.e., not as part of an integrated reengineering methodology as in our case. We also present recent work that addresses specifically reengineering to SOA.

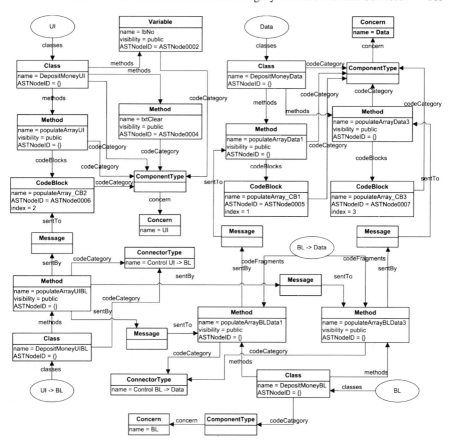

Fig. 7.14. Graph representing a subset of the BankSystem sample application after being transformed (from code block level until class level). The ellipses show the connections with Figure 7.13

Regarding the area of source code representation and reverse engineering, we briefly describe a few examples that show how this issue is dealt with in different contexts.

The Dagstuhl Middle Model (DMM) [325] was developed to solve interoperability issues of reverse engineering tools. Like our approach, it keeps traceability to the source code. The DMM is composed by sub-hierarchies that include an abstract view of the program and a source code model. The chosen way to relate these two is via a direct link. The Fujaba (From UML to Java And Back Again) tool suite [395] provides design pattern [190] recognition. The source code representation used for that process is based on an Abstract Syntax Graph (ASG). Another representation is put forward with the Columbus Schema for C++ [173]. Here an AST conforming to the C++ model/schema is built, and a higher level semantic information is derived from types. The work of Ramalingam et al., from IBM research, in [426], addresses

```
package SoftwareEvolutionBookChapter.ControlUIBL;

import SoftwareEvolutionBookChapter.UI.DepositMoneyUI;
import SoftwareEvolutionBookChapter.BL.DepositMoneyBL;

public class DepositMoneyUIBL {

    private int rows = 0;
    private int total = 0;

    DepositMoneyUI depositMoneyUI = new DepositMoneyUI();
    DepositMoneyBL depositMoneyBL = new DepositMoneyBL();

    void populateArrayUIBL() {
        try {
            depositMoneyBL.populateArrayBL1(rows);
        } catch (Exception e) {
            rows = depositMoneyBL.getRows();
            total = rows;
            if (total == 0) {
                depositMoneyUI.populateArrayUI();
            } else {
                depositMoneyBL.populateArrayBL3();
            }
        }
    }
}
```

Fig. 7.15. Code Transformed (Package ControlUIBL)

the reverse engineering of OO data models from programs written in weakly-typed languages like Cobol. In their work, the links between the model and the code are represented in a reference table. This table establishes the link between each model element and the line of code having no intermediate representation. One major difference between our methodology and the above approaches is that ours uses a categorisation step that will make possible the automated transformation to a new architectural style.

The ARTISAn framework, described by Jakobac, Egyed and Medvidovic in [250], like our approach, categorises source code. It uses an iterative user-guided method to achieve this. The code categories used are: "processing", "data" and "communication". The approach differs from ours in several aspects. Firstly, the goal of the framework is program understanding and not the creation of a representation that is aimed to be used as input for the transformation part of a reengineering methodology. Another important difference is that in ARTISAn the categorisation process (called "labeling") is based in clues that result in the categorisation of classes only. In our approach we need, and support, the method and code block granularity levels.

The next related area is program transformation, which can occur in different levels of abstraction. The source-to-source level of transformation is the most established one, both in research and in industrial implementations. There are several research ideas that led to successful industrial tools. Examples from research include TXL [126] and ASF+SDF [513]. DMS from Semantic Designs [46] and Forms2Net from ATX Software [12] are program transformation tools being successfully applied in the industry. Transformations at the detailed design level, due to its applications as

```
package SoftwareEvolutionBookChapter.UI;

import javax.swing.JOptionPane;
import javax.swing.JTextField;

public class DepositMoneyUI {

    private JTextField txtNo, txtName, txtDeposit;
    private int rows = 0;

    public int getRows() { return rows; }

    public void populateArrayUI() {
        JOptionPane.showMessageDialog (null, "Records File is Empty.\n
                                    Enter Records First to Display.",
            "BankSystem - EmptyFile", JOptionPane.PLAIN_MESSAGE);
        btnEnable ();

    }

    //Function use to Clear all TextFields of Window.
    void txtClear () {
        txtNo.setText ("");
        txtName.setText ("");
        txtDeposit.setText ("");
        txtNo.requestFocus ();
    }

    void btnEnable() {
        // ...
    }

}
```

Fig. 7.16. Code Transformed (Package UI)

maintenance techniques, have an increasing interest that is following the same path. Practices such as refactoring [183] are driving the implementation of functionalities that automate detailed design level transformations. These are mainly integrated in development environments as is the case of Eclipse [494] and IntelliJ [255]. However, there is still a lot of ongoing research in this area, for instance, in the determination of dependencies between transformations [368].

Work in the area of architecture transformation is broad and diverse. It includes a few works based on model transformation, automated code transformation, or graph transformation and re-writing, which are closely related to the work in this chapter. The approaches found in the literature vary in three main things: first, the levels of abstraction used for describing the system (architecture models only or interlinked architecture and implementation models), second, the way the architecture models are represented and third, the method and tools used for representing and executing architecture transformation rules. Available case studies are either only concerned with the transformation of high level architecture representations or limited to very specific source and target architectures and programming languages combinations.

Kong et al. [288] developed an approach for software architecture verification and transformation based on graph grammar. First, the approach requires translating

```
package SoftwareEvolutionBookChapter.BL;

import SoftwareEvolutionBookChapter.Data.DepositMoneyData;

public class DepositMoneyBL {

    DepositMoneyData depositMoneyData = new DepositMoneyData();

    public int getRows() { return depositMoneyData.getRows(); }

    public void populateArrayBL1(int rows) throws Exception {
        depositMoneyData.populateArrayData1(rows);
    }

    public void populateArrayBL3() {
        depositMoneyData.populateArrayData3();
    }

}
```

Fig. 7.17. Code Transformed (Package ControlBLData)

```
package SoftwareEvolutionBookChapter.Data;

import java.io.DataInputStream;
import java.io.FileInputStream;

public class DepositMoneyData {

    private FileInputStream fis;
    private DataInputStream dis;

    private String records[][] = new String [500][6];
    private int rows = 0;

    public int getRows() { return rows; }

    public void populateArrayData1(int p_rows) throws Exception {
        rows = p_rows;
        fis = new FileInputStream ("Bank.dat");
        dis = new DataInputStream (fis);
        while (true) {
            for (int i = 0; i < 6; i++) {
                records[rows][i] = dis.readUTF();
            }
            rows++;
        }
    }

    public void populateArrayData3() {
        try {
            dis.close();
            fis.close();
        }
        catch (Exception exp) { }
    }

}
```

Fig. 7.18. Code Transformed (Package ControlData)

UML diagrams describing the system architecture (or acquiring a description for it) to reserved graph grammar formalism (RGG). Then, the properties of the RGG description can be checked automatically. Also, automatic transformation can also be applied but only at the architecture description level and not at the implementation level.

Ivkovic and Kontogiannis [244] proposed a framework for quality-driven software architecture refactoring using model transformations and semantic annotations. In this method, first, conceptual architecture view is represented as a UML 2.0 profile with corresponding stereotypes. Second, instantiated architecture models are annotated using elements of the refactoring context, including soft-goals, metrics, and constraints. A generic refactoring context is defined using UML 2.0 profiles that includes "semanticHead" stereotype for denoting the semantic annotations. These semantic annotations are related to system quality improvements. Finally, the actions that are most suitable for the given refactoring context are applied after being selected from a set of possible refactorings. Transformations in this method occur at the conceptual architecture view level using Fowler [183] refactorings.

Fahmy et al. [165] used graph rewriting to specify architectural transformations. They used PROGRES tool [70] to formulate executable graph-rewriting specifications for various architectural transformations. They represent architecture using directed typed graphs that represent system hierarchy and component interaction. The assumption is that the architecture is extracted using some extraction tool. Their work is at the architecture description level and no actual transformation is performed on the code.

Unlike the three previous works, the approach of Carrière et al. [106] implements architectural transformations at the code level using automated code transformation. Their first step is reconstructing the existing software architecture by extracting architecturally important features from the code and aggregating the extracted (low-level) information into an architectural representation. The next step is defining the required transformations. In this work, they were interested in transforming the connectors of a client-server application to separate the client and server sides as much as possible and reduce their mutual dependence. Next, the Reasoning SDK (formerly Refine/C), which provides an environment for language definition, parsing and syntax tree querying and transformation, is used to implement the required connector transformations at code level on the AST of the source system. The major difference from our work relies on the fact that we use code categorisation to relate the original source code with the intended target architecture. We also transform at model level while this approach does it at code level.

Regarding code generation, there is a significant number of research work and tools available. A comprehensive list is already too long to specify in the context of this chapter so we only name a few. The already mentioned Fujaba tool suite supports the generation of Java sourcecode from the design in UML resulting in an executable prototype. The Eclipse Modeling Framework (EMF) [495] can generate Java code from models defined using the Ecore meta-model. This has a number of possible uses such as to help develop an editor for a specific type of models. UModel [8], from Altova, can generate C# and Java source code from UML class or component diagrams. In the Code Generation Network website there is a very extensive list of available tools [120].

Work in the area of reengineering to SOA is new. It primarily focuses on identifying and extracting services from legacy code bases and then wrapping them for deployment on a SOA. A key assumption in this area is that an evaluation of the legacy system will be conducted to assess if there are valuable reusable and reliable functionalities embedded that are meaningful and useful to be exposed in the service-oriented environment and that are fairly maintainable. Sneed [465] presents a tool supported method for wrapping legacy PL/I, COBOL, and C/C++ code behind an XML shell which allows individual functions within the programs, to be offered as web services to any external user. The first step is identifying candidate functionality for wrapping as a web service. The second step is locating the code of the functionality, with the aid of reverse engineering tools. The third step is extracting that code and reassembling it as a separate module with its own interface. This is done by copying the impacted code units into a common framework and by placing all of the data objects they refer to into a common data interface. The fourth step is wrapping the component extracted with a WSDL interface. The last step is linking the web service to overlying business processes by means of a proxy component.

A lighter code-independent approach was developed by Canfora et al. [100], which wraps only the presentation layer of legacy form-based user interfaces (and not the code) as services. In form-based user interfaces, the flow of data between the system and the user is described by a sequence of query/response interactions or forms with fixed screen organisation. There wrappers interacts with the legacy system as though it were a user, with the help of a Finite State Automata (FSA) that describes the interaction between the user and the legacy system. Each use case of the legacy system is described by a FSA and is reengineered to a web service. The FSA states correspond to the legacy screens and the transitions correspond to the user actions performed on the screen to move to another screen. The wrapper derives the execution of the uses cases on the legacy system by providing it with the needed flow of data and commands using the FSA of the relevant use case. Of particular relevance to our work is the service identification and extraction task, which is closely related to the vertical dimension mentioned earlier in this chapter, but not reported here. This task is essential for any code-wrapping approach to reengineering to SOA. Some works focus primarily on this aspect. For example, Del Grosso et al. [145] proposed an approach to identify, from database-oriented applications, pieces of functionality to be potentially exported as services. The identification is performed by clustering, through formal concept analysis, queries dynamically extracted by observing interactions between the application and the database. Zhang et al. [565] proposed an approach for extracting reusable object-oriented legacy code segments with combined formal concept analysis and slicing techniques for service integration. Firstly, an evaluation of legacy systems is performed to confirm the applicability of this approach and to determine other re-engineering activities. Secondly, the legacy system is decomposed into component candidates via formal concept analysis. Static program slicing is applied to further understand these component candidates. Then, component candidates are extracted, refined and encapsulated.

7.6 Conclusion

Most of the ongoing research in the context of automated software transformation, as well as existing industrial tools, focus on textual and structural transformation techniques that intend to solve very specific problems within well defined domains (e.g. program restructuring, program renovation, language-platform migration). Our experience indicates that such techniques fall short of addressing, in a systematic way, the complexity of the architecture-based transformation problem. In practice, when such a problem arises, these approaches have to be combined in a trial and error fashion, the success of which often depends on the experience of the reengineering team and on the specific problem at hand. On the other hand, there exist techniques and tools that work well at the architectural level, but with the main goal of documenting and visualising the architecture of applications rather than supporting increased levels of automation in architecture-based transformations. Although such tools can provide a very good starting point and facilitate the subsequent effort, in industry projects a reengineering approach that starts with redocumenting architectures is often limited given the time and budget constraints.

SOA is becoming a prevailing software engineering practice and presents challenges that add to the difficulty of the architectural transformation process. In this work we have presented a systematic approach in order to explicitly address these issues. This chapter has reported in detail our approach: the code annotation process, code representation, architectural transformation using graph transformation techniques.

While in this chapter we presented an instantiation of the technique to transform Java 2-tier applications to 3-tier to address the technological dimension of SOA, the general technique can be used in a variety of contexts, tailored to the specific requirements of a particular redesign problem by adapting the code annotation and transformation rules. Possible instantiations include, for example, the migration of monolithic applications into thin-client 2-tier architectures or of 3-tier applications into SOA. Our current implementation serves as a demonstration of the methodology and is incomplete in the sense that more categorisation rules may have to be added to allow a more complete automation of the step 1 of the methodology, and that code generation is not yet automated. However, from our experiments, we can see the potential of using this methodology in industry.

Presently we are in the process of completing the tools in order to apply them to a large real-world scenario. Another branch of work is to develop an instantiation of the methodology to address the functional dimension of SOA. By applying it in sequence in both dimensions it will be possible to transform legacy systems to Service-Oriented Architectures.

Acknowledgement. R. Correia and C. Matos are Marie-Curie Fellows seconded to the University of Leicester as part of the Transfer of Knowledge, Industry Academia Partnership Leg2Net (MTK1-CT-2004-003169). This work has also been supported by the IST-FET IP SENSORIA (IST-2005-16004).

G. Koutsoukos participated in the development of the presented reengineering methodology while at ATX Software. M. El-Ramly contributed to this work while lecturer at the University of Leicester.

## Part III

Novel Trends in Software Evolution

8

On the Interplay Between Software Testing and Evolution and its Effect on Program Comprehension

Leon Moonen[1], Arie van Deursen[1,2], Andy Zaidman[1], and Magiel Bruntink[2,1]

[1] Delft University of Technology, The Netherlands
[2] CWI, The Netherlands

Summary. We know software evolution to be inevitable if the system is to survive in the long-term. Equally well-understood is the necessity of having a good test suite available in order to (1) ensure the quality of the current state of the software system and (2) to ease future change. In that light, this chapter explores the interplay that exists between software testing and software evolution, because as tests ease software evolution by offering a safety net against unwanted change, they can equally be experienced as a burden because they are subject to the very same forces of software evolution themselves.

In particular, in this chapter, we describe how typical refactorings of production code can invalidate tests, how test code can (structurally) be improved by applying specialized test refactorings. Building upon these concepts, we introduce "test-driven refactoring", or refactorings of production code that are induced by the (re)structuring of the tests. We also report on typical source code design metrics that can serve as indicators for testability. To conclude, we present a research agenda that contains pointers to—as yet—unexplored research topics in the domain of testing.

8.1 Introduction

Lehman has taught us that a software system must evolve, or it becomes progressively less satisfactory [317, 321]. We also know that due to ever changing surroundings, new business needs, new regulations and also due to the people working with the system, the software is in a semi-permanent state of flux [319]. Combined with the increasing life-span of most software systems [56], this leads to a situation where an ever higher fraction of the total budget of a software system is spent during the maintenance or evolution phase of a software system, considerably outweighing the initial development costs of a system [329].

For many people, evolving a software system has become a synonym for adapting the source code as this concept stands central when thinking of software. Software, however, is multidimensional, and so is the development process behind it. This multidimensionality lies in the fact that to develop high-quality source code, other artifacts are needed. Examples of these are: specifications, which are needed

T. Mens, S. Demeyer (eds.), *Software Evolution.*
DOI 10.1007/978-3-540-76440-3, © Springer 2008

to know what should be developed, constraints, which are defined so that the software has to adhere to them, documentation, which needs to be written to ease future evolution, and tests, which need to be set up and exercised to ensure quality [436]. The central question then is how evolution should happen: in a unidimensional way, where only the source code is changed, or in a multidimensional way, where (all) the other artifacts are also evolved?

Within this chapter we will explore two dimensions of the multidimensional software evolution space, as we will focus on how the production software evolves with regard to the accompanying tests of the software system. To characterize why tests are so important during evolution, we first discuss some general focal points of tests:

Quality assurance Tests are typically engineered and run to ensure the quality of a software system [131]. Other facets that are frequently tested are the robustness and stress-resistance of a software system.

Documentation In *agile software development* methods such as *extreme programming* (XP), tests are explicitly used as a form of documentation, and as such, the tests serve as a means of communication between developers [516, 149].

Confidence At a more psychological level, test code can help the software (re-) engineer become more confident, because of the safety net that is provided by the tests. Furthermore, the confidence within the development team can be improved when they see that the system they are trying to deliver, is working correctly [119, 149].

An aspect of testing that cannot be neglected is the impact on the software development process: testing is known to be very time-intensive, thus driving up the total costs of the software system. Estimates by Brooks put the total time devoted to testing at 50% of the total allocated time [85, 447], while Kung et al. suggest that 40 to 80% of the development costs of building software is spent in the testing phase [301].

Several types of testing activities can be distinguished. The focus of this chapter is on *developer testing* (often also called *unit testing*), i.e., testing as conducted by the development team in order to assess that the system that is being built is working properly. In some cases, such tests will be set up with knowledge of the inner workings of the system (*white box* testing)—in others the test case will be based on component requirements, (design) models or public interfaces (black box testing) [66, 346].

One of the alternatives to developer testing is *acceptance testing*, i.e., testing as conducted by end user representatives in order to determine whether the system meets the stated criteria. Although acceptance testing is not the primary focus of this chapter, it has many techniques in common with developer testing (as observed by Binder [66]), which is why we believe that the results that we discuss will to a large extent be valid for acceptance testing as well.

Having discussed the necessity of a software system's evolution and also the importance of having a test suite available for a system, we can turn our attention to the interactions that occur between tests and the system under evolution. To this end, we define a number of research questions that we will investigate in the remainder of this chapter:

1. How does a system's test suite influence the program comprehension process of a software engineer trying to understand a given system? What are the possible side effects with regard to evolving the software system?
2. Are there typical code characteristics that indicate which test code resists evolution? And if so, how can we help alleviate these, so called, *test smells*?
3. Given that production code evolves through e.g. refactorings—behavior preserving changes—, what is the influence of these refactorings on the associated test code? Does that test code need to be refactored as well or can it remain in place unadapted? And what will happen to its role as safety net against errors?
4. Can we use metrics to understand the relation between test code and production code? In particular, can object-oriented metrics on the production code be used to predict key properties of the test code?

In order to find answers to the above questions, we have studied how the test suites of a number of applications evolve through time. We have specifically looked at software developed using agile software development methods since these methods explicitly include a number of evolutionary steps in their development process. Furthermore, such projects typically make use of testing frameworks, such as JUnit [49, 262]. To sketch this context, we give a short introduction to agile methods in Section 8.2.

The four research questions introduced above, are discussed in Sections 8.3 through 8.6: we investigate the effects of test suites on comprehension in Section 8.3. We present a catalogue of test smells and test refactorings in Section 8.4. In Section 8.5 we make a classification of classical refactorings [183] into categories, so that one can easily see which refactorings (possibly) break a test. Finally, we discuss a study that shows how certain object-oriented metrics correlate to testing effort in Section 8.6.

In our concluding remarks (Section 8.7) we present a retrospective and touch upon a number of unexplored research tracks.

8.2 Agile Software Development Methods

Agile software development methods (or Agile methods in short) refer to a collection of "lightweight" software development methodologies that adhere to the ideas in the Agile Manifesto [233]. Agile methods aim at minimizing risk and achieving customer satisfaction through a short (development) feedback loop.

Agile methods recognize that continuous change of software systems is natural, inevitable and actually a desirable aspect of successful software systems. Agile software development is typically done in short iterations, lasting only a few weeks. Each iteration includes all software engineering activities, such as planning, design, coding, and testing, that are needed to add a (small) piece of functionality to the system. Agile methods aim at having a working product (albeit not functionally complete) deliverable to the customer after each iteration.

Agile software development builds upon various existing and common sense practices and principles, such as code reviewing, testing, designing and refactoring. However, these practices are done *continuously* rather than at dedicated phases of the software process only. On the other hand, the need for extensive documentation on an agile project is reduced by several of its practices: test-driven development and a focus on acceptance testing ensures that there is always a test suite that shows that your system works and fulfills the requirements implemented to that point. For the developers, these tests act as significant documentation because it shows how the code actually works [9], and how it should be invoked.

A particular agile method that is studied in more detail in this chapter is *Extreme Programming* (XP). XP is one of the initial and most prominent of the agile methods and applies many of the agile practices to "extreme levels". It is a lightweight methodology for small teams of approximately 10 people developing software in the face of vague or rapidly changing requirements [50]. XP is performed in short *iterations*, which are grouped into larger *releases*. The planning process is depicted as a game in which business and development determine the scope of releases and iterations. The customer describes features via *user stories*, informal use cases that fit on an index card. The developers estimate each of the user stories. User stories are the starting point for the planning, design, implementation, and acceptance test activities conducted in XP.

Two key practices of XP play an important role within the scope of our study, namely testing and refactoring. In XP (and most other agile methods) *tests* are written in parallel with (or even *before*) the production code by the programmers. The tests are collected and they must all pass at any time. Customers write acceptance tests for the stories in an iteration, if needed supported by the development team. Tests are typically fully automatic, making it cheap to run them frequently. To write tests, testing frameworks such as JUnit [49] are used (see the next section).

The second key practice of interest is *refactoring*: improving the design of existing code without changing functionality. The guiding design principle is "do the simplest thing that could possibly work". In XP, continuous refactoring during coding replaces the traditional (big) up front design effort.

Note that although this chapter uses agile software development methods and XP to discuss the interaction between software evolution and software testing, this does not mean that the issues observed only apply to agile methods; they are just as likely to come up in any other development process where developer testing and refactoring plays an important role. We choose agile methods as showcase because of its explicit focus on testing and inclusion of evolutionary steps in the development cycle.

8.3 Program Comprehension

A major cost factor in the life cycle of a software system is *program understanding*: trying to understand an existing software system for the purpose of planning, designing, implementing, and testing changes. Estimates put the total cost of the understanding phase at 50% of the total effort [125]. This suggests that paying attention to program comprehension issues in the software process could well pay off in terms of higher quality, longer life time, fewer defects, lower costs, and higher job satisfaction.

This is especially true in the case of extreme programming since the need for people to understand pieces of code is at the very core of XP.

Based upon a thorough analysis of (1) literature on XP [50, 254, 48]; (2) online discussion covering XP subjects[3]; and (3) our own experiences made during an ongoing (industrial) extreme programming project[4], we made the following observation:

Observation 1   An extensive test suite can stimulate the program comprehension process, especially in the light of continuously evolving software.

For our study, we specifically focus on how program comprehension and unit tests interact in the XP software process. We analyze risks and opportunities, look at the effect on the team (whether and how the team gets a better understanding of the code) as well as on the source code (whether and how the code gets more understandable).

8.3.1 Program Understanding

We define program understanding (comprehension) as *the task of building mental models of an underlying software system at various abstraction levels, ranging from models of the code itself to ones of the underlying application domain, for software maintenance, evolution, and re-engineering purposes* [383].

An important research area in program understanding deals with the cognitive processes involved in constructing a mental model of the software system (see, e.g., [530]). A common element of such cognitive models is generating hypotheses about code and investigating whether they hold or must be rejected. Several *strategies* can be used to arrive at relevant hypotheses, such as bottom up (starting from code), top down (starting from a high-level goal and expectations), and opportunistic combinations of the two [125]. Strategies guide two understanding mechanisms that produce information: *chunking* creates new, higher level abstraction structures from lower level structures, and *cross referencing* relates different abstraction levels [530]. We will see how the XP practices relate to these program understanding theories.

The construction of mental models at different levels of abstraction can be supported by so called software exploration tools [378]. These tools use reverse engineering techniques to (1) identify a system's components and interrelationships; and (2) create representations of a system in other forms or at higher levels of abstraction [112].

8.3.2 Unit Testing and XP

Unit testing is at the heart of XP. Unit tests are written by the developers, using the same programming language used to build the system itself. Tests are small, take a white box view on the code, and include a check on the correctness of the

---

[3] Most notably, the *C2 wiki* at http://www.c2.com/cgi/wiki and http://groups.yahoo.com/group/extremeprogramming/. Last visited January, 2007.

[4] Program understanding tools by the *Software Improvement Group*: http://www.software-improvers.com/.

results obtained, comparing actual results with expected ones. Tests are an explicit part of the code, they are put under revision control, and all tests are shared by the development team (any one can invoke any test). A unit test is required to run in almost zero time. This makes it possible (and recommended) to run all tests before and after any change, however minor the change may be.

Testing is typically done using a testing framework such as *JUnit* developed by Beck and Gamma [49, 262]. The framework caters for invoking all test methods of a test class automatically, and for collecting test cases into test suites. Test results can be checked by invoking any of the *assert* methods of the framework with which expected values can be compared to actual values. Testing success is visualized through a graphical user interface showing a growing green bar as the tests progress: as soon as a test fails, the bar becomes red.

The XP process encourages writing a test class for every class in the system. The test code/production code ratio may vary from project to project and in practice we have seen ratios as high as 1:1. Moreover, XP encourages programmers to use tests for documentation purposes, in particular if an interface or method is unclear, if the implementation of a method is complicated, if there are circumstances in which the code should work in a special way, and if a bug report is received [50]. In each of these situations, the test is written *before* the corresponding method is written (or modified) [52].

Also, tests can be added while understanding existing code. In particular, whenever a programmer is tempted to type something into a print statement or debugger instruction, XP advises to write a test instead and add it to the system's test suite [49].

8.3.3 Comprehension Benefits

This section discusses a number of benefits that an automated unit testing regime has for program comprehension.

First, *XP's testing policy encourages programmers to explain their code using test cases.* Rather than explaining the behavior of a function using prose in comments or documentation, the extreme programmer adds a test that explicitly shows the behavior.

Second, *the requirement that all tests must run 100% at all times, ensures that the documentation via unit tests is kept up-to-date.* With regular technical documentation and comments, nothing is more difficult than keeping them consistent with the source code. In XP, all tests must pass before and after every change, ensuring that what the developer writing the tests intended to communicate remains valid.

Third, *adding unit tests provides a repeatable program comprehension strategy.* If a programmer needs to change a piece of code that he is not familiar with, he will try to understand the code by inspecting the test cases. If these do not provide enough understanding, the programmer will try to understand the nature of the code by developing and testing a series of hypotheses, as we have seen in Section 8.3.1. The advise to write tests instead of using print statements or debugger commands applies here as well: *program understanding hypotheses can be translated into unit tests*, which then can be run in order to confirm or refute the hypotheses.

Fourth, *a comprehensive set of unit tests reduces the comprehension space when modifying source code.* To a certain extent a programmer can just try a change and see whether the tests still run. This reduces the risks and complexity of conducting a painstakingly difficult impact analysis. Thus, the XP process attempts to minimize the *size* of the mental model that needs to be build and maintained since the tests help the programmer to see what parts are not affected by the current modifications.

Last but not least, *systematic unit testing helps build team confidence.* In the XP literature, it is said that the tests help the team to develop *courage* to change the code [344].

The XP testing process not only affects the way the team works, it also has a direct effect on the understandability of the production code written [254, p.199]. *Writing unit tests requires that the code tested is split into many small methods each responsible for a clear and testable task.*

In addition, if the tests are written after the production code, it is likely that the production code is difficult to test. For that reason, XP requires that the unit tests are written *before* the code (the "test-driven" approach) [52]. In this way, *testing code and production code are written hand-in-hand, ensuring that the production code is set up in a testable manner.*

8.3.4 Comprehension Risks

Using tests for documentation leads to the somewhat paradoxical situation that in order to understand a given piece of code a programmer has to read another piece of code. Thus, to support program comprehension, XP increases the code base and this code needs to be maintained as well. We experienced that maintaining such test code requires special skills and refactorings, which we describe in Section 8.5.

Also of importance is that tests are automated (with the possible exception of exploratory tests), as non-automated tests probably require knowledge or skill to activate the tests. Knowledge which is possibly not available during (initial) program comprehension [131].

Another concern is that XP uses the tests (in combination with oral communication and code written to display intent) as a *replacement* for technical documentation. The word "documentation" is mentioned once in Beck's book, where he explains why he decided *not* to write documentation [50, p. 156]. For addressing subjects not easily expressed in the tests or code of the system under development, a *technical memorandum* can be written [134]. These are short (one or two pages) papers expressing key ideas and motivations of the design. However, if the general tendency is not to write documentation, it is unlikely that the technical memoranda actually get written, leaving important decisions undocumented.

A final concern is that some types of code are inherently hard to test, the best known examples being user interfaces and database code. Writing tests for such code requires skill, experience, and determination. This will not be always available, leaving the hardest code without tests and thus without documentation.

A possible solution for these cases can be the use of so called *mock objects* which are "simulated" objects that can mimic the behavior of complex objects in a controlled way (often using a form of capture and replay) [336]. Setting up such a mock object can then serve as documentation of the interaction with the real object.

8.4 Test Smells and Refactorings

Continuous refactoring, one of the key practices of extreme programming and most other agile methods, is advocated for bringing the code into the simplest state possible. To aid in the refactoring process a catalog of "code smells" and a wide range of refactorings is available, varying from simple modifications up to ways to systematically introduce design patterns in existing code [273].

From our own experiences we know however that test code is different from production code and this has led us to the following observations:

> **Observation 2**   Test code has a distinct set of smells, dealing with the ways in which test cases are organized, how they are implemented, and how they interact with each other.

> **Observation 3**   Improving test code involves a mixture of applying refactorings as identified by Fowler [183] specialized to test code improvements, as well as a set of additional refactorings, involving the modification of test classes and the way of grouping test cases.

In this section we describe a set of *test smells* indicating trouble in test code, and a collection of *test refactorings* explaining how to overcome some of these problems through a simple program modification.

For the remainder of this chapter, we assume some familiarity with the *x*Unit framework [49] and refactorings as described by Fowler [183]. We will refer to refactorings described in this book using *Name (F:page#)* and to our test specific refactorings described in Section 8.4.2 using *Name (#)*.

8.4.1 Test Code Smells

This section gives an overview of bad code smells that are specific for test code.

Smell 1: *Mystery Guest*.
When a test uses external resources, such as a file containing test data, the test is no longer self contained. Consequently, there is not enough information to understand the tested functionality, making it hard to use that test as documentation.

Moreover, using external resources introduces hidden dependencies: if some force changes or deletes such a resource, tests start failing. Chances for this increase when more tests use the same resource.

The use of external resources can be eliminated using the refactoring *Inline Resource* (1). If external resources are needed, you can apply *Setup External Resource* (2) to remove hidden dependencies.

Smell 2: *Resource Optimism.*
Test code that makes optimistic assumptions about the existence (or absence) and state of external resources (such as particular directories or database tables) can cause non-deterministic behavior in test outcomes. Situations where tests run fine at one time and fail miserably the next time are not where you want to find yourself in. Use *Setup External Resource* (2) to allocate and/or initialize all resources that are used.

Smell 3: *Test Run War.*
Such wars arise when the tests run fine as long as you are the only one testing but fail when more programmers run them. This is most likely caused by resource interference: some tests in your suite allocate resources such as temporary files that are also used by others. Apply *Make Resource Unique* (3) to overcome interference.

Smell 4: *General Fixture.*
In the *JUnit* framework a programmer can write a setUp method that will be executed before each test method to create a fixture for the tests to run in.

Things start to smell when the setUp fixture is too general and different tests only access part of the fixture. Such set-ups are harder to read and understand and may make tests run more slowly (because they do unnecessary work). The danger of having tests that take too much time to complete is that testing starts interfering with the rest of the programming process and programmers eventually may not run the tests at all.

The solution is to use setUp only for that part of the fixture that is shared by all tests using Fowler's *Extract Method (F:110)* and put the rest of the fixture in the method that uses it using *Inline Method (F:117)*. If, for example, two different groups of tests require different fixtures, consider setting these up in separate methods that are explicitly invoked for each test, or spin off two separate test classes using *Extract Class (F:149)*.

Smell 5: *Eager Test.*
When a test method checks several methods of the object to be tested, it is hard to read and understand, and therefore more difficult to use as documentation. Moreover, it makes tests more dependent on each other and harder to maintain.

The solution is simple: separate the test code into test methods that test only one method using Fowler's *Extract Method (F:110)*, using a meaningful name highlighting the purpose of the test. Note that splitting into smaller methods can slow down the tests due to increased setup/teardown overhead.

Smell 6: *Lazy Test.*
This occurs when several test methods check the same method *using the same fixture* (but for example check the values of different instance variables). Such tests often only have meaning when considering them together so they are easier to use when joined using *Inline Method (F:117)*.

Smell 7: *Assertion Roulette.*
You know *something* is wrong because your tests fail but it is unclear *what*. This smell comes from having a number of assertions in a single test method that do not

have a distinct explanation. If one of the assertions fails, you do not know which one it is. Use *Add Assertion Explanation* (5) to remove this smell.

Smell 8: *Indirect Testing.*
A test class is supposed to test its counterpart in the production code. It starts to smell when a test class contains methods that actually perform tests on other objects (for example because there are references to them in the class-to-be-tested). Such indirection can be moved to the appropriate test class by applying *Extract Method (F:110)* followed by *Move Method (F:142)* on that part of the test. The fact that this smell arises also indicates that there might be problems with data hiding in the production code.

Note that opinions differ on indirect testing. Some people do not consider it a smell but a way to guard tests against changes in the "lower" classes. We feel that there are more losses than gains to this approach: it is much harder to test anything that can break in an object from a higher level and understanding and debugging indirect tests is much harder.

Smell 9: *For Testers Only.*
When a production class contains methods that are only used by test methods, these methods either (1) are not needed and can be removed, or (2) are only needed to set up a fixture for testing. Depending on functionality of those methods, you may not want them in production code where others can use them. If this is the case, apply *Extract Subclass (F:330)* to move these methods in the testcode and use that subclass to perform the tests on. You will often find that these methods have names or comments stressing that they should only be used for testing.

Fear of this smell may lead to another undesirable situation: a class without corresponding test class. The reason then is that the developer (1) does not know how to test the class without adding methods that are specifically needed for the test and (2) does not want to pollute his production class with test code. Creating a separate subclass helps to deal with this problem.

Smell 10: *Sensitive Equality.*
It is fast and easy to write equality checks using the `toString` method. A typical way is to compute an actual result, map it to a string, which is then compared to a string literal representing the expected value. Such tests, however may depend on many irrelevant details such as commas, quotes, spaces, etc. Whenever the `toString` method for an object is changed, tests start failing. The solution is to replace `toString` equality checks by real equality checks using *Introduce Equality Method* (6).

Smell 11: *Test Code Duplication.*
Test code may contain undesirable duplication. In particular the parts that set up test fixtures are susceptible to this problem. Solutions are similar to those for normal code duplication as described by Fowler [183, p. 76]. The most common case for test code will be duplication of code in the same test class. This can be removed using *Extract Method (F:110)*. For duplication across test classes, it may be helpful to mirror the class hierarchy of the production code into the test class hierarchy. A word of caution

however: moving duplicated code from two separate classes to a common class can introduce (unwanted) dependencies between tests.

A special case of code duplication is *test implication*: test *A* and *B* cover the same production code, and *A* fails if and only if *B* fails. A typical example occurs when the production code gets refactored: before this refactoring, *A* and *B* covered different code, but afterwards they deal with the same code and it is not necessary anymore to maintain both tests. Because it fails to distinguish between the various cases, test implication impedes comprehension and documentation.

8.4.2 Test Refactorings

Bad smells seem to arise more often in production code than in test code. The main reason for this is that production code is adapted and refactored more frequently, allowing these smells to escape.

One should not, however, underestimate the importance of having fresh test code. Especially when new programmers are added to the team or when complex refactorings need to be performed, clear test code is invaluable. To maintain this freshness, test code also needs to be refactored.

We define *test refactorings* as changes (transformations) of test code that: (1) do not add or remove test cases, and (2) make test code better understandable/readable and/or maintainable [518].

The remainder of this section presents refactorings that we encountered while working on test code. Not all of these refactorings are directly linked with the elimination of the test smells of Section 8.4.1, but when a link is there, it is described.

Refactoring 1: *Inline Resource*.
To remove the dependency between a test method and some external resource, we incorporate that resource in the test code. This is done by setting up a fixture in the test code that holds the same contents as the resource. This fixture is then used instead of the resource to run the test. A simple example of this refactoring is putting the contents of a file that is used into some string in the test code.

If the contents of the resource are large, chances are high that you are also suffering from *Eager Test* (5) smell. Consider conducting *Extract Method (F:110)* or *Reduce Data* (4) refactorings.

Refactoring 2: *Setup External Resource*.
If it is necessary for a test to rely on external resources, such as directories, databases, or files, make sure the test that uses them explicitly creates or allocates these resources before testing, and releases them when done (take precautions to ensure the resource is also released when tests fail).

Refactoring 3: *Make Resource Unique*.
A lot of problems originate from the use of overlapping resource names, either between different tests run done by the same user or between simultaneous test runs done by different users.

Such problems can easily be prevented (or repaired) by using unique identifiers for all resources that are allocated, e.g. by including a time-stamp. When you also include the name of the test responsible for allocating the resource in this identifier, you will have less problems finding tests that do not properly release their resources.

Refactoring 4: *Reduce Data.*
Minimize the data that is setup in fixtures to the bare essentials. This will have two advantages: (1) it makes them better suitable as documentation, and (2) your tests will be less sensitive to changes.

Refactoring 5: *Add Assertion Explanation.*
Assertions in the JUnit framework have an optional first argument to give an explanatory message to the user when the assertion fails. Testing becomes much easier when you use this message to distinguish between different assertions that occur in the same test. Maybe this argument should not have been optional...

Refactoring 6: *Introduce Equality Method.*
If an object structure needs to be checked for equality in tests, add an implementation for the "equals" method for the object's class. You then can rewrite the tests that use string equality to use this method. If an expected test value is only represented as a string, explicitly construct an object containing the expected value, and use the new equals method to compare it to the actually computed object.

8.4.3 Other Test Smells and Refactorings

Fowler [183] presents a large set of bad smells and refactorings that can be used to remove them. Our work focuses on smells and refactorings that are typical for test code, whereas Fowler focuses more on production code. The role of unit tests in [183] is also more geared towards proving that a refactoring did not break anything than to be used as documentation of the production code.

Instead of focusing on cleaning test code which already has bad smells, Schneider [454] describes how to prevent these smells right from the start by discussing a number of best practices for writing tests with JUnit.

The C2 Wiki contains some discussion on the decay of unit test quality and practice as time proceeds [98], and on the maintenance of broken unit tests [542]. Opinions vary between repairing broken unit tests, deleting them completely, and moving them to another class in order to make them less exposed to changes (which may lead to our *Indirect Testing* (8) smell).

Van Rompaey et al. present an approach in which test smells are detected and then ranked according to their relative significance [521]. For this, they rely on a metric-based heuristic approach. They focus on the "General Fixture" and "Eager Test" test smells (Smell 4 & 5 in Section 8.4.1).

Besides the test smells we described earlier, Meszaros [372] discusses an additional set of process-oriented test smells and their refactorings.

8.5 How Refactoring Can Invalidate Its Safety Net

When evolving a piece of software, the change activities can roughly be divided into two categories. The first category consists of those operations that preserve behavior, i.e. refactorings, while the second category contains those changes that do not necessarily preserve behavior. Intuitively, when non-behavior-preserving changes are applied to production code, one would expect that the associated test code would need to evolve as well, as the end-result of the computation is bound to be different.

When thinking of refactorings of production code however, the picture is not that clear whether the associated unit tests need to evolve as well. Refactoring, which aims to improve the internal structure of the code, happens e.g. through the removal of duplication, simplification, making code easier to understand, adding flexibility, ... Fowler describes it as: *"Without refactoring, the design of software will decay. Regular refactoring helps code retain its shape."* [183, p.55].

One of the dangers of refactoring is that a programmer unintentionally changes the system's behavior. Ideally, it can be verified that this did not happen by checking that all the tests pass after refactoring. In practice, however, we have noticed that there are refactorings that will invalidate tests, as tests often rely, to a certain extent, on the code structure, which may have been affected by the refactoring (e.g., when a method is moved to another class and the test still expects it in the original class).

From this perspective, we observed the following:

Observation 4   The refactorings as proposed by Fowler [183] can be classified based on the type of change they make to the code, and therefore on the possible change they require in the test code.

Observation 5   In parallel to test-driven design, *test-driven refactoring* can improve the design of production code by focusing on the desired way of organizing test code to drive refactoring of production code (i.e., refactor for testing).

To explore the relationship between unit testing and refactorings, we take the following path: we first set up a classification of the refactorings described by Fowler [183], identifying exactly which of the refactorings affect class interfaces, and which therefore require changes in the test code as well (see Section 8.5.1). Subsequently, we look at the video store example from [183], and assess the implications of each refactoring on the test code (Section 8.5.2). We explore *test-driven refactoring*, which analyzes the test code in order to arrive at code level refactorings (Section 8.5.3), before we discuss the relationship between code-level refactorings and test-level refactorings (Section 8.5.4). We then integrate our results via the notion of a *refactoring session* which is a coherent set of steps resulting in refactoring of both the code and the tests (Section 8.5.5).

8.5.1 Types of Refactoring

Refactoring a system should not change its observable behavior. Ideally, this is verified by ensuring that all the tests pass before and after a refactoring [50, 183].

In practice, it turns out that such verification is not always possible: some refactorings restructure the code in such a way that tests only can pass after the refactoring if they are modified. For example, refactoring can move a method to a new class while some tests expect it in the original class (in that case, the code will probably not even compile).

This unfortunate behavior was also noted by Fowler: "Something that is disturbing about refactoring is that many of the refactorings do change an interface." [183, p.64]. Nevertheless, we do not want to change the tests together with a refactoring since that will make them less trustworthy for validating correct behavior afterwards.

In the remainder of this section, we will look in more detail at the refactorings described by Fowler [183] to analyze in which cases problems might arise because the original tests need to be modified.

Taxonomy

If we start with the assumption that refactoring does not change the behavior of the system, then there is only one reason why a refactoring can break a test: *because the refactoring changes the interface that the test expects*. Note that the interface extends to all visible aspects of a class (fields, methods, and exceptions). This implies that one has to be careful with tests that directly inspect the fields of a class since these will more easily change during a refactoring[5].

So, initially, we distinguish two types of refactoring: refactorings that do not change any interface of the classes in the system and refactorings that do change an interface. The first type of refactorings has no consequences for the tests: since the interfaces are kept the same, tests that succeeded before refactoring will also succeed after refactoring (if the refactoring indeed preserves the tested behavior).

The second type of refactorings can have consequences for the tests since there might be tests that expect the old interface. Again, we can distinguish two situations:

Incompatible: the refactoring destroys the original interface. All tests that rely on the old interface must be adjusted.

Backwards Compatible: the refactoring extends the original interface. In this case the tests keep running via the original interface and will pass if the refactoring preserves tested behavior. Depending on the refactoring, we might need to add more tests covering the extensions.

A number of incompatible refactorings that normally would destroy the original interface can be made into backwards compatible refactorings. This is done by extending the refactoring so it will retain the old interface, for example, using the *Adapter* pattern or simply via delegation. As a side-effect, the new interface will already partly be tested. Note that this is common practice when refactoring a published interface to prevent breaking dependent systems. A disadvantage is that a larger interface has to be maintained but when delegation or wrapping was used, that should not be too much work. Furthermore, language features like deprecation can be used to signal that this part of the interface is outdated.

---

[5] In fact, direct inspection of fields of a class is a test smell that could better be removed beforehand [518].

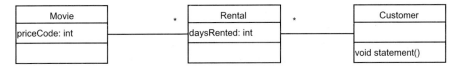

Fig. 8.1. Classes before refactoring

Classification

We have analyzed the refactorings in [183] and divided them into the following classes:

A. *Composite:* The four big refactorings *Convert Procedural Design to Objects, Separate Domain from Presentation, Tease Apart Inheritance,* and *Extract Hierarchy* will change the original interface, but we will not consider them in more detail since they are performed as series of smaller refactorings.

B. *Compatible:* Refactorings that do not change the original interface. Refactorings in this class are listed in Table 8.1.

C. *Backwards Compatible:* Refactorings that change the original interface and are inherently backwards compatible since they extend the interface. Refactorings in this class are listed in Table 8.2.

D. *Make Backwards Compatible:* Refactorings that change the original interface and can be made backwards compatible by adapting the new interface to the new one. Refactorings in this class are listed in Table 8.3.

E. *Incompatible:* Refactorings that change the original interface and are not backwards compatible (for example, because they change the types of classes that are involved). Refactorings in this class are listed in Table 8.4.

Note that the refactorings *Replace Inheritance with Delegation* and *Replace Delegation with Inheritance* are listed both in the *Compatible* and *Backwards Compatible* tables since they can be of either category, depending on the actual case.

8.5.2 Revisiting the Video Store

In this section, we study the relationship between testing and refactoring using a well-known example of refactoring. We revisit the video store code used by Fowler [183, Chapter 1], extending it with an analysis of what should be going on in the accompanying video store test code.

The video store class structure before refactoring is shown in Figure 8.1. It consists of a *Customer*, who is associated with a series of *Rentals*, each consisting of a *Movie* and an integer indicating the number of days the movie was rented. The key functionality is in the Customer's *statement* method printing a customer's total rental cost. Before refactoring, this statement is printed by a single long method. After refactoring, the statement functionality is moved into appropriate classes, resulting in the structure of Figure 8.2 taken from [183, p. 51].

Fowler emphasizes the need to conduct refactorings as a sequence of small steps. At each step, you must run the tests in order to verify that nothing essential has

Table 8.1. Compatible refactorings (type B)

Change Bidirectional Association to Unidirectional	Replace Exception with Test
Replace Nested Conditional with Guard Clauses	Change Reference to Value
Replace Magic Number with Symbolic Constant	Split Temporary Variable
Consolidate Duplicate Conditional Fragments	Decompose Conditional
Replace Conditional with Polymorphism	Introduce Null Object
Replace Inheritance with Delegation	Preserve Whole Object
Replace Delegation with Inheritance	Remove Control Flag
Replace Method with Method Object	Substitute Algorithm
Remove Assignments to Parameters	Introduce Assertion
Replace Data Value with Object	Extract Class
Introduce Explaining Variable	Inline Temp

Table 8.2. Backwards compatible refactorings (type C)

Replace Inheritance with Delegation	Replace Temp with Query	Push Down Method
Replace Delegation with Inheritance	Duplicate Observed Data	Push Down Field
Consolidate Conditional Expression	Self Encapsulate Field	Pull Up Method
Replace Record with Data Class	Form Template Method	Extract Method
Introduce Foreign Method	Extract Superclass	Pull Up Field
Pull Up Constructor Body	Extract Interface	

Table 8.3. Refactorings that can be made backwards compatible (type D)

Change Unidirectional Association to Bidirectional	Remove Middle Man
Replace Parameter with Explicit Methods	Remove Parameter
Replace Parameter with Method	Add Parameter
Separate Query from Modifier	Rename Method
Introduce Parameter Object	Move Method
Parameterize Method	

Table 8.4. Incompatible refactorings (type E)

Replace Constructor with Factory Method	Remove Setting Method
Replace Type Code with State/Strategy	Encapsulate Downcast
Replace Type Code with Subclasses	Collapse Hierarchy
Replace Error Code with Exception	Encapsulate Field
Replace Subclass with Fields	Extract Subclass
Replace Type Code with Class	Hide Delegate
Change Value to Reference	Inline Method
Introduce Local Extension	Inline Class
Replace Array with Object	Hide Method
Encapsulate Collection	Move Field

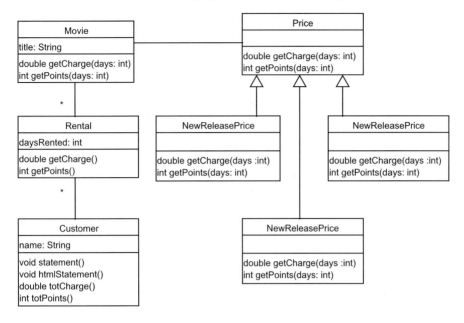

Fig. 8.2. Class structure after refactoring

changed. His testing approach is the following: "I create a few customers, give each customer a few rentals of various kinds of films, and generate the statement strings. I then do a string comparison between the new string and some reference strings that I have hand checked" [183, p. 8]. Although Fowler does not list his test classes, this typically should look like the code in Figure 8.3.

Studying this string-based testing method, we make the following observations:

• The setup is complicated, involving the creation of many different objects.
• The documentation value of the test is limited: it is hard to relate the computation of the charge of 4.5 for movie m1 to the way in which charges are computed for the actual movies rented (in this case a children's and a regular movie, each with their own price computation).
• The tests are brittle. All test cases include a full statement string. When the format changes in just a very small way, all existing tests (!) must be adjusted, an error prone activity we would like to avoid.

Unfortunately, there is no other way to write tests for the given code. The poor structure of the long method necessarily leads to an equally poor structure of the test cases. From a testing perspective, we would like to be able to separate computations from report writing. The long statement method prohibits this: it needs to be refactored in order to be able to improve the testability of the code.

This way of reasoning naturally leads to the application of the *Extract Method* refactoring to the *statement* method. Fowler comes to the same conclusion, based on the need to write a new method printing a statement in HTML format. Thus, we

```
Movie m1 = new Movie("m1",Movie.CHILDRENS);
Movie m2 = new Movie("m2", Movie.REGULAR);
Movie m3 = new Movie("m3", Movie.NEW_RELEASE);
Rental r1 = new Rental(m1, 5);
Rental r2 = new Rental(m2, 7);
Rental r3 = new Rental(m3, 1);
Customer c1 = new Customer("c1");
Customer c2 = new Customer("c2");

public void setUp() {
  c1.addRental(r1);
  c1.addRental(r2);
  c2.addRental(r3);
}

public void testStatement1() {
  String  expected =
    "Rental Record for c1\n" +
    "\tm1\t4.5\n" +
    "\tm2\t9.5\n" +
    "Amount owed is 14.0\n" +
    "You earned 2 frequent renter points";
  assertEquals(expected, c1.statement());
}
```

Fig. 8.3. Initial sample test code

extract *getCharge* for computing the charge of a rental, and *getPoints* for computing the "frequent renter points".

Extract Method is of type C, the *backwards compatible* refactorings, so we can use our existing tests to check the refactoring. However, we have created new methods, for which we might like to add tests that document and verify their specific behavior. To create such tests, we can reuse the setup of movies, rentals, and customers used for testing the *statement* method. We end up with a number of smaller test cases specifically addressing either the charge or rental point computations.

Since the correspondence between test code and actual code is now much clearer and better focused, we can apply white box testing, and use our knowledge of the structure of the code to determine the test cases needed. Thus, we see that the *getCharge* method to be tested distinguishes between 5 cases, and we make sure our tests cover these cases.

This has solved some of the problems. The tests are better understandable, more complete, much shorter, and less brittle. Unfortunately, we still have the complicated setup method. What we see is that the setup mostly involves rentals and movies, while the tests themselves are in the customer testing class. This is because the extracted method is in the wrong class: applying *Move Method* to *Rental* simplifies the set up for new test cases. Again we use our analysis of the test code to find refactorings in the production code.

The *Move Method* is of type D, refactorings that can be made backwards compatible by adding a wrapper method to retain the old interface. We add this wrapper so we can check the refactoring with our original tests. However, since the documentation of the method is in the test, and this documentation should be as close as possible to the method documented, we want to move the tests to the method's new location. Since there is no test class for Rental yet, we create it, and move the test methods for *getCharge* to it. Depending on whether the method was part of a published interface, we might want to keep the wrapper (for some time), or remove it together with the original test.

Fowler discusses several other refactorings, moving the charge and point calculations further down to the *Movie* class, replacing conditional logic by polymorphism in order to make it easier to add new movie types, and introducing the *state* design pattern in order to be able to change movie type during the life time of a movie.

When considering the impact on test cases of these remaining video store refactorings, we start to recognize a pattern:

- Studying the test code and the smells contained in it may help to identify refactorings to be applied at the production code;
- Many refactorings involve a change to the structure of the unit tests as well: in order to maintain the documenting value of these unit tests, they should be changed to reflect the structure of the code being tested.

In the next two sections, we take a closer look at these issues.

8.5.3 Test-Driven Refactoring

In *test-driven refactoring*, we try to use the existing test cases in order to determine the code-level refactorings. Thus, we study *test* code in order to find improvements to the *production* code.

This calls for a set of *code smells* that helps to find such refactorings. A first category is the set of existing code smells discussed in Fowler's book [183]. Several of them, such as long method, duplicated code, long parameter list, and so on, apply to test code as well as they do to production code. In many cases solving them involves not just a change on the test code, but first of all a refactoring of the production code.

A second category of smells is the collection of *test smells* discussed in Section 8.4 (also see [518]). In fact, in our movie example we encountered several of them already. Our uneasy feeling with the test case of Figure 8.3 is captured by the *Sensitive Equality* smell [518, Smell 10]: comparing computed values to a string literal representing the expected value. Such tests depend on many irrelevant details, such as commas, quotes, tabs, ... This is exactly why the customer tests of Figure 8.3 become brittle.

Another *test smell* we encountered is called *Indirect Testing* [518, Smell 8]: a test class contains methods that actually perform tests on other objects. Indirect tests make it harder to understand the relationship between test and production code. While moving the *getCharge* and *getPoints* methods in the class hierarchy (using *Move Method*), we also moved the corresponding test cases, in order to avoid *Indirect Testing*.

The test-driven perspective may lead to the formulation of additional test smells. For example, we observed that setting up the fixture for the CustomerTest was complicated. This indicates that the tests are in the wrong class, or that the underlying business logic is not well isolated. Another smell appears when there are many test cases for a single method, indicating that the method is too complex.

Test-driven refactoring is a natural consequence of test-driven design. Test-driven design is a way to get a good design by thinking about test cases first when adding functionality. Test-driven refactoring is a way to improve your design by rethinking the way you structured your tests.

In fact, Beck's work on test-driven design [51, 52] contains an interesting example that can be transferred to the refactoring domain. It involves testing the construction of a mortality table. His first attempt requires a complicated setup, involving separate "person" objects. He then rejects this solution as being overly complex for testing purposes, and proposes the construction of a mortality table with just an age as input. His example illustrates how test case construction guides design when building new code; likewise, test case refactoring guides the improvement of design during refactoring.

8.5.4 Refactoring Test Code

In our study of the video store example, we saw that many refactorings on the code level can be completed by applying a corresponding refactoring on the test case level. For example, to avoid *Indirect Testing*, the refactoring *Move Method* should be followed by "*Move Test*". Likewise, in many cases *Extract Method* should be followed by "*Extract Test*". To retain the documentation value of the unit tests, their structure should be in sync with the structure of the source code.

In our opinion, it makes sense to extend the existing descriptions of refactorings with suggestions on what to do with the corresponding unit tests, for example in the "mechanics" part.

The topic of refactoring test code is discussed extensively in Section 8.4. An issue of concern when changing test code is that we may "lose" test cases. When refactoring production code, the availability of tests forms a safety net that guards us from accidentally losing code, but such a safety net is not in place when modifying test code. A solution is to measure coverage [346] before and after changing the tests, e.g. with the help of Clover [108] or Emma [469]. One step further is *mutation testing*, using a tool such as Jester [379, 470]. Jester automatically makes changes to conditions and literals in Java source code. If the code is well-tested, such changes should lead to failing tests. Running Jester before and after test case refactorings helps to verify that the changes did not affect test coverage.

8.5.5 Refactoring Sessions

The meaningful unit of refactoring is a sequence of steps involving changes to both the code base and the test base. We propose the notion of a *refactoring session* to capture such a sequence. It consists of the following steps:

1. Detect *smells* in the code or test code that need to be fixed. In test-driven refactoring, the test set is the starting point for finding such smells.
2. Identify candidate refactorings addressing the smell.
3. Ensure that all existing tests run.
4. Apply the selected refactoring to the code. Provide a backwards compatible interface if the refactoring falls in category D. Only change the associated test classes when the refactoring falls in category E.
5. Ensure that all existing tests run. Consider applying mutation testing to assess the coverage of the test cases.
6. Apply the testing counterpart of the selected refactoring.
7. Ensure that the modified tests still run. Check that the coverage has not changed.
8. Extend the test cases now that the underlying code has become easier to test.
9. Ensure the new tests run.

The integrity of the code is ensured since (1) all tests are run between each step; (2) each step changes either code or tests, but never both at the same time (unless this is impossible).

8.6 Measuring Code and Test Code

In the previous sections we have seen how test suites affect program comprehension, how test suites themselves can be subjected to refactoring, and how refactoring of the production code is reflected in the test code. The last thing we investigate is whether there is a relation (correlation) between certain properties of the production code and those of the test code. We look at one property in particular, namely the *testability* of production code, based on our earlier work on finding testability metrics for Java systems [89].

For our investigation, we take advantage of the popularity of the JUnit framework [262]. JUnit's typical usage scenario is to test each Java class C by means of a dedicated test class C_T, generating pairs of the form $\langle C, C_T \rangle$. The route then that we pursue is to use these pairs to find source code metrics on C that are good predictors of test-related metrics on C_T.

To elaborate this route, we first define the notion of testability that we address, then describe the experimental design that can be used to explore the hypothesis, followed by a discussion of initial experimental results.

8.6.1 Testability

The ISO defines testability as "attributes of software that bear on the effort needed to validate the software product" [240]. Binder [65] offers an analysis of the various factors that contribute to a system's testability, which he visualizes using the fish bone diagram as shown in Figure 8.4. The major factors determining test effort that Binder distinguishes include the test adequacy criterion that is required, the usefulness of the documentation, the quality of the implementation, the reusability and structure of the test suite, the suitability of the test tools used, and the process capabilities.

Of these factors, we are concerned with the structure of the implementation, and with source code factors in particular. One group of factors we distinguish are *test case generation* factors, which influence the *number* of test cases required. An example is the testing criterion (test all branches, test all inherited methods), but directly related are characteristics of the code itself (use of if-then-else statements, use of inheritance). The other group of factors we distinguish are *test case construction factors*, which are related to the effort needed to create a particular test case. Such factors include the complexity of creating instances for a given class, or the number of fields that need to be initialized.

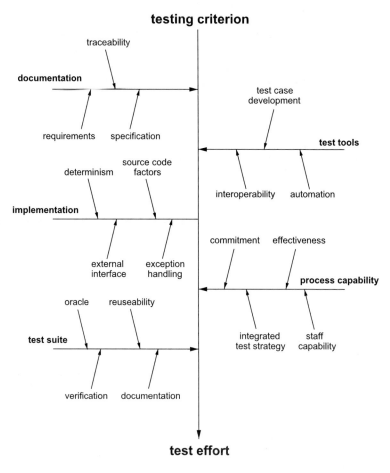

Fig. 8.4. The testability fish-bone [65, 89]

8.6.2 Experimental Design

Our goal is to assess the capability of a suite of object-oriented metrics to predict testing effort. We assess this capability from a class level perspective, i.e., we assess whether or not the values of object-oriented metrics for a given class can predict the required amount of effort needed for unit testing that class. The particular environment in which we conduct the experiments consists of Java systems that are unit tested at the class level using the JUnit testing framework.

To help us translate the goal into measurements, we pose questions that pertain to the goal:

Question 1: Are the values of the object-oriented metrics for a class associated with the required testing effort for that class?

To answer this question, we must first quantify "testing effort." To indicate the testing effort required for a class we use the size of the corresponding test suite. Well-known cost models such as Boehm's COCOMO [72] and Putnam's SLIM model [421] relate development cost and effort to software size. Test suites are software in their own right; they have to be developed and maintained just like 'normal' software. Below we will see which metrics we use to measure the size of a test suite.

Next, we can refine our original question, and obtain the following new question:

Question 2: Are the values of the object-oriented metrics for a class associated with the size of the corresponding test suite?

From these questions we can derive a hypothesis that our experiments test:

$\mathbf{H_0}(m,n)$**:** There is *no* association between object-oriented metric m and test suite metric n,

$\mathbf{H_1}(m,n)$**:** There is an association between object-oriented metric m and test suite metric n,

where m ranges over our set of object-oriented metrics, and n over our set of test-suite based metrics.

As a candidate set of object-oriented metrics, we use the suite proposed by Binder [65] as a starting point. Binder is interested in testability as well, and uses a model distinguishing "complexity" and "scope" factors, which are similar to our test case construction and generation factors. The metrics used by Binder are based on the well known metrics suite provided by Chidamber and Kemerer [111], who for some of their metrics (such as the Coupling Between Objects and the Response for Class) already suggested that they would have a bearing on test effort. The metrics that we have used in our experiments are listed in Table 8.5.

For our experiments we propose the dLOCC (Lines Of Code for Class) and dNOTC (Number of Test Cases) metrics to indicate the size of a test suite. The 'd' prepended to the names of these metrics denotes that they are the *dependent* variables of our experiment, i.e., the variables we want to predict. The dLOCC metric is defined like the LOCC metric.

Table 8.5. Metrics suite used for assessing testability of a class c

Metric	Description
DIT	Depth of inheritance tree
FOUT	Fan out, nr of classes used by c
LCOM	Lack of cohesion in methods—which measures how fields are used in methods
LOCC	Lines of code per class
NOC	Number of children
NOF	Number of fields
NOM	Number of methods
RFC	Response for class—Methods in c plus the number of methods invoked by c.
WMC	Weighted methods per class—sum of McCabe's cyclomatic complexity number of all methods.

The dNOTC metric provides a different perspective on the size of a test suite. It is calculated by counting the number of invocations of JUnit 'assert' methods that occur in the code of a test class. JUnit provides the tester with a number of different 'assert' methods, for example 'assertTrue', 'assertFalse' or 'assertEqual'. The operation of these methods is the same; the parameters passed to the method are tested for compliance to some condition, depending on the specific variant. For example, 'assertTrue' tests whether or not its parameter evaluates to 'true'. If the parameters do not satisfy the condition, the framework generates an exception that indicates a test has failed. Thus, the tester uses the set of JUnit 'assert' methods to compare the expected behavior of the class-under-test to its current behavior. Counting the number of invocations of 'assert' methods, gives the number of comparisons between expected and current behavior which we consider an appropriate definition of a test case.

Conducting the measurements yields a series of values $\langle m,n \rangle$ of object-oriented metric m and test suite metric n for a series of pairs $\langle C,C_T \rangle$ of a class C and its corresponding test class C_T. To test the hypotheses, we calculate Spearman's rank-order correlation (which does not require a normal distribution of the data), yielding values $r_s(m,n)$ for metrics m and n. The significance (related to the number of observations made) of the value of r_s found is subsequently determined by calculating the t-statistic, yielding a value p indicating the chance that the observed value is the result of a chance event, allowing us to accept $H_1(m,n)$ with confidence level $1 - p$.

8.6.3 Experimental Results

Experiments were conducted on five software systems, of which four were closed source software products developed at the Software Improvement Group (SIG)[6]. Additionally, we included Apache Ant [18], an open source automation tool for software development. All systems are written in Java and the systems totaled over 290 KLOC.

---

[6] http://www.sig.nl.

The key results for the Ant case study are shown in Table 8.6; similar results were obtained for the other case studies. The experiment shows that there is a significant correlation between test level metrics dLOCC (Lines of Code for Class) and dNOT (Number of Testcases) and various class level metrics:

- There are several metrics related to *size*, in particular LOCC, NOM, and WMC. Since size can be considered a test case generation (we need more test cases) as well as a test case construction factor (larger classes become harder to test), it is natural that these metrics are correlated with test effort.
- The inheritance related metrics DIT (depth of inheritance tree) and NOC (number of subclasses) are *not* correlated with test metrics. In principle, test strategies in which, for example, extra subclasses lead to more intensive testing of the superclass, could cause NOC or DIT to be predictors of test effort. Apparently in the case studies these strategies were not adopted.
- Two metrics measuring external dependencies are Fan Out (FOUT) and Response-for-Class (RFC). Both are clearly correlated with both test suite metrics.
- The metrics LCOM (Lack of Cohesion of Methods) and NOF (Number of Fields) are correlated with the test metrics for the Ant case as well, but not for the four commercial case studies. One can expect NOF to be an indicator for test effort, for example, for initializing fields in a class. In cases where NOF is not an indicator, this may be due to the fact that the NOF metric only measures fields introduced in a particular class, and not fields inherited from superclasses.

Based on these findings, we conclude with the following observation:

Observation 6   Traditional object-oriented source code metrics applied to production code can indicate the effort needed for developing unit tests.

We refer to Bruntink and Van Deursen for a full account of the experiments described above [89].

Table 8.6. Correlation values and confidence levels found for Ant

r_s	dLOCC	dNOTC		p	dLOCC	dNOTC
DIT	-.0456	-.201		DIT	.634	.0344
FOUT	.465	.307		**FOUT**	< .01	< .01
LCOM	.437	.382		**LCOM**	< .01	< .01
LOCC	.500	.325		**LOCC**	< .01	< .01
NOC	.0537	-.0262		NOC	.575	.785
NOF	.455	.294		**NOF**	< .01	< .01
NOM	.532	.369		**NOM**	< .01	< .01
RFC	.526	.341		**RFC**	< .01	< .01
WMC	.531	.348		**WMC**	< .01	< .01

8.7 Concluding Remarks

In this section we first look back on the interplay between software testing and evolution. We then present a research agenda with a number of future research tracks, which are currently left unexplored.

8.7.1 Retrospective

Based upon *Observation 1* (see page 177), which states that an extensive test suite can stimulate the program comprehension process in the light of continuously evolving software, we have investigated the interactions between software evolution, software testing and program comprehension that exist in extreme programming in Section 8.3. Naturally, some (or all) of these elements are used in other development processes as well. For example, Humphrey stresses the importance of inspections, software quality assurance, and testing [236]. The Rational Unified Process emphasizes short iterations, architecture centric software development, and use cases [299]. Key publications on extreme programming [50, 254, 48] cover many issues related to comprehension, such as code expressing intent, feedback from the system, and tests to document code.

From our observation that test code has a distinct set of smells (see *Observation 2*, page 180), we looked at test code from the perspective of refactoring. Our own experiences are that the quality of test code is not as high as the quality of the production code. Test code was not refactored as mercilessly as production code, following Fowler's advice that it is acceptable to copy and edit test code, trusting our ability to refactor out truly common items later [183, p. 102]. When at a later stage we started refactoring test code more intensively, we discovered that test code has its own set of problems (which we translated into smells) as well as its own repertoire of solutions (which we formulated as test refactorings).

For each test smell that we identified, we have provided a solution, using either a potentially specialized variant of an existing refactoring from Fowler [183] or a dedicated test refactoring. We believe that the resulting smells and refactorings provide a valuable starting point for a larger collection based on a broader set of projects. This is in line with our *Observation 3* (see page 180).

Observation 4 (see page 185) states that when applying the refactorings as proposed by Fowler [183] on production code, a classification can be made based on whether these refactorings necessitate refactoring the test code as well. In Section 8.5 we have analyzed which of the documented refactorings affect the test code. It turns out that the majority of the refactorings are in category D (requiring explicit actions to keep the interface compatible) and E (necessarily requiring a change to the test code). We have shown the implications of refactoring tests with the help of Fowler's video store example. We then proposed the notion of *test-driven refactoring*, which uses the existing test cases as the starting point for finding suitable code level refactorings.

We have argued for the need to extend the descriptions of refactorings with a section on their implications on the corresponding test code. If the tests are to maintain their documentation value, they should be kept in sync with the structure of the code. As outlined in *Observation 5* (see page 185), we propose, as a first step, the notion of a *refactoring session*, capturing a coherent series of separate steps involving changes to both the production and the test code.

The impact of program structure on test structure is further illustrated through *Observation 6* (page 197), which suggests that traditional object-oriented metrics can be used to estimate test effort. We described an experiment to assess which metrics can be used for this purpose. Note that some of the metrics identified (such as fan-out or response-for-class) are also indicators for class complexity. This suggests that high values for such metrics may call for refactorings, which in turn may help to reduce the test effort required for unit testing these classes.

From our studies we have learned that the interplay between software evolution and software testing is often more complex than meets the eye. The interplay that we witnessed works in two directions: software evolution is hindered by the fact that when evolving a system, the tests often need to co-evolve, making the evolution more difficult and time-intensive. On the other hand, many software evolution operations cannot safely take place without adequate tests being present to enable a safety net. This leads to an almost paradoxical situation where tests are essential for evolving software, yet at the same time, they are obstructing that very evolution.

Another important factor in this interplay is *program comprehension*, or the process of building up knowledge about a system under study, which is of critical importance during software evolution. In this context, having a test suite available can be a blessing, as the tests provide documentation about how the software works. At the same time, when no tests are available, writing tests to understand the software is a good way of building up comprehension.

We have seen that software evolution and testing are intertwined at the very core of (re)engineering software systems and continue to provide interesting and challenging research topics.

8.7.2 Research Agenda

During our study we came across a number of research ideas in the area of software testing and software evolution that are as yet still unexplored. The topics we propose can be seen as an addition or refinement to the topics that were addressed by Harrold in her "Testing: A Roadmap" [224].

Model Driven Engineering

MDE [453] is a modeling activity, whereby the traditional activity of writing code manually is replaced by modeling specifications for the application. Code generation techniques then use these models to generate (partial) code models of the application. This setup ensures the alignment between the models and the executable implementation. A similar approach can be followed when it comes to testing the application: modeling both the application and the tests through specifications. Muccini et al. consider this as the next logical step [381]. Recently, Pickin et al. have picked up on this research topic in the context of distributed systems [415].

Aspect Oriented Programming

AOP [276] is a programming paradigm that aims to offer an added layer of abstraction that can modularize system-level concerns (also see Chapter 9). However, when these aspects are woven into the base code, some unexpected effects can occur that are difficult to oversee. This can happen (1) when the pointcut is not defined precisely enough, resulting in an aspect being woven in at an unexpected place in the base program, or (2) because of unexpected results because of aspect composition, when the advice of two separate aspects is woven in. McEachen et al. describe a number of possible fault scenarios that can occur [357], but further research into this area is certainly warranted to prevent such fault scenarios through testing.

Test Case Isomorphism

Various sources indicate that test cases should be independent of each other because this decreases testing time, increases test output comprehensibility and having concise and focused tests increases their benefit as documentation of a specific aspect of the code [149, 131].

As said, having concise and focused tests decreases the testing time, which partly alleviates the problem of having to do selective regression testing [444, 445]. Another problem situation that is overcome, is the one described by Gaelli et al., whereby broken unit tests are ordered, so that the most specific unit test can be dealt with first [189].

Research questions of interest are how we can characterize and measure this isomorphism and what refactorings can be used to improve this isomorphism. These are related to detecting and removing the test implication smell described earlier.

Service-Orientation

The current trend is to build software systems from loosely coupled components or services (see Chapter 7). These services have mostly not been designed to co-exist with each other from their phase of inception and their "integration" often depends on the configuration of parameters at run-time. Although the components (or services) themselves will probably be of a higher quality, due to the fact that these are shared by many different projects (this can e.g. be in the case of *Commercial Off The Shelf* (COTS) components), testing the integration of these components or services is all the more important.

Although work related to testing components [212, 539] is readily available, not so much can be found on testing service-orientation. Although it is probable that many existing testing techniques can be adapted to work in this context, additional research is warranted. One of the first attempts at tool support for testing services is Coyote [507]. Commercial tool-support comes from SOAPSonar and Ikto's LISA and also Apache's Jakarta JMeter is useful when testing services [467].

Empirical Studies

Although many testing techniques are currently in circulation, there are few academic publications documenting how these testing techniques are exactly used and combined in industrial projects. Performing empirical studies that involve professional software developers and testers can lead to a better understanding of how software testing techniques or strategies are used (e.g., the study of Erdogmus et al. [161]). The results from this research can be used to build the next generation of testing techniques and test tools. An added benefit of this line of research is that by providing cutting-edge testing techniques to the industrial partners helps with knowledge and technology transfer about testing from academia to industry.

Repository Mining

The a posteriori analysis of software evolution, through the mining of e.g. versioning systems, provides a view on how the software *has* evolved and on how the software *might* evolve in the future (also see Chapter 3).

Up until recently however, no specific research has been carried out in this context that looks at the co-evolution of the software system and its associated test suite. Zaidman et al. performed an initial study on how this co-evolution happens in open source software systems [562]. They offer three separate views that show (1) the commit behavior of the developers, (2) the growth evolution of the system and (3) the coverage through time. The major observation that was made is that testing is mostly a *phased* activity, whereas development is more continuous.

In the same context, further research might provide answers to questions such as:
- Is every change to the production code backed up by a change to the test suite? Are there specific reasons why this should or should not happen?
- Can IDE's provide warnings when adaptations to the production code lead to reduced quality of the test suite?

Test Coverage

Even when continuous testing is becoming more and more commonplace in the development process [448], determining the test coverage [346, Chapter 7] is often not part of the fixed testing routine. In combination with the findings of Elbaum et al. [159], who have determined that even minor changes to production code can have a serious impact on the test coverage, this might lead to situations where the testing effort might prove to be insufficient. As such, the development of features in integrated developments environments that preemptively warn against drops in test coverage will lead to a more efficient and thorough test process.

Regression Testing

Regression testing provides you with a safety net when letting software evolve, because it guards against introducing bugs into functionality that previously worked fine. Ideally, these tests should be run after each modification, but regression testing is often very expensive. Rothermel and Harrold provide a detailed survey of research in regression testing techniques, particularly in the domain of *selective* regression testing [445], where only that part of the regression test pertaining to the modification is re-run. Although selective regression testing can save costs, the process of determining which tests should be re-run is still expensive and the ultimate gain is thus relatively small. Further research into this topic is certainly warranted.

9

Evolution Issues in Aspect-Oriented Programming

Kim Mens[1] and Tom Tourwé[2]

[1] Université catholique de Louvain, Belgium
[2] Eindhoven University of Technology, The Netherlands

Summary. This chapter identifies evolution-related issues and challenges in aspect-oriented programming. It can serve as a guideline for adopters of aspect technology to get a better idea of the evolution issues they may confront sooner or later, of the risks involved, and of the state-of-the-art in the techniques currently available to help them in addressing these issues. We focus in particular on the programming level, although some of the issues and challenges addressed may apply to earlier software development life-cycle phases as well. The discussed issues range from the exploration of crosscutting concerns in legacy code, via the migration of this code to an aspect-oriented solution, to the maintenance and evolution of the final aspect-oriented program over time. We discuss state-of-the-art techniques which address the issues of aspect exploration, extraction and evolution, and point out several issues for which no adequate solutions exist yet. We conclude that, even though some promising techniques are currently being investigated, due to the relative immaturity of the research domain many of the techniques are not out of the lab as yet.

9.1 Introduction

Just like the industrial adoption of object orientation in the early nineties led to a demand for migrating software systems to an object-oriented solution—triggering a boost of research on software evolution, reverse engineering, reengineering and restructuring—the same is currently happening for the aspect-oriented paradigm. *Aspect-oriented software development* (AOSD) is a novel paradigm that addresses the problem of the *tyranny of the dominant decomposition* [490]. This problem refers to a software engineer's inability to represent in a modular way certain concerns in a given software system, when those concerns do not fit the chosen decomposition of the software in modules. Such concerns are said to be *crosscutting* as they cut across the dominant decomposition of the software. Consequently, the source code implementing crosscutting concerns gets *scattered* across and *tangled* with the source code of other concerns. Typical examples of crosscutting concerns are tracing [88], exception handling [91] or transaction management [164].

In absence of aspect-oriented programming techniques, crosscutting concerns often lead to duplicated code fragments throughout the software system. As argued by

T. Mens, S. Demeyer (eds.), *Software Evolution.*
DOI 10.1007/978-3-540-76440-3, © Springer 2008

Koschke in Chapter 2, duplication tends to have a negative impact on software quality. Crosscutting concerns are thus believed to negatively affect evolvability, maintainability and understandability, because understanding and changing a crosscutting concern requires touching many different places in the source code. Although the few studies that have explored this negative relation between crosscutting concerns and software quality do not contradict this claim (see Subsection 9.3.3), there is currently not enough empirical evidence of this claim yet. Nevertheless, aspect-oriented programming (AOP) does propose a solution to this acclaimed problem by introducing the notion of *aspects*, which are designated language constructs that allow a developer to localise a concern's implementation, and thus improve modularity, understandability, maintainability and evolvability of the code.

Adopting a new software development technology brings about particular risks, however, and aspect-oriented programming forms no exception. In his article "AOP myths and realities" [302], Laddad refutes 15 often-heard 'myths' that are said to hinder the adoption of AOP, such as "debugging aspects is hard" and "aspects cannot be unit tested". As convincing as his arguments may be, they mainly focus on currently existing AOP technology, and try to prove it sufficiently mature for widespread adoption.

However, a much larger opportunity and obstacle for adopting AOP technology is the fact that it has to be introduced into *existing* software systems. Most software systems today are not developed from scratch, but rather are enhanced and maintained *legacy systems*. Awareness is growing that aspects can and should be used not only to modularise crosscutting concerns in newly developed software; the vast majority of existing software systems suffers from the tyranny of the dominant decomposition as well, making them hard to maintain and evolve. As such, legacy software systems form an important range of applications which may benefit from the advantages that AOP claims to offer. We predict that real widespread adoption of AOP will only be achieved if the risks and consequences of adopting AOP in existing software are studied, and if the necessary tools and techniques are available for dealing with those risks.

This chapter addresses the issues and challenges related to such adoption of AOP from a software evolution perspective. We present a series of questions and challenges that are relevant to new adopters of aspect technology in an evolutionary context and summarise existing research that addresses some of these issues. In this way, potential adopters are given an overview of the existing research efforts and can assess the usefulness and maturity of existing tools and techniques. Additionally, fellow researchers are presented with an overview of the research domain, which can help them in posing new research questions and tackling problems still left open.

As illustrated by Figure 9.1 we distinguish 3 different phases: *aspect exploration*[3], *aspect extraction* and *aspect evolution*.

---

[3] As in the survey paper [272], we deliberately reserve the term *aspect mining* for the more specific activity of (semi-)automatically identifying aspect candidates from the source code of a software system. We propose the term *aspect exploration* as a more general term which does not imply these restrictions and also encompasses manual approaches as well as techniques that try to discover aspects from earlier software life-cycle artefacts.

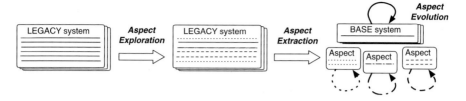

Fig. 9.1. Software evolution and AOSD

Aspect exploration. Before introducing aspects in existing software, one should explore whether that software actually exhibits any crosscutting concerns that are worthwhile being extracted into aspects. The tyranny of the dominant decomposition implies that large software is likely to contain crosscutting concerns. During the aspect exploration phase we try to discover *aspect candidates* in the software, i.e., we try to discover what the crosscutting concerns are, where and how they are implemented, and what their impact on the software's quality is.

Aspect extraction. Once the crosscutting concerns have been identified and their impact on software quality has been assessed, we can consider migrating the software to an aspect-oriented version. We refer to this activity as aspect extraction. If we do decide to migrate the software towards an aspect-oriented solution, we need a way of turning the aspect candidates, i.e., the crosscutting concerns that were identified in the exploration phase, into actual aspects. At the same time, we need techniques for testing the migrated software to make sure that the new version of the software still works as expected, as well as techniques to manage the migration step, for example to ensure that we can still keep on using the software during the transition phase.

Aspect evolution. According to Belady and Lehman's first *law of software evolution* [320], every software system that is used will continuously undergo changes or become useless after a period of time. There is no reason to believe that this law does not hold for aspect-oriented software too. But to what extent is evolution of aspect-oriented software different from evolution of traditional software? Can the same techniques that are used to support evolution of traditional software be applied to aspect-oriented software? Do the new abstraction mechanisms introduced by AOP give rise to new types of evolution problems that require radically different solutions?

Before taking a closer look at each of these phases, in Section 9.2 we provide a brief introduction to AOP for the non-initiated readers. In the subsequent three sections we then discuss the challenges, risks and issues related to each of the three phases of aspect exploration, extraction and evolution. Each section has the same format:

1. *Rationale:* A more precise description and definition of the activity, and why it is important and needed, from an end-user perspective.

2. *Challenges and risks:* What are the challenges and risks that need to be dealt with or will be encountered when conducting this activity?
3. *Existing techniques:* What existing techniques help in supporting the activity? What challenges do these techniques address and to what extent?
4. *Open issues:* To what extent do available techniques address the aforementioned risks and challenges? What challenges and risks are not addressed by any technique?
5. *Case study:* To obtain a better intuition of some of the issues, challenges and risks pertaining to the activity, we discuss some of our experiences gained on a realistic case.

9.2 Aspect-Oriented Programming

The goal of aspect-oriented programming is to provide an advanced modularisation scheme to separate the core functionality of a software system from system-wide concerns that cut across the implementation of this core functionality. To this extent, AOP introduces a new abstraction mechanism, called an aspect. An aspect is a special kind of module that represents a crosscutting concern. Aspects are defined independently from the core functionality of the system and integrated with that *base program* by means of a dedicated *aspect weaver*, a dedicated tool similar to a compiler that merges aspect code and base code in the appropriate way. Figure 9.2 illustrates this idea.

In most current-day aspect languages, of which AspectJ is the most well-known, aspects are composed of *pointcuts* and *advices*. Whereas advices correspond to the

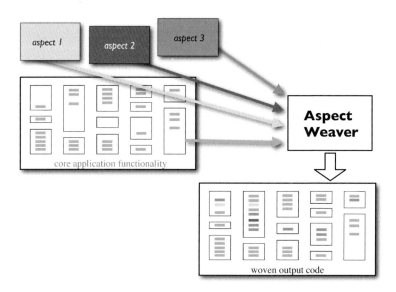

Fig. 9.2. The AOP idea

```
class Point extends Shape {

  public void setX(int x) throws IllegalArgumentException {
    if ( x < MIN_X || x > MAX_X )
      throw new IllegalArgumentException("x is out of bounds.");
    ...
  }
  public void setY(int y) throws IllegalArgumentException {
    if ( y < MIN_Y || y > MAX_Y )
      throw new IllegalArgumentException("y is out of bounds.");
    ...
  }
}

class FigureElement extends Shape {

  public void  setXY(int, int) throws IllegalArgumentException {
    if ( x < MIN_X || x > MAX_X )
      throw new IllegalArgumentException("x is out of bounds.");
    if ( y < MIN_Y || y > MAX_Y )
      throw new IllegalArgumentException("y is out of bounds.");
    ...
  }
}
```

Fig. 9.3. Bounds checking concern for moving points

code fragments that would crosscut an entire program, pointcuts correspond to the
locations in the source code of the program where the advice will be applied (i.e.,
where the crosscutting code will be woven). A pointcut essentially specifies a set
of *joinpoints*, which are well-defined locations in the structure or execution flow of
a program where an aspect can weave in its advice code. Typical AspectJ joinpoints
are method invocations or field accesses, for example.

To illustrate these notions, consider the Java code fragments in Figure 9.3 that
implement bounds checking for operations that move points in a graphical drawing
application. Because the application has been decomposed into classes and methods according to the different graphical elements that can be drawn, such as points
and figures, the bounds checking code cuts across this dominant decomposition
and does not align with these classes and methods. This results in scattering and
tangling: bounds checking code is implemented in different methods and classes,
which clutters and interferes with the other code implemented by those methods and
classes.

To modularise this bound checking concern, a PointBoundsChecking aspect can
be defined as in Figure 9.4. For didactic purposes, we kept the definition of this aspect very simple; a more intelligent definition is given further on. This code defines
two pointcuts: the setX pointcut captures all executions of methods that change the
x value, while the setY pointcut captures all executions of methods that change the
y value. In addition to these pointcuts, the advice code is defined: the first 'before'

```
aspect PointBoundsChecking {

  pointcut setX(int x):
    (execution(void FigureElement.setXY(int, int)) && args(x, *))
    || (execution(void Point.setX(int)) && args(x));

  before(int x): setX(x) {
    if ( x < MIN_X || x > MAX_X )
      throw new IllegalArgumentException("x is out of bounds.");
  }

  pointcut setY(int y):
    (execution(void FigureElement.setXY(int, int)) && args(*, y))
    || (execution(void Point.setY(int)) && args(y));

  before(int y): setY(y) {
    if ( y < MIN_Y || y > MAX_Y )
      throw new IllegalArgumentException("y is out of bounds.");
  }
}
```

Fig. 9.4. An extensional bounds checking aspect

advice specifies that before every execution of a method captured by the setX point-cut, the appropriate bound needs to be checked. The advice for the setY pointcut is defined analogously.

Note that the advice code references an actual parameter of the method it advices in order to check its value, i.e., the x and y parameters. The pointcut exposes this parameter to the advice code, by providing an appropriate name. Moreover, when the method has more than one parameter, as is the case for the setXY method, the pointcut needs to make sure that the appropriate parameter is exposed. All this is achieved by using the args construct. For example, args(x, *) exposes the variable x, which corresponds to the first argument of the method, to the advice code. Similarly, args(*,y) exposes a variable y that corresponds to the last argument of the method.

The setX and setY pointcuts defined in Figure 9.4 are examples of *extensional* or *enumeration-based* pointcuts, since they explicitly enumerate the signatures of *all* methods they need to capture. Such pointcuts are brittle and can break easily when the base program evolves. More robust pointcut definitions can be obtained by mentioning explicitly only the information that is absolutely required and using wildcard patterns to hide implementation details that do not matter. For instance, in Figure 9.5 we use the wildcard * to hide the exact return types of the method joinpoints and the pattern Shape+ to hide the precise name of the implementing class while still requiring that it belongs to the Shape class hierarchy. However, we do not use a wildcard in the method names, but match against the exact names, because their intension-revealing nature is likely to help us in capturing the correct pointcuts. Using more abstract names might result in accidentally capturing the wrong joinpoints.

```
pointcut setX(int x):
   (execution(* Shape+.setXY(int, int)) && args(x, *))
   || (execution(* Shape+.setX(int)) && args(x));

pointcut setY(int y):
   (execution(* Shape+.setXY(int, int)) && args(*, y))
   || (execution(* Shape+.setY(int)) && args(y));
```

Fig. 9.5. An intensional pointcut definition for the bounds checking aspect

Pointcuts that use wildcards patterns or other mechanisms to abstract over certain implementation details are called *intensional* or *pattern-based* pointcuts. They are said to be more robust toward evolution, because of the abstractions they use. For example, when a setXY method would be added to another class in the Shape hierarchy, it will still be adviced and the bounds of its parameters will be checked. Similarly, when the return type of such a method would change, it would still be captured by the pointcut.

In summary, pointcuts, whether they are extensional or intensional, specify those places in the code or its execution where the advice code needs to be woven. This means that aspects are not *explicitly* invoked by the program. The *base program* (i.e., the program without the aspects) is not aware of the aspects that apply to it. Instead, it is the aspects themselves that specify when and where they act on the program. This has been referred to as the *obliviousness* property of aspect orientation [176], and is one of the most essential characteristics of an aspect-oriented programming language.

9.3 Aspect Exploration

Migrating a legacy software system into an aspect-oriented one is a non-trivial endeavour. The sheer size and complexity of many existing systems, combined with the lack of documentation and knowledge of such systems render it practically infeasible to *manually* transform their crosscutting concerns into aspects. To alleviate this problem, a growing body of research exists that proposes a number of tools and techniques to assist software engineers in semi-automatically migrating crosscutting concerns to aspects. Most of these approaches distinguish two phases in this migration process: aspect exploration and aspect extraction. Whereas Section 9.4 will focus on the aspect extraction phase, the current section discusses issues and challenges related to aspect exploration, as well as existing techniques to address some of those issues.

9.3.1 Rationale

We define *aspect exploration* as the activity of identifying and analysing the crosscutting concerns in a non aspect-oriented system. A distinction can be made between manual exploration supported by special-purpose browsers and source-code navigation tools, on the one hand, and aspect mining techniques that try to automate this process of aspect discovery and propose their user one or more aspect candidates, on the other hand.

9.3.2 Challenges and Risks

What (Kind of) Crosscutting Concerns Can Be Discovered?

Examples of crosscutting concerns that are often mentioned in literature, and exemplified by small-scale example projects, include simple and basic functionalities like tracing, logging or precondition checking. Do such simple concerns actually occur in industrial code? Is AOP only suited to implement such simple concerns? Do industrial software systems contain more complex crosscutting concerns? How good is AOP at tackling those?

How Are Crosscutting Concerns Implemented in Absence of Aspects?

Since crosscutting concerns in a traditional software system are per definition not well-localised, they need to be implemented over and over again. To minimise this implementation overhead, developers tend to rely on a variety of programming idioms and naming and coding conventions. What (kind of) crosscutting concerns are implemented by which programming idioms and conventions?

(How) Do Crosscutting Concerns Affect Software Quality?

When crosscutting concerns occur in a software system, (how) do they affect the quality of that software? How can we measure their impact on quality factors like understandability, maintainability and adaptability? How can these measures help us assess whether extracting the concerns into aspects is beneficial?

How to Find Where Crosscutting Concerns Are Located in the Code?

When we want to turn a crosscutting concern into an aspect, we need to know where exactly it is located in the code. This knowledge is important to determine an appropriate pointcut for the extracted aspect. How can we be sure that we have found all relevant crosscutting concerns, that we have covered them completely, that there are no false positives or negatives?

9.3.3 Existing Research

Over the last few years, aspect exploration has become quite an active research domain and a whole range of different approaches, techniques and tools for supporting or automating the activity of aspect exploration have been proposed.

Crosscutting Concerns in Practice

In most research papers, tutorials and textbooks on AOP, the examples of crosscutting concerns given show simple and basic concerns (like logging), implemented in small-scale software systems or as illustrative examples only. Consequently, one may wonder whether more complex concerns exist, whether such concerns actually occur in industrial software systems, and whether AOP is only suited for addressing simple small-scale crosscutting concerns.

Several examples of more complex crosscutting concerns occurring in real-world software have been described in literature as well, however. Bruntink et al. [91] discuss how *exception handling* is a crosscutting concern in a large-scale embedded software system, and show how its implementation is prone to errors. Colyer and Clement [122] present a study in which they separated support for Enterprise Java-Beans from the other functionality contained within an application server of several millions of lines of code. Coady et al. [118] refactored the *prefetching* concern from the FreeBSD UNIX operating system kernel.

This shows that complex crosscutting concerns do occur in practice, and that large-scale industrial software systems also exhibit such concerns. Hence, when exploring a system for crosscutting concerns, one should not limit the search for well-known concerns only, but one should look for scattered and tangled code of any nature.

Implementing Crosscutting Concerns

Since crosscutting concerns are not well-modularised, to reduce the effort of implementing, maintaining and evolving them developers rely on *structural regularities* like naming and coding conventions, programming idioms and design patterns.

Bruntink et al. [88, 91, 90] discuss an industrial software system that implements crosscutting concerns by means of programming idioms. Idioms are simple code templates for the implementation of a concern, that are prescribed in architecture manuals and that a developer can copy-paste and then adapt to his particular needs and wishes. The bounds checking concern presented in the previous section is an example of such an idiom: all methods that move points need to test the new value first, and need to raise the appropriate exception whenever the value is not within a specified range. As the authors observed, such an approach leads to code duplication, is prone to errors and is time- and effort-consuming.

In [364], we observed that, when implementing crosscutting concerns, developers often rely on naming conventions and thus provide valuable hints about the locations of such crosscutting concerns. We studied the JHotDraw application framework and grouped classes and methods that share identifiers in their name. This lightweight approach turned out to be capable of detecting several interesting concerns, such as for example an *Undo* and a *Persistence* concern. Shepherd et al [460] discuss a similar approach based on *lexical chaining*, a natural language processing technique, to identify crosscutting concerns in the PetStore application.

Marin et al. [347] introduce *crosscutting concern sorts*, a classification system for crosscutting functionality. For each sort of crosscutting concern they indicate how it could be implemented by using traditional modularisation mechanisms. For example, they define a *role superimposition* sort, a construction that implements a specific secondary role or responsibility for a class, and observed that this is often implemented by using interfaces (in Java). Other examples of implementation techniques that are used to implement sorts are several design patterns, such as the Observer, Decorator and Adapter design pattern, and a design by contract approach in a language that supports explicit pre- and postconditions.

Again, when exploring a software system for crosscutting concerns and reasoning about them, discovering such regularities helps. Additionally, such information is also useful for program comprehension, as it provides interesting information on how the software is structured.

Crosscutting Concerns and Software Quality

Few studies exist that explore the relation between crosscutting concerns and software quality.

Bruntink et al. [91, 90] assessed the quality of the *exception handling* and *parameter checking* concerns, implemented by means of idioms in an industrial context. They observed that the implementation of both concerns exhibited several faults, but were unable to conclude whether these were due to the crosscutting nature of the implementation or to the inherent complexity of the concern itself. Moreover, they acknowledge that faults are not failures, and hence they are not sure about the severity of the discovered faults.

Kulesza et al. [300] performed a study in which they computed metrics for both object-oriented and aspect-oriented versions of a medium-scale software system, and compared them in order to quantify the difference. They observed that the aspect-oriented versions resulted in fewer lines of code, improved separation of concerns, weaker coupling and lower intra-component complexity. However, they also found that the number of operations and components in the aspect-oriented version increased, and observed a lower cohesion for the aspect-oriented components.

A number of authors have studied whether the implementation quality of popular design patterns could be improved by using aspect-oriented programming [222, 193]. It turns out that such an improvement can be achieved, and comes primarily from enhanced modularisation, which makes the implementation more localised, reusable, composable and pluggable. However, these results have been observed in small and illustrative cases only, and no evidence has yet been provided that these results can be generalised to large-scale industrial software.

Gibbs et al. [198] conducted a broad case study where they compared the maintainability and evolvability of a version of a software system that was restructured with traditional abstraction mechanisms against a version of that same system which was restructured by means of aspects. They then considered a 'big bang' type of evolution that implied many changes to the code being crosscut. Their conclusion was that, in the particular case they studied, overall the aspect-oriented version performed either better or not worse than the other (non aspect-oriented) version at dealing with those changes.

Locating Crosscutting Concerns

Kellens et al. [272] distinguish three main categories of techniques that can help in locating the crosscutting concerns in a software system:

Early aspect discovery techniques: Research on 'early aspects' tries to discover aspects in the early phases of the software life-cycle [35] like requirements and domain analysis [34, 431, 492] and architecture design [42]. Although these techniques can help to identify some of the crosscutting concerns in a software system, early aspect discovery techniques may be less promising than approaches that focus on source code, when applied to existing software systems where requirements and architecture documents are often outdated, obsolete or no longer available.

Dedicated browsers: A second class of approaches are the advanced special-purpose code browsers that aid a developer in manually navigating the source code of a system to explore crosscutting concerns. These techniques typically start from a location in the code, a so-called "seed", as point-of-entry from which they guide their users by suggesting other places in the code which might be part of the same concern. This way, the user iteratively constructs a model of the different places in the code that make up a crosscutting concern. Examples of such approaches are Concern Graphs [442], Intensional Views [363], Aspect Browser [211], (Extended) Aspect Mining Tool [221, 563], SoQueT [347] and Prism [564].

Aspect mining techniques: Complementary to dedicated browsers, a number of techniques exist that have as goal to automate the aspect identification process and that propose their user one or more aspect candidates. To this end, they reason about the system's source code or execution traces. All techniques seem to have at least in common that they search for symptoms of crosscutting concerns, using either techniques from data mining and data analysis like formal concept analysis and cluster analysis, or more classic code analysis techniques like program slicing, software metrics and heuristics, clone detection and pattern matching techniques, dynamic analysis, and so on. For an extensive survey and an initial classification of aspect mining techniques which semi-automatically assist a developer in the activity of mining the crosscutting concerns from the source code of an existing system, we refer to [272].

9.3.4 Open Issues

From the discussions in the previous subsection, it is clear that several researchers have studied complex crosscutting concerns that occur in real-world industrial software systems, and that they are starting to get an idea about how such concerns are implemented in the absence of aspect-oriented programming techniques. Nevertheless, more such studies on industrial-size software systems would be welcome. Similarly, although preliminary research attempts have been undertaken for the remaining two challenges (i.e., how crosscutting concerns affect software quality and how to locate them in the software), more research is needed in order to come up with satisfying answers and solutions.

For example, more empirical work and quantitative studies are needed on how crosscutting concerns affect software quality. The impact of crosscutting concerns on software quality factors like evolvability is not yet clear, and has been investigated mostly on small-scale example software only. Part of the problem stems from the fact that AOP is a relatively young paradigm, and hence little historical information (in the form of revision histories etc.) is available for study. Another problem is that, more often than not, a traditional version and an AOP version of the same software system are not available, making it hard to conduct objective comparisons.

As for the identification of crosscutting concerns, all known techniques are only partly automated and still require a significant amount of user intervention. In addition, most aspect mining techniques are only academic prototypes and, with few exceptions, have not been validated on industrial-size software yet. Although this may hinder industrial adoption, the existence of such techniques is obviously a step forward as opposed to having no tool support at all. Another issue with applying automated aspect mining techniques is that preferably the user should have some knowledge about the system being mined for aspects. Indeed, different aspect mining techniques rely on different assumptions about *how* the crosscutting concerns are implemented.

9.3.5 Exploration in Practice

As a concrete practical case study of aspect exploration, in this subsection we summarise a larger experiment that was conducted by Bruntink et al. [92, 93] to evaluate the suitability of clone detection techniques for automatically identifying crosscutting concern code. They considered a single component of a large-scale, industrial software system, consisting of 16,406 non-blank lines of code.

In a first phase, the programmer of this component manually marked five different concerns that occur in it, consisting of 4,182 lines of code, or 25,5% of the total lines of code. The concerns that were considered were memory handling, null pointer checking, range checking, exception handling and tracing. The details are in the second column of Table 9.1.

In a second phase, three different clone detection techniques were applied to the component: an AST-based, a token-based and a PDG-based one. In order to evaluate how well each of the three techniques succeeded in finding the code that implemented the five crosscutting concerns, the third phase then consisted of measuring precision and recall of the results of each of these clone detection techniques with respect to the manually marked occurrences of the different crosscutting concerns. *Recall* was used to evaluate how much of the code of each crosscutting concern was found by each clone detector, while *precision* was used to determine the ratio of

Table 9.1. Line counts and average precision for the five concerns

Concern	Line Count (%)	AST-based	Token-based	PDG-based
Memory handling	750 (4.6%)	.65	.63	.81
Null pointer checking	617 (3.8%)	.99	.97	.80
Range checking	387 (2.4%)	.71	.59	.42
Exception handling	927 (5.7%)	.38	.36	.35
Tracing	1501 (9.1%)	.62	.57	.68

crosscutting concern code to code unrelated to the crosscutting concern found. Table 9.1 shows the average precision of the three clone detection techniques for each of the five concerns considered, whereas Table 9.2 shows their recall.

The results of this experiment were rather disparate. For the null pointer checking concern, which is somewhat similar to the bounds checking example presented earlier, all clone detectors obtained excellent results, identifying all concern code at near-perfect precision and recall, as can be seen from the corresponding rows in Table 9.1 and 9.2.

For the other concerns, such as the exception handling concern, none of the clone detectors achieve satisfying recall and precision, as can be seen from the corresponding rows in Tables 9.1 and 9.2. It appeared that this was related to the amount of tangling of the concerns. Clone detectors achieved higher precision and recall for concerns that exhibited relatively low tangling with other concerns or with the base code, than for concerns that exhibited high tangling.

This experiment illustrates several of the issues identified in subsection 9.3.2. First of all, it shows that simple concerns, such as logging, as well as more complex concerns, such as exception handling, are present in industrial software systems. Second, the experiment shows a particular way of implementing crosscutting concerns in the absence of an aspect-like language constructs: cloning small pieces of idiomatic code. This knowledge was used to verify whether clone detection techniques can be used to identify *where* crosscutting concerns are implemented. Last, the experiment shows some of the effects of crosscutting concerns on software quality. In particular, it confirms the common belief that crosscutting concerns are, at least in some cases, implemented by using similar pieces of code, that are scattered throughout the software. It also shows that up to 25% of the code can be attributed to crosscut-

Table 9.2. Recall for the each of the clone detection techniques on the five concerns

Concern	AST-based	Token-based	PDG-based
Memory handling	.96	.95	.98
Null pointer checking	1.0	1.0	1.0
Range checking	.89	.96	.92
Exception handling	.79	.97	.95
Tracing	.76	.85	.90

ting concern code. The negative effect of code duplication on software quality, and in particular on maintainability and evolvability, has already been investigated (see Chapter 2).

9.4 Aspect Extraction

Once we have identified the crosscutting concerns and have obtained an idea of their impact on code quality, a decision needs to be made whether or not to extract the concern code into aspects. Concerns which occur in only a few places or with limited scattering and tangling, may be less important to extract into aspects than concerns that have a high impact on software quality factors like understandability, modularity and maintainability. You should not feel compelled to migrate towards aspects if there is no real need to. It may be that aspect exploration revealed that there are no significant opportunities for introducing aspects, or that there is no clear evidence that introducing them will improve the quality of your code. Also, even if during aspect exploration some interesting crosscutting concerns were discovered, maybe you are happy with just documenting these crosscutting concerns, and keeping them in sync with the code, using a dedicated environment based on *multi-dimensional separation of concerns* [490], *concern graphs* [442] or *intensional views* [363]. However, when you do decide that it would be useful to actually turn the identified crosscutting concerns into aspects, then you enter the aspect extraction phase.

9.4.1 Rationale

Aspect extraction is the activity of separating the crosscutting concern code from the original code, by moving it to one or more newly-defined aspects, and removing it from the original code. Since an aspect is typically defined as a collection of pointcuts and associated advice code, extraction entails the identification of suitable pointcuts and the definition of the appropriate advice code corresponding to the crosscutting concern code.

Although aspect extraction is often referred to as *aspect refactoring* in existing literature, we believe that term to be ambiguous. Indeed, Fowler [183] defined refactoring as "the process of modifying source code without changing its external behaviour". When applying this definition to aspect-oriented programs, the term "source code" could either refer to the code from which an aspect is extracted, or to the code of an existing aspect that evolves. Therefore, we will use the term *aspect extraction* for the activity of turning a traditional crosscutting concern into an aspect and reserve the term *aspect refactoring* for the activity of refactoring an already existing aspect.

Research in aspect extraction thus focusses on how to automate the activity of extracting aspects from existing source code. Only with an automated approach, an extraction that is both *efficient* and *correct* can be achieved. Existing software systems often consist of millions of lines of code, and a real-world crosscutting concern thus easily consists of thousands of lines of code. Manually extracting aspects from these crosscutting concerns, if feasible at all, would not only be very time-consuming, but prone to errors as well. A correct aspect weaves the appropriate code at the appropriate joinpoints, and hence requires correct advice code and correct pointcuts. These are hard to construct, given the scattered and tangled nature of crosscutting concerns, and the size of current-day software systems.

9.4.2 Challenges and Risks

In order to be able to extract crosscutting concerns code from the original code into the appropriate aspects, the following questions need to be addressed:

How to Separate Crosscutting Concerns from Original Source Code?

Sophisticated program analysis and manipulation techniques are needed to separate crosscutting concern code, since by definition such code is tangled with other code. Depending on the kind and the amount of tangling, some code is easier to separate than other code. Tracing code, for example, is often relatively independent of the code surrounding it, whereas Bruntink et al.'s experiment [91] showed that exception handling code exhibits significantly more tangling.

How to Determine Appropriate Joinpoint(s) for Extracted Aspects?

An aspect needs to specify the exact location where advice code needs to be woven, by means of a (set of) pointcut(s) that select(s) the appropriate joinpoints. However, aspect languages impose certain restrictions on the locations in the static or dynamic software structure that can be made available as joinpoints. Hence, determining the appropriate joinpoints requires significant attention.

How to Determine Appropriate Pointcut(s) for Extracted Aspects?

Assuming that appropriate joinpoints can be found, the next problem is that of determining the appropriate pointcut(s) that describes these joinpoints. Additionally, the pointcuts need to expose the appropriate context information for the advice code.

How to Determine Appropriate Advice Code for Extracted Aspects?

The crosscutting concern code typically cannot be transformed "as is" into advice code. Small modifications are often required, due to the code being defined in a different context, but also due to small variations in the scattered snippets of crosscutting concern code.

How to Ensure Correctness of Extracted Code?

The correctness requirement is of course related to *behaviour preservation*, i.e., extracting aspects from existing source code is expected to preserve the external behaviour of that code. Even for traditional refactorings this is already considered a non-trivial problem [404]; when extracting aspects from traditional programs the problem only becomes harder. Obviously, automating the transformations that are applied can help meeting this requirement, as automated transformations can be proven correct by using preconditions [404]. Additionally, appropriate test suites are of great value, but are not always present in (legacy) software. Furthermore, since the extraction process affects the original code structure, certain tests that rely on that structure may need to be restructured as well. In particular, certain tests may need to be transformed into their aspect-oriented equivalent.

9.4.3 Existing Techniques

Research on aspect extraction is still in its infancy, as most researchers focussed primarily on aspect exploration first. Nonetheless, work exists that contributes to the growing body of aspect extraction research [88, 375, 376, 163, 67, 223, 220]. Most of this work does not clearly distinguish between aspect extraction and aspect evolution, however. In this section, we only consider those parts of this work that deal with extraction.

Separating Crosscutting Concern Code

Separating the crosscutting concern code from the original code requires taking tangling into account: the code might use local variables that are defined by the ordinary code, or might modify variables that are used by the ordinary code. Hence, all separation techniques need to include a way to deal with such local references.

Both Monteiro and Fernandes [375] and Hanenberg et al. [220] discuss an *extract advice* transformation, that is responsible for separating the concern code but is not automated. Both mention that particular attention should be paid to local variables used in the crosscutting concern code. Hanenberg et al. take the position that either the developer should check whether such variables are not referenced outside the crosscutting code, in which case the variable declaration can be moved safely to the advice code, or else the transformation cannot be applied. Monteiro and Fernandes suggest that the code fragment should be isolated first using *Extract Method* or *Replace Method with Method Object* refactorings [183]. Binkley et al [67] present automated transformations, but propose the same approach as Monteiro and Fernandes. It is not clear, however, if this would work in practice, as these refactorings themselves might not be applicable when dealing with the problem of local variables.

The work of Ettinger and Verbaere [163] is currently the only one proposing an automated solution to the problems encountered when separating concern code from the original code. They propose to use program slicing [538] to untangle concern code and ordinary code. Program slicing is a technique that singles out those statements that may have affected the value of a given variable and that outputs a set of statements, called a *slice*. The idea is that this slice contains all code that is related to the concern, including references to local variables and how their values are computed, and can be factored out by means of an *extract slice* transformation [352]. This transformation can either fully extract all statements from the original code, or can leave some statements where they are, if they are relevant for the original code. It is not clear whether such a transformation is feasible to implement, however.

Determining Appropriate Joinpoints

After having separated the crosscutting concern code from the original code, we need to map those locations where that code was originally located to an appropriate set of joinpoints. The possible joinpoint locations that can be specified by a given AOP language are often limited: not every node in the structure or execution flow graph can be selected by an aspect. Hence, the required mapping is not always possible.

A possible solution for this problem is to extend the pointcut language so that more joinpoints can be exposed. However, a trade-off exists between the completeness of the joinpoint model and the performance of the produced software. The execution of aspect-oriented software would slow down considerably if an aspect could select any node in the structure or execution flow graph. Consequently, a complete joinpoint model is considered impractical.

Another alternative is to restructure the code before extracting the crosscutting concern code, to make it fit the joinpoint model offered by the AOP language. This is the approach taken by both Binkley et al [67] and Monteiro and Fernandes [375], who suggest to apply traditional refactorings first in order to make the code more "aspect friendly". For example, concern code occurring in between a set of statements is impossible to separate using most existing AOP languages. Hence, as depicted in Figure 9.6, this concern code can be extracted first using an *Extract Method* refactoring, for example, producing additional joinpoints that an aspect can use. There is considerable discussion in the AOSD community about this issue, as it interferes with the obliviousness property of AOSD, as explained in Section 9.2: the ordinary code should not "know" about the aspects that apply to it. Clearly, transforming the code with the sole intent of making it "aspect friendly" breaks this assumption. However, the experiments of Binkley et al. [67] suggest that only 20% of the cases requires performing a traditional refactoring first. The authors acknowledge the fact that performing such transformation should be seen as the "extreme recourse that solves all problems", since the transformation might reduce code familiarity and quality in general.

Determining Appropriate Pointcuts

Having determined the appropriate joinpoints, we need to define the appropriate pointcuts that capture those joinpoints. The simplistic solution is to use extensional pointcuts which merely enumerate all joinpoints. However, as explained in Section 9.2, we prefer more intensional pointcut definitions which are more robust towards evolution.

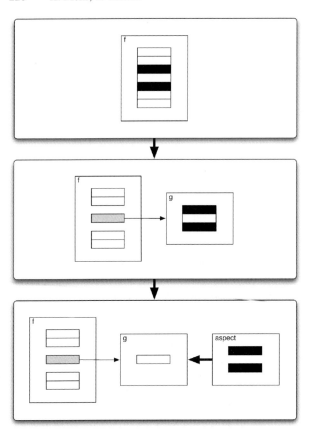

Fig. 9.6. Making code aspect friendly

Authors that propose non-automated extraction transformations generally do not pay sufficient attention to the definition of appropriate pointcuts. Hanenberg et al [220] consider extracting crosscutting concern code from a single method only, and describe that "a pointcut that targets the relevant method" has to be defined. Monteiro and Fernandes [375] provide a bit more sophistication, saying that a pointcut "should capture the intended set of joinpoints", and that if the intended pointcut is already under construction, it should be extended so that it includes the joinpoint related to the code fragment currently being extracted. The responsibility of defining a good pointcut thus rests completely with the developer, who needs detailed knowledge of the structure and the behaviour of the software.

Binkley et al. [67] tackle the problem of determining "sensible" pointcuts automatically, and describe 7 extraction transformations with the particular pointcuts they generate. For example, they define an *Extract Before Call* transformation, depicted in Figure 9.7, that extracts a block of code that always occurs before a particular method call. In the aspect B, the pointcut p intercepts the call to h that occurs within the execution of method f. A before-advice reintroduces the call to g at the proper execution point.

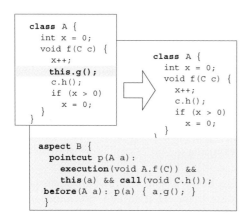

Fig. 9.7. The Extract Before Call transformation

Although not explained explicitly in the paper, it is clear that applying their extraction transformations yield extensional pointcuts: when extracting code from many different locations, the transformations extract the code from one location at a time, and combine the pointcut of each individual location with the already existing pointcut, in order to form a new pointcut.

Braem et al. [79] present an experiment where they use *inductive logic programming* in order to uncover "patterns" in, and generate intensional pointcuts from, a given set of joinpoints. Inductive logic programming is a machine-learning technique that requires positive as well as negative examples and background information, so as to define a logic rule that captures all positive but none of the negative examples. For this experiment, the authors use joinpoints corresponding to the crosscutting concern code as positive examples, all other joinpoints occurring in the program as negative examples, and structural information about the program, such as the classes in which methods are defined and which methods a particular method calls, as background information. The resulting induced pointcuts look similar to a pointcut that a developer would define when confronted with the same task.

Determining Appropriate Advice Code

The advice code of an aspect definition consists of the code that should be woven at the joinpoints selected by the aspect's pointcuts. Although we discuss the problem of how to determine that advice code separately here, it is strongly overlapping with the problem of separating the crosscutting concern code from the original code, which we discussed earlier on. The advice code corresponds to the crosscutting concern code that was separated from the original source code, but cannot be used as advice code as is. In general, the crosscutting concern code makes use of the context in which it is implemented: it may contain references to local variables or use instance variables or methods of a class. To determine the appropriate advice code, the crosscutting concern code needs to be inspected for such context-specific references, and the pointcut and advice code need to be adapted adequately to the new (aspect) context.

Most aspect languages provide dedicated constructs to allow aspects to expose context information associated to the joinpoint at which the aspect applies, such that this information can be used in the advice code. The args construct used in Figure 9.4 was an example of such a construct and allowed a method joinpoint to pass the actual value of the method's argument to the advice. Other examples are constructs to expose the name of the method corresponding to the joinpoint, the names of its formal parameters, or a reference to its defining class. In general, the pointcut definition that captures the appropriate joinpoints is extended with dedicated predicates and parameters in order to be capable of exposing the necessary information to the advice code.

This can be a quite complex undertaking, however, due to limitations in the context information exposed by aspects. For example, the crosscutting concern code may use temporary variables local to the method or function in which it is contained, and most aspect languages do not provide constructs to expose such information. Additionally, in an object-oriented language, the crosscutting concern code may reference private instance variables and/or methods, and visibility rules may prevent an aspect from accessing or extracting such private information.

Hanenberg et al. [220] and Monteiro and Fernandes [375] touch upon the problem of references to (private) instance variables and methods when dealing with their *extract advice* and *extract introduction* transformations. Their solution consists of declaring an aspect privileged, meaning it can bypass visibility rules, and of using additional this and target pointcuts in order to resolve self and super calls in the advice code. Additionally, Monteiro and Fernandes [375] consider the problem of crosscutting concern code that uses local variables, and propose to turn such variables into instance variables if necessary. The consequences of adapting the code in this way with the sole intent of making it "aspect friendly" is not elaborated upon, nor is made clear what its impact would be on large code bases or on the code quality, and whether this solution is always feasible.

Binkley et al. [67] explicitly mention the context exposure problem when defining their extraction transformations, and provide a precise description of how these transformations generate pointcuts that expose the necessary context. Because these transformations are automated and reason about the crosscutting concern code, they either generate a correct pointcut that exposes the necessary context, or are not applicable at all. Hence, the resulting aspect is always correct, which is not the case for the other (manual) approaches.

9.4.4 Open Issues

The issues identified above and our overview of the current state of the research show that the major issues and problems related to aspect extraction have been identified, but that no satisfactory solutions exist yet. Most existing techniques touch upon a specific part of a particular problem, but no single technique provides a complete solution to all problems identified. This is no surprise, as research on aspect extraction is only just emerging.

First of all, the level of automation of current extraction techniques is poor, and all issues touched upon in the previous subsection could benefit significantly from more automation. Clearly, more effort is needed in this area, since automated extraction techniques are indispensable when dealing with large-scale software, in order to achieve efficiency and correctness. A technique such as the use of inductive logic programming to automatically produce intensional pointcut definitions [79] is definitely a step forward. However, this technique was validated only on a single example and it remains to be investigated how it performs on more complex cases.

Second, the issue of preserving the behaviour of the software after extraction has not yet been tackled explicitly. Proving the correctness of aspects that were extracted manually is practically impossible. Automated techniques, however, could be proven correct. Given Opdyke's experience in this matter [404], it is clear that constructing formal proofs for the complex extraction transformations is far from trivial. However, formally defining the necessary preconditions for such transformations should be feasible, but has currently not yet been realised.

Related to testing behaviour-correctness of performing aspect extraction, the issue of migrating the original test suites to the migrated software system remains. Unfortunately, little work exists on testing aspect-oriented systems (notable exceptions are the works of Xu and Xu [555] and Xie and Zhao [549]), let al.one on the migration of the original tests to their aspect-oriented equivalent. Chapter 8 of this book also mentions this explicitly as a topic that warrants further investigation.

Finally, little or no empirical validation of the proposed techniques on large-scale, real-world software systems has been performed. This makes it hard to assess whether the techniques actually work in practice, what their advantages and disadvantages are, whether they scale to large industrial software, and whether the extraction actually improves the quality of the software.

9.4.5 Extraction in Practice

As is apparent from the previous subsections, most work on aspect extraction is focused on the technical level, i.e., it describes new transformations that extract crosscutting concerns into aspects. With the notable exception of the work by Binkley et al. [67], none of these transformations have been applied extensively on real-world systems. Binkley's work does not present any concrete details of the case study either, and focuses mainly on the transformations themselves.

In this subsection, we summarise an experiment by Bruntink et al. [88], where they studied the *tracing* crosscutting concern in a 80.000 lines subset of an industrial software system. The goal of their experiment was to study whether this concern was implemented in a sufficiently systematic way, so that it could be expressed easily in terms of appropriate pointcuts and advice. Such an investigation could be regarded as a preliminary step before performing an actual extraction.

As an illustration of their approach, taken from [88], consider the idiomatic implementation of the tracing concern in Figure 9.8. A developer needs to trace input parameters of a function at the beginning, and output parameters at the end of that function. The trace function implements tracing and is a variable-argument function.

```
int f(chuck_id* a, scan_component b) {
    int result = OK;
    char* func_name = "f";
    ...
    trace(CC, TRACE_INT, func_name, "> (b = %s)",
          SCAN_COMPONENT2STR(b));
    ...
    trace(CC, TRACE_INT, func_name, "< (a = %s) = %d",
          CHUCK_ID_ENUM2STR(a), result);
    return result;
}
```

Fig. 9.8. Code fragment illustrating the tracing idiom in Bruntink et al..'s case study

Its first four arguments denote, respectively, the component in which the function to be traced is defined, whether the tracing is internal or external to that component, the name of the function for which the parameters are being traced, and a `printf`-like format string that specifies the format in which the parameters should be traced. Optional arguments specify the input or output parameters that need to be traced. Parameters of a complex type (as opposed to a basic type like `int` or `char`) need to be converted to a string representation. Typically, this is done by using a dedicated function or macro, such as `SCAN_COMPONENT2STR` and `CHUCK_ID_ENUM2STR` in the example of Figure 9.8.

In order to study whether the concern was implemented consistently throughout their case study, Bruntink et al. proposed a method based on formal concept analysis, applied on typical attributes associated with the concern under study. For the tracing concern, they studied both *function-level* and *parameter-level* variability, and tuned the concept analysis algorithm so that it grouped all functions that invoked tracing in a similar way, and all parameters that are converted in the same way, respectively.

Without going into all details, the results of running the experiment on four components of the software system are described in Table 9.3. The most striking observation (second row) was that only 40 out of 704 (5.7%) of all functions invoke tracing in the 'standard' way. The first row shows that 29 different tracing variants are used in the four components. In addition, the authors observed that none of these 29 variants could be considered as the 'standard' variant, with the other variants being simple deviations from the general rule.

As for parameter-level variability (lower half of the table), the study showed that 37.7% of the parameter types (94 out of 249) were traced in an inconsistent way, i.e. a single parameter type is converted into a string representation in more than one way. Only 16% (40 out of 249) was traced consistently, and 115 parameter types were not traced at all. Some inconsistency arises because not all functions need to trace, however, and hence some parameter types are converted using one single converter function in many different functions, while not traced in other functions. To take this into account, those parameter types are excluded from the number of inconsistently-

Table 9.3. Function-level and parameter-level variability results (taken from [88], ©ACM, 2007)

	CC1	CC2	CC3	CC4	total	global
Function-level variability						
#tracing variants	6	4	19	2	31	29
#functions w. std. tracing	13	1	26	0	40	40
% of total functions	4	0.7	15	0		5.7
Parameter-level variability						
#not traced	61	49	4	16	130	115
#consistently traced	15	5	16	19	55	40
#inconsistently traced	32	17	45	14	108	94
#w.o. not traced	11	6	39	8	64	57

traced parameter types. Hence, the fourth row shows the parameter types that are converted using more than one converter function, and the authors concluded that 42.5% (57 out of 134) of all parameter types were not traced consistently, and 57.5% (77 out of 134) were traced consistently.

An additional advantage of their method is that formal concept analysis produces concept lattices that can be visually inspected. Figure 9.9, again taken from [88], illustrates this: it clearly shows that the component uses three different ways to specify the component name (CC, "CC2" and CC2_CC), and that there is one function that uses both CC and "CC2", i.e. there are two trace statements in that function, and each statement specifies the component name in a different way.

The most appealing result of this experiment was the observation that the implementation of the tracing concern was not consistent at all, contained much more variability than expected, and could thus not be expressed as one single aspect. This came as a surprise, given the fact that tracing is a relatively simple concern, which is often used as the prototypical example of a concern that can easily be turned into

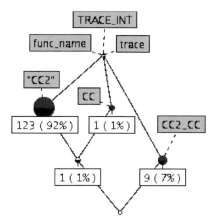

Fig. 9.9. Function-level variability in the CC2 component

an aspect. Since current aspect extraction tools and techniques that are proposed do not take these observations into account, they are not yet ready to be used on real-world systems. Granted, since a study of this kind was never conducted before, these issues could not have been identified yet. But it clearly illustrates the complexity of the activity of aspect extraction.

9.5 Aspect Evolution

Once the crosscutting concerns in the original software system have been explored and the system has been migrated to a new aspect-oriented version, the system enters a new phase in which it will need to be continuously maintained and evolved in order to cope with changing requirements and environments. In this section, we highlight some of the issues and problems related to such evolution of aspect-oriented systems.

9.5.1 Rationale

As was argued in the introductory section, AOSD overcomes some of the problems related to software evolution, in particular the problems related to maintaining and evolving independently the different (crosscutting) concerns in a system. But since all software systems are subject to evolution (remember the first law of software evolution), aspect-oriented systems themselves too will eventually need to evolve. We define *aspect evolution* as the process of progressively modifying the elements of an aspect-oriented software system in order to improve or maintain its quality over time, under changing contexts and requirements.

9.5.2 Challenges and Risks

While research on aspect exploration is only starting to produce its first results and research on aspect extraction is still gaining momentum, research on aspect evolution is even younger. This is largely due to the fact that few large-scale aspect-oriented software systems exist today. Even if they would exist, they would be too young in order for them to be the subject of a rigorous scientific study regarding their long-term evolution problems.

Despite the immaturity of the field, some initial research questions have been raised, related to how the evolution of aspect-oriented software differs from evolving traditional software and whether techniques and tools, successful in supporting traditional software evolution, can still be applied to the evolution of aspect-oriented software. It seems that the very techniques that AOP provides to solve or limit some of the evolution problems with traditional software, actually introduce a series of new evolution problems. This phenomenon is sometimes called the *evolution paradox* of AOP [505].

9.5.3 Existing Techniques and Open Issues

Evolving aspect-oriented software differs in at least two ways from evolving traditional software:

1. First of all, evolving the base code in any way may impact the aspects that work on that code (see Figure 9.10). Evolution normally involves adding and removing classes, methods and instance variables, or changing them in some way. By doing so, the set of joinpoints associated to the program changes too: new joinpoints are added and existing joinpoints are removed or changed. This clearly affects the aspects which select joinpoints by means of pointcuts. Hence, when evolving the base code, care has to be taken to assess the impact this evolution has on the aspects.
2. Conversely, the aspects themselves can be subject to evolution too (Figure 9.11). Since concerns are easier to evolve when they are separated into aspects instead of being implemented by means of coding conventions and idioms, it seems natural to assume that aspects may therefore evolve more often. However, like any other software artefact, aspects evolve for a variety of different reasons. For example, pointcuts could be generalised to make them less brittle, abstract aspects could be introduced to make the aspect-oriented code more reusable, or advice code could be restructured to make it more comprehensible. Hence, the introduction of AOP introduces new types of evolution that where previously impossible or difficult to achieve.

These issues were already identified by a number of authors. Hanenberg et al. [220] introduce *aspect-aware* and *aspect-oriented* refactorings. The former are traditional refactorings that are extended to take aspects into account, such as *Rename method* and *Extract method* that need to make sure an aspect's pointcuts are updated appropriately. Such refactorings tackle the first issue presented above. The latter refactorings are newly-defined and refactor the aspect code instead of the base code. They

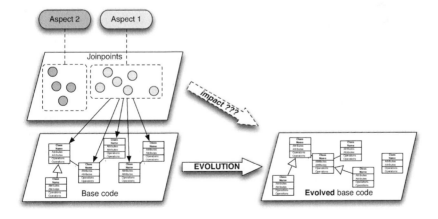

Fig. 9.10. Impact of base code evolution on the aspects

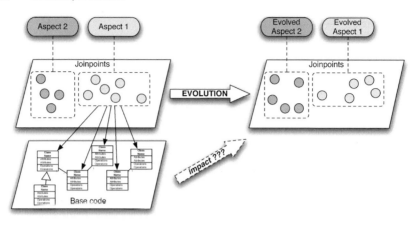

Fig. 9.11. Impact of aspect evolution on the base code

thus tackle the second issue. An example is the *Separate pointcut* refactoring, that extracts the common parts of several pointcuts into a new pointcut, so that it can be reused properly.

Monteiro and Fernandes [376] follow an approach similar to Fowler [182] where they identify several *bad (aspect) smells*, and define refactorings that alleviate these. They divide the different refactorings into three categories, as shown in Table 9.4: for extracting crosscutting concerns, for restructuring the internals of aspects, and for dealing with generalisation. The first category of refactorings has been explained in Section 9.4. The second category contains refactorings that are often applied after an aspect has been extracted from a crosscutting concern, and needs tidying up, whereas the third category contains refactorings that should make an aspect definition more general and hence more reusable. The distinction between the last two categories is rather arbitrary, and the refactorings presented are not automated. Since they are rather high-level refactorings, they are probably difficult to automate at all.

Not only does AOP lead to new types of evolution, it also introduces new kinds of evolution problems. In particular, several authors have identified and suggested solutions for the *fragile pointcut problem* [293, 477, 482, 362]. This problem occurs when pointcuts accidentally capture or miss particular joinpoints as a consequence of their fragility with respect to seemingly safe modifications to the base program. We will illustrate and discuss this problem in more detail in Subsection 9.5.4.

Another danger to evolution of aspect-oriented programs is what is sometimes called the *aspect composition problem* [226]. When combining into the same application two aspects that have been developed independently, they may interact in undesired ways. For example, suppose we want to combine a simple logging and synchronisation aspect. For those joinpoints that are captured by both aspects, do we only want to log and synchronise the base code? Do we want the logging aspect to log the synchronisation code as well? Or do we want the synchronisation aspect to synchronise the logging code? Languages like AspectJ propose language

Table 9.4. Three categories of refactorings as defined by Monteiro and Fernandes (Adapted from [376]), ©ACM, 2005

Restructuring aspect internals	
Extend marker interface with signature	
Generalise target type with marker interface	
Introduce aspect protection	
Replace inter-type field with aspect map	
Replace inter-type method with aspect method	
Tidy up internal aspect structure	

Extracting crosscutting concerns	Dealing with generalisation
Change abstract class to interface	Extract superaspect
Extract feature into aspect	Pull up advice
Extract fragment into advice	Pull up declare parents
Extract inner class to standalone	Pull up inter-type declaration
Inline class within aspect	Pull up marker interface
Inline interface within aspect	Pull up pointcut
Move field from class to inter-type	Push down advice
Move method from class to inter-type	Push down declare parents
Replace implements with declare parents	Push down inter-type declaration
Split abstract class into aspect and interface	Push down marker interface
	Push down pointcut

constructs to define how to combine aspects, for example by providing priority rules and permitting a developer to declare in what order to apply the aspects. However, when combining more complex aspects, often these constructs do not suffice and more intricate compositions are desired. Lopez-Herrejon et al. [331] and others propose alternative composition models, based on program transformations, that support step-wise development, retain the power of AspectJ and simplify program reasoning using aspects. Such composition models align aspect-oriented software development with component-based software engineering in order to offer the best of both worlds. Chapter 10 also briefly touches upon these issues.

To conclude, it is clear that aspect evolution is still an emerging research area, in which not all important research questions have been identified, let al.one answered. Nevertheless, it is important to mention that an awareness of the problem is growing inside the AOSD community, and that more and more researchers in that community are starting to investigate such problems.

9.5.4 Aspect Evolution in Practice: The Fragile Pointcut Problem

As a concrete example of an aspect evolution problem, this section touches upon the *fragile pointcut problem*, proposes a possible solution, and discusses a small case study on which an initial validation of this solution was conducted.

In Section 9.2 we already illustrated the distinction between extensional pointcuts, which merely enumerate the joinpoints in the source code, and intensional pointcuts that are defined in terms of more high-level structural or behavioural properties of the program entities to which they refer. The tight coupling of extensional pointcut definitions to the base program's structure hampers evolvability of the software [482] since it implies that all pointcuts of each aspect need to be checked and possibly revised whenever the base program evolves. Due to changes to the base program, the pointcuts may unanticipatedly capture joinpoints that were not supposed to be captured, or may miss certain joinpoints that were supposed to be affected by the aspect. This problem has been coined the fragile pointcut problem [293, 477].

Kellens et al. [362] address the fragile pointcut problem by replacing the intimate dependency of pointcut definitions on the base program by a more stable dependency on a conceptual model of the program. This is illustrated schematically in Figure 9.12. Their *model-based pointcut* definitions are less likely to break upon evolution, because they are no longer defined in terms of how the program happens to be structured at a certain point in time, but rather in terms of a model of the program that is more robust to evolution.

To validate their approach, they defined two simple aspects on an initial release of the SmallWiki application. The 'action logging' aspect extended SmallWiki with basic logging functionality for the different actions that occur in the wiki system. A second 'output' aspect altered the way (font) in which text in wiki documents was rendered. They implemented each of these two aspects once with aspects defined in terms of traditional pointcuts and once in terms of model-based pointcuts defined over a conceptual model of the application. Then they considered two more recent versions of the SmallWiki application (a version one month and another about one year after the initial release) and assessed the impact of the aspects in those versions.

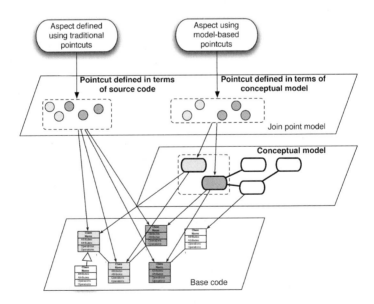

Fig. 9.12. Managing the fragile pointcut problem with model-based pointcuts

As it happened, some occurrences of the fragile pointcut problem appeared. In the solution with traditional aspects this resulted in an erroneous behaviour of the aspectualised application. More specifically, some actions that should have been logged were not and some text outputting that should have been altered was not. With the model-based pointcut approach, however, these fragile pointcut problems were detected as mismatches between the evolved code and the conceptual model that was defined on top of it. As such, the conflicts could be detected early and solved by the aspect programmer before actually applying the aspects.

On the downside, the approach does not detect all occurrences of the fragile pointcut problem: a lot depends on the level of detail of the conceptual model in terms of which the pointcuts are defined. The more detailed the model, the more mismatches can be detected. Also, since the approach has only been illustrated an a relatively small case on two simple aspects, it remains to be investigated how well it performs on real aspect-oriented systems.

9.6 Summary

In this chapter, we summarised important evolution-specific issues and challenges related to the adoption of aspect-oriented programming, and presented an overview of the state-of-the-art research that addresses these. We identified three different stages that adopters of AOP may need to go through: exploration, extraction and evolution.

The exploration stage is a preliminary phase that studies whether the software actually exhibits important crosscutting concerns that can or should be extracted into aspects. We showed that exploring a software system for crosscutting concerns means looking for more than the well-known and simple crosscutting concerns often documented in the research literature. Moreover, particular coding conventions and idioms can help in identifying important crosscutting concerns, as they are often used to make up for the lack of aspects. Additionally, we described how some of the existing exploration tools make use of the very same information in order to automatically mine a software system for crosscutting concerns. However, even those automated tools typically require quite a lot of manual inspection of the produced results, due to the relatively low precision and recall of the proposed techniques. Regarding crosscutting concerns and software quality, we discussed some preliminary work that hints at a positive impact on the software quality of implementing crosscutting concerns by means of aspects, but no definitive conclusions can be drawn yet and more experimental validation is clearly needed.

The extraction stage follows the exploration stage, and considers how crosscutting concern code can be extracted from the ordinary code and defined into the appropriate aspects. We identified the issues related to this extraction, in particular separating the concern code from the base code and turning it into advice code, and determining the appropriate joinpoints and pointcuts. Existing work that tackles (part of) these issues was described, which showed that this area of research is still young and needs significantly more work before it can be useful in an industrial context.

Nonetheless, these techniques show the feasibility of automating, at least partly, the process of aspect extraction.

The evolution stage then deals with the evolution of the final aspect-oriented software, and how this differs from the evolution of ordinary software. We showed that evolving aspect-oriented software involves evolving the ordinary code as well as the aspect code, and that this gives rise to extensions of existing techniques that support evolution, as well as new techniques to support aspect evolution. Additionally, we explained that the adoption of AOP gives rise to new evolution-related problems, such as the fragile pointcut problem and the aspect composition problem. Solutions to those problems are under active research by the AOP community.

The overall conclusion that can be drawn is that aspect-oriented software development is still a young paradigm, that still needs to mature and requires much more rigourous research. Nonetheless, it is a promising paradigm that receives a lot of attention, and gives rise to several tools and techniques that already provide at least some kind of support for early adopters.

Acknowledgement. This chapter builds on the work of a vast community of people working on evolution-related issues in the domain of AOP. We are grateful to all authors of the work referred to in this text for having implicitly or explicitly provided us the necessary material for writing this chapter. Given the broad range of topics and issues covered by this chapter, it is inevitable that some important references may be missing. We are equally grateful to those researchers for advancing the state-of-the-art in this exciting research area.

Software Architecture Evolution

Olivier Barais[1], Anne Françoise Le Meur[2], Laurence Duchien[2], and Julia Lawall[3]

[1] Université de Rennes 1/IRISA/INRIA, Triskell project - France
[2] Université de Lille 1, LIFL/INRIA ADAM project - France
[3] DIKU, University of Copenhagen, Denmark

Summary. Software architectures must frequently evolve to cope with changing requirements, and this evolution often implies integrating new concerns. Unfortunately, when the
new concerns are crosscutting, existing architecture description languages provide little or no
support for this kind of evolution. The software architect must modify multiple elements of
the architecture manually, which risks introducing inconsistencies.

   This chapter provides an overview, comparison and detailed treatment of the various state-
of-the-art approaches to describing and evolving software architectures. Furthermore, we discuss one particular framework named TranSAT, which addresses the above problems of software architecture evolution. TranSAT provides a new element in the software architecture
descriptions language, called an architectural aspect, for describing new concerns and their
integration into an existing architecture. Following the early aspect paradigm, TranSAT allows the software architect to design a software architecture stepwise in terms of aspects at
the design stage. It realises the evolution as the weaving of new architectural aspects into an
existing software architecture.

10.1 Introduction

The role of software architecture in the engineering of software-intensive systems
is becoming increasingly important and widespread. A software architecture models
the structure and behavior of a system, including the software elements and the relationships between them. It is the basis of the design process, a guide for the software
development process and one of the main inputs to drive the development of integration tests. There are currently a number of Architecture Description Languages
(ADLs) [358], which enable an architect to specify a software architecture. During
the design process, the architect uses an ADL to create the software architecture
of a system by constructing and combining increasingly complex components and
connectors.

   An ADL makes it easy to construct an initial description of the architecture of
a system. In practice, however, so that an architecture can remain useful over time, it
must be able to evolve in response to the changing and often conflicting requirements
of the many diverse stakeholders. An architecture can thus not be viewed as simply

T. Mens, S. Demeyer (eds.), *Software Evolution.*
DOI 10.1007/978-3-540-76440-3, © Springer 2008

a description of a static software structure, but as a description of the space in which this software structure can dynamically evolve. Most ADLs, however, do not provide support for describing the evolution of a software system.

Software systems undergo two main kinds of evolution: *internal evolution* and *external evolution*. Internal evolution models the changes in the topology of the components and interactions as they are created or destroyed during execution. As such, it captures the dynamics of the system. External evolution models the changes in the specification of the components and interactions that are required to cope with new stakeholder requirements. It entails adaptation of the software architecture. In the first part of this chapter, we study a number of approaches that address these issues of evolution in a software architecture. We furthermore classify the approaches according to the kind of evolution that is supported.

In the second part of this chapter, we focus on the issue of separation of concerns in the context of the external evolution of a software architecture. Software architectures are designed around the concepts of components and their interactions, and thus suffer from the "tyranny of the dominant decomposition" [490], in which some concerns cannot be adequately modularised because they crosscut the chosen dimension of decomposition. Evolutions in such concerns require pervasively modifying the ADL specification, at all points affected by the concerns, which can be tedious and difficult. In the context of implementations, Aspect-Oriented Software Development (AOSD) [276], has been proposed to improve the separation of concerns [153]. At the architecture level, several approaches have proposed to follow the spirit of AOSD, by putting the description of each concern in a separate architecture construct, that can automatically be integrated into an existing software architecture by a *weaver*. However, because architectures are complex and aspects are invasive, many transformations may be needed to integrate or modify a concern, making the specification of the transformation highly error prone. We present in detail the system TranSAT [36, 38], which detects inconsistencies that may be introduced by such an architectural aspect as early as possible.

The rest of this chapter is organised as follows. Section 10.2 presents several software architecture languages in order to identify the key concepts of these languages and their advantages and shortcomings. Sections 10.3 and 10.4 present several initial solutions to cope with internal and external evolution. Section 10.5 presents the TranSAT approach, showing how an explicit specification of weaving can help guarantee the consistency of the resulting architecture. Section 10.6 describes some related work and finally Section 10.7 concludes and presents some remaining critical issues.

10.2 Component-Based Software Architecture: Concepts and Open Issues

The software architecture of a software system describes its high level structure and behavior. In a software architecture specification, a system is represented as a set of software components, their connections, and their behavioral interactions. Creating a software architecture promotes a better understanding of the system, and thus facilitates the design process. A software architecture is described using an architectural description language (ADL). Such a language can be a graphical textual, or both. The use of an ADL allows rigorously specifying the global architecture of a system, that can then be analyzed by automated tools. ADLs are typically both human and machine readable and provide a high level of abstraction. An ADL can provide features that support the automatic generation of parts of a software system.

Many ADLs have been developed by either academic or industrial groups [115]. While the various ADLs differ in many points, the ADL community generally agrees that the key elements of an ADL are abstractions for describing components, connectors, and configurations [358]. A component represents a computational element with multiple ports, allowing it to communicate with its environment. A connector models the interaction between components. Finally, a configuration describes how components and connectors are arranged into a system.

In this section, we focus on three significant directions in the design of ADLs: (i) the specification and analysis of the interaction between distributed components, as illustrated by Darwin [339] and Wright [5], (ii) the strong link with the implementation of the software system, as may be found in ArchJava [4], Fractal [87] and SOFA [96], and (iii) the building of an architecture-driven software development environment, as promoted by ArchStudio [141], AcmeStudio [556] and SafArchie [37]. Finally, we evaluate these works in terms of their support for evolution.

Architecture Specification and Analysis

Some ADLs, such as Wright [5], Darwin [339] and Rapide [334], focus on the specification and analysis of component interaction. Wright provides a formal model based on CSP for architectural description. Based on this model, it defines a set of standard consistency and completeness properties that can be checked using standard model checking technology to increase the architect's confidence in the design of a system. Darwin has been built with the same spirit and goals as Wright. It is a formal language for describing software structures and network topologies in the context of dynamic distributed systems. It uses Finite State Process (FSP) Languages to specify system behavior [340]. FSP provides a concise way of describing Labelled Transition Systems (LTSs).

System Configuration and Code Generation

Many ADLs decouple the implementation from the architecture, which can lead to a situation in which the implementation and the architecture are inconsistent. ArchJava [4], Fractal [87], and SOFA [96] have the goal of unifying software architecture with implementation.

ArchJava is an extension to Java that unifies the software architecture with the implementation by focusing on a property known as *communication integrity*. This property requires that the implementations of components only communicate along the channels declared in the architecture. ArchJava uses a type system to ensure this property in the implementation code.

The Fractal component model distinguishes two kinds of components: *primitives*, which contain actual code, and *composites*, which are only used as a mechanism to group components into a whole. Fractal provides an XML-based ADL that provides constructs to specify component types, primitive templates and composite templates. A tool can parse a Fractal ADL specification and instantiate the corresponding components to create an implementation [315]. One of the implementations of Fractal, Julia, is a Java library that enables the specification and manipulation of components and architectures at runtime. In Julia, primitives can be standard Java classes that conform to some coding conventions.

SOFA (SOFtware Appliances) provides a platform for developing applications with primitive and composite software components. A component is described by its *frame* and its *architecture*. The frame is a component interface and the *architecture* is an abstract implementation. A frame specifies the services that are provided and required by the component, and can be implemented by more than one architecture. The architecture of a composite describes the structure of the component by instantiating direct subcomponents and specifying the interconnections between them. A primitive has no architecture but an implementation that can be a binary. SOFA provides a text-based ADL called Component Definition Language (CDL), which is based on OMG IDL [397]. This ADL allows specifying the communication among SOFA components and embeds a process algebra called *behavior protocols* to express the behavior of each component.

The ADLs ArchJava and Fractal provide a tight link between the architecture and the implementation, but unlike Darwin or Wright do not provide any facilities for behavior specification and analysis. Indeed, the only check on the interaction between components is to ensure that connected ports provide and require services with compatible signatures. The language CDL used with SOFA, however, additionally allows specifying behavior protocols in terms of regular expressions on sequences of events, which constrains the set of admissible traces of the component.

Architecture-Centric Integrated Development Environments

Finally, some work has focused on the design of ADLs that are targeted towards use with architecture-centric software development tools, with the goal of improving the use of software architecture concepts in the software industry. Some of these ADLs are ArchStudio [141], AcmeStudio [556], and SafArchie [37].

ArchStudio is a software development environment that focuses on software development from the perspective of software architecture. It supports the C2 architectural style [491]. A C2 architecture is a hierarchical network of concurrent components linked together by connectors (message routing devices) in accordance with a set of style rules. C2 components communicate via message passing. ArchStudio is extensible, and many extensions have been developed to analyze, refine, or deploy architecture specifications.

AcmeStudio is a customizable editing environment and visualization tool for software architectural designs based on the Acme ADL. Acme is extensible and is intended to be used as a common interchange format for architecture design tools and as a foundation for developing new architectural design and analysis tools. Acme-Studio allows the designer to define new Acme families and customise the environment to work with those families by defining diagram styles.

SafArchie Studio is a tool suite for the SafArchie component model [37] and is built as a set of modules for ArgoUML [19]. SafArchie provides a hierarchical component model, including primitive and composite components. Each component interface is associated with a contract. These contracts clarify both the structure and the external behavior of the components, describing its interactions with its environment. SafArchie Studio allows a designer to describe an architecture and then to check its properties using either a built-in model checker or the verification tool LTSA [340]. Finally, it can generate code for use with ArchJava or Fractal.

Overall, these tools vary in the underlying architectural style that is targeted, but they have the common goal of providing a complete tool suite to build, deploy and refine a software architecture, in order to transform ADLs into an effective vehicle for communication and analysis of a software system.

Evaluation: Managing Software Architecture Evolution

The various languages presented in this section support the static description of a software architecture. From this description, tools can check the correctness of the model and can generate code. They can furthermore guarantee the consistency between a design and an implementation. However, none of these languages and associated tools take evolution into account. Thus, a software architecture, once implemented in the software system, can be prohibitively expensive to change. Due to the lack of a first-class artefact that manages the evolution, architectures become obsolete quickly and their use degenerates to that of an outdated documentation of the system.

If we consider the problem of evolution in the context of each of the different languages presented in this section, we can notice that:

- these languages cannot describe the internal evolution (dynamics) of a system. They give a snapshot view of the system that can become obsolete.
- these languages do not take care of external evolutions. For example, the architecture analysis tools do not support incremental checks when an architect integrates a new concern. Consequently, for each modification, the model checker has to re-check the entire system. At the implementation level, component-based software platforms suffer greatly from tangled code because many functions that relate to crosscutting concerns are spread out and repeated over different components. Consequently, the integration or the modification of a new concern is difficult and error-prone. Finally, the different architecture development environments do not provide any facilities for easily integrating or modifying a concern that crosscuts several components in the architecture.

In the next sections, we will study several initial solutions to handle the internal and external evolutions of component-based software architectures.

10.3 Dynamic Software Architecture Description

A running system may create new components and interactions, causing it to diverge from its initial architecture. Because such changes may interact in subtle ways with the rest of the system, it is desirable for the architecture to document and allow reasoning about the changes that can occur during the system execution. A number of approaches have been proposed to address the dynamics of a system at the architecture level [78]. These can be divided into two main categories: either the ADL can support an explicit specification of the software architecture's dynamics in which all of the possible evolutions of the system are foreseen in the software architecture description, or the ADL can define the space of potential evolutions of the software architecture.

10.3.1 Explicit Specification of the Software Architecture Dynamics

Wright

The first approach to address the problem of expressing the dynamics of a software architecture was an extension of Wright [6]. This extension reuses the behavior notation of Wright to model reconfiguration. It allows the architect to view the architecture in terms of a set of possible architectural snapshots, each with its own steady-state behavior. Transitions between these snapshots are represented by reconfiguration-triggering events. To introduce dynamism in an architecture description, the architect has to extend the interface of each component, i.e., its alphabet and port descriptions, to describe when reconfigurations are permitted in each protocol in which it participates. A manager of reconfiguration, called a "reconfiguration view," consumes these events to trigger reconfigurations. This extension allows the designer to simulate the evolution of the software architecture. Each potential snapshot can be checked by the Wright model checker.

This extension is especially tailored for dynamic software architectures. However, two main problems limit its use in a industrial system development. First, the need to modify the component breaks the separation of concerns principle because the reconfiguration is expressed at the same level as the functional behavior of the component. Second, this approach is limited to modelling and to simulating dynamic systems with a finite number of configurations.

Fractal/FScript

The execution model of Fractal is highly dynamic, as components or bindings can be instantiated programmatically at runtime and the configuration of a composite can be changed. Nevertheless, Fractal ADL, described in Section 10.2, only allows expressing a single instantiation of the system, indicating how its components are instantiated and interconnected. The scripting language FScript [142], however, can be used to program reconfigurations of Fractal components. The language guarantees various properties of reconfigurations by considering them as transactions: *termination* (a reconfiguration cannot be infinite), *atomicity* (reconfiguration is executed either completely or not at all), *consistency* (the Fractal system resulting from a successful FScript reconfiguration is structurally consistent) and *isolation* (there are no concurrent reconfigurations). Each FScript program can be triggered by an event occurring inside the application itself using reactive rules modelled after the *Event-Condition-Action* paradigm (ECA). Combined with Fractal ADL, FScript allows modelling of the dynamics of a system.

ArchJava

ArchJava, described in Section 10.2, only allows statically defined components to be dynamically instantiated and connected. At creation time, each component records the component instance that created it as its parent component. ArchJava enforces the property of communication integrity, to ensure that the implementation remains coherent with the model. Thus, each component must explicitly document the kinds of architectural interactions that are permitted between its subcomponents. This is done using a *connection pattern*, which describes the set of connections that can be declared at runtime. ArchJava does not support the explicit component or connector destruction.

AADL

AADL (Architecture Analysis & Design Language) is a new international standard for predictable model-based engineering of real-time and embedded software [25]. It is mainly inspired by MetaH [526], which has been designed to analyze and combine software and hardware components to form a complete computer system, and targets control systems in the automotive, avionics, and space industries. AADL is a lower-level modelling language than the ADLs presented in the previous section. The main concepts manipulated by this language are components, ports, threads, and the communication bus. It models software topologies, execution platform topologies and the relationships between them. AADL was one of the first ADLs to model quality of service, including timing properties and resources consumption.

AADL provides a mechanism of *mode* to model the reconfiguration of statically-known systems. These modes can be associated with any AADL component. Modes represent alternative configurations of the component implementation. Only one mode is active at a time. At the level of system and process a mode represents possibly overlapping (sub-)sets of active threads and port connections, alternative configurations of execution platform components, as well as alternative bindings of application components to execution platform components. Mode changes are specified as a state transition diagram whose states are the modes, and the transitions are triggered by events.

Evaluation

The languages presented in this section make dynamic architectures explicit. These approaches are based on a limited version of the CRUD (Create, Retrieve, Update,

Delete) primitives, i.e., they can create or destroy components or connections. However, although the reconfiguration policies are separated of the rest of the software architecture for Fractal/FScript and AADL, these policies are completely tangled into the components for ArchJava, and partially for Wright. Furthermore, these approaches currently do not describe the dynamics with the same goal. The Wright extension and AADL model the dynamics to be able to simulate and check the evolution of the software architecture. Fractal and ArchJava focus on implementing a dynamic software architecture. Finally, the exhaustive specification of all the possible reconfigurations can be tricky and limits the real dynamics of the software architecture.

10.3.2 A Frame for Dynamic Software Architecture

Rather than explicitly specifying the set of potential snapshots of the system configuration, some ADLs allow delimiting the space of potential evolutions in what we call a *frame* for dynamic software architecture.

UML 2.0

UML 2.0 [398] permits the specification of logical components, e.g., business components and process components, through the composite structure diagram, and deployed components (such as artefacts and nodes) through the deployment diagram. It models a system as a hierarchy of nested components that provide and require interfaces. It provides support for decomposition through the notion of *structured classifiers*. A structured classifier is a classifier (a type) that can be internally decomposed (Classes, Collaboration, and Components). Constructs to support decomposition include: Part, Connectors, and Ports. In a UML 2.0 composite structure diagram, a component is viewed as a *"self-contained unit that encapsulates state + behavior of a set of classifiers"*[398]. It may have its own behavior specification and specifies a contract of provided/required services, through the definition of ports. To model the nested hierarchy, a component can be seen as parts because a component is a structured classifier. In this case, a part has type and a lower/upper bound multiplicity. Consequently, a connector does not represent a connection at the instance level but a potential connection at the type level. This kind of diagram is most relevant to designing a frame for software architecture. The variability of the software architecture is confined within the lower and the upper bound of subcomponents. Besides, each connection between component instances must match a connection pattern declared in the enclosing component between component types. However, UML 2.0 provides usual intentional points of variation. This kind of diagram is optional, and the nested hierarchy can be modelled only with instances that have a fixed cardinality. In this last case, UML 2.0 does not provide any frame to mark out the software architecture dynamics.

SafArchie

In the same spirit, SafArchie defines the concept of an *architecture type*. An architecture type defines a set of constraints on component interfaces and the interaction between them that must be respected by the software architectures. Architecture types are used to check structural and behavioral compatibility between components. An architecture type is composed of six main elements: port type, component type, composite type, bindings, operation, and attribute. A port type specifies the set of signatures of the operations that the port should provide or require. A component type defines all port types of the component and the minimum and maximum cardinality for each one. A composite type identifies all the component types that the composite should contain and the minimum and maximum cardinality for each one. It defines the allowed interactions between these component types through the binding concept. A binding defines a possible interaction between two port types belonging to one or two component types that belong to the same composite type. An architecture type is a set of structured constraints in terms of composite type, component type, and port type. Each typed software architecture should respect these constraints.

ACL

Tibermacine et al. [498] present an Architectural Constraint Language (ACL) as a means to formally describe architectural choices at all the stages of the component-based software development process. This language is based on the UML's Object Constraint Language (OCL) [399], but limits the scope of an OCL constraint to a particular component, by slightly modifying the syntax and semantics of the context part in OCL. At the syntactic level, every constraint context should introduce an identifier, corresponding to the name of a particular instance of the meta-class cited in the context. At the semantic level, ACL interprets a constraint with the meaning it would have in the context of the metaclass, but limiting its scope only to the instance cited in the context. A component is thus able to define constraints on its own structure. Finally, ACL can only express invariants; as compared to OCL, pre- and post-conditions are removed from the language.

ACL can be used to define a frame for a software architecture by defining a set of invariants that have to be respected by all configurations of the system. The architect has more work to do when using UML 2.0 or SafArchie because he has to define constraints for each component instances. ACL allows expressing more accurate constraints. Indeed, like OCL, which has been shown useful to improve the comprehensibility and the maintainability of models [81], ACL is easier for the designer to define and to read than a formal language.

ArchStudio

An early version of ArchStudio [406] proposes a mechanism for restricting runtime changes that compromise system integrity. It uses constraints to confine not only the set of changes that can occur but also when these changes may occur. ArchStudio supports transactional modifications. The constraints are only checked at the end of a transactional modification, thus allowing the system architecture to be in an invalid state within a transaction. This allows imposing precise constraints, without limiting how modifications are implemented.

Evaluation

These four approaches tackle the issue of the software architecture dynamics by limiting the allowed variability. They, however, suffer from two main limitations. The first problem is that there is insufficient connection with component-based platforms. Indeed, these models could be seen as a repository which could evaluate if an explicit evolution is permitted. But, currently, no approach combines a scripting language to make explicit the dynamics at the platform level and an architecture type or a set of constraints to check if the proposed evolutions are correct from the modelling point of view. The second problem concerns the number of valid architectures that are defined with a set of constraints or an architecture type. In many case, this number is infinite. Consequently, it is impossible to check the correctness of all of these architectures. Currently, model checkers do not support the evaluation of an infinite architecture family.

10.4 Aspect-Oriented Architectures Description Language

10.4.1 Issue

The notion of *architectural view/architectural layer/architectural aspect*, depending on the community, comes from a very natural analogy: Just as in the architecture of a building we have distinct *views/plans/blueprints* describing distinct concerns of the building structure (walls and spaces, electric wiring, water conduits), it seems reasonable to conceive a software architecture description as the composition of distinct concern specifications (*view, aspect, plan*) reflecting distinct perspectives on the same software system. Indeed the target audiences for an architecture description are the various stakeholders of the system. A stakeholder is any person, organization or other entity with a particular interest in the architecture of the system. Each of these stakeholders may have different interests and requirements.

A software architecture description already provides an implicit separation of concerns: by describing the component configuration and the component interface, it separates the dimensions of composition from interaction. Nevertheless, the separation of these dimensions is not sufficient to modularise concerns such as security that crosscut the software architecture. The insufficient modularity of crosscutting concerns complicates software evolution. To overcome this issue, this section presents several approaches that propose to integrate principles of Aspect-Oriented Software Development (AOSD) into ADLs. Through the description of these approaches, we will see how the improvement of the separation of concerns in a software architecture description can ease its evolution. We will also discuss the main issues raised by the introduction of AOSD into a software architecture.

10.4.2 Using Aspects in Architectural Description

IEEE 1471

IEEE Std 1471, named *Recommended Practice for Architectural Description of Software-Intensive Systems* [341], was the first formal standard to address what an architectural description (AD) is. It was developed by the IEEE Architecture Working Group between 1995 and 2000 by representatives from industry, other standards bodies and academia. In 2006, IEEE 1471 became a draft international standard (ISO/IEC DIS 42010) and is now undergoing joint revision by IEEE and ISO. It highlights the separation of concerns issue in a software architecture description.

IEEE 1471 is a conceptual framework. It establishes a set of content requirements on an architectural description. In IEEE 1471, an architecture description contains any collection of products used to document an architecture. IEEE 1471 specifies how architecture descriptions should be organised, and their information content. The three main principles of this framework are:

- abstracting away from specific media (e.g., text, HTML, XML);
- being method-neutral: It is being used with a variety of existing and new architectural methods and techniques;
- being notation-independent: IEEE 1471 recognises that diverse notations are needed for recording various facets of architectures.

An architecture description in IEEE 1471 is governed by a set of rules that define what it means for an AD to conform to the standard. Although IEEE 1471 does not provide the concept of aspect, it identifies the concept of architectural concerns which include: functionality, security, performance, reliability. All these concerns are generally regarded as aspects that can be managed at the design stage. Under the rules of IEEE 1471, an architectural description must explicitly identify the stakeholders of the system's architecture and enumerate each architectural concern. If an AD does not address all identified stakeholders' concerns, it is, by definition, incomplete.

In IEEE 1471, an AD is organised into one or more architectural views. An architectural view is defined to be *a representation of a whole system from the perspective of a related set of concerns*. Each view has a governing architectural viewpoint. The viewpoint provides the set of conventions for constructing, interpreting and analyzing a view, including the rules for determining whether it is well-formed. Each identified stakeholder concern must be covered by at least one of the architectural viewpoints selected for use in an AD; if not, the AD is incomplete.

With respect to this conceptual framework, we can see that it has identified as a key concept the issue of the different stakeholder management and the separation of concerns in a software architecture description. Currently, they do not propose to use Aspect-Oriented Modelling to compose this view. Consequently, they do not propose any clear join point model or pointcut language. The composition phase is furthermore not really formalised and thus this approach is not operational. However, we can imagine using IEEE 1471 as a framework associated to an ADL that supports AOSD.

Aspect-Oriented ADLs

Recently, to improve modularity and component reusability, several ADLs have been designed around the integration of Aspect-Oriented (AO) abstractions such as aspects, joinpoints, pointcuts and advice in order to address the modelling of crosscutting concerns.

As a software architecture description relies on a connector to express the interactions between components, an equivalent abstraction must be used to express the crosscutting interactions. An Architectural Aspect, which is composed of *aspectual connectors* and *aspectual components*, is a component that represents a crosscutting concern in a component-based architecture. The traditional connector cannot model the crosscutting interaction because the semantics between a binding of two components is different than the semantics of weaving an aspect into a base component. The first one usually defines a contract between a client and a supplier. The second one is more invasive. Due to the obliviousness principle [176], the base component must not be aware of the fact that it might be modified by an aspect component.

In order to express the crosscutting interaction, AspectualAcme [192] defines the Aspectual Connector, an architectural connection element that is based on the connector element but with a new kind of interface and a different semantics. The new interface makes a distinction between the different elements playing different roles in a crosscutting interaction, i.e., affected traditional components and aspectual components, and captures how they are interconnected.The interface of an aspectual component contains a glue clause, some base roles, and some crosscutting roles. The glue clause specifies how an aspectual component affects regular components. There are three types of glue clause: before, after, and around. The semantics is similar to that of advice composition in AspectJ [276]. The base roles can be linked to ports with a pointcut expression, which matches the different ports affected by the aspectual component. A crosscutting role identifies the aspectual component that affects the base components.

Similarly, Fractal Aspect Component (FAC) [413] extends the Fractal ADL with Aspect Components (AC). Aspect Components are responsible for specifying crosscutting concerns in a software architecture. Each aspect component can affect components by means of a special interception interface. Two kinds of bindings between components and ACs are offered: a direct crosscut binding declaring the component references and a crosscut binding using pointcut expressions based on component names, interface names and service names.

Contrary to FAC or AspectualAcme, PRISMA [412] is a symmetrical approach because it does not consider functionality as a kernel entity different from aspects and it does not constrain aspects to specify non-functional requirements; functionality is also specified as an aspect. As a result, PRISMA provides a homogeneous treatment of functional and non-functional requirements. In PRISMA, aspects are first-order citizens of software architectures and represent a specific behavior of a concern (e.g., safety, coordination, etc.) that may crosscut the software architecture.

10.4.3 Evaluation

Other analyzis of Aspect-oriented ADL can be found in [44, 422]. Complementary to these two studies, the approaches presented in this section illustrate that there is currently no consensus among existing approaches concerning the way to define an aspect in a software architecture. Some approaches consider that an aspect is composed of components, while others consider that an aspect is a kind of component or that a component is composed of aspects. However, most of them agree that the semantics of the composition has to be extended to incorporate aspects into an ADL. As in software architecture there is a consensus that a software connector is the element that mediates interactions between components; several approaches modify the semantics of the connector to reflect the concepts of AOSD in a software architecture description.

As illustrated by Mens et al. in [366], in addition to separating the different concerns during software development, AOSD can help to overcome many of the problems related to software evolution. Improving the separation at the architecture level can help to coordinate the requirements of the different stakeholders of the system and improve the ability to modify only one concern independently of the others. Nevertheless, integrating or modifying a concern requires invasively modifying the ADL specification, at all points affected by the concern. These modifications are low-level, tedious and error-prone, making the integration of such concerns difficult. As pointed out by the AOSD evolution paradox [505] (cf Section 10.6), the evolution of a concern can break the consistency of the software architecture. For this reason, we claim in the second part of this chapter that the consistency of a base architecture modified by an aspect is a key issue for the software architecture community. To illustrate the problem and evaluate an initial solution, we propose to study in depth TranSAT: a framework for integrating stepwise new concerns in a software architecture.

10.5 The Safe Integration of New Concerns in a Software Architecture

10.5.1 Overview of TranSAT

In this section, to motivate the breaking consistency issue, we present an overview of the TranSAT framework, through the example of a web travel agency software architecture. We first describe the architecture and then show how to use the TranSAT framework to extend this architecture with a session expiration concern. Finally, we consider some of the issues that confront an architect when specifying a crosscutting concern.

Example

Our example application of a web travel agency manages the booking of hotels and flight. This application is represented by the software architecture shown in Figure 10.1, which is specified using the SafArchie ADL (see Section 10.2).

Figure 10.1(a) gives the structural description of the web travel agency architecture. The structure is described in terms of composites (WebTravelAgency, ThirdPartyPartner), components (AuBoutDuMonde, Expedition, Voyage), ports (p1 to p5), delegated ports (dp1 to dp3) and bindings. A port contains operations; for example, the operations book and cancel are provided by the ports p4 and p5 respectively. A port must contain at least one operation, must be part of exactly one component, and must be bound to exactly one other port, in some other component. Operations are either provided or required. Bound ports must contain compatible operations; for example, port p2 requires the operations provided by port p4. Delegated ports do not contain any operations; they define the interface of a composite, exporting the operations of the composite's components.

Figure 10.1(b) gives the behavioral description of one of the components, AuBoutDuMonde. The behavior is specified in terms of an Input/Output Automaton [335] that describes the sequences of messages that a component may receive and emit. The notation used in these automata is as follows. For a provided operation

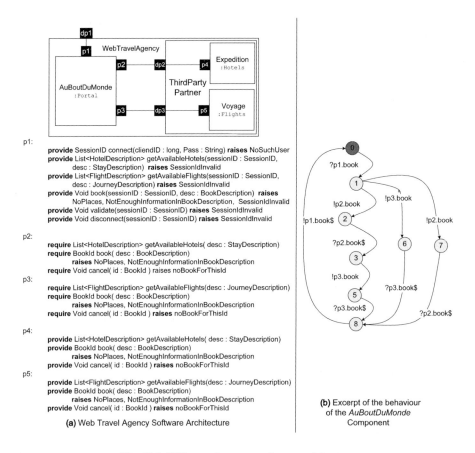

(a) Web Travel Agency Software Architecture

(b) Excerpt of the behaviour of the *AuBoutDuMonde* Component

Fig. 10.1. Web travel agency software architecture

op1, the message ?op1 represents the receipt of a request and the message !op1$ represents the sending of the response. ?op1 must precede !op1$, but they can be separated by any number of messages, representing the processing of op1. For a required operation op2, the message !op2 represents the sending of a call and the message ?op2$ represents the receipt of the response. Sending a call is a blocking operation, and thus !op2 must always be immediately followed by ?op2$. Using this notation, the behavior shown in Figure 10.1(b) specifies that when the AuBoutDu-Monde receives a book request, it makes a reservation of an hotel and/or a reservation of a flight.

Integrating a Session Expiration Concern Using the TranSAT Framework

The TranSAT framework manages the integration of a new concern, represented as an *architectural aspect*, into an existing architecture, referred to as a *basis plan*. The software architectural aspect represents the new concern in terms of a *plan*, a *join point mask*, and a set of *transformation rules*. The plan describes the structure and behavior of the new concern. The join point mask defines the structural and behavioral requirements that the basis plan must satisfy so that the new concern can be integrated. The transformation rules specify the means of composing the new plan with the basis plan. Given a software architectural aspect, the architect specifies where it should be added to the basis plan. The TranSAT *weaver* then checks that the selected point in the basis plan matches the join point mask, instantiates the transformation rules according to the architectural entities matched by the join point mask, and executes the instantiated transformation rules to compose the new concern into the basis plan.

As an example of the use of these constructs, we consider how to manage the automatic cancel of a trip if it is not confirmed. This concern is crosscutting, in that it affects the AuBoutDuMonde, the Expedition and Voyage components. The architectural aspect related to session expiration is shown in Figure 10.2. The new plan corresponding to the session expiration concern keeps a log of certain operations, sets a timer, and cancels some reservations when the timer expires. Specifically, the Manager components provide operations to keep a log and to retrieve information from this log. It also , and the Timer component triggers the Manager when a session duration is elapsed. The join point mask specifies that this plan can be composed in a context consisting of one component Cm1 attached to two other components Cm2 and Cm3. Some constraints (not shown) are also placed on the operations in the ports connecting these components.

In the web travel agency software architecture, the join point mask is compatible with the integration site consisting of the WebTravelAgency, Expedition and Voyage components. Finally, the transformation rules connect the ports of the plan to the ports of the selected integration site, and make other appropriate adjustments. In the case of the web travel agency architecture, the result of the composition is shown in Figure 10.3.

Issues

To specify the integration of a crosscutting concern, the architect must describe how to modify the component structure, behavior, and interfaces. This task is highly error prone, as many modifications are typically required, and these modifications can have both a local impact on the modified elements and a global impact on the consistency of the architecture.

Typically, a component model places a number of requirements on local properties of the individual architectural elements. For example, in SafArchie, the ADL on which TranSAT is built, it is an error to break a binding and then leave the affected port unattached, or to remove the last operation from a port, and then leave the port empty. The construction of the behavior automaton associated with each component is particularly error prone, because it must be kept coherent with the other elements of the component and because of the complexity of the automaton structure. For example, in SafArchie, all of the operations associated with the ports of a component must appear somewhere in the component's behavior automaton. When the ADL separates the structural and behavioral descriptions, it is easy to overlook one when adding or removing operations from the other. An automaton must also describe a meaningful behavior; at a minimum that for each operation, a call precedes a return and every call is eventually followed by a return from the given operation.

The architecture must also be globally coherent. The most difficult point raised by this consistency issue lies mainly in the behavior of the architecture. So that the application can run without deadlock, it must be possible to synchronize the behav-

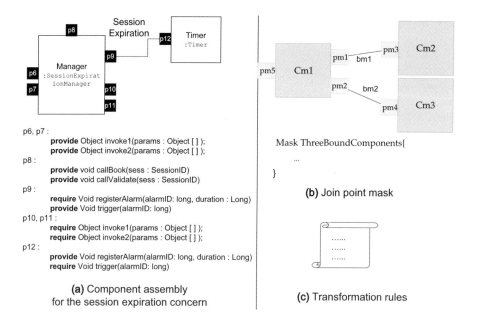

Fig. 10.2. Architectural aspect for the session expiration concern

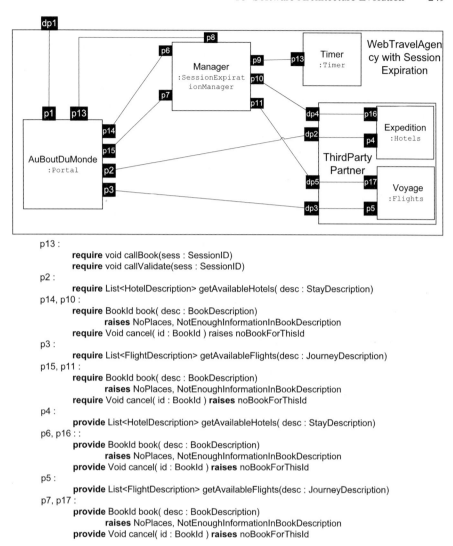

p13 :
        require void callBook(sess : SessionID)
        require void callValidate(sess : SessionID)
p2 :
        require List<HotelDescription> getAvailableHotels(desc : StayDescription)
p14, p10 :
        require BookId book(desc : BookDescription)
            raises NoPlaces, NotEnoughInformationInBookDescription
        require Void cancel(id : BookId) raises noBookForThisId
p3 :
        require List<FlightDescription> getAvailableFlights(desc : JourneyDescription)
p15, p11 :
        require BookId book(desc : BookDescription)
            raises NoPlaces, NotEnoughInformationInBookDescription
        require Void cancel(id : BookId) **raises** noBookForThisId
p4 :
        provide List<HotelDescription> getAvailableHotels(desc : StayDescription)
p6, p16 : :
        provide BookId book(desc : BookDescription)
            raises NoPlaces, NotEnoughInformationInBookDescription
        provide Void cancel(id : BookId) **raises** noBookForThisId
p5 :
        provide List<FlightDescription> getAvailableFlights(desc : JourneyDescription)
p7, p17 :
        provide BookId book(desc : BookDescription)
            raises NoPlaces, NotEnoughInformationInBookDescription
        provide Void cancel(id : BookId) **raises** noBookForThisId

Fig. 10.3. Transformed web travel agency software architecture

ior of each component with that of all of the components to which it is bound by its
ports. Any change in the behavior of a single component can impact the way it is synchronized with its neighbors, which in turn can affect the ability to synchronize their
behaviors with those of other components in the architecture. The interdependencies
between behaviors can make the source of any error difficult to determine.

10.5.2 A Specific Language for Software Architecture Transformation

In this subsection we present the TranSAT's transformation language for specifying
the elements of an architectural aspect: plan, join point mask and transformation
rules. The component assembly shown in Figure 10.2 (a) is an example of a plan,
showing only structural information. We also present the join point mask and the
transformation rules. The use of the language is illustrated through the definition of
the session expiration aspect.

The Join Point Mask

The join point mask describes structural and behavioral preconditions that a basis
plan must satisfy to allow the integration of the new concern. It consists of a series
of declarations specifying requirements on the structure and behavior of the components available at the integration site.

Figure 10.4 illustrates a join point mask suitable for use with the session expiration plan (Figure 10.2 (a)). For readability, some of the declarations are elided or
represented by the diagram at the top of the figure. The diagram specifies that some
component Cm1 must be connected to two other components Cm2 and Cm3. The remaining declarations define a series of placeholders for operations (line 3), specify
whether these operations must be declared as provided or as required (lines 4-13)
and specify that they must be associated with the ports pm1 to pm5 (lines 14-18).
Finally, lines 19-22 ensure that the operation opm1 is the inverse of operation opm5
in the bound port, and similarly for opm2 and opm6, opm3 and opm7, and opm4 and
opm8. Operations are inverse if they have the opposite polarity, the same name and
compatible types. In the web travel agency architecture, these constraints would, for
example, allow the architect to select the required operation book in port p2 as opm1
and the provided operation book in port p4 as opm5. In this example, the join point
mask does not specify any behavioral requirements. If needed, the constraints on the
behavior of a component mask can be specified in terms of a sequence of messages.

The Transformation Rules

The transformation rules describe precisely how to compose the new plan with a basis plan. They specify the various transformations to perform on the elements defined in the new plan and the join point mask, as well as their application order. The
language provides two kinds of transformation primitives: *computation transformation primitives* and *interaction transformation primitives*. The computation transformation primitives specify the introduction of new ports and operations in primitive
components, in order to adapt the component behavior. The interaction transformation primitives manage the insertion and deletion of component bindings and manage the composite content, in order to reconfigure the software architecture. Overall
TranSAT is targeted towards introducing new concerns into existing architectures
rather than removing existing functionalities. Thus, the language has been designed
to prevent transformations that remove existing behaviors.

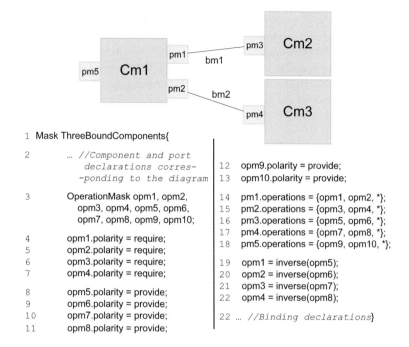

```
 1  Mask ThreeBoundComponents{

 2        ... //Component and port
               declarations corres-        12   opm9.polarity = provide;
              -ponding to the diagram      13   opm10.polarity = provide;

 3        OperationMask opm1, opm2,        14   pm1.operations = {opm1, opm2, *};
             opm3, opm4, opm5, opm6,       15   pm2.operations = {opm3, opm4, *};
             opm7, opm8, opm9, opm10;      16   pm3.operations = {opm5, opm6, *};
                                           17   pm4.operations = {opm7, opm8, *};
 4        opm1.polarity = require;         18   pm5.operations = {opm9, opm10, *};
 5        opm2.polarity = require;
 6        opm3.polarity = require;         19   opm1 = inverse(opm5);
 7        opm4.polarity = require;         20   opm2 = inverse(opm6);
                                           21   opm3 = inverse(opm7);
 8        opm5.polarity = provide;         22   opm4 = inverse(opm8);
 9        opm6.polarity = provide;
10        opm7.polarity = provide;         22   ... //Binding declarations}
11        opm8.polarity = provide;
```

Fig. 10.4. Join point mask definition

Computation Transformation Primitives

Table 10.1 shows the primitives used to manage the structural transformation of primitive component interfaces. These primitives allow the architect to create new ports and operations, to destroy empty ports and to move an operation from one port to another.

Adding an operation to a port has an impact on the behavior of the associated component. When a new copy of an operation is added to a port using the operation Operation Or = op in Pr, the architect must explicitly specify how the messages

Table 10.1. Computation transformations

	Port	Operation
create	Port Pr in Cp;	Operation $Or = op$ in Pr;
		Operation $Or_1 = op$ replaces Or_2;
destroy	Pr.destroy();	N/A
move	N/A	Or.move(Pr);

Cp: ComponentRef, Pr: PortRef, Or: OperationRef,
$op ::= Or \mid$ inverse(Or), N/A: Not applicable

associated with the newly added operation op fit into the behavior of the component
to which the operation is attached. The transformation of the behavior automaton is
specified using the pattern-matching syntax *template* => *result*. Such a rule inserts
the messages associated with the new operation, op, before, after, or around the calling or responding messages associated with some existing operation, m. The template
specifies the sequence of messages on m, possibly separated by any sequence of messages, x. The result describes how messages associated with the new operation, op,
are interleaved with this sequence.

The following lines illustrate the use of the automaton transformation rules:

$$?m \rightarrow x \rightarrow !m\$ \Rightarrow ?m \rightarrow !op \rightarrow ?op\$ \rightarrow x \rightarrow !m\$; \qquad 1$$
$$?m \rightarrow x \rightarrow !m\$ \Rightarrow ?m \rightarrow (!op \rightarrow ?op\$ \rightarrow x \mid x) \rightarrow !m\$; \qquad 2$$

In line 1, the template describes the receipt of a call to m followed by any number of
messages, followed by the sending of m's response. The result specifies that following the receipt of the call to m, the component sends a call to op and waits for the
response before performing any further computation. The use of the new operation
op at runtime can also be conditional. In line 2, the transformed component either
calls op, waits for the response, and then performs the sequence x, or performs x
alone, ignoring the added op operation.

Interaction Transformation Primitives

The interaction transformation primitives manage the reconfiguration of the software
architecture. As shown in Table 10.2, operators are provided to create and destroy
bindings, to create composites either at the top level or within another composite,
and to move one composite Cr_1 or one component Cp into another composite Cr_2.

Example

We use the session expiration example to illustrate the use of the computation and
interaction transformation primitives. In this example, composing the new plan requires (i) interposing the Manager component between the original component Cm1

Table 10.2. Interaction transformations

	Binding	Composite	Component
create	Binding $Br = \{Pr_1, Pr_2\}$;	Composite Cr; Composite Cr_1 in Cr_2;	N/A
destroy	Br.destroy();	N/A	N/A
move	N/A	Cr_1.move(Cr_2);	Cp.move(Cr_2);

Cp: ComponentRef, Cr: CompositeRef, Pr: PortRef,
Br: BindingRef, N/A: Not applicable

```
// Cm1 transformation                                                    1
Port  p14  in  Cm1;                                                      2
opm1 . move ( p14 );                                                     3
opm2 . move ( p14 );                                                     4
                                                                        5
... Similarly for the port p15 and the operation masks (opm3,opm4) of pm2   6
                                                                        7
// Cm2 transformation                                                    8
Port  p16  in  Cm2;                                                      9
opm5 . move ( p16 );                                                    10
opm6 . move ( p16 );                                                    11
... Similarly for the port p17 in Cm3 and the operation masks opm7 and opm8 of pm4   12
                                                                       13
// Port destruction                                                    14
pm1 . destroy ();                                                      15
pm2 . destroy ();                                                      16
pm3 . destroy ();                                                      17
pm4 . destroy ();                                                      18
... Ports are only destroyed if there are empty                        19
                                                                       20
// Manager transformation                                              21
                                                                       22
Operation  o6a  =  inverse ( opm1 )  replaces  p6 . invoke1 ;          23
Operation  o6b  =  inverse ( opm2 )  replaces  p6 . invoke2 ;          24
                                                                       25
... Similarly for the operations of the port p7                        26
                                                                       27
Operation  o10a=  inverse ( opm5 )  replaces  p10 . invoke1 ;          28
Operation  o10b=  inverse ( opm6 )  replaces  p10 . invoke2 ;          29
... Similarly for the operations of the port p11                       30
                                                                       31
// Introduction of p13 within Cm1                                      32
Port  p13  in  Cm1;                                                    33
Operation  o13a  =  inverse ( p8 . callBook )  in  p13 ;               34
Operation  o13b  =  inverse ( p8 . callValidate )  in  p13 ;           35
?opm9   →  x   →  !opm9$                                               36
          ⇒  ?opm9   →  x   →  !o13a  →  ?o13a$  →  !opm9$;             37
?opm10   →  x   →  !opm10$                                             38
          ⇒  ?opm10   →  x   →  !o13b  →  ?o13b$  →  !opm10$;           39
                                                                       40
// Component introduction                                              41
Manager . move ( Cm1 . parent );                                       42
Timer . move ( Cm1 . parent );                                         43
                                                                       44
// Binding creation                                                    45
Binding  b6  =  { p14 ,  p6 };                                         46
Binding  b7  =  { p15 ,  p7 };                                         47
                                                                       48
Binding  b18  =  { p13 ,  p8 };                                        49
                                                                       50
Binding  b10  =  { p10 ,  p16 };                                       51
Binding  b11  =  { p11 ,  p17 };                                       52
```

Fig. 10.5. Transformation rules for the session expiration concern

(instantiated as AuBoutDuMonde in the web travel agency case) and the operations
that are to be cancelled, and (ii) inserting this component between the components
Cm1 and (Cm2, Cm3) (instantiated as Expedition and Voyage in the web travel agency
case). Figure 10.5 shows the rules that carry out these transformations.

In the join point mask, the operations to be cancelled are specified to be in a port that may contain other operations, e.g., port pm1 includes the operations opm1, opm2, and some unknown list of operations * (line 14 in Figure 10.4). So that the session expiration concern does not have to take into account these other operations, lines 2–12 in Figure 10.5 move the operations into newly created ports, p14 to p17. This transformation may cause the ports matched by the join point mask to become empty. Accordingly, lines 15–18 apply the destroy operation to these ports, causing them to be destroyed if they are empty. When the session expiration concern is composed into the web travel agency software architecture, the ports matched by pm1 to pm4 are not destroyed because they contain the operations getFlightsDescription and getHotelsDescription.

The ports of the Manager are then updated with references to the operations to be cancelled. For each port, p6, p7, p10, and p11, the generic operations invoke1 and invoke2 are replaced by the inverses of the corresponding operations in the ports p14 to p17 (lines 20–30). These transformations implicitly update the Manager's behavior automaton by replacing the messages associated with the invoke operations by the messages associated with the new operations.

To insert the component Manager into the WebTravelAgency composite, a new port must be added to Cm1 and this ports must be instantiated with references to the callBook and callValidate operations. Lines 33–35 add the port p13 and copy the require counterpart of the Manager component's callBook and callValidate operations into this port. Because callBook and callValidate are new operations for Cm1, we must specify where they fit into Cm1's behavior. Lines 36–39 specify that Cm1 sends a call to this new operation whenever opm9 or opm10 are called.

The remaining rules transform the interaction between components. Lines 42–43 add the components of the plan to the basis plan. In these rules, for any outermost component or composite referenced by C in the join point mask, C.parent represents the parent of the element to which C is matched in the basis plan. As the component model is arborescent, each component or composite has at most one parent. If there is no parent, the enclosing transformation is not performed. Finally, lines 45–52 connect the components at the various ports. TranSAT automatically adds delegated ports, *e.g.,* dp4 in Figure 10.3, as needed. This behavior of the transformation engine improves the genericity of the architectural aspect. Applying these transformation rules to the join point between the AuBoutDuMonde, Voyage and Expedition components shown in Figure 10.1 (a) produces the software architecture shown in Figure 10.3 (structural information only).

10.5.3 Static Verification of the Transformation

A goal of TranSAT is to ensure that the composition of a new concern produces a valid software architecture. Accordingly, TranSAT statically checks various properties of the aspect at creation time and dynamically checks that the aspect is compatible with the insertion context when one is designated by the architect.

Static Properties and Checks

Given an aspect, TranSAT first checks that its various elements are syntactically and type correct. For example, a join point mask must declare that a port contains elements of type `Operation` and a `Binding` transformation must connect two ports. TranSAT then performs specific verifications for the plan, the join point mask, and the transformation rules.

Plan. TranSAT requires that the plan be a valid software architecture according to the component meta-model of SafArchie, except that it may contain unattached ports. For example, TranSAT checks that all bindings connect ports that contain compatible operations and that the automata describing the behaviors of the various components in the plan can be synchronized.

Join point mask. The variables declared by the join point mask represent the fragments of the basis architecture that can be manipulated by the transformation rules. Unlike the plan, the join point mask need not be an enriched architecture specification and thus TranSAT does not check that e.g. operations are specified for all ports or automata can be synchronized. These properties are, however, assumed to be satisfied by the elements matched in the basis architecture. TranSAT does verify the consistency of the information that is given, for example that any automaton provided uses operations in a manner consistent with their polarity.

Transformation rules. TranSAT ensures the safety of the transformation process by a combination of constraints on the transformation language and verifications performed statically on the transformation rules.

Compared to a general transformation languages, several features of the TranSAT transformation language have been designed to prevent the architect from expressing unsafe transformations. For example, the SafArchie component meta-model requires the insertion of delegated ports whenever a binding crosses a composite boundary. TranSAT introduces these delegated ports automatically, relieving the architect of the burden of identifying the composites between two ports, reducing the size of the transformation specification, and eliminating the need to fully specify composite nesting in the join point mask. The SafArchie component model also requires that each architectural element have a parent, except for the outermost components or composites. The transformation language enforces this constraint by combining the creation of a new element with a specification of where this element fits into the architecture; for example, `Port Pr in Cr` both creates a new port `Pr` and attaches this port to the composite `Cr`. Finally, a common transformation is to replace an operation in a port by another operation, which requires updating both the port structure and the automaton of the associated component. The transformation language combines both operations in the declaration `Operation Or`$_1$ `= op replaces Or`$_2$.

Other safety properties are not built into the syntax of the transformation language, but are checked by analyzis of the transformation rules. To do so, the operational semantics of the transformation language is formalised. Based on this formalization, the analyzis simulates the execution of the transformation rules on the various elements identified by the plan and the join point mask. At the end of the simulation, global post-conditions are checked to guarantee that the pattern will not break the software architecture consistency. For example, a post-condition guarantees that every element has at least one subelement except operations and join point mask elements for which no subelements are initially specified. A similar analyzis checks various properties of bindings: every port is connected to some other port by a binding, the connected ports are not part of the same component, the operations of the connected ports are compatible, etc. Another analyzis checks that for each component, the automaton and the set of operations in the various ports are kept consistent. A more detailed description of these checks is provided in [38].

10.5.4 Dynamic Verification

An architect integrates an aspect by designating a fragment of the existing architecture to which the aspect should be applied. TranSAT checks that the fragment matches the join point mask, to ensure that the fragment satisfies the assumptions under which the safety of the transformation rules has been verified. However, because the join point mask does not describe the entire basis architecture, the static checks of the different elements of the aspect are not sufficient to guarantee the correct composition of a new plan into a basis plan. Consequently, dynamic verifications of some structural and behavioral properties of the architecture are performed during the composition process.

The dynamic structural verification consists of checking the compatibility between the newly connected ports, according to the definition of the port compatibility of SafArchie [37]. Concretely, based on transformation rules that have been applied, the analyzis builds a list containing the newly created connections as well as the connections between ports that have been modified by the transformations. For each of these connections, the connected ports are verified to contain compatible operations. The other connections do not need to be checked as they are not affected by the transformations and their correctness has been previously verified during the analyzis of the basis plan or the aspect plan.

Adding new components and behaviors to a fragment of an architecture can change the synchronization at the interface of the fragment, and thus have an effect on the synchronization of the rest of the architecture. The use of an architectural aspect localises the modifications to a specified fragment of the existing architecture. The process of resynchronization thus starts from the affected fragment and works outward until reaching a composite for which the interface is structurally unchanged and the new automaton is bisimilar to the one computed before the transformation. The bismilarity relation ensures that the transformation has no impact on the observable behavior of the composite, and thus the resynchronization process can safely stop [520].

If the transformation of the architecture fails, any changes that were made must be rejected. Before performing any transformations, TranSAT records enough information to allow it to roll back to the untransformed version in this case.

10.5.5 Assessment

In Section 10.1, we observed that the architect who integrates a new concern without a dedicated framework, can use the general architecture analyzis tools to check the validity of the resulting architecture after the composition is complete. This approach, however, can give imprecise error messages, because the resulting architecture does not reflect the transformation step that caused the problem, and can be time consuming, due to the automaton synchronization that is part of this validation process. In this section, we briefly describe how a composition framework like TranSAT can address these issues.

Because the static verifications have a global view of the transformations that will take place, they can pinpoint the transformation rules that can lead to an erroneous situation. For example, if an operation is moved from a port of the join point mask, the port may become empty, resulting in an erroneous software architecture. While SafArchie would simply detect the empty port, TranSAT can, via an analyzis of the complete set of transformation rules, detect that there is a risk that a port contains only one operation, that a move is performed on the operation in this port, and that a destroy is not subsequently applied to this port. Using this information, TranSAT can inform the architect of problems in the transformation rules, before any actual modification of the architecture has taken place. Obtaining this feedback early in the composition process can reduce the overall time required to correctly integrate the new concern.

Because the dynamic verifications are aware of the exact set of components that are modified by the composition, they can target the resynchronization of the automata accordingly. As synchronization is expensive, reducing the amount of resynchronization required can reduce the amount of time required to integrate a new concern, making it easier for the architect to experiment with new variants.

10.5.6 Discussion and Tool Suite

Contrary to most AO-ADLs that create new first-class entities that extend the concept of *component* and *connector*, in TranSAT an architectural aspect is a composite entity that contains a set of components and connectors that must be inserted. Consequently, in TranSAT, weaving does not have a fixed semantics. Instead, the semantics of weaving is specified by the transformation rules contained in the architectural aspect description. This approach raises the issue of the difference between model weaving and model transformation. Indeed, this issue is not limited to the TranSAT approach. In many Aspect-Oriented Modelling approaches (AOM), a design is presented in terms of multiple user-defined views (aspects) and model composition is used to obtain a model that provides an integrated view of the design. In these approaches, model composition involves merging or weaving two or more models to obtain a single model. The apparent similarities between model weaving and model transformations have already been discussed elsewhere [45]. As a result, even if TranSAT can not be compared directly to others AO-ADLs, it can be classified as an AOM approach.

The TranSAT framework enriches the SafArchie tool suite to assist the architect during the specification of the system. For TranSAT, three main static modules have been developed. The first one permits the static checking of an architectural aspect. The second one assists the architect in composing an architectural aspect with an existing architecture by highlighting the different join points matched by the join point mask. Finally, the transformation engine weaves an architectural aspect into an architecture.

The static checking of the architectural aspect has been developed as an if-then clause in Drools [496] and in Prolog [484]. The Drools rules and the Prolog rules include the same conditions and the same consequences. The difference is that the rule is called explicitly in Prolog whereas it is chosen by the rule engine in Drools. Contrary to the Prolog implementation, the Drools implementation does not output the reason for the failure of a transformation rule. Although it is possible to check the reasons for the failure, it is not convenient to do so with forward-chaining. The time spent for the verification using the Prolog implementation is quite similar for both implementations. The rules check the initial state and the final state of the transformation environment and perform the structure and connection analyzis. The Drools implementation relies on 39 Drools rules. The Prolog implementation is composed of 21 Conditional Transformations [283] and 18 Prolog rules. Prolog and AGG rules were derived from the semantics of the transformation primitives defined in [36].

To detect the join point that can be matched by a join point expression, a module has been implemented in three ways with AGG [487], DROOLS and Prolog. The idea is the same for all the implementations. First we fill the knowledge base with facts that correspond to the elements of the software architecture. Then we transform the join point mask into a set of rules. Finally we provide these generated rules to the rule engine, which then finds all the matching facts in the knowledge base. The main difference between those implementations concerns the efficiency of the search. The AGG implementation is the slowest because of the graph matching process. The Drools implementation is slower than the Prolog implementation because of the time required to compile the Drools rules. Since the rules are generated from the join point mask, the cost of the rule compilation cannot be reduced.

Finally, the transformation engine has been developed with two concurrent techniques: AGG and Prolog. The AGG rules are generated from the TranSAT transformation rules. There are 158 graph transformation rules created for the session expiration composition. The host graph generated from the software architecture is composed of 75 nodes and of 84 edges. The transformed host graph contains 109 nodes and 130 edges. There are 34 conditional transformations that perform the TranSAT transformations. The software architecture is described by 172 predicates in the knowledge base. After the session expiration concern integration, the transformed software architecture is specified by 220 predicates. The session expiration integration in the reservation software architecture takes 50 times more time with AGG than with Prolog. Once again, the graph matching is responsible for the efficiency difference.

When considering how to implement the different weaving stages of TranSAT (static analyzis, join point resolution and transformation), we had two motivations:

First comparing existing transformation techniques as graph transformation engine and rules-based engine with backward chaining and forward chaining algorithms. Second, compare a domain specific framework as TranSAT to design architectural aspects with general transformation engine approaches. When comparing AGG, DROOLS and Prolog, the main differences are the techniques to communicate with the engine, the efficiency and the development complexity. Further differences among these techniques are discussed in [36]. Second, comparing TranSAT with these techniques, we can consider that our transformation engine and the join point mask are more close to the SafArchie language and semantics. Consequently, it is safer for an architect than using a general transformation approach; the language prevents the architect from making some errors; the static analyzer is more accurate thanks to the dedication of the transformation language. Finally, we plan to experiment with these different techniques to prove that in the context of building architectural aspects, TranSAT is easier to use and less verbose.

10.6 Related Work

Separation of Concerns in Software Modelling

In the Aspect Oriented Modelling domain, an important issue is how to compose the different concern models identified in the early stages of the development process. The major effort lies in being able to compose UML diagrams. For example, Reddy et al. [435] have developed a systematic approach for composing UML class diagrams in which a default composition procedure based on name matching can be customised by user-defined composition directives. The framework automatically identifies conflicts between models that have to be composed and solves them according to the composition directives. Composition directives, however, address weaving only from a structural point of view. They consider the composition as a model transformation. Besides, composition directives amount to a symmetric AOM approach that does not differentiate between aspect model and base model. Consequently, they do not provide a pointcut language to manage the composition.

Close to model composition directives, Muller et al. [382] present a means to build an information system with parametrised models. Model parametrisation allows the reuse of a model in multiple contexts. They use a model composition operator to combine models according to alternative and coherent ordering rules. However, as with model composition directives, their work only supports the composition of class diagrams and can not compose dynamic diagrams. This approach does not provide aspectual composition operators and as such does not support the composition of aspect models.

Along the same lines, Theme/UML extends UML to support the specification of symmetric concern models. In such a model, base and aspect concerns are defined in separate models at the same level of abstraction. At the modelling level, a base concern represents behaviors that are not crosscutting while an aspect concern represents behaviors that are primarily crosscutting. The Theme/UML approach introduces a *theme module* that can be used to represent a concern at the modelling level. Themes are declaratively complete units of modularization in which any of the diagrams available in the UML can be used to model one view of the structure and behavior that the concern requires for execution. Classes and methods defined in these diagrams describe the structure of these entities in the scope of the concern. Sequence diagrams describe the behavioral interactions that can occur between classes when the concern is executed. Aspects are represented as themes parametrised with templates that represent the join points at which behaviors in other themes are crosscut. In many ways, Theme/UML is very similar to TranSAT presented in this chapter. The main difference is in the target domain model. However, unlike TranSAT, Theme does not make any static guarantees on the result of the composition. KerTheme [245], however, proposes to validate the result of composition through testing.

Klein et al. [281] define an asymmetric operator that introduces the semantics-based weaving of scenarios. In this approach, an aspect is defined as a pair of scenarios, one for the join point designation (the "pointcut"), i.e., a scenario interpreted as a predicate over the semantics of MSCs (Message Sequence Charts) [243] satisfied by all join points (specification of the behavior to detect), and another for the advice, representing the expected behavior at the join point. Similarly to Aspect-J, where an aspectual behavior can be inserted around, before or after a join point, with this approach, an advice may complete the matched behavior or replace it with a new behavior to create a composed behavior. The operator proposed by Klein et al., is generic enough to be used to compose the behavioral part of an architectural aspect. It can for example be adapted to compose UML 2.0 sequence diagrams.

Less connected with UML, Roberto Lopez-Herrejon et al. [331] proposed an approach based on algebraic foundations. Here an aspect is seen as a model transformation function, i.e., a function that maps models to models, and the effects of the weaving process can be understood in terms of algebraic transformations. Around this definition, theoretical properties (commutativity, associativity and identity) are assigned to aspect compositions, and rules are generated (for example, precedence rules for compositions). This approach allows one to reason about composition, exposing its problems and leading to a partial solution for aspect reusability and problems that derive from the weaving process. The transformation language proposed in TranSAT to express the composition has the same goal.

The various approaches presented above focus on the problem of composition in the context of models. In considering a software architecture description as a model, some ideas such as the post directives described in [435] can inspire the architects to guarantee the correctness of an evolution step in a software architecture description. In the same way, the problem of building reusable model fragment can be addressed at the model level and specialised for the software architecture specification in a second stage.

AOSD Evolution Paradox

Despite the modularization provided by aspects, AOSD has been found to often hinder software evolution, and consequently to reduce software reliability. This problem is called AOSD-Evolution Paradox [505], and arises even when considering aspects at the architecture level. Essentially, the AOSD-Evolution Paradox is a consequence of the obliviousness property of aspects, which tries to make the use of aspects transparent for the base model. Because aspects include a description of each place at which they apply, they rely on the existing structure of the system, resulting in a tight coupling between the system and the aspects that advise it. When the system evolves, its structure changes and every crosscutting concern in every aspect needs to be checked to ensure that it still applies correctly, a tedious and error-prone task. For more details, we refer to Chapter 9.

Kellens et al. [362] present the idea of a *model-based pointcut definition*. These poincuts are defined in terms of a conceptual model of the base program, rather than referring directly to the implementation structure, thus reducing the coupling of the pointcut definition and the base model. These model-based pointcuts are useful to avoid the AOSD Evolution paradox. In TranSAT, the join point mask is based on the semantics of the software architecture. For example, when the join point mask defines two connected components, that are directly or indirectly connected are matched. Furthermore, a component mask matches either a component or a composite. This behavior of the join point mask improves the genericity of architectural aspects and limits the impact of structural changes on the weaving semantics.

10.7 Conclusion

Software architectures have the potential to provide a foundation for managing software evolution. However, if many ADLs support static description of a system, most of them currently provide no facilities for specifying architectural changes. In this chapter, we have identified two kinds of change: runtime architectural changes called internal software architecture evolution and changes managed by the architect called external software architecture evolution. For the first kind of evolution, two subcategories have been identified. The first one can express runtime reconfigurations to architectures but requires that the reconfigurations be specified explicitly. In contrast, other ADLs can accommodate unplanned reconfigurations of an architecture and incorporate behavior not anticipated by the original developers. These works propose to define architectural constraints to confine the potential evolution of the software architecture. On the other hand, to manage external evolution, ADLs suffer from the lack of support for modularity. This leads to a number of architectural breakdowns, such as increased maintenance overhead, reduced reuse capability, and architectural erosion over the lifetime of a system. As AOSD allows designers to modularise crosscutting concerns, promoting aspect-oriented software development principles into ADLs seems to be an attractive solution to overcome this external issue.

However, if applying AOSD to ADLs can help to overcome many of the problems related to software evolution, it pervasively modifies the semantics of the composition of software components. In the second part of this chapter, we argue that the integration of new concerns in a software architecture can break the software architecture consistency. Since a majority of existing ADLs have focused on design issues, they provide advanced static analyzis and system generation mechanisms. These mechanisms must be adapted to manage the new composition paradigm between aspects and components. Through SafArchie and TranSAT, this chapter proposes an initial solution to statically check that an aspect will not break the consistency of a software architecture. TranSAT is based on a specific architecture transformation language to describe the weaving. This language is carefully designed to make certain unsafe transformations impossible to express. Besides, it allows static verification of additional consistency properties before aspect weaving is performed. However, TranSAT and its transformation language are currently highly coupled with the SafArchie semantics.

To conclude this chapter, we claim that one of the future main steps of software architecture is to propose (i) a way to describe homogeneously internal and external software evolutions. (ii) This evolution description should be associated to a powerful analyzis model in order to be able to guarantee the consistency of a software architecture by checking only the parts of an architecture impacted by the changes. (iii) This approach should be generic in order to be adapted depending on the ADLs semantics. (iv) Any changes should be represented as first-class entities in the software architecture and it should, at least before system-deployment time, be possible to add, remove and modify a concern with a limited effort. The approaches presented in this chapter propose initial solutions to achieve these requirements. However, none addresses the evolution issue in its entirety in considering both the software evolution description, the analyzis impact of a change and its projection on a targeted platform.

11

Empirical Studies of Open Source Evolution

Juan Fernandez-Ramil[1], Angela Lozano[1], and Michel Wermelinger[1],
and Andrea Capiluppi[2]

[1] Computing Department, The Open University, United Kingdom
[2] Department of Computing & Informatics, Lincoln University, United Kingdom

Summary. This chapter surveys a sample of empirical studies of Open Source Software (OSS) evolution. According to these, the classical findings in proprietary software evolution, such as Lehman's laws of software evolution, might need to be revised, at least in part, to account for the OSS observations. The book chapter summarises what appears to be the empirical status of each of Lehman's laws with respect to OSS and highlights the threats to validity that frequently emerge in this type of research.

11.1 Introduction

Software evolution is the phenomenon of software change over years and releases, since inception (concept formation) to the decommissioning of a software system. The work on the evolution of larger software systems poses many challenges. Our assumption when studying software is that such work can be improved by taking into account the findings of empirical studies of long-lived software systems.

With the emergence of the open source paradigm, software evolution researchers have access to a larger number of evolving software systems for study than ever before. This has led to a renewed interest in the empirical study of software evolution. Some surprising findings in open source have emerged that appear to diverge from the classical view of software evolution. In this book chapter we attempt to examine this and, in doing so, propose research topics for further advance in this area.

The structure of this chapter is as follows. The remainder of this section briefly presents the results of the classic studies of proprietary software evolution and provides a short overview of the open source paradigm. Section 11.2 summarises the results of seven empirical studies of open source evolution. Section 11.3 attempts to compare the evolution of open and closed source systems based on such studies. Since addressing the threats to validity is a major challenge in order to make further progress in this line of research, Section 11.4 lists and briefly discusses the threats that are, in our view, the most common. Section 11.5 presents the main conclusions of this chapter and proposes topics for further research.

T. Mens, S. Demeyer (eds.), *Software Evolution.*
DOI 10.1007/978-3-540-76440-3, © Springer 2008

11.1.1 Classical Views of Proprietary Software Evolution

In the late 1960s and early 1970s Lehman and his collaborators pioneered the empirical study of the changes done to a software system after it has been released. They examined a number of proprietary systems, including the IBM 360-370 operating system. In the late 1970s and early 1980s they studied measurement data from several other systems [320]. Their initial focus of attention was the phenomenon of *large program growth dynamics*. Later they realised that the phenomenon was not only a property of large systems, partly because *largeness* cannot be unambiguously defined for software systems. What they observed was a process of change in which software systems were not only modified, but also acquired additional functionality. This process, they argued, could be legitimately called *software evolution*.

Lehman realised that software evolution, the continual change of a program, was not a consequence of bad programming, but something that was inevitably required to keep the software up-to-date with the changing operational domain. Continual software change was needed for the stakeholders' satisfaction to remain at an acceptable level in a changing world. This matched well with the software measurements that he and colleagues had collected. This realisation was so compelling that this observation was termed the *law* of continuing change. The use of the term *laws* was justified on the basis that the phenomena they described were beyond the control of individual developers. The forces underlying the laws were believed to be as strong as those of the laws of demand and supply in Economics. Other empirical observations were encapsulated in statements and similarly called laws. Initially three laws were postulated, followed by five that were added at various points later, giving a total of eight.

Despite the strong confidence on the validity of the laws, the matter of universality of the laws was not sufficiently well defined. Anyone could always recall a program that was developed, used only once or twice and then discarded. Hence, the first requisite for evolution is that there is a continual need for the program, i.e., there is a community of users for which running the program provides some value. Lehman's analysis, however, went deeper and led to the realisation that, strictly speaking, the laws only applied to a wide category of programs that Lehman called *E-type systems* [320], where the "E" stands for *evolutionary*. An E-type system is one for which the problem being addressed (and hence, the requirements and the program specification) cannot be fully defined. E-type software is always, to some degree, incomplete and addresses "open" problems. We say 'open' in the sense that the *change charter* has arbitrary boundaries that may move at any time and that the requirements specification can always be further refined or modified in some way as to seek to satisfy new or changed needs. The immediate consequence is that for an E-type program there is always a perceived need for change and improvement. Another characteristic of E-type systems is that the installation of the program in its operational domain *changes the domain*. The evolution process of an E-type program becomes a *feedback system* [320]. This is illustrated in Fig. 11.1.

E-type systems contrast with S-type programs, where the "S" stands for *specified*. In S-type programs the specification is complete and can be formally expressed us-

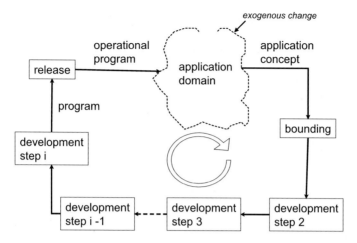

Fig. 11.1. Lehman's view of the E-type Software Process. This is a slightly modified version of the one in [174]

ing Mathematics. In S-type programs mathematical arguments can be used to prove that the program fully satisfies its specification. S-type programs represent the domain within which the application of formal verification methods is more meaningful and likely to be effective. However, the vast majority of systems used in businesses and by the general public (e.g., complex PC operating systems, word processors, spreadsheets, web browsers and servers, email systems) are of type E. Hence the importance of the type E and the laws that seek to be descriptions of their evolutionary characteristics. In its original classification [320], Lehman also identified a third type, called P, for *problem*. P-type problems are usually well-defined and can be formally described. However, the programs addressing such problems are based on heuristics rather than mathematical proof. They are generally characterised by some trade-offs in their requirements and their results are satisfactory only to certain level (not absolutely correct as in the case of S-type programs). The software used to generate schedules for trains and airline flights could be examples of the P-type. If a P-type program is actively used in a real-world application it is likely to acquire, at least to some extent, E-type properties. Traditionally, the software evolution research has concentrated on the most common, the type E.

Initially, the topic of empirical study of software evolution did not reach much momentum beyond Lehman's immediate circle of collaborators. To our knowledge, there were only two independent studies in the 1980s: one confirmatory by Kitchenham [279] and one, by Lawrence [314], which was mainly a critique. Lawrence [314] took a statistical approach and found support for one of the five laws, at that time. Three of the laws were not supported by his tests and he was not able to formulate one of the laws into proper statistical tests. In our view, a contribution of Lawrence's study was the realisation that laws were informal statements and that their formal testing against empirical data involved first their formalisation. However, because each law can be formalised in more than one different way, it may lead to more than one test for each law. We come back to this issue in subsection 11.2.7.

Despite these empirical challenges and the not uncommon view that software is not restricted by any natural laws, the wider software engineering community seemed to progressively realise that Lehman's laws were a legitimate attempt, possibly the most insightful so far, to describe why software evolves and what evolutionary trends software is likely to display. The laws appeared to match common experience and were discussed in popular software engineering textbooks and curricula [414, 468]. The laws should be considered, at the very least, hypotheses worth further studying.

In the late 1990s and early 2000s a fresh round of empirical studies by Lehman and colleagues took place (e.g., [323]). These involved five proprietary systems that were studied in the FEAST projects with results widely publicised [168]. FEAST led to the refinement of some of the laws, which, as we said, are currently eight in number. The laws are no longer isolated statements: the phenomena they describe are interrelated. The project realised that empirical data related to some of the laws were easier to extract than for others. Despite the difficulties, the laws were generally supported by the observations and seen as the basis for a *theory of software evolution*. The laws, in a recent post-FEAST wording [316], are listed in Table 11.1.

As can be seen in Table 11.1 a recent refinement of the fourth law included the text "The work rate of an organisation evolving an E-type software system tends to

Table 11.1. Laws of E-type Software Evolution, a slight revision from the version published in [316]

Number (year)	Name	Statement
I (1974)	Continuing change	An E-type system must be continually adapted otherwise it becomes progressively less satisfactory in use
II (1974)	Increasing complexity	As an E-type system is evolved its complexity increases unless work is done to maintain or reduce the complexity
III (1974)	Self regulation	Global E-type system evolution is regulated by feedback
IV (1978)	Conservation of organisational stability	The work rate of an organisation evolving an E-type software system tends to be constant over the operational lifetime of that system or segments of that lifetime
V (1991)	Conservation of familiarity	In general, the incremental growth (growth rate trend) of E-type systems is constrained by need to maintain familiarity
VI (1991)	Continuing growth	The functional capability of E-type systems must be continually enhanced to maintain user satisfaction over the system lifetime
VII (1996)	Declining quality	Unless rigorously adapted and evolved to take into account changes in the operational environment, the quality of an E-type system will appear to be declining
VIII (1971/96)	Feedback system	E-type evolution processes are multi-level, multi-loop, multi-agent feedback systems

be constant over the operational lifetime of that system *or segments of that lifetime"*, with the most recent addition in italics. This apparently minor addition recognised explicitly in the laws for the first time the possible presence of discontinuities in the lifetime of a software system and was a consequence of the observation in FEAST of breakpoints in growth and accumulated change trends. Other researchers [17, 57] seem to have independently arrived to similar views that software evolution is a discontinuous phenomenon. For example, Aoyama [17] studied the evolution of mobile phone software in Japan over a period of four years in the late 1990s. During this time mobile phones went through a fast evolution from voice communication devices to mobile Internet Java-enabled terminals. The code base studied by Aoyama increased its size by a factor of four in four years within which the software experienced significant structural changes at particular points. We share this author's view that dealing with discontinuities in evolution is an unresolved challenge. The immediate consequence is that it may not be sensible to simply extrapolate trends, such as growth or change rate into the future, to predict the future of a system. In other words, the analysis of quantitative data on growth and change rates, productivity, and so on needs to be done with care, and any quantitative prediction using historical trends should include the reservation "this might be so unless a discontinuity in the evolution of the system happens". (It is open to debate whether after discontinuities we are still dealing with the evolution of the "same" software, whether they lead to a new stage or even to a new system. One would expect a change of the software's name after a radical change that fundamentally transforms it, but software naming conventions might be driven by commercial and other non-technical considerations.)

In connection to the idea of discontinuity, an important addition to the description of how proprietary systems evolve came from Bennett and Rajlich [57], in the form of their *staged model of the software lifecycle*. A key idea contributed by these authors is that systems tend to go through distinctive phases, termed *initial development, evolution, servicing, phase-out* and finally *close-down*, with each of these phases involving specific management challenges. This is illustrated in Fig. 11.2. Bennett and Rajlich chose to call one of their phases *evolution*, possibly because according to them it is within this phase that software is actively enhanced and changed. During the so-called servicing phase, only minor fixes are implemented to keep the system running (possibly while a replacement is on its way) before phasing out the software.

As a summary, we can say that, when applied to software, *evolution* describes the process enacted by the people who are in charge of a software system after its first release when they seek to implement fixes (e.g., repairing the consequences of bad programming and other defects), enhancements in functionality and other valuable changes in the quality characteristics of the software, leading most of the time to a gradual phenomenon of change. We have also seen that there could also be discontinuities (even radical or revolutionary) in software evolution from time to time. It must be pointed out that software evolution is very different from Darwinian evolution and that the differences between software and biological entities are important. (For example, the changes in software are designed and implemented by intelligent humans. Such changes are not random. Biological entities are subject to physical and chemical laws but software isn't.) Software evolution is very much a phenomenon

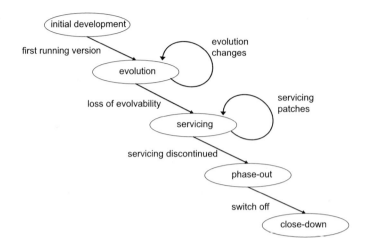

Fig. 11.2. Staged model of the software life-cycle [57], taken from [174] © 2000 IEEE

on its own that has been studied during the last three or four decades, mainly using data from proprietary systems. This section has presented a brief account of the situation with regards to empirical studies of such systems. With the emergence of open source, software evolution researchers can access vast amounts of software evolution data which is now available for study. Some of the initial findings (e.g. [206]) were concerning because they suggested that open source evolutionary patterns can be different to the ones suggested by the laws and generally expected in proprietary software evolution. This and other open source case studies will be examined in the remainder of this chapter with the aim of providing the reader with an overall picture of the past and current empirical open source software evolution research.

11.1.2 The Emergence of Open Source

The emergence of *open source software* (OSS) and *free software* [3], has provided researchers with access to large amounts of code and other software artefacts (e.g., documentation, change-log records, defect databases, email conference postings) that they can use in their studies. For example, using OSS data researchers are able to test certain hypotheses about the effectiveness of a software engineering technique or the validity of theory. OSS has become an established approach to distribute software as a *common good*. This is the free software ideal defended by the Free Software Foundation and others. It is often emphasised that in free software, "free" is used as in "freedom", not as in "free beer". The following quotation from the Debian website (one of the largest Linux *distributions*) seems to capture well the open source philosophy:

---

[3] In this chapter we use "open source" and "free" as synonyms, even though there are slight differences in meaning (see their glossary entries).

"While free software is not totally free of constraints...it gives the user the flexibility to do what they need in order to get work done. At the same time, it protects the rights of the author. Now that's freedom."[4]

The OSS approach to software development has been documented in the literature [434]. The brief description that follows is based on our own experiences and on our discussions with colleagues. A defining property of OSS is that source code is openly shared with only some restrictions (e.g., normally any changes can only be released as OSS and under the same license restrictions as the original code). Many OSS contributors seem to be working in their free time with their own computing resources, even though companies are getting increasingly engaged in some OSS projects. The OSS process is lighter than the processes followed in companies involved in professional software development. In OSS, the code is the main artefact for sharing knowledge and understanding amongst contributors. OSS development is mostly about programming and testing. Other software engineering techniques and processes are often missing or done implicitly, like requirements analysis and specification, and detailed design. For this reason it is unlikely to find in OSS formal or informal requirements specification, a program specification or a formal representation of the architecture of a system. Release notes, email lists, defect databases and configuration management facilities are frequently provided by an OSS project. In some projects there are people that operate as gate keepers for any additions or changes to the code. Rules are set out by each project or community, regarding the submission of defect fixes, new functionality, and so on. The larger OSS projects tend to have scheduled releases and stated goals in terms of functionality to be achieved in coming releases. Frequently there are two evolving streams of code that are interrelated, the so-called "stable" or ready for distribution stream, and the developmental, which is the one currently being changed and enhanced. From time to time, development releases are promoted to stable and are distributed. Systematic testing (e.g., as when test cases are available) is not always present.

Particularly since the late 1990s, there have been OSS-related contributions to the literature. It is useful to distinguish here two types of studies. On the one hand, there are *technology-oriented* papers. These address mainly the "*how* view of evolution" [322]. These papers address a particular technical problem in implementing or supporting software evolution processes and propose a technique to address such problem. On the other hand, one encounters *empirical studies* that gather and analyse observations of the OSS evolution phenomenon and attempt their modelling and explanation, addressing the "*what and why* view of evolution" [322]. These empirical studies aim at characterising software evolution, identifying general or particular evolutionary patterns, in order to increase our understanding of the phenomenon or to inform good practice. The empirically-oriented papers that we have selected for our discussion examine sequences of code versions or releases and provide empirical observations that are comparable to those underlying the classical view of software evolution. These include OSS functional growth patterns and tests of compliance with Lehman's laws.

---

[4] http://www.debian.org/intro/free (as of Nov 2006).

11.2 Empirical Studies of Open Source Evolution

Pirzada's 1988 PhD thesis [418] was possibly the first study that singled out differences between the evolution of the Unix operating system and the systems studied by Lehman et al. [320]. Pirzada's work was still in the pre-Internet days and open source was yet to arrive. However, he should be credited with arguing, probably for the first time, that differences in development environments, in this case, differences in academic and industrial software development, could lead to differences in the evolutionary patterns. If Pirzada was right we should expect differences between OSS and proprietary evolution. Study of OSS evolution started 10 years or so later than Pirzada's thesis. In the next sections we summarise some of the most relevant empirical studies of OSS evolution to date.

11.2.1 The Linux Kernel Study by Godfrey and Tu [206]

Godfrey and Tu [206] studied the growth trend of the popular OSS operating system Linux, for which Unix was a precursor, with data covering Linux evolution since 1994 to 1999. Development of Linux started as a hobby by Linus Torvalds in Finland. The system was then publicly released and experienced an unprecedented popularity with hundreds of volunteers contributing to Linux. In 2000 more than 300 people were listed as having made significant contributions to the code. Godfrey and Tu found that Linux, a large system with about 2 million LOCs at that time, had been growing superlinearly. This essentially meant that the system was growing with an increasing growth rate. These authors found that the size of Linux followed a quadratic trend. This type of growth was fully in line with Lehman's sixth law, but the superlinear rate contradicted some consequences of the second law, such as a decrease in growth rate as complexity increases. It also appeared to contradict laws three (self-regulation) and five (conservation of familiarity). Godfrey and Tu's study was later replicated by Robles et al. [443] and Herraiz et al. [231] (see subsection 11.2.4 below), using independently extracted data from the Linux repository. These more recent studies also identified a superlinear growth trend in Linux.

Godfrey and Tu found that the growth rate was higher in one particular subsystem of Linux that holds the so-called *device drivers*, as can be seen in Fig. 11.3. Such device drivers enable a computer to communicate with a large variety of external or internal hardware components such as network adapters and video cards. Their explanation for Linux's high growth rate was that drivers tend to be independent of one another and that the addition of new drivers does not impact overall the complexity as when code is added to the *kernel*, the functional "heart" of the system. Another significant part of the Linux code base was the replicated implementation of features for different CPU types, giving the impression that the system was larger than it really was. The Linux kernel represents only a small part of the code repository. These authors recommended, in line with previous researchers [186], that evolution patterns should be visualised not only for the total system but also individually for each subsystem.

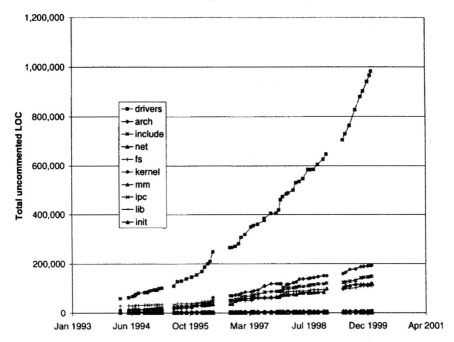

Fig. 11.3. Growth of Linux's major subsystems (development releases only), taken from [206]. ©2000 IEEE

11.2.2 The Comparative Study by Paulson et al. [411]

Paulson et al. [411] compared the evolution of three well-known OSS (the Linux kernel, the Apache HTTP web server, and the GCC compiler) and three proprietary systems in the embedded real time systems domain (the proprietary systems were described as "software protocol stacks in wireless telecommunication devices"). They chose to look at the Linux kernel because in their view it was more comparable to their three proprietary systems than the Linux system as a whole. The five hypotheses studied were: (1) OSS grows more quickly than proprietary software, (2) OSS projects foster more creativity, (3) OSS is less complex than proprietary systems, (4) OSS projects have fewer defects and find and fix defects more rapidly, and (5) OSS projects have better modularization. The measurements used to test these hypotheses were as follows:

1. For hypothesis 1, related to size (or growth): number of functions and lines of code (LOCs) added over time.
2. For hypothesis 2, related to creativity: functions added over time.
3. For hypothesis 3, related to complexity: overall project complexity, average complexity of all functions, average complexity of added functions.
4. For hypothesis 4, related to defects: functions modified over time, percentage of modified functions with respect to total.

5. For hypothesis 5, related to modularity: correlation between functions added and modified.

Only hypotheses (2) and (4) were supported by the measurements. However, with respect to hypothesis 2, it could be an oversimplification to assess creativity by simply looking at the number of functions added over time, without taking into consideration the number of developers. With respect to hypothesis 4, one would have expected some direct measure of defects or defect density, instead of simply looking at functions. For these reasons we conclude that these two hypotheses are not easy to investigate based on the measurements chosen and raise some questions. The investigation of the other three hypotheses seems to have been more straightforward. Paulson et al. found that the growth of the six systems analysed was predominantly linear. They compared their results with the averaged data by two other groups of researchers (see Fig. 11.4), finding that the slopes in the data by others matched well into the pattern they found. Paulson et al. also found, using three different complexity measures, that the complexity of the OSS projects was higher than that of the proprietary systems, concluding that the hypothesis that OSS projects are simpler than proprietary systems was not supported by their data. As said, one further aspect investigated was modularity. They looked at the growth and change rates, arguing that if modularity is low, adding a new function will require more changes in the rest of the system than if modularity is high. No significant correlation was found between the growth rate and change rate in proprietary systems, but such correlation was present in OSS projects. Hence, no support was found to the hypothesis that OSS projects are more modular than proprietary systems.

Whereas Godfrey and Tu (see subsection 11.2.1) found superlinear growth in Linux, Paulson et al. detected linear growth. These two findings do not necessarily contradict each other because the former study was looking at Linux as a whole, while the latter focused on the kernel, which is one of its subsystems and does not include drivers.

11.2.3 The Study of Stewart et al.[476]

Stewart et al. [476] explored the application of a statistical technique called *functional data analysis* (FDA) to analyse the dynamics of software evolution in the OSS context. They analysed 59 OSS projects in order to find out whether structural complexity increases over time or not. Two measurements of complexity were considered: coupling and lack of cohesion. The higher a program element is related to others, the higher the coupling. The higher the cohesion, the stronger will be the internal relationships within an element of a program. They considered that generally there is trade-off between the two measurements (i.e., increasing cohesion leads to a decrease in coupling). For this reason they used the product of the two attributes "coupling × lack of cohesion", as their measurement of interest. These authors found that FDA helped to characterise patterns of evolution in the complexity of OSS projects. In particular, they found two basic patterns: projects for which complexity either increased or decreased over time. When they refined their search for

Total Functions
Linear Approximation

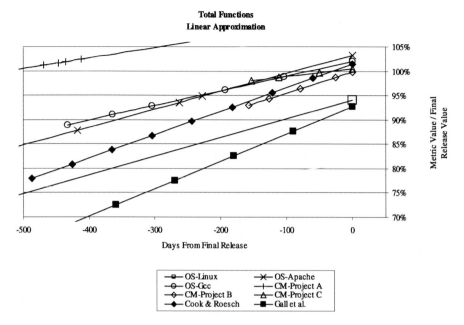

Fig. 11.4. Total size of systems studied by Paulson et al. and by other researchers (linear approximations), taken from [411]. ©2004 IEEE

patterns they actually found four patterns, as shown in Fig. 11.5. The names given to each of these patterns (and the number of projects under each) were *early decreasers* (13), *early increasers* (18), *midterm decreasers* (14) and *midterm increasers* (14).

Another differentiating factor, not represented in Fig. 11.5, was the period of time, shorter or longer, during which projects appeared to be most active. These researchers explored factors that might explain such patterns, as both functional growth and complexity reduction are desirable evolution characteristics. They discuss that, contrary to their hypotheses, neither the starting size nor the increase of size was significantly different between increasing and decreasing complexity clusters. Moreover, there was not a significant difference in the patterns on the average release frequency between increasing and decreasing complexity clusters. The authors hypothesise that the results may relate to the number of people involved in the project. Generally a correlation is expected between the number of contributors and the complexity. Projects with low complexity may initially attract and retain more people than others, but if they become very popular, their complexity may later increase. This may explain the midterm complexity increase pattern observed. However, in this study the number of contributors was not measured and this was suggested as an aspect for further work.

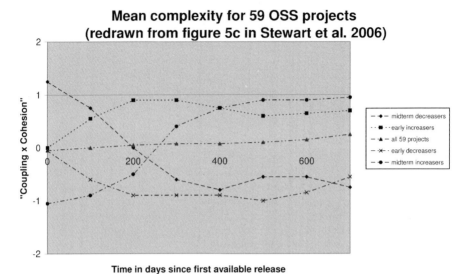

Fig. 11.5. Mean complexity for 59 OSS projects (line closest to zero) and for four specific clusters of such projects sample, as found by Stewart et al., taken from [476]

11.2.4 The Study by Herraiz et al. [231]

Herraiz et al. [231] examined the growth of 13 OSS systems. This sample included some of the largest packages in the Debian/Linux distribution. These authors concluded that the predominant mode of growth was superlinear. The choice of the large and popular Debian/Linux distribution was an attempt of achieving a representative sample of successful OSS projects. After various technical considerations, 13 projects were selected for study. Mathematical models were fit to the growth trends and the best fits were selected, determining that six projects where experimenting superlinear growth, four projects displayed linear growth and three projects were sublinear. The size measurements were made using number of files and number of lines or statements in the source code (SLOCs), with both measurements giving similar results. This study, looked at Linux growth data from 1991 to 2003 or so, confirming that Linux had still growing superlinearly since Godfrey and Tu's study [206] six years before. Table 11.2 lists the names of the OSS systems studied, their growth rates and the identified overall growth trends. In this table, growth rates are semiannual unless projects are labelled with an asterisk, indicating monthly growth rates. What is also relevant for growth rates is their sign[5]: positive, approximate zero or negative, which indicates predominantly superlinear, linear or sublinear growth.

---

[5] Herraiz et al. [231] fitted a quadratic polynomial to the SLOC and number of files data and looked at the coefficient of the quadratic term as an indication of the overall trend.

Table 11.2. Growth rates and overall growth trend in some Debian packages, taken from [231]. ©2006 IEEE

Project	Growth rate (SLOCs)	Growth rate (files)	Category
Amaya	1.45	-0.0055	linear
Evolution	-31.89	-0.17	sublinear
FreeBSD*	15.16	0.056	linear
Kaffe	77.13	0.71	superlinear
NetBSD*	152.74	1.04	superlinear
OpenBSD*	401.20	2.01	superlinear
Pre tools	4.31	0.044	superlinear
Python	18.43	-0.062	linear
Wine	50.06	0.064	linear
wxWidgets*	587.56	0.29	superlinear
XEmacs	-259.44	-0.60	sublinear
XFree86	-412.28	-1.47	sublinear
Linux*	186.21	0.71	superlinear

11.2.5 The Study by Wu et al.[548, 547]

Wu et al. [548, 547] analysed the evolution of three OSS systems (Linux, OpenSSH, PostgreSQL). One of the contributions of this work is to have put forward evidence that reinforces the observation that OSS evolution goes through periods of relatively stability where small, incremental changes are implemented, separated by periods of radical restructuring, where architectural changes take place. These are changes that may occur in relatively short periods of time and that virtually transform the architecture of an evolving system and the subsequent evolution dynamics. Fig. 11.6 presents one of the results derived by Wu [547] for Linux using the *evolution spectrograph* [548] visualisation technique. This type of graph shows the time on the x-axis, whereas the y-axis is mapped to elements (e.g., files) in the system. Files are ordered on the y-axis based on their creation date, from the bottom upwards. Every horizontal line in the graph describes the behavior of a property (e.g., number of dependencies) over time for each element. Whenever the property changes for an element at a point in time, that portion of the horizontal line is painted with strong intensity. If the property does not change or changes little, the intensity gradually decreases and the line fades away. Changes in colour intensity that can be seen vertically denote many elements having changes in that property. When vertical lines appear on the spectrograph, these indicate massive changes across the system. As one can see in Fig 11.6, there is evidence for at least four major Linux restructurings, identified with the release codes in the figure.

11.2.6 The Study of Capiluppi et al. [103, 104, 105]

Capiluppi et al. [103, 104, 105] studied the evolution of approximately 20 OSS systems using measurements such as growth in number of files, folders and functions;

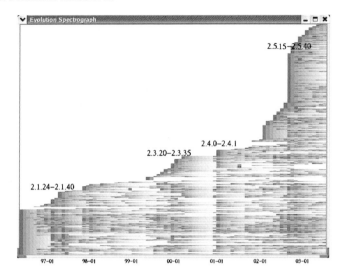

Fig. 11.6. Outgoing dependency changes in Linux, taken from [548].©2004 IEEE

complexity of individual functions using the McCabe index [354]; number of files handled (or touched) [320] and amount of *anti-regressive work* [320].

Segmented Growth Trends

One example of the systems studied is Gaim, a messenger program compatible with several operating systems: Linux, Windows, MacOS X and BSD. The growth trend of this system, in number of files and folders, is presented in Fig. 11.7.

In Gaim, one cannot easily identify its overall growth pattern. From day 1 to day 450 or so the growth pattern is superlinear. Then, growth essentially stops until day 1200, after which growth is resumed at a linear rate. It is difficult to predict what type of curve (linear, sublinear, or superlinear) will come out if this data is fed into a curve fitting algorithm. Gaim provides evidence of the fragmented nature of software growth patterns: growth patterns can be abstracted differently depending on the granularity of the observations. Another OSS system studied, Arla, showed a positive sublinear growth followed by stagnation (Fig. 11.8).

While the growth pattern of Arla is smoother than that of Gaim, overall it is a sublinear growth pattern. Nevertheless, it can also be seen as an initial superlinear trend, up to day 125, then followed by a sublinear trend, up to day 400 or so, followed by a short period of no growth, then followed by linear growth until day 1,000, and, more recently, a period of no growth. As in the Gaim case, in Arla, the interpretation of a fragmented growth trend as an arbitrary sequence of superlinear, linear and sublinear trends is plausible.

Both Fig. 11.7 and 11.8 display the growth in number of folders which overall follows the file growth trend but tends to be more discontinuous, with the big jumps possibly indicating architectural restructuring or other major changes, such as when

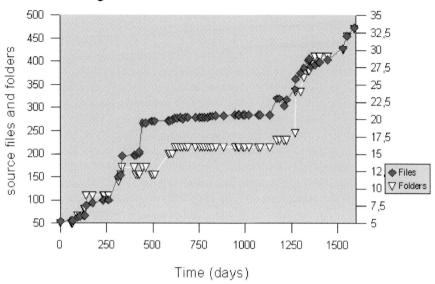

Fig. 11.7. Growth of the OSS Gaim system both in number of files and number of folders [428]

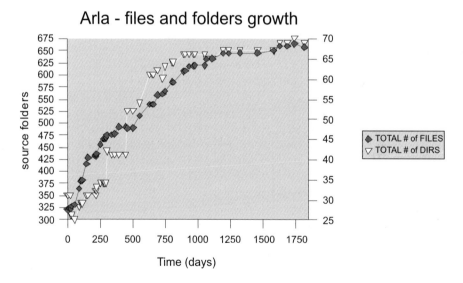

Fig. 11.8. Growth of the OSS Arla system both in number of files and number of folders [428]

large portions of code are transferred from another application. There is tendency for large jumps (e.g., growth greater than 10 percent) in number of folders to precede a period of renewed growth at the file level and it appears that one could use, to a certain extent, the folder size measurement to identify periods of restructuring, even though it does not always work.

Anti-Regressive Work in OSS

One finding of these studies [105] was that, based on metric evidence, the so called anti-regressive work, actually takes place in the OSS projects studied. These authors measured anti-regressive work by comparing two successive releases and counting how many functions had a lower cyclomatic complexity index [354] than in the previous release. Anti-regressive work is related to what has been more recently called *refactoring* [183]. Refactoring consists in modifying portions of the code which appear to be too difficult to understand or too complex, without changing the functionality that such code implements. The actual amount, role and impact of anti-regressive work (and refactoring) on the long-term evolution of software systems (including OSS) is not well-known. If one could generalise the results from a small sample of systems studied by Capiluppi et al., one would say that in general OSS projects invest on average only a small portion of the effort in anti-regressive work, even though some large peaks of such activity occur from time to time. In two OSS systems, Mozilla and Arla, for which anti-regressive work was measured, the portion of changes that can be considered as anti-regressive was less than 25 percent of the total changes in a given release. This is illustrated in Fig. 11.9 that presents the approximate amount of anti-regressive work in Arla. The figure shows high variance in anti-regressive work with high peaks but low running average [105]. Note that the presence of a peak in anti-regressive work does not imply that the activity for that

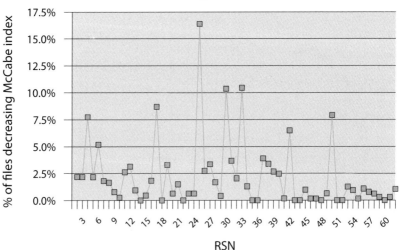

Fig. 11.9. Estimated amount of complexity reduction work as a percentage of all the files touched in a given release [105]. ©2004 IEEE

month or period was predominantly such. New functionality or other changes could have been implemented during the same interval.

11.2.7 The Study by Smith et al. [461, 462]

One important aspect, not considered by Lawrence [314] in his critique, is that the phenomena described by all the laws operate in the real-world in a parallel fashion. The important point to make here is that *testing each law in isolation and independently of the other laws and their assumptions can lead to erroneous results*. This is why, in our opinion, simulation models remain as the most promising way of empirically validating the laws. In this line of work, Smith et al. [462] examined 25 OSS systems by looking at the following attributes: functional size, number of files touched and average complexity. The research question was to test whether the growth patterns in OSS were similar to those predicted by three simulation models previously studied [429]. This was an indirect way of testing the empirical support for some of Lehman's laws, as these models were three different interpretations or refinements of some of Lehman's laws, in particular those related to system growth and complexity. Simulation models seem to be a reasonable way to test the empirical validity of the laws as a whole. This is important because the laws interact with each other. Moreover, because the laws are informally stated in natural language, their formalisation can vary and lead to multiple simulation models.

This work used *qualitative abstraction*. The key idea is to abstract from the detail of the data and focus on a high level characteristic (e.g., overall pattern of growth). One possible way of applying qualitative abstraction is by finding out whether a trend is superlinear, linear, or sublinear by checking the value of the first and second differences in a time series. The symbols used are presented in Fig. 11.10.

Since growth trends in OSS systems display discontinuities, a characteristic already discussed in Section 11.2.6, the authors allowed for a sequence of multiple growth trends to be considered. Fig. 11.11 shows the results obtained for 25 systems. Two types of growth trends were considered for each system: size in files per release, called *un-scaled* trend, and a trend where the incremental growth in number of files was divided by the number of files touched during the interval, called *scaled* trend.

Sign of first difference dm/dt	Sign of 2nd difference $\sim d^2m/dt^2$	Symbol	Segment name
[0]	[0]	–	Constant
[+]	[0]	/	Linear growth
]	[0]	\	Linear decrease
[+]	[+]	J	Super-linear increase
[+]	[−]	⌠	Sub-linear increase
[−]	[−]	⌡	Super-linear decrease
[−]	[+]	⌊	Sub-linear decrease
[0]	[+]	∪	Minimum reached
[0]	[−]	∩	Maximum reached

Fig. 11.10. Symbols used to represent abstracted trends and the corresponding signs for the first and second differences of the variable, taken from [461]. ©2005. Copyright John Wiley & Sons Limited. Reproduced with permission

System	Unscaled Growth Segments (true.smooth.simplified.collapsed)	Scaled Growth Segments (scaled.smooth.simplified.collapsed)
Arla	/{} {/} {∩} {}∩−/}{} {}/}	/{}/{∩{}−}/}∩}/}
Ganymede	/∩−/	/∩−/
Gwydion-Dylan	−/}/}	−/}/}
Ghemical	∩	?∩?
Gimprint	−/{−∪}−}/{{−∪}{∩−/{−{}	−/{−∪}−}/{{−∪}{∩{−/{−{}
Gist	{}{}/{	{}{}
Grace	/−{}{/{∩}{{−	/−{}{/{∩}{{−
HtDig	}/}{∩	/}{∩
Ksi	{\	{∩
Lerzo	/−}/}{}/{}∪{}∪−/}{/	{∩−{/}{/}{}∩}−}//
Linuxconf	/{}{}{∩−}−∩/	/{}{}{/}{∩−}−{∩/
Mit-Scheme	{∩−/}{∩}	{∩−/}{∩}{
Motion	∩}−/−/∩−/}∪−	∩}−/−/∩−/}∪−
Mozilla	{/−}{}{}{}−	{/−}{}{}−
Mutt	{{}{∩−/∪{−{}{−/{}∪−}	{{}{∩−/∪{−{}{−/{}∪−{
Nicestep	/}{}	}/{}
Parted	{∩−∩−∩−/−/∪}/{}−∪−	{∩−}∩−∩−}−/−/}∪−}{}−∪−
Pliant	/}{/−/{/{}{}{}	/}{/−/{/{}{}{}
Quakeforge	{{}/{	{{}/{/{
Rblcheck	}−	{∩−
Rdrtool	{∩−/−	{∩−/−
Siagofoffice	}{}−{}{}{∪{	{}/−{}{}/}∪
Vovida Sip	}/}{	/}/{
Weasel	∩}−{/	∩}−{/
Xfce	/}/{∩−}/}−{\/}	/{/{∩−}}/{/{/{/

Fig. 11.11. Qualitative behaviors for system growth identified in empirical data from 25 OSS systems, taken from [461]. ©2005. Copyright John Wiley & Sons Limited. Reproduced with permission

The scaled trend was intended in order to remove the effect of the effort applied, hoping that any impact of the evolving complexity will be more evident. In fact, however, both scaled and un-scaled patterns were quite similar, as can be appreciated in Fig. 11.11.

The results in Fig. 11.11 show a variety of segment sequences (or patterns). These 25 OSS systems display greater variability in their segmented sequences of growth than the proprietary systems studied in [429]. In the OSS systems, increasing patterns predominated over non-growth or decreasing patterns. None of three qualitative simulation models, built and run using a tool called QSIM, was able to predict the OSS observed trends, with the latter being richer and more complex than those predicted by the models. This meant that none of the software evolution "theories" proposed for proprietary systems (and reflected in the qualitative simulation models) was able to explain the behaviors observed in OSS evolution. This implies that there is a need for new and refined theories of OSS evolution. (The interested reader is referred to [461] for details on how this type of analysis was carried out.) The search for such "new theories" has led to the development of a *multi-agent model* to study how size, complexity and effort relate to each other in OSS [462]. In this model, a large number of contributors, represented in the model as agents, generate, extend, and re-factor code modules independently and in parallel. To our knowledge, this was the first simulation model of OSS evolution that included the complexity of software modules as a limiting factor in productivity (second law), the fitness of the software to its requirements (seventh law), and the motivation of developers (a new factor).

Evaluation of the model was done by comparing the simulated results against four measures of software evolution (system size, proportion of highly complex modules, level of complexity control work, and distribution of changes) for four OSS systems (Arla, Gaim, MPlayer, Wine). The simulated results resembled the observed data, except for system size: three of the OSS systems showed alternating patterns of super-linear and sub-linear growth, while the simulations produced only super-linear growth. However, the fidelity of the model for the other measures suggests that developer motivation, and the limiting effect of complexity on productivity, are likely to have a significant effect on the development of OSS systems and should be considered in further simulation models of OSS development [462].

11.3 Comparing the Evolution of Open and Closed Source Software Systems

This discussion brings out to the question of comparing the evolution of OSS and proprietary systems. It is always challenging to compare the empirical results from research that looked at different attributes, using different samples and measurements. However, one can attempt to make a high-level summary of major points. Such summary will be temporary and subject to change as results of future, hopefully more comprehensive studies, are published. With such caveat in mind, we can observe the following:

- The laws were proposed when most of the systems were developed in-house by a dedicated group of engineers working in the same place, under some form of hierarchical management control and following a waterfall-like process. The software systems of the 70s and 80s were in many cases monolithic and there was little reuse from other systems. OSS challenges many of these assumptions[6].
- The laws are difficult to test empirically, because they are informal statements. One can formalise them making assumptions but many different formalisations are possible. Moreover, the phenomena described by the laws happen in parallel, with some of the laws related to the others. This calls for the use of techniques such as simulation models to test the laws. Qualitative simulation and multi-agent simulations are promising techniques.
- Growth patterns of OSS systems seem to be less regular than those of proprietary systems studied in the past[7]. This could be due to the open system, in the system-theoretic sense, nature of OSS systems: contributors can come and go from wherever in the world, code can be easily duplicated or transferred from one application to the other. There are less restrictive rules than in traditional organisations. All these appear to contribute to a richer and more chaotic phenomenon.

---

[6] Current proprietary systems are less monolithic and there are serious (e.g. Agile) process model alternatives to the waterfall. This is likely to affect the validity of the laws even for proprietary systems.

[7] Ideally one would like to compare data from both recent proprietary and recent OSS. However, access to data on proprietary systems is restricted.

- OSS evolutionary trends are in general more difficult to predict than those of traditional systems. Paradoxically, this does not imply more risk for those using OSS. Since they have access to the source code, they have a degree of control on the evolution of a system that users of proprietary systems do not have. OSS users can eventually implement their own features and fix defects, or even create and evolve their own version if they need to.
- There is evidence for discontinuity in OSS evolution (see subsection 11.2.6). Evolutionary stages are present in OSS but these have not been fully characterised. Models such as the one by Bennett and Rajlich [57] might need to be revised to accommodate OSS observations. One such revision is proposed in [102].

Table 11.3 is an attempt to summarise the applicability of each of the laws to successful OSS projects, based on the empirical evidence so far collected. The laws do not apply to many OSS projects which remain in the initial development or proposal stage. Some of the possible reasons for a project to become successful have been investigated in [123] and this is an important topic for the understanding of OSS evolution.

It is worth mentioning here that the laws refer to common properties across evolving E-type systems *at a very high level of abstraction*. For example, under the laws, the fact that two software systems display functional increase over time or over releases, means that they share one property: positive functional growth. Growth is a rather straightforward and global characteristic that can be studied across a large number of systems. However, there is empirical research where investigators are looking to much more detailed characteristics (e.g., types of design patterns in software systems), perhaps looking for statistical regularities in these, which might be more challenging to generalise across systems than the simple properties which are the concern of the laws. This also means that two systems may share some properties at a high level of abstraction but when one studies the details they might be highly different. One needs to keep the issues of the level of abstraction in mind when one is referring to common or different characteristics across software systems. The same applies when one is discussing whether software evolution is predictable or not. Some characteristics at a high level of abstraction may be predictable but as we get concerned of more detailed properties (e.g., the precise evolution in requirements that a software application will experience in two years time), characteristics are likely to be much more difficult to predict.

11.4 Threats to Validity

Empirical studies are frequently subject to some threats to validity and it is seen as a duty of authors to discuss these to the best of their knowledge [280]. The validity of the results of the empirical studies of OSS evolution, and in some cases also of proprietary software evolution, is constrained by a number of factors such as the following ones:

Incomplete or Erroneous Records

Chen et al. [110] found that in three different OSS systems studied, the omissions in change-logs ranged from 3 to almost 80 percent and conclude that change-logs are not a reliable data source for researchers. This is obviously a concern because some studies may use change-logs as a data source. Other data sources may be subject similarly to missing or mistaken entries. Quantification of the error (or uncertainty) due to missing, incomplete or erroneous records tends to be difficult and, unfortunately, not common. This is a factor that requires increasing attention in order for empirical studies of software evolution to become more disciplined, scientific and relevant.

Biased Samples

When projects selected for study were not randomly chosen there is a risk of having selected more projects of some type than others. For example, we know that only a small percentage of OSS projects achieve a mature and stable condition where there is a large number of contributions. The vast majority of OSS projects do not reach such stage [123]. Similarly, many software projects are cancelled for one reason or another before initial delivery to users and hence never achieve evolution. Strictly speaking, one should be referring to many studies as empirical studies of *successful* software evolution.

Errors in Data Extraction

Data extraction from raw sources (e.g., code repositories and configuration management systems) can be complex and error prone. Assumptions may have made that are not clearly indicated. Data extraction and parsing and visualisation tools may contain errors.

Data Extraction Conventions

Whereas classic studies of proprietary systems use time series, where each measurement was taken for a given release, most of OSS studies follow a contemporary trend of using time series based on actual time of the measurement. Some authors like [411] have argued that this is more appropriate. However, the question remains as to what extent the release sequence is more or less informative than actual dates (real-time) and how these different data can be compared.

External Validity

In many studies it is not clear how the systems studied were selected and to what extent the systems analysed are representative of typical OSS, or whether such a typical OSS actually exists. Some empirical evidence [123] suggests that the type of application influences the stability and success on an OSS project. Whether and how application domains relate to evolutionary patterns remains an open question for further research.

Table 11.3. Applicability of the laws of software evolution to successful OSS projects

Number	Name	Empirical Support	Comment on applicability to Open Source Evolution
I	Continuing change	YES	Seems to apply well to those OSS projects which have achieved maturity. Many projects do not pass the initial development stage. However, even successful projects experience periods of no change or little change
II	Increasing complexity	?	Evidence is so far contradictory. There are some OSS systems that show increasing complexity and others of decreasing complexity. There is evidence of complexity control but it is not clear how this affects the overall complexity trend. Structural complexity has many dimensions and only a handful of them have been measured so far
III	Self regulation	?	Not clear whether this law applies to OSS or not. For example, the influence of individuals like Linus Torvalds in the evolution of a system is very significant. On the other hand, there are forces from the entire multi-project eco-system which may affect the growth, change and other rates
IV	Conservation of organisational stability	?	There are different degrees and types of control by small groups of lead developers and how their policies and loose organisation affect evolution is still not understood. Segmented growth suggests less stability than in proprietary systems. Mechanism that influence the joining in and departure of contributors need to be better understood
V	Conservation of familiarity	?	Everyone, including users, can access the code and the documents available. The need to familiarise with a new release might be less relevant in OSS than in proprietary systems because many users are at the same time contributors and have a more in-depth knowledge of the application or participated in the implementation of the latest release
VI	Continuing growth	YES	The law seems to describe well successful OSS where despite irregularity in patterns there is a tendency to grow in functionality. Some successful OSS systems like Linux display superlinear growth. However, many OSS projects also display none or little growth

Table 11.3. (continued)

Number	Name	Empirical Support	Comment on applicability to Open Source Evolution
VII	Declining quality	Possibly, but not tested yet	This law is difficult to test because it depends on the measurement of quality. At least it should consider in addition to defect rates, the number of requirements waiting to be implemented at a given moment in time. These variables are difficult to study in OSS since, in general, there are no formal requirements documents
VIII	Feedback system	YES, but different type of feedback system	This law seems to apply well to OSS evolution. However the nature of the feedback in proprietary and open source systems may be different, leading to more variety, perhaps more chaotic behavior, in OSS evolution

Granularity

There is evidence that evolutionary behavior at the total system level and at the level of individual subsystems is different [206]. This may affect the internal validity of any results. Moreover, there is little knowledge on how the behavior observed at the total system level relates to the behavior observed at the subsystem level.

Initial Development

Many OSS projects are started as closed-source projects before made available as OSS on the Internet. Little is known about what happens during this initial phase and how it influences the later evolution phases. Most of the empirical data do not capture this hidden initial development phase, which is possibly more similar to proprietary initial development than the later time when a system becomes OSS.

Confounding Variables and Co-Evolution

There might exist other known or unknown variables that impact on the observed behaviors different to those considered in the studies. This could be due to measurement difficulties, because the researchers could not take additional variables into account for practical reasons or because these additional variables are unknown. One example of these is the amount of code that is duplicated, sometimes called *code cloning*, or ported from another system. This is an example of *network externality* [450]. Scacchi et al. [450] refer to OSS as a *software eco-system*. In such eco-system one should not study individual systems, but one should look at the complex co-evolution of multiple software projects in order to make sense of the evolutionary trends.

Project Sample Definition

There is no general agreement about the definition of a successful OSS project. This makes difficult to identify objectively a sample of projects for study. In the majority of the cases the reference to *successful* OSS projects seems to be based on an *ad-hoc* definition of the term or considering attributes such as high popularity and the existence of a lively community. Feitelson et al. [170] studied a very large sample of OSS projects from SourceForge. Based on that study, they proposed an empirically-derived criterion of OSS project success based on a discontinuity that they observed in the distribution of the number of downloads. Such distribution suggested "natural" thresholds. These authors determined that, from the 41,608 projects with more than one download, 85 were "superprojects", which had been downloaded more than 1 million times. Some 10,000 projects were called "successful" (having been downloaded from about 1,000,000 to 1,681 times) and some 31,000 projects or so that they called "struggling projects" (only a few downloads). The definition of Feitelson et al., if widely accepted and used, could provide an objective way of defining samples of OSS projects for future empirical study.

The above list is not complete and other factors may also become threats to validity. Future studies will need to consider and handle these factors in detail. For the moment, we assume that the empirical results are the best description we have at hand of OSS evolution. The fact that some studies have been replicated or point towards the same type of phenomena, however, enhances the validity of the current OSS empirical research, despite the many threats that we have mentioned in this section.

11.5 Conclusions and Further Work

Open source software (OSS) has made software evolution accessible for wider study. Empirical studies of open source software is a vast area and this chapter has discussed a small sample of studies that are concerned with the evolution of OSS, which is, as someone put it, what happens when one looks at the dynamic changes in software characteristics over time. By studying how OSS changes over time one might understand better the specific challenges of OSS evolution and how to address them in different ways, by inventing specific tools, for example.

Empirical studies of OSS evolution, the focus of this chapter, tell us that the classical results from the studies of proprietary software evolution, which have laid a foundational stone in our collective understanding of software evolution, need to be reconciled with some of the evidence coming from OSS. From Table 11.3 it is clear that the OSS evolution phenomenon is not completely inconsistent with the laws, but it is opening up new questions which challenge the assumptions of the laws and it could well be that we are facing a paradigm-shift in our understanding of software evolution. Scacchi et al. [450] have put forward the view that OSS evolution should be viewed as an eco-system. If this were so, we would need to get a better understanding of the personal attitudes, rules and "good practice" that make the OSS ecosystem work successfully. Multi-agent simulation models [462] may be particularly useful here and perhaps the software evolution and biological evolution analogies, discussed in the 70s and 80s [320], may need to be revisited. We add a precautionary note here since fundamental differences are likely to remain between the two domains: software evolution is done by people using programming languages and technologies that themselves evolve, unconstrained by any physical laws, while biological evolution is constrained by the physical and chemical properties of molecules such as the DNA.

Section 11.4 addressed a number of important threats to the validity of the empirical studies of OSS evolution. A key issue is to find out which should be the "first-class entity" in the software evolution research. While classical studies of software evolution concentrated in a single software system as the first-class entity, in OSS (and in some proprietary environments too) there is high code reuse and software evolves within interrelated multi-project environments. Because many OSS software systems can be strongly related through reuse and the importing and exporting of code, various systems co-evolve and influence the evolution of each other. This suggests that we should conduct future empirical studies on families of OSS systems.

Even a superficial analysis makes evident that understanding OSS evolution requires a multi-disciplinary approach that involves economics, social science and other disciplines in addition to computing. All this entails plenty of challenges for developers and researchers and the need to establish links to other research communities (e.g. information systems, economics, complexity science, psychology) with whom wider questions and interests could be shared. This is a prerequisite to any major progress in understanding and improving OSS evolution.

Acknowledgement. Many of the ideas in this chapter came from discussion and interactions with colleagues, to whom we are grateful. In particular, J. Fernandez-Ramil wishes to acknowledge the discussions and collaborative work with Professor M.M. Lehman, who introduced him to this field. We are also grateful to the anonymous reviewers for their comments, which helped to improve this chapter. Any errors remain the responsibility of the authors.

Appendices

A

Resources

In this appendix we listed a number of additional resources for those readers that wish to gain more detailed information on particular topics addressed in this book.

Books

Over the years, many books have been published on the topics of software maintenance, software evolution and related areas. It is not our intent to provide a complete list of such books here, especially since many of the older books are either outdated or out of print. Therefore, we have preferred to present in chronological order our personal, subjective, list of books that we feel relevant for the interested reader.

- *Program Evolution: Processes of Software Change* [320]. This book, written by Lehman and Belady, is one of the very first that has been published on the topic of software evolution. Although it is no longer available, electronic versions of the book may be downloaded for free on the internet (for example, from the *Publications* section on the website of the *ERCIM Working Group on Software Evolution* – http://w3.umh.ac.be/evol).
- *Software Evolution: The Software Maintenance Challenge* [24]. Another important milestone in software evolution, written by Arthur. Unfortunately no longer available.
- *Software Reengineering* [23]. A book containing a collection of scientific articles on the topic of software reengineering.
- *Migrating Legacy Systems: Gateways, Interfaces and the Incremental Approach* [84]. This book illustrates how one should avoid risks while migrating legacy systems, namely by doing small successive steps (i.e., "Chicken Little").
- *Software Change Impact Analysis* [74]. A book containing a collection of scientific articles on the topic of software change impact analysis.
- *Refactoring: Improving the design of existing code* [183]. Martin Fowler's well-known book on refactoring object-oriented programs, an important subdomain of software restructuring.

- *Design and Use of Software Architectures - Adopting and Evolving a Product Line Approach* [75]. Bosch describes how to set-up and maintain a product line architecture: a framework which allows to develop a series of products derived from a reusable core.
- *Managing the Change: Software Configuration and Change Management* [225]. This book, written by Haug et al. offers a variety of perspectives on software configuration/change management and requirements engineering.
- *Object-Oriented Reengineering Patterns* [149]. This book, written by Demeyer, Ducasse and Nierstrasz, provides a number of practical guidelines for re-engineering object-oriented legacy systems.
- *Software Maintenance: Concepts and Practice* [213]. The second edition of this textbook comprehensively covers the breadth of software maintenance issues.
- *Modernizing Legacy Systems: Software Technologies, Engineering Processes, and Business Practices* [457]. This book provides a roadmap to implement a successful software modernization strategy. The proposed incremental approach encompasses changes in software technologies, engineering processes, and business practices. It exemplifies a case study of migrating legacy Cobol code to J2EE.
- *Refactoring to patterns* [273]. This book explains how to introduce design patterns in your code, by listing typical code smells and ways to refactor them away. An appealing way to teach reluctant designers how to clean up their code base.
- *Working Effectively with Legacy Code* [169]. Feathers shows how to deal with the "testing vs. reengineering" dilemma. Before you reengineer you need a good suite of regression tests to ensure that the system does not break. However, the design of a system that needs reengineering typically makes testing very difficult and would benefit from reengineering.
- *Refactoring Databases: Evolutionary Database Design* [10]. This book applies the ideas of refactoring to database schemas.
- *Software Evolution and Feedback: Theory and Practice* [338]. This book scientifically explores what software evolution is and why it is inevitable. It addresses the phenomenological and technological underpinnings of software evolution, and it explains the role of feedback in software development and maintenance.
- *Software Maintenance Management: Evaluation and Continuous Improvement* [11]. This book focuses on the managerial aspects of software maintenance. It shows how process improvement models can be applied to software maintenance, and proposes a Software Maintenance Maturity Model to achieve this.

Websites

The most important website related to the research domain on software evolution is undoubtedly www.planet-evolution.org. It contains a wealth of data on people, events, tools, and much more relevant information related to software evolution.

Another website containing a wealth of information on software evolution and related research is Tao Xie's Software Engineering Research Links www.csc.ncsu.edu/faculty/xie/seresearchlinks.html

Journals

The only dedicated international journal on the topic of software evolution and software maintenance is Wiley's *Journal on Software Maintenance and Evolution: Research and Practice* (JSME).

Other international journals in which scientific articles on software maintenance and evolution are published occasionally are: IEEE's *Transactions on Software Engineering*, ACM's *Transactions on Programming Languages and Systems* and *Transactions on Software Engineering and Methodology*, Kluwer's journal on *Automated Software Engineering*, Elsevier's journal on *Systems and Software* and Wiley's journal entitled *Software: Practice and Experience*.

Standards

The following standards are very relevant in the field of software evolution, though some of them may be a bit outdated compared to the current state-of-the-art in research:

- The ISO/IEC 14764 standard on "Software Maintenance" [242]
- The ISO/IEC 12207 standard (and its amendments) on "Information Technology - Software Life Cycle Processes" [241]
- The ANSI/IEEE 1042 standard on "Software Configuration Management" [13]
- The IEEE 1219 standard on "Software Maintenance" [239]
- The ISO/IEC 9126 standard on "Information technology – Software product evaluation – Quality characteristics and guidelines for their use" [240]

Events

There are many events being organised each year around the themes of software evolution, software maintenance and reengineering, or related areas. We will only list the most well-known international events here.

Conferences

A number of international conferences are organised each year, devoted to the topics of software evolution, software maintenance, reverse engineering and reengineering:

CSMR The *European Conference on Software Maintenance and Reengineering*
ICPC The annual *International Conference on Program Comprehension*
ICSM The *International Conference on Software Maintenance*
WCRE The *Working Conference on Reverse Engineering*

In addition, many other international conferences are being organised that include contributions on software evolution. We list only those conferences here that have been cited frequently in the various chapters of this book:

AOSD The international conference on *Aspect-Oriented Software Development*
ASE The international conference on *Automated Software Engineering*
COMPSAC The international *Computer Software and Applications Conference*
ECMDA The *European Conference on Model-Driven Architectures*
ECOOP The *European Conference on Object-Oriented Programming*
ESEC The *European Software Engineering Conference*
FASE The ETAPS conference *Fundamental Approaches to Software Engineering*
FSE The ACM SIGSOFT International Symposium on the *Foundations of Software Engineering*
ICSE The *International Conference on Software Engineering*
MODELS The international conference on *Model Driven Engineering Languages and Systems*
OOPSLA The international conference on *Object-Oriented Programming Systems, Languages and Applications*

Workshops

A wide range of international workshops are organised each year on the topic of software evolution or a subdomain thereof:

EVOL The annual workshop on software evolution organised by the ERCIM Working Group on Software Evolution
IWPSE The annual *International Workshop on Principles of Software Evolution*
SCAM The annual workshop on *Source Code Analysis and Manipulation*
SCM The annual workshop on *Software Configuration Management*
SETra The bi-annual workshop on *Software Evolution through Transformations*
WOOR The annual ECOOP *Workshop on Object-Oriented Reengineering*
WSE The annual international workshop on *Web Site Evolution*

B

Glossary of Terms

This appendix contains a glossary of terms that have been introduced in the various chapters contributing to this book.

Abstract syntax tree. Compilers often construct an abstract syntax tree (AST) for the semantic analysis. Its nodes are programming language constructs and its edges express the hierarchical relation between these constructs. From [295]: "The structure of an AST is a simplification of the underlying grammar of the programming language, e.g., by generalization or by suppressing chain rules. (...) This structure can be generalized so that it can be used to represent programs of different languages."

Advice. *Aspect* definitions consist of *pointcuts* and *advices*. Advices are the code that crosscuts the *dominant decomposition* of a software system.

Agile software development. According to Scott W. Ambler, respected authority in the agile methods community, *agile software development* "is an iterative and incremental (evolutionary) approach to software development which is performed in a highly collaborative manner with "just enough" ceremony that produces high quality software which meets the changing needs of its stakeholders. *Agile methods* refer to a collection of "lightweight" software development methodologies that are basically aimed at minimising risk and achieving customer satisfaction through a short feedback loop.

Anti-regressive work. Term introduced by Lehman [320] to describe the work done to decrease the complexity of a program without altering the functionality of the system as perceived by users. Anti-regressive work includes activities such as code rewriting, refactoring, reengineering, restructuring, redocumenting, and so on.

Architecture. The architecture of a software system is the set of principal design decisions about the system. It is the structural and behavioural framework on which all other aspects of the system depend. It is the organisational structure of a software system including components, connections, constraints, and rationale.

Architectural style. David Garlan states that an *architectural style* "defines constraints on the form and structure of a family of architectural instances".

Aspect. A modular unit designed to implement a *(crosscutting) concern.* In other words, an aspect provides a solution for abstracting code that would otherwise be spread throughout (i.e., cross-cut) the entire program. Aspects are composed of *pointcuts* and *advices.*

Aspect exploration. The activity of locating opportunities for introducing *aspects* in non aspect-oriented software. A distinction can be made between manual exploration supported by special-purpose browsers and source-code navigation tools, and *aspect mining* techniques that try to automate this process of aspect discovery and propose the user one or more aspect candidates.

Aspect extraction. The activity that turns potential aspects into actual aspects in some aspect-oriented language, after a set of potential aspects have been identified in the aspect exploration phase.

Aspect evolution. The process of progressively modifying the elements of an aspect-oriented software system in order to improve or maintain its quality over time, under changing contexts and requirements.

Aspect migration. The process of *migrating* a software system that is written in a non aspect-oriented way into an aspect-oriented equivalent of that system.

Aspect mining. The activity of semi-automatically discovering those *crosscutting concerns* that potentially could be turned into *aspects,* from the source code and/or run-time behaviour of a software system.

Aspect-oriented software development. An approach to software development that addresses limitations inherent in other approaches, including object-oriented programming. The approach aims to address *crosscutting concerns* by providing means for systematic identification, separation, representation and composition. Crosscutting concerns are encapsulated in separate modules, known as *aspects,* so that localization can be promoted. This results in better support for modularization hence reducing development, maintenance and evolution costs.

Aspect weaving. The process of composing the core functionality of a software system with the *aspects* that are defined on top of it, thereby yielding a working system.

Bad smell. According to Kent Beck [183] a bad smell is a structure in the code that suggests, and sometimes even scream for, opportunities for refactoring.

Case study. According to [171], a *case study* is a research technique where you identify key factors that may affect the outcome of an activity and then document the activity: its inputs, constraints, resources, and outputs. Case studies usually look at a typical project, rather than trying to capture information about all possible cases; these can be thought of as "research in the typical". Formal experiments, case studies and surveys are three key components of empirical investigation in software engineering.

However, the term *case study* is also often used in an engineering sense of the word. Testing a given technique or tool on a representative case against a predefined list of criteria and reporting about the lessons learned.

CASE tool. A software tool that helps software designers and developers specify, generate and maintain some or all of the software components of an application. Many popular CASE tools provide functions to allow developers to draw database schemas and to generate the corresponding code in a data description language (DDL). Other CASE tools support the analysis and design phases of software development, for example by allowing the software developer to draw different types of UML diagrams.

Change charter. This term is used sometimes when developing a new system (or evolving an existing system) to refer to what can be potentially changed. It may be used as a synonym of "scope".

Change log. Record with some of the information related to one or several amendments (i.e., *changes*) made to the code or to another software artefact. The record generally includes the responsible, the date and some explanation (e.g., reasons for which a change was made).

Clone. A *software clone* is a special kind of *software duplicate*. It is a piece of software (e.g., a code fragment) that has been obtained by *cloning* (i.e., duplicating via the copy-and-paste mechanism) another piece of software and perhaps making some additional changes to it. This primitive kind of software reuse is more harmful than it is beneficial. It actually makes the activities of debugging, maintenance and evolution considerably more difficult.

Clone detection. The activity of locating duplicates or fragments of code with a high degree of similarity and redundancy.

Component. In [459], Mary Shaw and David Garlan define software components as "the loci of computation and state. Each component has an interface specification that defines its properties, which include the signatures and functionality of its resources together with global relations, performance properties, and so on. (...)"

Complexity. *Structural complexity* refers to the degree to which a program is difficult to understand by human developers in order to, for example, inspect the program, or modify it. There are other types of complexity (e.g., algorithmic complexity). Different measures of software complexity exist. One of the best known is McCabe's cyclomatic complexity [354].

Connector. In [459], Mary Shaw and David Garlan state that connectors are "the loci of relations among components. They mediate interactions but are not things to be hooked up (rather, they do the hooking up). Each connector has a protocol specification that defines its properties, which include rules about the types of interfaces it is able to mediate for, assurances about properties of the interaction, rules about the order in which things happen, and commitments about the interaction (...)."

Consistency. Consistency is the absence of **inconsistencies** in or between software artefacts. If the software artefact under consideration is a program, we talk about *program (in)consistency*, if the software artefact is a model, we talk about *model (in)consistency*. If the software artefact is a (program or model) transformation, we talk about *transformation (in)consistency*.

Crosscutting concerns. *Concerns* that do not fit within the *dominant decomposition* of a given software system, and as such have an implementation that cuts across that decomposition. *Aspect-oriented programming* is intended to be a solution to modularise such crosscutting concerns.

Database conversion. In database migration, we can distinguish between two migration strategies.

Physical database conversion is a straightforward migration strategy according to which each source schema object (e.g., a record type or a data field) is converted to the closest construct of the target DMS model (e.g., a table or a column). This strategy is sometimes called one-to-one migration. This approach is fast, simple and inexpensive but generally yields a database with poor performance and weak maintainability.

Conceptual database conversion is a migration strategy that transforms the source database into a clean and normalized target database that exploits the expressive power of the target DMS. This strategy comprises a reverse engineering phase, through which the conceptual schema of the database is recovered, followed by a forward engineering towards the new DMS. This approach is slow, expensive and relies on skilled developers, but its output is a high quality database that will be easy to maintain and to evolve.

Database reverse engineering. *Database reverse engineering* is a special kind of *reverse engineering*. It is the process through which the logical and conceptual schemas of a legacy database, or of a set of files, are recovered from various information sources such as DDL code, data dictionary contents, database contents, or the source code of application programs that use the database.

Database model and database schema. In the database realm, a *model M* is a formal system comprising a closed set of abstract object categories and a set of assembly rules that states which arrangements of objects are valid. Since M is supposed to describe the structure, the properties and the behaviour of a class S of external systems, the semantics of M is specified by a mapping of M onto S. Any arrangement m of objects which is valid according to M describes a specific system s of class S. m is called a *schema* while s is the application domain or the *universe of discourse*. Among the most popular conceptual models we can mention the Entity-Relationship models, Object-Role models, relational models and UML class models. Among DBMS models, the SQL, CODASYL, IMS, Object-relational and XML models are currently the most widely used.

We can essentially distinguish three types of database schemas:

Conceptual schema. A structured technology-independent description of the information about an application domain such as a company or a library. By extension, it is also an abstract representation of the existing or project database that is made up of the data of this domain.

Logical schema. The description of the data structures of a database according to the model of a specific technology, e.g., a RDBMS. The logical schema of a database is the implementation of its conceptual schema. Application programs know the database through its logical schema.

Physical schema. The technical description of a database where all the physical constructs (such as indexes) and parameters (such as page size or buffer management policy) are specified. The physical schema of a database is the implementation of its logical schema.

Decay. Decay is the antithesis of evolution. While the evolution process involves progressive changes, the changes are degenerative in the case of decay.

Dominant decomposition. The dominant decomposition is the principle decomposition of a program into separate modules. The *tyranny of the dominant decomposition* [490] refers to restrictions imposed by the dominant decomposition on a software engineer's ability to represent particular concerns in a modular way. Many kinds of concerns do not align with the chosen decomposition, so that the concerns end up scattered across many modules and tangled with one another.

Duplicate. A software duplicate is a code fragment that is redundant to another code fragment; often due to copy and paste. A negative consequence of duplication is that if one fragment is changed, each duplicate may need to be adjusted, too.

Note that a the term software *duplicate* is preferred over software *clone*. In English, clone suggests that one fragment is derived/copied from the other one. However, this is just one special type of software redundancy. Code fragments could also be similar by accident.

E-type system. One of the three types of software described by Lehman in his SPE program classification [320]. The distinctive properties of E-type systems are:
- the problem that they address cannot be formally and completely specified;
- the program has an imperfect model of the operational domain embedded in it;
- the program reflects an unbounded number of assumptions about the real world;
- the installation of the program changes the operation domain;
- the process of developing and evolving E-type system is driven by feedback.

Evolution. According to Lehman and Ramil (chapter 1 of [338]), the term *evolution* reflects "a process of *progressive*, for example beneficial, change in the attributes of the evolving entity or that of one or more of its constituent elements. What is accepted as progressive must be determined in each context. It is also appropriate to apply the term evolution when long-term change trends are beneficial even though isolated or short sequences of changes may appear degenerative. For example, an entity or collection of entities may be said to be evolving if their value or fitness is increasing over time. Individually or collectively they are becoming more meaningful, more complete or more adapted to a changing environment."

Evolutionary process model. A software process model that explicitly takes into account the iterative and incremental nature of software development. A typical example is the so-called spiral software process model [71].

Externality. Term used mainly in economics to refer to the break-down of markets due to external influences. In open source software, network externalities have been used to refer to code importing, replication, tailoring or code sharing between projects which can lead to superlinear functional growth.

Extreme programming. *Extreme programming* (XP) is a specific instance of *agile software development* that aims to simplify and expedite the process of developing new software in a volatile environment of rapidly-changing requirements. XP is a lightweight process that offers a set of values, principles and practices for developing software that provides the highest value for the customer in the fastest way possible.

Feedback. In engineering, *feedback* refers to the case when at least some part of the output(s) of the system are fed back to the input, normally for control purposes. In systems thinking and related disciplines (e.g., system dynamics), feedback describes a property of many complex systems in which the outputs determine the inputs.

Forward engineering. Forward engineering is the traditional process of moving from high-level abstractions and logical, implementation-independent designs to the physical implementation of a system [149].

Fragile pointcut problem. This problem arises in *aspect-oriented software development* when *pointcuts* unintentionally capture or miss particular *joinpoints* as a consequence of their fragility with respect to seemingly safe modifications to the base program.

Free software. A popular mode of software distribution as a common good in which users can access, modify and re-distribute the code, under the terms of the license and some parts (e.g., notices) that should not been modified.

Graph transformation. *Graph transformation* (also known as *graph rewriting* or *graph grammars*) is a theory and set of associated tools that allows to modify graph-based structures by means of transformation rules, and to reason about the formal properties of these rules. It is an extension of the theory of *term rewriting*. One of its many useful applications is to formalize model transformations in the context of model-driven software engineering.

Graph transformation rule. A *graph transformation rule* is composed of a Left-Hand Side (LHS) and a Right-Hand Side (RHS). The LHS of the rule specifies the pre-conditions that must be satisfied so that the rule can be applied. The RHS corresponds to the post-conditions of applying the rule. Executing a *graph transformation rule* consists of finding an occurrence (or match) of the LHS and transforming it into the RHS.

Implicit construct. In a database, a data structure or an integrity constraint that holds, or should hold, among the data, but that has not been explicitly declared in the DDL code of the database. Implicit compound and multivalued fields as well as implicit foreign keys are some of the most challenging constructs to chase when recovering the logical schema of a database.

Inconsistency. Paraphrased from [471], an inconsistency is a situation in which two or more overlapping elements of one or different software artefacts make assertions about aspects of the system they describe that are not jointly satisfiable.

Information system. The subsystem of an organization aimed at collecting, memorizing, processing and distributing the information that is necessary to support the business and management processes of this organization. According to a limited meaning, an information system is a business software system comprising a database and the programs that use it.

Joinpoint. A joinpoint is a well-defined place in the structure or execution flow of a program where additional behaviour can be attached.

Legacy software. According to [84], a *legacy system* is any system that significantly resists modifications and change.

According to [149], *legacy software* is valuable software that you have inherited. It may have been developed using an outdated programming language or an obsolete development method. Most likely it has changed hands several times and shows signs of many modifications and adaptations.

Maintenance. According to the ISO Standard 12207 [241], the software product undergoes modification to code and associated documentation due to a problem or the need for improvement. The objective of software maintenance is to modify the existing software while preserving its integrity.

According to the IEEE Standard 1219 [239], *software maintenance* is the modification of a software product after delivery to correct faults, to improve performance or other attributes, or to adapt the product to a modified environment. In the ISO/IEC Standard 14764 [242], maintenance is further subdivided into four categories:

Perfective maintenance is any modification of a software product after delivery to improve performance or maintainability.

Corrective maintenance is the reactive modification of a software product performed after delivery to correct discovered faults.

Adaptive maintenance is the modification of a software product performed after delivery to keep a computer program usable in a changed or changing environment.

Preventive maintenance refers to software modifications performed for the purpose of preventing problems before they occur. This type of maintenance, that does not alter the system functionality, is also referred to as *anti-regressive work*.

Metamodel. According to the Meta-Object Facility (MOF) standard [396], a *metamodel* is a model that defines the language for expressing a model.

Metric. According to the IEEE Standard [238], a *metric* is a quantitative measure of the degree to which a system, component or process possesses a given attribute.

Migration. Migration is a particular variant of re-engineering. In the context of software systems, *migration* refers to the process of moving a software system from one technological environment to another one that is, for some reason, considered to be better. Migrations can be very diverse in nature: changing the hardware infrastructure, changing the underlying operating system, moving data to another kind of database (database migration), changing the programming language in which the software has been written, and so on.

Model. A *model* is a simplified representation of a system on a higher level of abstraction. It is an abstract view on the actual system emphasizing those aspects that are of interest to someone. Depending on the system under consideration, we talk about *software models* (for software systems), *database models* (for database systems), and so on.

Model-driven engineering. A software engineering approach that promotes the use of models and transformations as primary artefacts throughout the software development process. Its goal is to tackle the problem of developing, maintaining and evolving complex software systems by raising the level of abstraction from source code to models. As such, model-driven engineering promises reuse at the domain level, increasing the overall software quality.

Open source software. Software of which the source code is available for users and third parties to be inspected and used. It is made available to the general public with either relaxed or non-existent intellectual property restrictions. It is generally used as a synonym of free software even though the two terms have different connotations. *Open* emphasises the accessibility to the source code, while *free* emphasises the freedom to modify and redistribute under the terms of the original license.

Outlier. An entity's metric value that is beyond a predefined threshold.

Pointcut. *Aspect* definitions consist of *pointcuts* and *advices*. Pointcuts define those points in the source code of a program where an *advice* will be applied (i.e., where crosscutting code will be "woven").

Precision. In data mining or information retrieval, *precision* is defined as the proportion of retrieved and relevant data or documents to all the data or documents retrieved:

$$precision = \frac{|\{\text{relevant documents}\} \cap \{\text{retrieved documents}\}|}{|\{\text{retrieved documents}\}|}$$

Precision is a measure of how well the technique performs in *not* returning non-relevant items. Precision is 100% when every document returned to the user is relevant to the query. Being very precise usually comes at the risk of missing documents that are relevant, hence precision should be combined with recall.

Program representation. A *program representation* consists of properties of a program specified in an alternate means to source code. Kontogiannis, in his article [292], states that "Program representation is a key aspect for design recovery as it serves as the basis for any subsequent analysis chosen. Some of the most common program representation methods include (a) abstract syntax trees (...); (b) Prolog rules (...); (c) code and concept objects (...); (d) code action frames (...); (e) attributed data flow graphs (...); (f) control and data flow graphs (...). Most of these approaches represent and refer to the structural properties of a program."

Program understanding. *Program understanding* or *program comprehension* is "the task of building mental models of an underlying software system at various abstraction levels, ranging from models of the code itself to ones of the underlying application domain, for software maintenance, evolution, and re-engineering purposes" [383].

Recall. In data mining or information retrieval, *recall* is defined as the proportion of relevant data or documents retrieved, out of all relevant data or documents known or available:

$$recall = \frac{|\{\text{relevant documents}\} \cap \{\text{retrieved documents}\}|}{|\{\text{relevant documents}\}|}$$

Recall is 100% when every relevant item is retrieved. In theory, it is easy to achieve good recall: simply return every item in the collection, thus recall by itself is not a good measure and should be combined with precision.

Redesign. *Redesign*, in the context of software engineering, is the transformation of a system's structure to comply to a given set of constraints. *Architectural redesign* is a transformation at model level with the goal of achieving conformance to a specific architectural style.

Redundancy. Software redundancy is the superfluous repetition of code or data. Note that there is also "healthy" redundancy. For example, many programming languages force us to specify an interface of a module, the declarations in the module body are then redundant to the interface items, and this is a desirably property.

Re-engineering. According to [112], *re-engineering* is the examination and alteration of a subject system to reconstitute it in a new form and the subsequent implementation of the new form. Re-engineering generally includes some form of *reverse engineering* (to achieve a more abstract description) followed by some form of *forward engineering* or *restructuring*. This may include modifications with respect to new requirements not met by the original system.

Refactoring. *Refactoring* is the object-oriented equivalent of *restructuring*. According to [183], refactoring is [the process of making] a change to the internal structure of software to make it easier to understand and cheaper to modify without changing its observable behaviour. If applied to programs, we talk of *program refactoring*. If applied to models, we talk of *model refactoring*. If applied to aspects, we talk of *aspect refactoring*.

Release. A release is a version of a software system that has been approved and distributed to users outside the development team.

Restructuring. According to [112], *restructuring* is the transformation from one representation form to another at the same relative abstraction level, while preserving the system's external behaviour.

Reverse engineering. According to [112], *reverse engineering* is the process of analyzing a subject system to identify the system's components and their interrelationships and create representations of the system in another form or at a higher level of abstraction. Reverse engineering generally involves extracting design artefacts and building or synthesizing abstractions that are less implementation-dependent.

Scattering and tangling. Occurs when the code needed to implement a given concern is spread out (*scattered*) over and clutters (is *tangled* with) the code needed to satisfy one or more other concern. Scattering or tangling are typically the result of a program's inability to handle what is called a *crosscutting concern*.

Schema refinement. The process within database reverse engineering that attempts to recover all, or at least most, implicit constructs (data structures and integrity constraints) of a physical or logical schema.

Schema conceptualisation. The process within database reverse engineering that aims at deriving a plausible conceptual schema from the logical schema of a legacy database. Also called *schema interpretation*.

Schema transformation. A rewriting rule that replaces a set of constructs of a database schema with another set of constructs. Such a transformation comprises two parts: a schema rewriting rule (structural mapping) and a data conversion rule (instance mapping). The latter transforms the data according to the source schema into data complying with the target schema.

Service-oriented architecture. According to Thomas Erl [162], SOA is "a model in which automation logic is decomposed into smaller, distinct units of logic. Collectively, these units comprise a larger piece of business automation logic. Individually, these units can be distributed. (...) (SOA) encourages individual units of logic to exist autonomously yet not isolated from each other. Units of logic are still required to conform to a set of principles that allow them to evolve independently, while still maintaining a sufficient amount of commonality and standardization. Within SOA, these units of logic are known as *services*."

Some of the key principles of service-orientation are: loose coupling, service contract, autonomy, abstraction, reusability, composability, statelessness and discoverability.

Software engineering. The term *software engineering* was defined for the first time during a conference of the NATO Science Committee [391] as "the establishment and use of sound engineering principles in order to obtain economically software that is reliable and works efficiently on real machines." Alternatively, the IEEE standard 610-12 [238] defines software engineering as "the application of a systematic, disciplined, quantifiable approach to the development, operation, and maintenance of software; that is, the application of engineering to software."

Testability. The ISO/IEC standard 9126 defines *testability* as "attributes of software that bear on the effort needed to validate the software product" [240].

Testing. We can distinguish different kinds of software testing [66]:

Regression testing. Tests which seek to reveal cases where software functionality that previously worked as desired, stops working or no longer works in the same way that was previously planned.

Developer testing. Preliminary testing performed by the software engineers who design and/or implement the software systems. Stands in contrast with *independent testing*, or testing performed by software engineers who are not directly involved with designing or implementing the software system.

Black box testing. The use of specified or expected responsibilities of a unit, subsystem, or system to design tests. Synonymous with specification-oriented, behavioural, functional, or responsibility-based test design.

Acceptance testing. Formal testing conducted to determine whether or not a system satisfies its acceptance criteria and to enable the customer to determine whether or not to accept the system.

White box testing. The use of source code analysis to develop test cases. Synonymous with structural, glass box, clear box, implementation-based test design.

Unit testing. Testing of individual software units, or groups of related units. A test unit may be a module, a few modules, or a complete computer program.

Traceability. The property of software design and development that makes it possible to link any abstract artefact to the technical artefacts that implement it, and conversely. In addition, this link explains how and why this implementation has been chosen.

In the database realm, traceability allows a programmer to know exactly which conceptual object a definite column is an implementation of. Conversely, it informs on how a conceptual object type has been implemented.

Transformation rule. A rewriting rule through which the instances of some pattern of an abstract or concrete specification are replaced with instances of another pattern. Depending on the type of artefact that needs to be transformed, different types of transformation can be considered: schema transformation (for database schemas), term rewriting (for tree-based structures), graph transformation (for graph-based structures), and so on.

Transformational software engineering. A view of software engineering through which the production and evolution of software can be modelled, and practically carried out, by a chain of transformations which preserves some essential properties of the source specifications. Program compilation, but also transforming tail recursion into an iterative pattern are popular examples. This approach is currently applied to software evolution, reverse engineering and migration. The transformational paradigm is one of the most powerful approaches to formally guarantee *traceability*.

Threshold. A fixed value (typically an upper bound or lower bound) that distinguishes normal values from abnormal metric values. Typically used when applying software metrics to detect anomalies.

Uniqueness. *Uniqueness* is the property of model or program transformations to deliver a unique result upon termination.

Version. A version is a snapshot of a certain software system at a certain point in time. Whenever a change is made to the software system, a new version is created. The *version history* is the collection of all versions and their relationships.

Version repository. A kind of database, file system or other kind of repository in which the version history of a software system are stored. The repository may be used to store source code, executable code, documentation or any other type of software artefact of which different versions may exist over time (or even at the same time).

Web service. The World Wide Web Consortium (W3C), in [544], states that "A web service is a software system designed to support interoperable machine-to-machine interaction over a network. It has an interface described in a machine-processable format (specifically WSDL). Other systems interact with the web service in a manner prescribed by its description using SOAP-messages, typically conveyed using HTTP with an XML serialization in conjunction with other web-related standards."

Well-definedness. *Well-definedness* is the property of model or program transformations to terminate with a unique and correct result when given a consistent input.

Wrapper. A software component that encapsulates a system component (a procedure, a program, a file, an API) in order to transform its interface with its environment. For instance, a wrapper associated with a legacy program can give the latter an object-oriented interface.

In a database setting, a *data wrapper* is a software component that encapsulates a database or a set of files in order to change its model and the API through which the data can be manipulated. For example, a data wrapper built on top of a standard file can allow application programs to access the contents of the file as if it were a relational table or a collection of XML documents.

C

List of Acronyms

This appendix contains a list of acronyms that have been used throughout the various contributing chapters.

ACM *Association for Computing Machinery.*
ADL *Architectural Description Language.*
AOP *Aspect-Oriented Programming.*
AOSD *Aspect-Oriented Software Development.*
API *Application Programming Interface.*
ASF *Algebraic Specification Formalism.*
AST *Abstract Syntax Tree.*
CASE *Computer-Aided Software Engineering.*
DBMS *Database Management System.*
DDL *Data Description Language.*
DML *Data Manipulation Language.*
DMS *Data Management System.*
ERCIM *European Research Consortium on Informatics and Mathematics.*
FEAST *Feedback, Evolution And Software Technology.*
IEEE *Institute of Electrical and Electronics Engineers.*
ISO *International Standards Organisation.*
L-CARE *Legacy Computer Aided Reengineering Environment.*
LOC *Lines of Code.*
MDA *Model-Driven Architecture.*
MDE *Model-Driven Engineering.* Sometimes, the acronym *MDD* or *MDSD* is used in literature, for *Model-Driven (Software) Development*, but both terms are largely interchangeable.
OMG The *Object Management Group.*
OSS *Open Source Software.*
RDBMS *Relational Database Management System.*
SDF *Syntax Definition Formalism.*
SOA *Service-Oriented Architecture.*
SQL *Structured Query Language.*

SWEBOK The IEEE *Software Engineering Body of Knowledge* [2].
UML The *Unified Modeling Language* [398].
W3C *World Wide Web Consortium.*
WSDL *Web Service Description Language.*
XML *eXtensible Markup Language.*
XP *Extreme Programming.*

References

1. Abran, A., Nguyen, K.: Measurement of the maintenance process from a demand-based perspective. Software Maintenance and Evolution: Research and Practice **5**(2) (1993) 63–90 [7]
2. Abran, A., Moore, J.W., Bourque, P., Dupuis, R., Tripp, L.L.: Guide to the Software Engineering Body of Knowledge (SWEBOK). IEEE (2004) [3, 93, 97, 308]
3. Advani, D., Hassoun, Y., Counsell, S.: Extracting refactoring trends from open-source software and a possible solution to the 'related refactoring' conundrum. In: Proc. Symposium on Applied computing, ACM Press (2006) 1713–1720 [96]
4. Aldrich, J., Chambers, C., Notkin, D.: ArchJava: Connecting software architecture to implementation. In: Proc. Int'l Conf. Software Engineering (ICSE), New York, ACM Press (May 19–25 2002) 187–197 [235]
5. Allen, R.: A Formal Approach to Software Architecture. PhD thesis, School of Computer Science, Carnegie Mellon University (January 1997) Issued as CMU Technical Report CMU-CS-97-144. [235]
6. Allen, R., Douence, R., Garlan, D.: Specifying and analyzing dynamic software architectures. In: Proc. Int'l Conf. Fundamental Aspects of Software Engineering (FASE). (1998) Lisbon, Portugal. [238]
7. Alonso, G., Casati, F., Kuno, H., Machiraju, V.: Web Services. Springer-Verlag (2003) [139]
8. Altova: UModel UML software development tool. http://www.altova.com/products/umodel/uml_tool.html (2007) [167]
9. Ambler, S.W.: Agile modeling: Effective Practices for Extreme Programming and the Unified Process. John Wiley & Sons (2001) [176]
10. Ambler, S.W., Sadalage, P.J.: Refactoring Databases: Evolutionary Database Design. Addison-Wesley (2006) [292]
11. April A., Abran A.: Software Maintenance Management: Evaluation and Continuous Improvement, Wiley (2008) [292]
12. Andrade, L., Gouveia, J., Antunes, M., El-Ramly, M., Koutsoukos, G.: Forms2Net – Migrating Oracle Forms to Microsoft .NET. In Lämmel, R., Saraiva, J., Visser, J., eds.: Generative and Transformational Techniques in Software Engineering. Volume 4143 of Lecture Notes in Computer Science., Springer-Verlag (2006) [164]
13. ANSI/IEEE: Standard ANSI/IEEE 1042-1987 on Software Configuration Management. IEEE Press (1987) [293]

14. Antoniol, G., Casazza, G., Di Penta, M., Merlo, E.: Modeling clones evolution through time series. In: Proc. Int'l Conf. Software Maintenance (ICSM), IEEE Computer Society Press (2001) 273–280 [23]

15. Antoniol, G., Villano, U., Merlo, E., Di Penta, M.: Analyzing cloning evolution in the Linux kernel. Information and Software Technology **44**(13) (2002) [23]

16. Antoniol, G., Caprile, B., Potrich, A., Tonella, P.: Design-code traceability recovery: selecting the basic linkage properties. Science of Computer Programming **40**(2-3) (2001) 213–234 [9]

17. Aoyama, M.: Metrics and analysis of software architecture evolution with discontinuity. In: Proc. Int'l Workshop on Principles of Software Evolution (IWPSE), Orlando, Florida (2002) 103–107 [267]

18. Apache Ant: Apache ant.
    http://ant.apache.org (2007) [196]

19. ArgoUML: Cookbook for developers of ArgoUML.
    http://argouml.tigris.org/files/documents/4/0/argouml-0.14/cookbook-0.14.pdf   (2006) [55, 237]

20. Arisholm, E., Sjoberg, D.: Evaluating the effect of a delegated versus centralized control style on the maintainability of object-oriented software. IEEE Trans. Software Engineering **30**(8) (2004) 521–534 [97]

21. Arnold, R.S.: An introduction to software restructuring. In Arnold, R.S., ed.: Tutorial on Software Restructuring. IEEE Press (1986) [6]

22. Arnold, R.S.: Software restructuring. In: Proc. IEEE. Volume 77. IEEE Computer Society Press (April 1989) 607–617 [5]

23. Arnold, R.S.: Software Reengineering. IEEE Computer Society Press (1993) [5, 291]

24. Arthur, L.J.: Software Evolution: The Software Maintenance Challenge. John Wiley & Sons (1988) [2, 291]

25. As-2 Embedded Computing Systems Committee SAE: Architecture Analysis & Design Language (AADL). SAE Standards n^o AS5506 (November 2004) [239]

26. Astels, D.: Refactoring with UML. In: Proc. Int'l Conf. eXtreme Programming and Flexible Processes in Software Engineering (XP). (2002) 67–70 Alghero, Sardinia, Italy. [96]

27. Bailey, J., Burd, E.: Evaluating clone detection tools for use during preventative maintenance. In: Proc. Workshop Source Code Analysis and Manipulation (SCAM), IEEE Computer Society Press (2002) 36–43 [29]

28. Baker, B.S.: A program for identifying duplicated code. In: Computer Science and Statistics: Proc. Symp. on the Interface. (March 1992) 49–57 [18]

29. Baker, B.S.: On finding duplication and near-duplication in large software systems. In Wills, L., Newcomb, P., Chikofsky, E., eds.: Proc. Working Conf. Reverse Engineering (WCRE), Los Alamitos, California, IEEE Computer Society Press (July 1995) 86–95 [15, 19, 27, 29, 30]

30. Baker, B.S.: Parameterized pattern matching: Algorithms and applications. Computer System Science **52**(1) (February 1996) 28–42 [27]

31. Balazinska, M., Merlo, E., Dagenais, M., Laguë, B., Kontogiannis, K.: Partial redesign of Java software systems based on clone analysis. In: Proc. Working Conf. Reverse Engineering (WCRE), IEEE Computer Society Press (1999) 326–336 [19, 25]

32. Balazinska, M., Merlo, E., Dagenais, M., Laguë, B., Kontogiannis, K.: Advanced clone analysis to support object-oriented system refactoring. In: Proc. Working Conf. Reverse Engineering (WCRE), IEEE Computer Society Press (October 2000) 98–107 [19, 25]

33. Balazinska, M., Merlo, E., Dagenais, M., Laguë, B., Kontogiannis, K.: Measuring clone based reengineering opportunities. In: Proc. IEEE Symp. Software Metrics, IEEE Computer Society Press (November 1999) 292–303 [19]

34. Baniassad, E., Clarke, S.: Theme: An approach for aspect-oriented analysis and design. In: Proc. Int'l Conf. Software Engineering (ICSE), Washington, DC, USA, IEEE Computer Society Press (2004) 158–167 [213]
35. Baniassad, E., Clements, P.C., Araujo, J., Moreira, A., Rashid, A., Tekinerdogan, B.: Discovering early aspects. IEEE Software 23(1) (January-February 2006) 61–70 [213]
36. Barais, O.: Construire et Maîtriser l'Évolution d'une Architecture Logicielle à base de Composants. PhD thesis, LIFL, Université des Sciences et Technologies de Lille (Novembre 2005) [234, 258, 259]
37. Barais, O., Duchien, L.: SafArchie studio: An ArgoUML extension to build safe architectures. In: Architecture Description Languages. Springer-Verlag (2005) 85–100 [235, 236, 237, 256]
38. Barais, O., Le Meur, A.F., Duchien, L., Lawall, J.: Safe integration of new concerns in a software architecture. In: Proc. IEEE Int'l Symp. and Workshop on Engineering of Computer Based Systems (ECBS), IEEE Computer Society Press (2006) 52–64 [234, 256]
39. Basili, V.R., Briand, L.C., Melo, W.L.: A validation of object-oriented design metrics as quality indicators. IEEE Trans. Software Engineering 22(10) (October 1996) 751–761 [7, 73]
40. Basili, V.R., Shull, F., Lanubile, F.: Building knowledge through families of experiments. IEEE Trans. Software Engineering 25(4) (1999) 456–473 [86, 87]
41. Bass, L., Clements, P., Kazman, R.: Software Architecture in Practice. Addison-Wesley (1998) [99]
42. Bass, L., Klein, M., Northrop, L.: Identifying aspects using architectural reasoning. Position paper presented at Early Aspects 2004: Aspect-Oriented Requirements Engineering and Architecture Design, Workshop of the 3rd Int'l Conf. Aspect-Oriented Software Development (AOSD) (2004) [213]
43. Batini, C., Ceri, S., Navathe, S.B.: Conceptual Database Design : An Entity-Relationship Approach. Benjamin/Cummings (1992) [115]
44. Batista, T., Chavez, C., Garcia, A., Rashid, A., Sant'Anna, C., Kulesza, U., Filho, F.C.: Reflections on architectural connection: seven issues on aspects and ADLs. In: Proc. Int'l workshop on Early Aspects (EA), Int'l Conf. Software Engineering, New York, NY, USA, ACM Press (2006) 3–10 [245]
45. Baudry, B., Fleurey, F., France, R., Reddy, R.: Exploring the relationship between model composition and model transformation. In: Proc. Int'l Workshop on Aspect-Oriented Modeling (AOM), MoDELS 2005, Montego Bay, Jamaica (October 2005) [257]
46. Baxter, I., Pidgeon, C., Mehlich, M.: DMS®: Program transformations for practical scalable software evolution. In: Proc. Int'l Conf. Software Engineering (ICSE), Washington, DC, USA, IEEE Computer Society Press (2004) 625–634 [164]
47. Baxter, I.D., Yahin, A., Moura, L., Sant'Anna, M., Bier, L.: Clone detection using abstract syntax trees. In: Proc. Int'l Conf. Software Maintenance (ICSM), IEEE Computer Society Press (1998) 368–377 [27, 29, 30]
48. Beck, K., Fowler, M.: Planning Extreme Programming. Addison-Wesley (2001) [177, 198]
49. Beck, K., Gamma, E.: Test infected: Programmers love writing tests. Java Report 3(7) (1998) 51–56 [175, 176, 178, 180]
50. Beck, K.: Extreme Programming Explained: Embrace Change. Addison-Wesley (1999) [3, 93, 176, 177, 178, 179, 185, 198]
51. Beck, K.: Aim, fire: Kent beck on test-first design. IEEE Software 18(5) (September/October 2001) 87–89 [192]

52. Beck, K.: Test-Driven Development: By Example. Addison-Wesley (2003) [178, 179, 192]

53. Behm, A., Geppert, A., Dittrich, K.: On the migration of relational schemas and data to object-oriented database systems. In: Proc. Re-Technologies in Information Systems, Klagenfurt, Austria (December 1997) [110]

54. Bellon, S.: Vergleich von Techniken zur Erkennung duplizierten Quellcodes. Diploma thesis, no. 1998, University of Stuttgart (Germany), Institute for Software Technology (September 2002) [29, 30]

55. Bellon, S., Koschke, R., Antoniol, G., Krinke, J., Merlo, E.: Comparison and evaluation of clone detection tools. IEEE Trans. Software Engineering **33**(9) (September 2007) 577–591 [29, 30]

56. Bennett, K.: Legacy systems: Coping with success. IEEE Software **12**(1) (1995) 19–23 [173]

57. Bennett, K.H., Rajlich, V.T.: Software Maintenance and Evolution: A Roadmap. In: The Future of Software Engineering. ACM Press (2000) 75–87 [2, 3, 4, 267, 268, 282]

58. Bevan, J., Whitehead, E.J., Kim, S., Godfrey, M.: Facilitating software evolution research with Kenyon. In: Proc. European Software Engineering Conf. and Foundations of Software Engineering (ESEC/FSE), New York, NY, USA, ACM Press (2005) 177–186 [44, 45]

59. Beyer, D., Hassan, A.E.: Animated visualization of software history using evolution storyboards. In: Proc. Working Conf. Reverse Engineering (WCRE), Washington, DC, USA, IEEE Computer Society (2006) 199–210 [60]

60. Bezem, M., Klop, J.W., de Vrijer, R., eds.: Term Rewriting Systems. Cambridge Tracts in Theoretical Computer Science. Cambridge University Press (March 2003) [150]

61. Bhat, T., Nagappan, N.: Building scalable failure-proneness models using complexity metrics for large scale software systems. In: Proc. Asia Pacific Software Engineering Conf. (APSEC), Washington, DC, USA, IEEE Computer Society Press (2006) 361–366 [87]

62. Bianchi, A., Caivano, D., Visaggio, G.: Method and process for iterative reengineering of data in a legacy system. In: Proc. Working Conf. Reverse Engineering (WCRE), IEEE Computer Society Press (2000) 86– [110]

63. Biggerstaff, T.J., Mitbander, B.G., Webster, D.E.: Program understanding and the concept assignment problem. Comm. ACM **37**(5) (May 1994) 72–82 [99]

64. Biggerstaff, T.J., Mittbander, B.G., Webster, D.: The concept assignment problem in program understanding. In: Proc. Int'l Conf. Software Engineering (ICSE), IEEE Computer Society Press (1993) 482–498 [99]

65. Binder, R.: Design for testability in object-oriented systems. Comm. ACM **37**(9) (1994) 87–101 [193, 194, 195]

66. Binder, R.V.: Testing Object-Oriented Systems: Models, Patterns, and Tools. Object Technology Series. Addison-Wesley (1999) [6, 98, 174, 304]

67. Binkley, D., Ceccato, M., Harman, M., Ricca, F., Tonella, P.: Automated refactoring of object oriented code into aspects. In: Proc. Int'l Conf. Software Maintenance (ICSM), IEEE Computer Society Press (2005) 27–36 [218, 219, 220, 222, 223]

68. Bird, C., Gourley, A., Devanbu, P., Gertz, M., Swaminathan, A.: Mining email social networks. In: Proc. Int'l Workshop on Mining Software Repositories (MSR), New York, NY, USA, ACM Press (2006) 137–143 [51]

69. Bisbal, J., Lawless, D., Wu, B., Grimson, J.: Legacy information systems: Issues and directions. IEEE Software **16**(5) (September/October 1999) 103–111 [107]

70. Blostein, D., Schürr, A.: Computing with Graphs and Graph Rewriting. Software – Practice and Experience, John Wiley & Sons **29**(3) (1999) 1–21 [167]

71. Boehm, B.W.: A spiral model of software development and enhancement. IEEE Computer **21**(5) (1988) 61–72 [2, 299]
72. Boehm, B.: Software Engineering Economics. Prentice Hall (1981) [7, 195]
73. Boger, M., Sturm, T., Fragemann, P.: Refactoring browser for UML. In: Proc. Int'l Conf. eXtreme Programming and Flexible Processes in Software Engineering (XP). (2002) 77–81 Alghero, Sardinia, Italy. [93, 95, 96]
74. Bohner, S.A., Arnold, R.S.: Software Change Impact Analysis. IEEE Computer Society Press (1996) [6, 291]
75. Bosch, J.: Design and Use of Software Architectures – Adopting and Evolving a Product Line Approach. Addison-Wesley (2000) [292]
76. Bottoni, P., Parisi Presicce, F., Taentzer, G.: Specifying integrated refactoring with distributed graph transformations. Lecture Notes in Computer Science **3062** (2003) 220–235 [94]
77. Bouktif, S., Gueheneuc, Y.G., Antoniol, G.: Extracting change-patterns from CVS repositories. In: Proc. Working Conf. Reverse Engineering (WCRE), Washington, DC, USA, IEEE Computer Society Press (2006) 221–230 [59]
78. Bradbury, J.S., Cordy, J.R., Dingel, J., Wermelinger, M.: A survey of self-management in dynamic software architecture specifications. In: Proc. ACM SIGSOFT workshop on Self-managed systems (WOSS), New York, NY, USA, ACM Press (2004) 28–33 [238]
79. Braem, M., Gybels, K., Kellens, A., Vanderperren, W.: Automated pattern-based pointcut generation. In: Proc. Int'l Symp. Software Composition (SC), Springer-Verlag (2006) 66–81 [221, 223]
80. Breu, S., Zimmermann, T.: Mining aspects from version history. In: Proc. Int'l Conf. Automated Software Engineering (ASE), Washington, DC, USA, IEEE Computer Society Press (2006) 221–230 [59]
81. Briand, L.C., Labiche, Y., Yan, H.D., Pent, M.D.: A controlled experiment on the impact of the object constraint language in UML-based development. icsm (2004) 380–389 [241]
82. Briand, L.C., Wüst, J., Ikonomovski, S.V., Lounis, H.: Investigating quality factors in object-oriented designs: an industrial case study. In: Proc. Int'l Conf. Software Engineering (ICSE), Los Alamitos, CA, USA, IEEE Computer Society Press (1999) 345–354 [74]
83. Brito e Abreu, F., Melo, W.: Evaluating the impact of object-oriented design on software quality. In: Proc. IEEE Symp. Software Metrics. (March 1996) 90–99 [7]
84. Brodie, M.L., Stonebraker, M.: Migrating Legacy Systems. Gateways, Interfaces, and the Incremental Approach. Morgan Kaufmann (1995) [91, 106, 107, 111, 123, 137, 291, 301]
85. Brooks, F.P.: The Mythical Man-Month: Essays on Software Engineering. 20th anniversary edn. Addison-Wesley (1995) [7, 174]
86. Brown, W.J., Malveau, R.C., McCormick, H.W., Mowbray, T.J.: AntiPatterns: Refactoring Software, Architectures, and Projects in Crisis. John Wiley & Sons (1998) [99, 102]
87. Bruneton, E., Coupaye, T., Leclercq, M., Quema, V., Stefani, J.B.: An open component model and its support in Java. In: Component-Based Software Engineering. (2004) 7–22 [235]
88. Bruntink, M., D'Hondt, M., van Deursen, A., Tourwé, T.: Simple crosscutting concerns do not exist. In: Proc. Int'l Conf. Aspect-Oriented Software Development (AOSD), ACM Press (2007) 199–211 [203, 211, 218, 223, 225]
89. Bruntink, M., van Deursen, A.: An empirical study into class testability. Systems and Software **79**(9) (2006) 1219–1232 [193, 194, 197]

90. Bruntink, M., van Deursen, A., Tourwé, T.: Isolating Idiomatic Crosscutting Concerns. In: Proc. Int'l Conf. Software Maintenance (ICSM), IEEE Computer Society Press (2005) 37– 46 [211, 212]

91. Bruntink, M., van Deursen, A., Tourwé, T.: Discovering faults in idiom-based exception handling. In: Proc. Int'l Conf. Software Engineering (ICSE), ACM Press (2006) 242–251 [203, 211, 212, 217]

92. Bruntink, M., van Deursen, A., van Engelen, R., Tourwé, T.: An evaluation of clone detection techniques for identifying crosscutting concerns. In: Proc. Int'l Conf. Software Maintenance (ICSM), IEEE Computer Society (2004) 200–209 [20, 34, 214]

93. Bruntink, M., van Engelen, R., Tourwé, T.: On the use of clone detection for identifying crosscutting concern code. IEEE Trans. Software Engineering 31(10) (2005) 804–818 [30, 34, 109, 214]

94. Buckley, J., Mens, T., Zenger, M., Rashid, A., Kniesel, G.: Towards a taxonomy of software change. Software Maintenance and Evolution: Research and Practice 17(5) (September/October 2005) 309–332 [5]

95. Bugzilla: Bugzilla.
http://www.bugzilla.org (2007) [41]

96. Bures, T., Hnetynka, P., Plasil, F.: Sofa 2.0: Balancing advanced features in a hierarchical component model. In: Proc. Int'l Conf. Software Engineering Research, Management and Applications (SERA), Washington, DC, USA, IEEE Computer Society Press (2006) 40–48 [235]

97. Buschmann, F., Meunier, R., Rohnert, H., Sommerlad, P., Stal, M.: Pattern-Oriented Software Architecture – A System of Patterns. John Wiley & Sons (1996) [98]

98. C2 Wiki: Two year itch.
http://c2.com/cgi/wiki?TwoYearItch (January 20 2007) [184]

99. Canfora, G., Cimitile, A., Munro, M.: An improved algorithm for identifying objects in code. Software – Practice and Experience, John Wiley & Sons 26(1) (1996) 25–48 [109]

100. Canfora, G., Fasolino, A.R., Frattolillo, G., Tramontana, P.: Migrating interactive legacy systems to web services. In: Proc. European Conf. Software Maintenance and Reengineering (CSMR), Washington, DC, USA, IEEE Computer Society Press (2006) 24–36 [168]

101. Canfora, G., Santo, G.D., Zimeo, E.: Developing and executing Java AWT applications on limited devices with TCPTE. In: Proc. Int'l Conf. Software Engineering (ICSE), New York, NY, USA, ACM Press (2006) 787–790 [109]

102. Capiluppi, A., Gonzales-Barahona, J., Herraiz, I., Robles, G.: Adapting the "staged model for software evolution" to free/libre/open source software. In: Proc. Int'l Workshop on Principles of Software Evolution (IWPSE), Dubrovnik, Croatia (3-4 Sept. 2007) [282]

103. Capiluppi, A., Morisio, M., Ramil, J.F.: The evolution of source folder structure in actively evolved open source systems. In: Proc. IEEE Symp. Software Metrics, IEEE Computer Society Press (2004) 2–13 [275]

104. Capiluppi, A., Morisio, M., Ramil, J.F.: Structural evolution of an open source system: A case study. In: Int'l Workshop on Program Comprehension (IWPC). (2004) 172–182 [275]

105. Capiluppi, A., Ramil, J.F.: Studying the evolution of open source systems at different levels of granularity: Two case studies. In: Proc. Int'l Workshop on Principles of Software Evolution (IWPSE), IEEE Computer Society Press (2004) 113–118 [275, 278]

106. Carrière, S.J., Woods, S.G., Kazman, R.: Software architectural transformation. In: Proc. Working Conf. Reverse Engineering (WCRE), IEEE Computer Society Press (1999) 13–23 [167]

107. Casais, E.: Automatic reorganization of object-oriented hierarchies: a case study. Object Oriented Systems **1** (1994) 95–115 [93]

108. Cenqua: Clover.
http://www.cenqua.com/clover/ (January 20 2007) [192]

109. Chapin, N., Hale, J., Khan, K., Ramil, J., Than, W.G.: Types of software evolution and software maintenance. Software Maintenance and Evolution: Research and Practice **13** (2001) 3–30 [5]

110. Chen, K., Schach, S.R., Yu, L., Offutt, A.J., Heller, G.Z.: Open-source change logs. Empirical Software Engineering **9**(3) (2004) 197–210 [283]

111. Chidamber, S.R., Kemerer, C.F.: A metrics suite for object-oriented design. IEEE Trans. Software Engineering **20**(6) (June 1994) 476–493 [73, 195]

112. Chikofsky, E.J., Cross, J.H.: Reverse engineering and design recovery: A taxonomy. IEEE Software **7**(1) (1990) 13–17 [5, 106, 177, 303]

113. Chou, A., Yang, J., Chelf, B., Hallem, S., Engler, D.R.: An empirical study of operating system errors. In: Proc. Symp. Operating Systems Principles. (2001) 73–88 [22]

114. Church, K.W., Helfman, J.I.: Dotplot: A program for exploring self-similarity in millions of lines for text and code. Journal of American Statistical Association, Institute for Mathematical Statistics and Interface Foundations of North America **2**(2) (June 1993) 153–174 [31]

115. Clements, P.: A survey of architecture description languages. In: Proc. Int'l Workshop on Software Specification and Design, IEEE Computer Society Press (March 1996) 16–25 [235]

116. Cleve, A., Hainaut, J.L.: Co-transformations in database applications evolution. In: Generative and Transformational Techniques in Software Engineering. Volume 4143 of Lecture Notes in Computer Science. Springer-Verlag (2006) 409–421 [116]

117. Cleve, A., Henrard, J., Hainaut, J.L.: Data reverse engineering using system dependency graphs. In: Proc. Working Conf. Reverse Engineering (WCRE), Washington, DC, USA, IEEE Computer Society Press (2006) 157–166 [132]

118. Coady, Y., Kiczales, G., Feeley, M., Smolyn, G.: Using AspectC to improve the modularity of path-specific customization in operating system code. In: Proc. European Software Engineering Conf. (ESEC), ACM Press (2001) 88–98 [211]

119. Cockburn, A.: Agile Software Development. Addison-Wesley (2001) [3, 8, 174]

120. Code Generation Network: List of code generators.
http://www.codegeneration.net/generators.php (2007) [168]

121. Collberg, C., Kobourov, S., Nagra, J., Pitts, J., Wampler, K.: A system for graph-based visualization of the evolution of software. In: Proc. ACM Symp. Software Visualization, New York, NY, USA, ACM Press (2003) 77–86 [65]

122. Colyer, A., Clement, A.: Large-scale AOSD for middleware. In: Proc. Int'l Conf. Aspect-Oriented Software Development (AOSD), ACM Press (2004) 56–65 [211]

123. Comino, S., Manenti, F.M., Parisi, M.L.: From planning to mature: on the determinants of open source take off. Technical report, Trento University, Dept. of Economics (January 2005) [282, 283]

124. Cooper, K., McIntosh, N.: Enhanced code compression for embedded RISC processors. In: Proc. ACM Conf. on Programming Language Design and Implementation, ACM Press (May 1999) 139–149 [34]

125. Corbi, T.A.: Program understanding: Challenge for the 1990s. IBM Systems Journal **28**(2) (1989) 294–306 [176, 177]

126. Cordy, J., Dean, T., Malton, A., Schneider, K.: Source transformation in software engineering using the TXL transformation system. Information and Software Technology **44**(13) (2002) 827–837 [164]

127. Cordy, J.R., Dean, T.R., Synytskyy, N.: Practical language-independent detection of near-miss clones. In: Proc. Conf. Centre for Advanced Studies on Collaborative research (CASCON), IBM Press (2004) 1–12 [27]

128. Cordy, J.: Comprehending reality: Practical challenges to software maintenance automation. In: Int'l Workshop on Program Comprehension (IWPC), IEEE Computer Society Press (2003) 196–206 [21, 22]

129. Corradini, A., Montanari, U., Rossi, F.: Graph processes. Fundamenta Informaticae **26**(3 and 4) (1996) 241–265 [148]

130. Counsell, S., Hassoun, Y., Loizou, G., Najjar, R.: Common refactorings, a dependency graph and some code smells: an empirical study of Java OSS. In: Proc. Int'l Symp. Empirical Software Engineering, ACM Press (2006) 288–296 [96]

131. Crispin, L., House, T.: Testing Extreme Programming. Addison-Wesley (2002) [174, 179, 200]

132. Cristianini, N., Shawe-Taylor, J.: An introduction to Support Vector Machines. Cambridge University Press (2000) [78]

133. Cubranic, D., Murphy, G.C.: Hipikat: recommending pertinent software development artifacts. In: Proc. Int'l Conf. Software Engineering (ICSE), Portland, Oregon, IEEE Computer Society Press (2003) 408–418 [43]

134. Cunningham, W.: Episodes: A pattern language of competitive development. In Vlissides, J., ed.: Pattern Languages of Program Design 2. Addison-Wesley (1996) [179]

135. CVS: Concurrent versions systems.
http://www.nongnu.org/cvs (2006) [40]

136. D'Ambros, M.: Software archaeology – reconstructing the evolution of software systems. Master thesis, Politecnico di Milano (April 2005) [40, 46]

137. D'Ambros, M., Lanza, M.: Reverse engineering with logical coupling. In: Proc. Working Conf. Reverse Engineering (WCRE), IEEE Computer Society Press (October 2006) 189–198 [52, 53, 56, 57, 58]

138. D'Ambros, M., Lanza, M.: Software bugs and evolution: A visual approach to uncover their relationship. In: Proc. European Conf. Software Maintenance and Reengineering (CSMR), IEEE Computer Society Press (2006) 227–236 [48]

139. D'Ambros, M., Lanza, M., Gall, H.: Fractal figures: Visualizing development effort for CVS entities. In: Proc. Int'l Workshop on Visualizing Software for Understanding (Vissoft), IEEE Computer Society Press (2005) 46–51 [46, 47, 48]

140. D'Ambros, M., Lanza, M., Lungu, M.: The evolution radar: Integrating fine-grained and coarse-grained logical coupling information. In: Proc. Int'l Workshop on Mining Software Repositories (MSR). (2006) 26–32 [52]

141. Dashofy, E.M., van der Hoek, A., Taylor, R.N.: An infrastructure for the rapid development of XML-based architecture description languages. In: Proc. Int'l Conf. Software Engineering (ICSE), New York, NY, USA, ACM Press (2002) 266–276 [235, 236]

142. David, P.C., Ledoux, T.: Safe dynamic reconfigurations of Fractal architectures with FScript. In: Proc. Fractal CBSE Workshop, ECOOP'06, Nantes, France (2006) [238]

143. DB-MAIN: The DB-MAIN official website.
http://www.db-main.be (2006) [129]

144. de Lucia, A., Lucca, G.A.D., Fasolino, A.R., Guerra, P., Petruzzelli, S.: Migrating legacy systems towards object-oriented platforms. In: Proc. Int'l Conf. Software Maintenance (ICSM), Los Alamitos, CA, USA, IEEE Computer Society Press (1997) 122 [109]

145. Del Grosso, C., Di Penta, M., Garcia-Rodriguez de Guzman, I.: An approach for mining services in database oriented applications. Proc. European Conf. Software Maintenance and Reengineering (CSMR) (2007) 287–296 [168]

146. Delcroix, C., Thiran, P., Hainaut, J.L.: Transformational approach to data reengineering. Ingénierie des Systèmes d'Information (December 2001) (in French). [130]

147. Demeyer, S., Bois, B.D., Rieger, M., Rompaey, B.V.: The LAN-simulation: A refactoring lab session. In: Proc. 1st Workshop on Refactoring Tools, University of Berlin (2007) [97]

148. Demeyer, S., Ducasse, S., Nierstrasz, O.: Finding refactorings via change metrics. In: Proc. ACM SIGPLAN Conf. Object-Oriented Programming, Systems, Languages and Applications (OOPSLA). Volume 35 of SIGPLAN Notices., ACM Press (October 2000) 166–177 [95]

149. Demeyer, S., Ducasse, S., Nierstrasz, O.: Object-Oriented Reengineering Patterns. Morgan Kaufmann, San Francisco, CA, USA (2002) [5, 92, 98, 99, 100, 102, 103, 139, 174, 200, 292, 300, 301]

150. Demeyer, S., Van Rysselberghe, F., Girba, T., Ratzinger, J., Marinescu, R., Mens, T., Du Bois, B., Janssens, D., Ducasse, S., Lanza, M., Rieger, M., Gall, H., El-Ramly, M.: The LAN-simulation: A refactoring teaching example. In: Proc. Int'l Workshop on Principles of Software Evolution (IWPSE), IEEE Computer Society Press (2005) 123–131 [97]

151. Di Lucca, G., Di Penta, M., Fasolino, A.: An approach to identify duplicated web pages. In: Proc. Int'l Computer Software and Applications Conf. (COMPSAC). (2002) 481–486 [27]

152. Dig, D., Johnson, R.: The role of refactorings in api evolution. In: Proc. Int'l Conf. Software Maintenance (ICSM), IEEE Computer Society Press (2005) 389–398 [96]

153. Dijkstra, E.W.: On the role of scientific thought (EWD447). In: Selected Writings on Computing: A Personal Perspective. Springer-Verlag (1982) 60–66 [234]

154. Du Bois, B.: A Study of Quality Improvements by refactoring. PhD thesis, University of Antwerp (September 2006) [97]

155. Duala-Ekoko, E., Robillard, M.: Tracking code clones in evolving software. In: Proc. Int'l Conf. Software Engineering (ICSE), ACM Press (2007) 158–167 [23]

156. Ducasse, S., Rieger, M., Demeyer, S.: A language independent approach for detecting duplicated code. In Yang, H., White, L., eds.: Proc. Int'l Conf. Software Maintenance (ICSM), IEEE Computer Society Press (September 1999) 109–118 [15, 26, 29, 30, 31]

157. Ehrig, H., Ehrig, K., Prange, U., Taentzer, G.: Fundamentals of Algebraic Graph Transformation. Springer-Verlag (2006) [148]

158. El-Ramly, M., Eltayeb, R., Alla, H.: An experiment in automatic conversion of legacy Java programs to C#. In: Proc. IEEE Int'l Conf. Computer Systems and Applications. (2006) 1037–1045 [108]

159. Elbaum, S., Gable, D., Rothermel, G.: The impact of software evolution on code coverage information. In: Proc. Int'l Conf. Software Maintenance (ICSM), IEEE Computer Society Press (2001) 170–179 [201]

160. Endres, A., Rombach, D.: A Handbook of Software and Systems Engineering. Pearson Addison-Wesley (2003) [70, 72]

161. Erdogmus, H., Morisio, M., Torchiano, M.: On the effectiveness of the test-first approach to programming. IEEE Trans. Software Engineering 31(3) (2005) 226–237 [201]

162. Erl, T.: Service-Oriented Architecture: Concepts, Technology, and Design. Prentice Hall, Upper Saddle River, NJ, USA (2005) [9, 140, 304]

163. Ettinger, R., Verbaere, M.: Untangling: a slice extraction refactoring. In: Proc. Int'l Conf. Aspect-Oriented Software Development (AOSD), ACM Press (March 2004) 93–101 [218]

164. Fabry, J.: Modularizing Advanced Transaction Management – Tackling Tangled Aspect Code. PhD thesis, Vrije Universiteit Brussel (September 2005) [203]

165. Fahmy, H., Holt, R.C., Cordy, J.R.: Wins and losses of algebraic transformations of software architectures. In: Proc. Int'l Conf. Automated Software Engineering (ASE), Washington, DC, USA, IEEE Computer Society Press (2001) 51– [167]

166. Fanta, R., Rajlich, V.: Removing clones from the code. Software Maintenance and Evolution: Research and Practice 11(4) (July/Aug. 1999) 223–243 [24]

167. Favre, J.M.: Languages evolve too! Changing the software time scale. In: Proc. Int'l Workshop on Principles of Software Evolution (IWPSE), Los Alamitos, CA, USA, IEEE Computer Society (2005) 33–44 [9]

168. FEAST: Feedback, evolution and software technology projects website. http://www.doc.ic.ac.uk/ mml/feast/ (Sept 2001) [266]

169. Feathers, M.C.: Working Effectively with Legacy Code. Prentice Hall (2005) [100, 104, 292]

170. Feitelson, D.G., Heller, G.Z., Schach, S.R.: An empirically-based criterion for determining the success of an open-source project. In: Proc. Australian Software Engineering Conf. (ASWEC). (21 April 2006) 6 pp. [286]

171. Fenton, N., Pfleeger, S.L.: Software Metrics: A Rigorous and Practical Approach. 2nd edn. International Thomson Computer Press, London, UK (1997) [7, 296]

172. Fenton, N.E., Ohlsson, N.: Quantitative analysis of faults and failures in a complex software system. IEEE Trans. Software Engineering 26(8) (2000) 797–814 [73, 87]

173. Ferenc, R., Beszédes, Á.: Data exchange with the Columbus schema for C++. In: Proc. European Conf. Software Maintenance and Reengineering (CSMR), Washington, DC, USA, IEEE Computer Society Press (2002) 59–66 [163]

174. Fernandez-Ramil, J., Hall, P.: Maintaining and Evolving Software. M882 Course on Managing the Software Enterprise, Learning Space, The Open University, http://openlearn.open.ac.uk/course/view.php?id=1698 (2007) Work licensed under a Creative Commons Attribution-NonCommercial-ShareAlike 2.0 Licence. [265, 268]

175. Ferrante, J., Ottenstein, K., Warren, J.: The program dependence graph and its use in optimization. ACM Trans. Programming Languages and Systems 9(3) (July 1987) 319–349 [28]

176. Filman, R., Friedman, D.: Aspect-oriented programming is quantification and obliviousness (2000) October 2000, Minneapolis. http://ic-www.arc.nasa.gov/ic/darwin/oif/leo/filman/text/oif/aop-is.pdf. [209, 244]

177. Fioravanti, F., Nesi, P.: Estimation and prediction metrics for adaptive maintenance effort of object-oriented systems. IEEE Trans. Software Engineering 27(12) (2001) 1062–1084 [7]

178. Fischer, M., Gall, H.: EvoGraph: A lightweight approach to evolutionary and structural analysis of large software systems. In: Proc. Working Conf. Reverse Engineering (WCRE), Washington, DC, USA, IEEE Computer Society (2006) 179–188 [60]

179. Fischer, M., Pinzger, M., Gall, H.: Populating a release history database from version control and bug tracking systems. In: Proc. Int'l Conf. Software Maintenance (ICSM), Los Alamitos CA, IEEE Computer Society Press (September 2003) 23–32 [40]

180. Flammia, G.: On the internet, software should be milked, not brewed. IEEE Expert 11(6) (December 1996) 87–88 [34]

181. Foote, B., Yoder, J.W.: Big ball of mud. In Harrison, N., Foote, B., Rohnert, H., eds.: Pattern Languages of Program Design. Volume 4. Addison-Wesley (2000) 654–692 [98, 102]

182. Fowler, M.: Analysis Patterns: Reusable Object Models. Addison-Wesley (1997) [98, 228]

183. Fowler, M.: Refactoring: Improving the Design of Existing Code. Addison-Wesley, Boston, MA, USA (1999) [6, 21, 35, 92, 93, 96, 101, 104, 165, 167, 175, 180, 182, 184, 185, 186, 187, 189, 191, 198, 216, 218, 278, 291, 296, 303]

184. G. Sunyé, Pollet, D., LeTraon, Y., Jézéquel, J.M.: Refactoring UML models. In: Proc. UML. Volume 2185 of Lecture Notes in Computer Science., Springer-Verlag (2001) 134–138 [93, 95, 96]

185. Gall, H., Hajek, K., Jazayeri, M.: Detection of logical coupling based on product release history. In: Proc. Int'l Conf. Software Maintenance (ICSM), IEEE Computer Society Press (November 1998) [59]

186. Gall, H., Jazayeri, M., Klösch, R., Trausmuth, G.: Software evolution observations based on product release history. In: Proc. Int'l Conf. Software Maintenance (ICSM), IEEE Computer Society Press (September 1997) 160–166 [270]

187. Gall, H., Jazayeri, M., Krajewski, J.: CVS release history data for detecting logical couplings. In: Proc. Int'l Workshop on Principles of Software Evolution (IWPSE), Los Alamitos CA, IEEE Computer Society Press (2003) 13–23 [59]

188. Gall, H., Jazayeri, M., Riva, C.: Visualizing software release histories: The use of color and third dimension. In Yang, H., White, L., eds.: Proc. Int'l Conf. Software Maintenance (ICSM), Oxford, UK, IEEE Computer Society (1999) 99–108 [65]

189. Galli, M., Lanza, M., Nierstrasz, O., Wuyts, R.: Ordering broken unit tests for focused debugging. In: Proc. Int'l Conf. Software Maintenance (ICSM), IEEE Computer Society Press (2004) 114–123 [200]

190. Gamma, E., Helm, R., Johnson, R., Vlissides, J.: Design Patterns: Elements of Reusable Object-Oriented Languages and Systems. Addison-Wesley (1994) [98, 163]

191. Garcez, A., Russo, A., Nuseibeh, B., Kramer, J.: Abductive reasoning and inductive learning to evolve requirements specifications. IEE Proceedings – Software **150**(1) (February 2003) 25–38 [8]

192. Garcia, A., Chavez, C., Batista, T., Sant'Anna, C., Kulesza, U., Rashid, A., de Lucena, C.J.P.: On the modular representation of architectural aspects. In: Proc. European Workshop on Software Architecture (EWSA). (2006) 82–97 [244]

193. Garcia, A., Sant'Anna, C., Figueiredo, E., Kulesza, U., Lucena, C., von Staa, A.: Modularizing design patterns with aspects: a quantitative study. In: Proc. Int'l Conf. Aspect-Oriented Software Development (AOSD), ACM Press (2005) 3–14 [212]

194. Gartner Group: Gartner. http://www.gartner.com (2007) [139]

195. German, D.: Mining CVS repositories, the softChange experience. In: Proc. Int'l Workshop on Mining Software Repositories (MSR). (2004) 17–21 [43, 45]

196. German, D., Hindle, A., Jordan, N.: Visualizing the evolution of software using softChange. In: Proc. Int'l Conf. on Software Engineering & Knowledge Engineering (SEKE), New York NY, ACM Press (2004) 336–341 [43]

197. German, D.M.: A study of the contributors of PostgreSQL. In: Proc. Int'l Workshop on Mining Software Repositories (MSR), New York, NY, USA, ACM Press (2006) 163–164 [43]

198. Gibbs, C., Liu, C.R., Coady, Y.: Sustainable system infrastructure and big bang evolution: Can aspects keep pace? In: Proc. European Conf. Object-Oriented Programming (ECOOP), Springer-Verlag (2005) 241–261 [212]

199. Giesecke, S.: Clone-based Reengineering für Java auf der Eclipse-Plattform. Diplomarbeit, Carl von Ossietzky Universität Oldenburg, Department für Informatik, Abteilung Software Engineering, Germany (2003) [24]

200. Gilb, T.: Evolutionary development. ACM Software Engineering Notes **6**(2) (April 1981) 17– [2]

201. Girard, J.F., Koschke, R., Schied, G.: A metric-based approach to detect abstract data types and state encapsulations. Automated Software Engineering **6**(4) (1999) 357–386 [109]

202. Gîrba, T., Ducasse, S., Lanza, M.: Yesterday's weather: Guiding early reverse engineering efforts by summarizing the evolution of changes. In: Proc. Int'l Conf. Software Maintenance (ICSM), Chicago, Illinois, IEEE Computer Society Press (2004) 40–49 [53]

203. Gîrba, T., Kuhn, A., Seeberger, M., Ducasse, S.: How developers drive software evolution. In: Proc. Int'l Workshop on Principles of Software Evolution (IWPSE), IEEE Computer Society Press (2005) 113–122 [50, 51]

204. Gitchell, D., Tran, N.: Sim: a utility for detecting similarity in computer programs. In: Proc. Technical Symp. Computer Science Education (SIGCSE), ACM Press (1999) 266–270 [27]

205. Godfrey, M., Tu, Q.: Growth, evolution and structural change in open source software. In: Proc. Int'l Workshop on Principles of Software Evolution (IWPSE). (September 2001) [23, 35]

206. Godfrey, M.W., Tu, Q.: Evolution in open source software: A case study. In: Proc. Int'l Conf. Software Maintenance (ICSM), Los Alamitos, California, IEEE Computer Society Press (2000) 131–142 [8, 35, 268, 270, 271, 274, 286]

207. Godfrey, M.W., Zou, L.: Using origin analysis to detect merging and splitting of source code entities. IEEE Trans. Software Engineering **31**(2) (2005) 166–181 [95]

208. Grady, R.B.: Successful Software Process Improvement. 1st edn. Prentice Hall (1997) [8]

209. Graves, T.L., Karr, A.F., Marron, J., Siy, H.: Predicting fault incidence using software change history. IEEE Trans. Software Engineering **26**(7) (April 2000) 653–661 [82, 87]

210. Grier, S.: A tool that detects plagiarism in Pascal programs. SIGSCE Bulletin **13**(1) (1981) 15–20 [34]

211. Griswold, W., Kato, Y., Yuan, J.: Aspect browser: Tool support for managing dispersed aspects. In: Workshop on Multi-Dimensional Separation of Concerns in Object-oriented Systems. (1999) [213]

212. Gross, H.G.: Component-Based Software Testing with UML. Springer-Verlag (2005) [200]

213. Grubb, P., Takang, A.A.: Software Maintenance: Concepts and Practice. 2nd edn. World Scientific (2003) [292]

214. Hainaut, J.L.: Introduction to Database Reverse Engineering. 3rd edn. LIBD Publish., Namur (2002) [120]

215. Hainaut, J.L., Englebert, V., Henrard, J., Hick, J.M., Roland, D.: Database reverse engineering: From requirements to CARE tools. Automated Software Engineering **3** (1996) 9–45 [112, 120, 129]

216. Hainaut, J.L.: Specification preservation in schema transformations – application to semantics and statistics. Data Knowledge Engineering **19**(2) (1996) 99–134 [115]

217. Hainaut, J.L.: The transformational approach to database engineering. In Lämmel, R., Saraiva, J., Visser, J., eds.: Generative and Transformational Techniques in Software Engineering. Volume 4143 of Lecture Notes in Computer Science., Springer-Verlag (2006) 95–143 [113, 114]

218. Hainaut, J.L., Henrard, J., Hick, J.M., Roland, D., Englebert, V.: Database design recovery. In: Proc. Int'l Conf. Advances Information System Engineering (CAiSE). Volume 1080 of Lecture Notes in Computer Science., Springer-Verlag (1996) 272–300 [116]

219. Hainaut, J.L., Hick, J.M., Henrard, J., Roland, D., Englebert, V.: Knowledge transfer in database reverse engineering: A supporting case study. In: Proc. Working Conf. Reverse Engineering (WCRE), IEEE Computer Society Press (1997) [120]

220. Hanenberg, S., Oberschulte, C., Unland, R.: Refactoring of aspect-oriented software. In: Proc. Int'l Conf. Object-Oriented and Internet-based Technologies, Concepts, and Applications for a Networked World (Net.ObjectDays), Springer-Verlag (2003) 19–35 [218, 220, 222, 227]

221. Hannemann, J., Kiczales, G.: Overcoming the prevalent decomposition in legacy code. In: Workshop on Advanced Separation of Concerns, Int'l Conf. Software Engineering (ICSE). (2001) [213]

222. Hannemann, J., Kiczales, G.: Design pattern implementation in Java and AspectJ. In: Proc. ACM SIGPLAN Conf. Object-Oriented Programming, Systems, Languages and Applications (OOPSLA), ACM Press (2002) 161–173 [212]

223. Hannemann, J., Murphy, G.C., Kiczales, G.: Role-based refactoring of crosscutting concerns. In: Proc. Int'l Conf. Aspect-Oriented Software Development (AOSD), ACM Press (2005) 135–146 [218]

224. Harrold, M.J.: Testing: a roadmap. In: The Future of Software Engineering (ICSE 2000), ACM Press (2000) 61–72 [199]

225. Haug, M., Olsen, E.W., Cuevas, G., Rementeria, S.: Managing the Change: Software Configuration and Change Management: v. 2. Springer-Verlag (2001) [292]

226. Havinga, W., Nagy, I., Bergmans, L.: An analysis of aspect composition problems. In: Proc. European Workshop on Aspects in Software. (August 2006) 1–8 [228]

227. Heckel, R., Wagner, A.: Ensuring consistency of conditional graph grammars: A constructive approach. Electronic Notes in Theoretical Computer Science 1 (1995) [149]

228. Henrard, J., Hick, J.M., Thiran, P., Hainaut, J.L.: Strategies for data reengineering. In: Proc. Working Conf. Reverse Engineering (WCRE), Washington, DC, USA, IEEE Computer Society Press (2002) 211–220 [110]

229. Henrard, J.: Program Understanding in Database Reverse Engineering. PhD thesis, University of Namur (2003) [129, 138]

230. Henry, S.M., Kafura, D.G.: Software structure metrics based on information flow. IEEE Trans. Software Engineering 7(5) (1981) 510–518 [74]

231. Herraiz, I., Robles, G., Gonzalez-Barahona, J.M., Capiluppi, A., Ramil, J.F.: Comparison between SLOCs and number of files as size metrics for software evolution analysis. In: Proc. European Conf. Software Maintenance and Reengineering (CSMR), Bari, Italy (21–24 March 2006) [7, 270, 274, 275]

232. Hick, J.M., Hainaut, J.L.: Database application evolution: A transformational approach. Data & Knowledge Engineering 59 (December 2006) 534–558 [116]

233. Highsmith, J., Fowler, M.: The agile manifesto. Software Development Magazine 9(8) (2001) 29–30 [175]

234. Higo, Y., Ueda, Y., Kamiya, T., Kusumoto, S., Inoue, K.: On software maintenance process improvement based on code clone analysis. In: Proc. Int'l Conf. Product Focused Software Process Improvement. Volume 2559 of Lecture Notes in Computer Science., Springer-Verlag (2002) 185–197 [27]

235. Horwitz, S., Reps, T., Binkley, D.: Interprocedural slicing using dependence graphs. ACM Trans. Programming Languages and Systems 12(1) (January 1990) 26–60 [132]

236. Humphrey, W.: Managing the Software Process. Addison-Wesley (1989) [198]

237. Hunt, J.: Extensible, Language Aware Differencing and Merging. Dissertation, University of Kaiserslautern (2001) [35]

238. IEEE. In: Standard 610.12-1990: Glossary of Software Engineering Terminology. Volume 1. IEEE Press (1999) [73, 301, 304]

239. IEEE. In: Standard IEEE Std 1219-1999 on Software Maintenance. Volume 2. IEEE Press (1999) [1, 7, 293, 301]

240. International Standards Organisation (ISO): International standard ISO/IEC 9126. information technology: Software product evaluation: Quality characteristics and guidelines for their use (1991) [193, 293, 304]

241. International Standards Organisation (ISO): Software life cycle processes. In: ISO 12207 Information Technology. ISO (1995) [293, 301]

242. International Standards Organisation (ISO): Standard 14764 on Software Engineering – Software Maintenance. ISO/IEC (1999) [3, 4, 7, 293, 301]

243. ITU: Recommendation Z.120: Message Sequence Chart (MSC). Ø Haugen (ed.), Geneva (1999) [260]

244. Ivkovic, I., Kontogiannis, K.: A framework for software architecture refactoring using model transformations and semantic annotations. In: Proc. European Conf. Software Maintenance and Reengineering (CSMR), Washington, DC, USA, IEEE Computer Society Press (2006) 135–144 [167]

245. Jackson, A., Klein, J., Baudry, B., Clarke, S.: Testing aspect models. In: Model Driven Development and Model Driven Testing workshop at ECMDA. (2006) [260]

246. Jackson, J.E.: A Users Guide to Principal Components. John Wiley & Sons (2003) [76]

247. Jacobson, I., Ng, P.W.: Aspect-Oriented Software Development with Use Cases. Addison-Wesley (2004) [8]

248. Jacoby, R., Masuzawa, K.: Test coverage dependent software reliability estimation by the HGDmodel. In: Proc. Int'l Symp. Software Reliability Engineering (ISSRE). (1992) 193–204 [73]

249. Jahnke, J.H., Wadsack, J.: Varlet: Human-centered tool support for database reengineering. In: Proc. Working Conf. Reverse Engineering (WCRE), IEEE Computer Society Press (May 1999) [109]

250. Jakobac, V., Egyed, A., Medvidovic, N.: Improving system understanding via interactive, tailorable, source code analysis. In Cerioli, M., ed.: Proc. Int'l Conf. Fundamental Aspects of Software Engineering (FASE). Volume 3442 of Lecture Notes in Computer Science., Springer-Verlag (2005) 253–268 [164]

251. Jankowitz, H.T.: Detecting plagiarism in student Pascal programs. Computer Journal 1(31) (1988) 1–8 [34]

252. Jazayeri, M.: On architectural stability and evolution. In: Proc. Reliable Software Technologies-Ada-Europe. Volume 2361 of Lecture Notes in Computer Science., Vienna, Austria, Springer-Verlag (2002) 397–420 [9]

253. Jazayeri, M., Ran, A., Van Der Linden, F.: Software Architecture for Product Families: Principles and Practice. Addison-Wesley (2000) [9]

254. Jeffries, R., Anderson, A., Hendrickson, C.: Extreme Programming Installed. Addison-Wesley (2000) [177, 179, 198]

255. JetBrains: IntelliJ IDEA.
http://www.jetbrains.com/idea/ (2007) [165]

256. Jeusfeld, M.A., Johnen, U.A.: An executable meta model for re-engineering of database schemas. In: Proc. Conf. on the Entity-Relationship Approach, Manchester (December 1994) [109]

257. Jiang, L., Misherghi, G., Su, Z., Glondu, S.: Deckard: Scalable and accurate tree-based detection of code clones. In: Proc. Int'l Conf. Software Engineering (ICSE), ACM Press (2007) 96–105 [28]

258. Johnson, J.H.: Identifying redundancy in source code using fingerprints. In: Proc. Conf. Centre for Advanced Studies on Collaborative research (CASCON), IBM Press (1993) 171–183 [26]

259. Johnson, J.H.: Substring matching for clone detection and change tracking. In: Proc. Int'l Conf. Software Maintenance (ICSM), IEEE Computer Society Press (1994) 120–126 [26]

260. Johnson, J.H.: Visualizing textual redundancy in legacy source. In: Proc. Conf. Centre for Advanced Studies on Collaborative research (CASCON), IBM Press (1994) 32–41 [31, 32]

261. Jörgensen, M.: Experience with the accuracy of software maintenance task effort prediction models. IEEE Trans. Software Engineering **21**(8) (1995) 674–681 [7]

262. JUnit: JUnit.
http://www.junit.org (2007) [175, 178, 193]

263. Kamiya, T., Kusumoto, S., Inoue, K.: CCFinder: A Multi-Linguistic Token-based Code Clone Detection System for Large Scale Source Code. IEEE Trans. Software Engineering **28**(7) (2002) 654–670 [27, 29, 30]

264. Kapser, C., Godfrey, M.: A taxonomy of clones in source code: The re-engineers most wanted list. In: Proc. Working Conf. Reverse Engineering (WCRE), IEEE Computer Society Press (2003) [19, 20]

265. Kapser, C., Godfrey, M.W.: Toward a taxonomy of clones in source code: A case study. In: Proc. Int'l Workshop on Evolution of Large Scale Industrial Software Architectures (ELISA). (2003) 67–78 [19, 20]

266. Kapser, C., Godfrey, M.W.: "Clones considered harmful" considered harmful. In: Proc. Working Conf. Reverse Engineering (WCRE), IEEE Computer Society Press (2006) 19–28 [20, 21]

267. Kapser, C.J., Godfrey, M.W.: Supporting the analysis of clones in software systems: Research articles. Software Maintenance and Evolution: Research and Practice **18**(2) (2006) 61–82 [19]

268. Karp, R.M.: Combinatorics, complexity, and randomness. Comm. ACM **29**(2) (February 1986) 98–109 [26]

269. Karp, R.M., Rabin, M..: Efficient randomized pattern-matching algorithms. IBM Journal Research and Development **31**(2) (March 1987) 249–260 [26]

270. Kazman, R., Carrière, S.J.: Playing detective: Reconstructing software architecture from available evidence. Automated Software Engineering **6**(2) (1999) 107–138 [99]

271. Kazman, R., Woods, S., Carrière, J.: Requirements for integrating software architecture and reengineering models: CORUM II. In: Proc. Working Conf. Reverse Engineering (WCRE), Washington, DC, USA, IEEE Computer Society Press (1998) 154–163 [5, 140]

272. Kellens, A., Mens, K., Tonella, P.: A survey of automated code-level aspect mining techniques. Trans. Aspect-Oriented Software Development (2007) To be published. [204, 213]

273. Kerievsky, J.: Refactoring to patterns. Addison-Wesley (2004) [101, 180, 292]

274. Khoshgoftaar, T.M., Allen, E.B., Goel, N., Nandi, A., McMullan, J.: Detection of software modules with high debug code churn in a very large legacy system. In: Proc. Int'l Symp. Software Reliability Engineering (ISSRE), Washington, DC, USA, IEEE Computer Society Press (1996) 364–371 [87]

275. Khoshgoftaar, T.M., Szabo, R.M.: Improving code churn predictions during the system test and maintenance phases. In: Proc. Int'l Conf. Software Maintenance (ICSM), Washington, DC, USA, IEEE Computer Society Press (1994) 58–67 [87]

276. Kiczales, G., Lamping, J., Mendhekar, A., Maeda, C., Lopes, C.V., Loingtier, J.M., Irwin, J.: Aspect-oriented programming. In Aksit, M., Matsuoka, S., eds.: Proc. European Conf. Object-Oriented Programming (ECOOP). Volume 1241 of Lecture Notes in Computer Science., Springer-Verlag (1997) 220–242 [200, 234, 244]

277. Kim, M., Bergman, L., Lau, T., Notkin, D.: An ethnographic study of copy and paste programming practices in OOPL. In: Proc. Int'l Symp. Empirical Software Engineering, IEEE Computer Society Press (2004) 83–92 [19, 21]

278. Kim, M., Sazawal, V., Notkin, D., Murphy, G.C.: An empirical study of code clone genealogies. In: Proc. European Software Engineering Conf. and Foundations of Software Engineering (ESEC/FSE). (2005) 187–196 [23]

279. Kitchenham, B.A.: System evolution dynamics of VME/B. ICL Tech. J. (May 1982) 42–57 [265]

280. Kitchenham, B.A., Pfleeger, S.L., Hoaglin, D.C., Rosenberg, J.: Preliminary guidelines for empirical research in software engineering. IEEE Trans. Software Engineering **28**(8) (August 2002) 721– 734 [282]

281. Klein, J., Hélouêt, L., Jézéquel, J.M.: Semantic-based weaving of scenarios. In: Proc. Int'l Conf. Aspect-Oriented Software Development (AOSD), New York, NY, USA, ACM Press (2006) 27–38 [260]

282. Kleinbaum, D.G., Kupper, L.L., Nizam, A., Muller, K.E.: Applied Regression Analysis and Multivariable Methods. 4th edn. Duxbury Press (2007) [75]

283. Kniesel, G.: Conditional transformation. http://roots.iai.uni-bonn.de/research/jtransformer/cts (2003) [258]

284. Kniesel, G.: Type-safe delegation for runtime component adaptation. In Guerraoui, R., ed.: Proc. European Conf. Object-Oriented Programming (ECOOP). Volume 1628 of Lecture Notes in Computer Science., Springer-Verlag (1999) 351–366 [9]

285. Kniesel, G., Koch, H.: Static composition of refactorings. Science of Computer Programming **52**(1-3) (2004) 9–51 [95]

286. Komondoor, R., Horwitz, S.: Using slicing to identify duplication in source code. In: Proc. Int'l Symp. Static Analysis. (July 2001) 40–56 [28, 30]

287. Komondoor, R., Horwitz, S.: Eliminating duplication in source code via procedure extraction. Technical report 1461, UW-Madison Dept. of Computer Sciences (December 2002) [24]

288. Kong, J., Zhang, K., Dong, J., Song, G.: A graph grammar approach to software architecture verification and transformation. Proc. Int'l Computer Software and Applications Conf. (COMPSAC) (2003) 492– [165]

289. Kontogiannis, K., DeMori, R., Bernstein, M., Galler, M., Merlo, E.: Pattern matching for design concept localization. In: Proc. Working Conf. Reverse Engineering (WCRE), IEEE Computer Society Press (July 1995) 96–103 [27]

290. Kontogiannis, K., Martin, J., Wong, K., Gregory, R., Müller, H., Mylopoulos, J.: Code migration through transformations: an experience report. In: Proc. Conf. Centre for Advanced Studies on Collaborative research (CASCON), IBM Press (1998) 13 [108]

291. Kontogiannis, K., Mori, R.D., Merlo, E., Galler, M., Bernstein, M.: Pattern matching for clone and concept detection. Automated Software Engineering **3**(1/2) (June 1996) 79–108 [15, 27]

292. Kontogiannis, K.: Program representation and behavioural matching for localizing similar code fragments. In: Proc. Conf. Centre for Advanced Studies on Collaborative research (CASCON), IBM Press (1993) 194–205 [302]

293. Koppen, C., Störzer, M.: PCDiff: Attacking the fragile pointcut problem. In Gybels, K., Hanenberg, S., Herrmann, S., Wloka, J., eds.: European Interactive Workshop on Aspects in Software (EIWAS). (September 2004) [228, 230]

294. Koschke, R., Falke, R., Frenzel, P.: Clone detection using abstract syntax suffix trees. In: Proc. Working Conf. Reverse Engineering (WCRE), IEEE Computer Society Press (2006) 253–262 [28]

295. Koschke, R., Girard, J.F.: An intermediate representation for reverse engineering analyses. In: Proc. Working Conf. Reverse Engineering (WCRE), IEEE Computer Society Press (1998) 241–250 [295]

296. Koskinen, J.: Software maintenance costs.
http://www.cs.jyu.fi/ koskinen/smcosts.htm (2003) [7]

297. Kramer, J., Magee, J.: The evolving philosophers problem: Dynamic change management. IEEE Trans. Software Engineering 16(11) (November 1990) 1293–1306 [9]

298. Krinke, J.: Identifying Similar Code with Program Dependence Graphs. In: Proc. Working Conf. Reverse Engineering (WCRE), IEEE Computer Society Press (2001) 301–309 [28, 29]

299. Kruchten, P.: The Rational Unified Process. An Introduction. Addison-Wesley (1998) [198]

300. Kulesza, U., Sant'Anna, C., Garcia, A., Coelho, R., von Staa, A., Lucena, C.: Quantifying the effects of aspect-oriented programming: A maintenance study. In: Proc. Int'l Conf. Software Maintenance (ICSM), IEEE Computer Society Press (2006) 223–233 [212]

301. Kung, D.C., Gao, J., Kung, C.H.: Testing Object-Oriented Software. IEEE Computer Society Press (1998) [174]

302. Laddad, R.: AOP@Work: AOP myths and realities – beyond hype and misunderstandings. Published as article in IBM's developerWorks series
http://www.ibm.com/developerworks (February 2006) [204]

303. Laguë, B., Proulx, D., Merlo, E.M., Mayrand, J., Hudepohl, J.: Assessing the benefits of incorporating function clone detection in a development process. In: Proc. Int'l Conf. Software Maintenance (ICSM), IEEE Computer Society Press (1997) 314–321 [15, 24, 25, 27]

304. Lämmel, R., Verhoef, C.: Semi-automatic Grammar Recovery. Software – Practice & Experience 31(15) (December 2001) 1395–1438 [131]

305. Lämmel, R.: Towards generic refactoring. In: Proc. ACM SIGPLAN workshop on Rule-based programming (RULE), ACM Press: New York NY (2002) 15–28 [93]

306. Lämmel, R.: Coupled software transformations (ext. abstract). In: Proc. Int'l Workshop on Software Evolution Transformations (SETra). (Nov. 2004) [116]

307. Lanubile, F., Mallardo, T.: Finding function clones in web applications. In: Proc. European Conf. Software Maintenance and Reengineering (CSMR). (2003) 379–386 [27]

308. Lanza, M.: The evolution matrix: Recovering software evolution using software visualization techniques. In: Proc. Int'l Workshop on Principles of Software Evolution (IWPSE), Vienna, Austria, ACM (September 2001) 37–42 [65, 66]

309. Lanza, M., Ducasse, S.: Polymetric views – a lightweight visual approach to reverse engineering. IEEE Trans. Software Engineering 29(9) (September 2003) 782–795 [32, 47, 61]

310. Lanza, M., Ducasse, S., Gall, H., Pinzger, M.: Codecrawler – an information visualization tool for program comprehension. In: Proc. Int'l Conf. Software Engineering (ICSE), ACM Press (2005) 672–673 [48]

311. Lanza, M., Marinescu, R.: Object-Oriented Metrics in Practice. Springer-Verlag (2006) [103, 104]

312. Larman, C., Victor R. Basili: Iterative and incremental development: A brief history. IEEE Computer 36(6) (June 2003) 47–56 [3]

313. Lauder, A., Kent, S.: More legacy system patterns. In Henderson, P., ed.: Systems engineering for business process change: new directions. Springer-Verlag, New York, NY, USA (2002) 225–240 [103]

314. Lawrence, M.: An examination of evolution dynamics. In: Proc. Int'l Conf. Software Engineering (ICSE), IEEE Computer Society Press (13–16 Sep 1982) 188–196 [265, 279]

315. Leclercq, M., Ozcan, A.E., Quema, V., Stefani, J.B.: Supporting heterogeneous architecture descriptions in an extensible toolset. Proc. Int'l Conf. Software Engineering (ICSE) (2007) 209–219 [236]

316. Lehman, M.M., Fernandez-Ramil, J.: Software evolution and feedback: Theory and practice. John Wiley & Sons, Chichester, U.K. (2006) 7–40 [266]

317. Lehman, M.M.: On understanding laws, evolution and conservation in the large program life cycle. Systems and Software 1(3) (1980) 213–221 [2, 173]

318. Lehman, M.M.: Programs, life cycles, and laws of software evolution. Proc. IEEE 68(9) (September 1980) 1060–1076 [2, 8]

319. Lehman, M.M.: Software's future: Managing evolution. IEEE Software 15(1) (January/February 1998) 40–44 [173]

320. Lehman, M.M., Belady, L.A.: Program Evolution: Processes of Software Change. Apic Studies In Data Processing. Academic Press (1985) [VII, 2, 82, 205, 264, 265, 270, 276, 287, 291, 295, 299]

321. Lehman, M.M., Ramil, J.F., Wernick, P., Perry, D.E., Turski, W.M.: Metrics and laws of software evolution – the nineties view. In: Proc. IEEE Symp. Software Metrics, IEEE Computer Society Press (1997) 20–32 [173]

322. Lehman, M., Ramil, J.F., Kahen, G.: Evolution as a noun and evolution as a verb. In: Proc. Workshop on Software and Organisation Co-evolution (SOCE). (July 2000) [4, 269]

323. Lehman, M., Ramil, J.: An overview of some lessons learnt in FEAST. In: Proc. Workshop on Empirical Studies of Software Maintenance (WESS). (October 2002) [266]

324. Leitao, A.M.: Detection of redundant code using R2D2. In: Proc. Workshop Source Code Analysis and Manipulation (SCAM), IEEE Computer Society Press (2003) 183–192 [28]

325. Lethbridge, T., Tichelaar, S., Plödereder, E.: The Dagstuhl middle metamodel: A schema for reverse engineering. Electronic Notes in Theoretical Computer Science 94 (2004) 7–18 [163]

326. Li, P.L., Herbsleb, J.D., Shaw, M.: Finding predictors of field defects for open source software systems in commonly available data sources: A case study of OpenBSD. In: Proc. IEEE Symp. Software Metrics, IEEE Computer Society Press (2005) 32 [87]

327. Li, Z., Lu, S., Myagmar, S., Zhou, Y.: CP-Miner: A tool for finding copy-paste and related bugs in operating system code. In: Operating System Design and Implementation. (2004) 289–302 [28]

328. Li, Z., Lu, S., Myagmar, S., Zhou, Y.: Copy-paste and related bugs in large-scale software code. IEEE Trans. Software Engineering 32(3) (March 2006) 176–192 [19, 23]

329. Lientz, B.P., Swanson, E.B.: Software maintenance management: a study of the maintenance of computer application software in 487 data processing organizations. Addison-Wesley (1980) [4, 7, 173]

330. Liu, Y., Stroulia, E., Erdogmus, H.: Understanding the open-source software development process: a case study with CVSChecker. In: Proc. Intl'l Conf. on Open Source Systems, NRC 47453 (2005) 154–161 [49, 50]

331. Lopez-Herrejon, R.E., Batory, D.S., Lengauer, C.: A disciplined approach to aspect composition. In: Proc. ACM SIGPLAN Symposium on Partial Evaluation and Program Manipulation (PEPM), New York, NY, USA, ACM Press (2006) 68–77 [229, 260]

332. Löwe, M., Korff, M., Wagner, A.: An algebraic framework for the transformation of attributed graphs. In Sleep, R., Plasmeijer, M., van Eekelen, M., eds.: Term Graph Rewriting: Theory and Practice. John Wiley & Sons (1993) 185–199 [148]
333. Lucia, A.D., Francese, R., Scanniello, G., Tortora, G., Vitiello, N.: A strategy and an Eclipse based environment for the migration of legacy systems to multi-tier web-based architectures. In: Proc. Int'l Conf. Software Maintenance (ICSM), Washington, DC, USA, IEEE Computer Society Press (2006) 438–447 [108]
334. Luckham, D.C., Kenney, J.J., Augustin, L.M., Vera, J., Bryan, D., Mann, W.: Specification and analysis of system architecture using Rapide. IEEE Trans. Software Engineering 21(4) (1995) 336–355 [235]
335. Lynch, N.A., Tuttle, M.R.: An introduction to input/output automata. CWI Quarterly 2(3) (1989) 219–246 [246]
336. Mackinnon, T., Freeman, S., Craig, P.: Endotesting: Unit testing with mock objects. In: Proc. Int'l Conf. eXtreme Programming and Flexible Processes in Software Engineering (XP). (2000) [180]
337. Madhavji, N.H.: Compare: a collusion detector for Pascal. Techniques et Sciences Informatiques 4(6) (1985) 489–497 [34]
338. Madhavji, N.H., Ramil, J.F., Perry, D.E.: Software Evolution and Feedback: Theory and Practice. John Wiley & Sons (2006) [4, 7, 292, 299]
339. Magee, J.: Behavioral analysis of software architectures using ltsa. In: Proc. Int'l Conf. Software Engineering (ICSE), IEEE Computer Society Press (1999) 634–637 [235]
340. Magee, J., Kramer, J., Giannakopoulou, D.: Behaviour analysis of software architectures. In: Proc. IEEE/IFIP Working Conf. Software Architecture (WICSA), Deventer, The Netherlands, The Netherlands, Kluwer Academic Publishers (1999) 35–50 [235, 237]
341. Maier, M.W., Emery, D., Hilliard, R.: ANSI-IEEE 1471 and systems engineering. Systens Engineering 7(3) (2004) 257–270 [243]
342. Malton, A.J.: The software migration barbell. In: ASERC Workshop on Software Architecture. (August 2001) [108]
343. Manber, U.: Finding similar files in a large file system. In: Proc. Winter Usenix Technical Conf. (1994) 1–10 [34]
344. Marchesi, M., Succi, G., Wells, D., Williams, L.: Extreme Programming Perspectives. Addison-Wesley (2003) [179]
345. Marcus, A., Maletic, J.: Identification of high-level concept clones in source code. In: Proc. Int'l Conf. Automated Software Engineering (ASE). (2001) 107–114 [26]
346. Marick, B.: The Craft of Software Testing. Prentice Hall (1995) [174, 192, 201]
347. Marin, M., Moonen, L., van Deursen, A.: A common framework for aspect mining based on crosscutting concern sorts. In Sim, S.E., Di Penta, M., eds.: Proc. Working Conf. Reverse Engineering (WCRE), IEEE Computer Society Press (2006) 29–38 [212, 213]
348. Marin, M., van Deursen, A., Moonen, L.: Identifying aspects using fan-in analysis. In: Proc. Working Conf. Reverse Engineering (WCRE), Washington, DC, USA, IEEE Computer Society Press (2004) 132–141 [109]
349. Marks, E., Bell, M.: Service-Oriented Architecture (SOA): A Planning and Implementation Guide for Business and Technology. John Wiley & Sons (2006) [140]
350. Martin, J., Müller, H.A.: Strategies for migration from C to Java. In: Proc. European Conf. Software Maintenance and Reengineering (CSMR). (2001) 200–209 [108]
351. Martin, R.C.: Agile Software Development: Principles, Patterns, and Practices. Prentice Hall (2002) [3, 8]
352. Maruyama, K.: Automated method-extraction refactoring by using block-based slicing. In: Proc. Symp. Software Reusability (SSR), ACM Press (2001) 31–40 [219]

353. Mayrand, J., Leblanc, C., Merlo, E.: Experiment on the automatic detection of function clones in a software system using metrics. In: Proc. Int'l Conf. Software Maintenance (ICSM). (1996) 244–253 [27, 29, 30]

354. McCabe, T.J.: A complexity measure. IEEE Trans. Software Engineering 2(4) (1976) 308–320 [276, 278, 297]

355. McCoy, D., Natis, Y.: Service-oriented architecture: Mainstream straight ahead. Technical Report LE-19-7652, Gartner Research (April 2003) [139]

356. McCreight, E.: A space-economical suffix tree construction algorithm. Journal of the ACM 32(2) (1976) 262–272 [27]

357. McEachen, N., Alexander, R.T.: Distributing classes with woven concerns: an exploration of potential fault scenarios. In: Proc. Int'l Conf. Aspect-Oriented Software Development (AOSD), ACM Press (2005) 192–200 [200]

358. Medvidovic, N., Taylor, R.N.: A classification and comparison framework for software architecture description languages. IEEE Trans. Software Engineering 26(1) (2000) 70–93 [233, 235]

359. Meier, A.: Providing database migration tools – a practitioner's approach. In: Proc. Int'l Conf. Very Large Data Bases (VLDB), San Francisco, CA, USA, Morgan Kaufmann (1995) 635–641 [110]

360. Meier, A., Dippold, R., Mercerat, J., Muriset, A., Untersinger, J.C., Eckerlin, R., Ferrara, F.: Hierarchical to relational database migration. IEEE Software 11(3) (1994) 21–27 [110]

361. Menhoudj, K., Ou-Halima, M.: Migrating data-oriented applications to a relational database management system. In: Proc. Int'l Workshop on Advances in Databases and Information Systems, Moscow (1996) [110]

362. Mens, K., Brichau, J., Gybels, K.: Managing the evolution of aspect-oriented software with model-based pointcuts. In Thomas, D., ed.: Proc. European Conf. Object-Oriented Programming (ECOOP). Volume 4067 of Lecture Notes in Computer Science., Springer-Verlag (2006) 501–525 [228, 230, 261]

363. Mens, K., Kellens, A., Pluquet, F., Wuyts, R.: Co-evolving code and design with intensional views – a case study. Computer Languages, Systems and Structures 32(2–3) (July-October 2006) 140–156 Special Issue: Smalltalk. [10, 213, 216]

364. Mens, K., Tourwé, T.: Delving Source Code with Formal Concept Analysis. Computer Languages, Systems and Structures 31(3) (2004) 183–197 [211]

365. Mens, T., Demeyer, S., Janssens, D.: Formalising behaviour preserving program transformations. In Corradini, A., Ehrig, H., Kreowski, H.J., Rozenberg, G., eds.: Proc. Int'l Conf. Graph Transformation (ICGT). Volume 2505 of Lecture Notes in Computer Science., Springer-Verlag (2002) 286–301 [94, 146, 148]

366. Mens, T., Mens, K., Tourwé, T.: Aspect-oriented software evolution. ERCIM News (58) (July 2004) 36–37 [245]

367. Mens, T., Taentzer, G., Müller, D.: Challenges in model refactoring. In: Proc. 1st Workshop on Refactoring Tools, University of Berlin (2007) [96]

368. Mens, T., Taentzer, G., Runge, O.: Analyzing refactoring dependencies using graph transformation. Software and Systems Modeling (2007) [152, 165]

369. Mens, T., Tourwé, T.: A survey of software refactoring. IEEE Trans. Software Engineering 30(2) (February 2004) 126–162 [94]

370. Mens, T., Van Eetvelde, N., Demeyer, S., Janssens, D.: Formalizing refactorings with graph transformations. Software Maintenance and Evolution: Research and Practice 17(4) (July/August 2005) 247–276 [94, 148, 159]

371. Mens, T., Wermelinger, M., Ducasse, S., Demeyer, S., Hirschfeld, R., Jazayeri, M.: Challenges in software evolution. In: Proc. Int'l Workshop on Principles of Software Evolution (IWPSE). (2005) [4]

372. Meszaros, G.: XUnit Test Patterns: Refactoring Test Code. Addison-Wesley (2007) [184]

373. Missaoui, R., Godin, R., Sahraoui, H.: Migrating to an object-oriented database using semantic clustering and transformation rules. Data Knowledge Engineering 27(1) (1998) 97–113 [110]

374. Monden, A., Nakae, D., Kamiya, T., Sato, S., Matsumoto, K.: Software quality analysis by code clones in industrial legacy software. In: Proc. IEEE Symp. Software Metrics. (2002) 87–94 [22]

375. Monteiro, M.P., Fernandes, J.M.: Object-to-aspect refactorings for feature extraction. In: Proc. Int'l Conf. Aspect-Oriented Software Development (AOSD), ACM Press (2004) [218, 219, 220, 222]

376. Monteiro, M.P., Fernandes, J.M.: Towards a catalog of aspect-oriented refactorings. In: Proc. Int'l Conf. Aspect-Oriented Software Development (AOSD), ACM Press (2005) 111–122 [218, 228, 229]

377. Moonen, L.: Generating robust parsers using island grammars. In: Proc. Working Conf. Reverse Engineering (WCRE), IEEE Computer Society Press (Oct. 2001) 13–22 [27]

378. Moonen, L.: Exploring Software Systems. PhD thesis, Faculty of Natural Sciences, Mathematics, and Computer Science, University of Amsterdam (December 2002) [177]

379. Moore, I.: Jester, JUnit test tester. In: Proc. Int'l Conf. eXtreme Programming and Flexible Processes in Software Engineering (XP). (2001) 84–87 [192]

380. Mossienko, M.: Automated Cobol to Java recycling. In: Proc. European Conf. Software Maintenance and Reengineering (CSMR), Washington, DC, USA, IEEE Computer Society Press (2003) 40–50 [139]

381. Muccini, H., Dias, M., Richardson, D.J.: Software architecture-based regression testing. Systems and Software 79(10) (2006) 1379–1396 [199]

382. Muller, A., Caron, O., Carré, B., Vanwormhoudt, G.: On some properties of parameterized model application. In: Proc. European Conf. Model-Driven Architectures: Foundations and Applications. (2005) 130–144 [259]

383. Müller, H.: Understanding software systems using reverse engineering technologies: Research and practice.
http://www.rigi.csc.uvic.ca/UVicRevTut/UVicRevTut.html (1996) ICSE-18 Tutorial. [177, 302]

384. Munson, J.C., Elbaum, S.G.: Code churn: A measure for estimating the impact of code change. In: Proc. Int'l Conf. Software Maintenance (ICSM), Washington, DC, USA, IEEE Computer Society Press (1998) 24–31 [82, 87]

385. Murphy, G.C., Notkin, D.: Reengineering with reflexion models: A case study. IEEE Computer 8 (1997) 29–36 [99]

386. Murphy, G.C., Notkin, D., Sullivan, K.: Software reflexion models: Bridging the gap between source and high-level models. SIGSOFT Software Engineering Notes 20(4) (1995) 18–28 [99]

387. Murray, A., Lethbridge, T.C.: Presenting micro-theories of program comprehension in pattern form. In: Int'l Workshop on Program Comprehension (IWPC), Washington, DC, USA, IEEE Computer Society Press (2005) 45–54 [100]

388. Musa, J.D.: Software Reliability Engineering. McGraw-Hill (1998) [72]

389. Nagappan, N., Ball, T.: Use of relative code churn measures to predict system defect density. In: Proc. Int'l Conf. Software Engineering (ICSE). (2005) 284–292 [82, 83, 84]

390. Nagappan, N., Ball, T., Zeller, A.: Mining metrics to predict component failures. In: Proc. Int'l Conf. Software Engineering (ICSE), New York, NY, USA, ACM Press (2006) 452–461 [75, 76]

391. Naur, P., Randell, B.: Software Engineering. NATO, Scientific Affairs Division, Brussels (1969) [1, 304]

392. Nelson, E.: Estimating software reliability from test data. Microelectronics and Reliability **17**(1) (1978) 67–74 [73]

393. Newcomer, E., Lomow, G.: Understanding SOA with Web Services. Addison-Wesley Professional (2004) [8, 140]

394. Nickell, E., Smith, I.: Extreme programming and software clones. In: Proc. Working Conf. Reverse Engineering (WCRE), IEEE Computer Society Press (2003) [36]

395. Niere, J., Schäfer, W., Wadsack, J.P., Wendehals, L., Welsh, J.: Towards pattern-based design recovery. In: Proc. Int'l Conf. Software Engineering (ICSE), IEEE Computer Society Press (May 2002) 338–348 [163]

396. Object Management Group: Meta object facility (MOF) specification. formal/2002-04-03 (April 2002) [301]

397. Object Management Group: Interface definition language, version 2.0. http://www.omg.org/gettingstarted/omg_idl.htm (2003) [236]

398. Object Management Group: Unified Modeling Language: Superstructure version 2.0. formal/2005-07-04 (August 2005) [148, 240, 308]

399. Object Management Group: UML 2 Object Constraint Language Specification. (March 2006) Version 2.0. [241]

400. O'Brien, L., Smith, D., Lewis, G.: Supporting migration to services using software architecture reconstruction. In: Proc. IEEE Int'l Workshop on Software Technology and Engineering Practice (STEP). (2005) 81–91 [109]

401. Ogawa, M.: Visualizing the Eclipse bug data. http://vis.cs.ucdavis.edu/~ogawa/eclipse/ (January 2007) [70]

402. Ohlsson, M.C., von Mayrhauser, A., McGuire, B., Wohlin, C.: Code decay analysis of legacy software through successive releases. In: Proc. IEEE Aerospace Conf. (1999) 69–81 [87]

403. Oman, P.W., Lewis, T.G.: Milestones in Software Evolution. IEEE Computer Society Press (1990) [2]

404. Opdyke, W.F.: Refactoring: A Program Restructuring Aid in Designing Object-Oriented Application Frameworks. PhD thesis, University of Illinois at Urbana-Champaign (1992) [93, 94, 218, 223]

405. Opdyke, W.F., Johnson, R.E.: Creating abstract superclasses by refactoring. In: Proc. ACM Computer Science Conf., ACM Press (1993) 66–73 [93]

406. Oreizy, P., Medvidovic, N., Taylor, R.N.: Architecture-based runtime software evolution. In: Proc. Int'l Conf. Software Engineering (ICSE), Washington, DC, USA, IEEE Computer Society Press (1998) 177–186 [241]

407. Organization for the Advancement of Structured Information Standards: Reference Model for Service Oriented Architecture 1.0. OASIS (July 2006) [140]

408. Ostrand, T.J., Weyuker, E.J., Bell, R.M.: Where the bugs are. In: Proc. ACM SIGSOFT Int'l Symp. Software Testing and Analysis (ISSTA), New York, NY, USA, ACM Press (2004) 86–96 [82, 87]

409. Papakonstantinou, Y., Gupta, A., Garcia-Molina, H., Ullman, J.: A query translation scheme for rapid implementation of wrappers. In: Proc. Int'l Conf. Declarative and Object-oriented Databases. (1995) [123]

410. Parnas, D.L.: Software aging. In: Proc. Int'l Conf. Software Engineering (ICSE), IEEE Computer Society Press (1994) 279–287 Sorento, Italy, May 16-21. [2]

411. Paulson, J.W., Succi, G., Eberlein, A.: An empirical study of open-source and closed-source software products. IEEE Trans. Software Engineering **30**(4) (2004) 246–256 [271, 273, 283]

412. Perez, J., Navarro, E., Letelier, P., Ramos, I.: A modelling proposal for aspect-oriented software architectures. In: Proc. IEEE Int'l Symp. and Workshop on Engineering of Computer Based Systems (ECBS), Washington, DC, USA, IEEE Computer Society Press (2006) 32–41 [244]

413. Pessemier, N., Seinturier, L., Coupaye, T., Duchien, L.: A model for developing component-based and aspect-oriented systems. In: Proc. Int'l Symp. Software Composition (SC). Volume 4089 of Lecture Notes in Computer Science., Vienna, Austria, Springer-Verlag (mar 2006) 259–273 [244]

414. Pfleeger, S.L.: Software Engineering: Theory and Practice. Prentice Hall (1998) [266]

415. Pickin, S., Jard, C., Jéron, T., Jézéquel, J.M., Traon, Y.L.: Test synthesis from UML models of distributed software. IEEE Trans. Software Engineering **33**(4) (2007) 252–269 [199]

416. Pigoski, T.M.: Practical Software Maintenance: Best Practices for Managing your Software Investment. John Wiley & Sons (1997) [7]

417. Pinzger, M., Gall, H., Fischer, M., Lanza, M.: Visualizing multiple evolution metrics. In: Proc. ACM Symp. Software Visualization, St. Louis, Missouri, ACM Press (2005) 67–75 [60]

418. Pirzada, S.S.: A Statistical Examination of the Evolution of the Unix System. PhD thesis, Department of Computing, Imperial College, London (1988) [270]

419. Plump, D.: Hypergraph rewriting: Critical pairs and undecidability of confluence. In Sleep, M.R., Plasmeijer, M.J., van Eekelen, M.C., eds.: Term Graph Rewriting: Theory and Practice. John Wiley & Sons (1993) 201–213 [150]

420. Prechelt, L., Malpohl, G., Philippsen, M.: JPlag: Finding plagiarisms among a set of programs. Technical report, University of Karlsruhe, Department of Informatics (2000) [29, 34]

421. Putnam, L.: A general empirical solution to the macrosoftware sizing and estimating problem. IEEE Trans. Software Engineering **4**(4) (1978) 345–61 [195]

422. Quintero, C.E.C., Rodríguez, M.P.R., de la Fuente, P., Barrio-Solórzano, M.: Architectural aspects of architectural aspects. In: Proc. European Workshop on Software Architecture (EWSA). (2005) 247–262 [245]

423. Rahm, E., Do, H.: Data cleaning: Problems and current approaches. Data Engineering Bulletin **23** (2000) 3–13 [121]

424. Rajlich, V.: A model for change propagation based on graph rewriting. In: Proc. Int'l Conf. Software Maintenance (ICSM), IEEE Computer Society Press (1997) 84–91 [6]

425. Rajlich, V., Gosavi, P.: Incremental change in object-oriented programming. IEEE Software **21**(4) (2004) 62–69 [6]

426. Ramalingam, G., Komondoor, R., Field, J., Sinha, S.: Semantics-based reverse engineering of object-oriented data models. In: Proc. Int'l Conf. Software Engineering (ICSE), New York, NY, USA, ACM Press (2006) 192–201 [163]

427. Ramil, J.F., Lehman, M.M.: Metrics of software evolution as effort predictors – a case study. In: Proc. Int'l Conf. Software Maintenance (ICSM). (October 2000) 163–172 [7]

428. Ramil, J., Capiluppi, A.: Metric-based studies of open source software evolution. Presentation Charts, Research Seminar, University of Leicester, UK (November 2004) [277]

429. Ramil, J.F., Smith, N.: Qualitative simulation of models of software evolution. Software Process: Improvement and Practice **7**(3–4) (September–December 2002) 95–112 [279, 280]

430. Randell, B.: System structure for software fault tolerance. IEEE Trans. Software Engineering **1**(2) (1975) 221–232 [80]

431. Rashid, A., Sawyer, P., Moreira, A.M.D., Araújo, J.: Early aspects: A model for aspect-oriented requirements engineering. In: Proc. Joint Int'l Conf. Requirements Engineering (RE), IEEE Computer Society Press (2002) 199–202 [213]

432. Ratzinger, J., Fischer, M., Gall, H.: Evolens: Lens-view visualizations of evolution data. In: Proc. Int'l Workshop on Principles of Software Evolution (IWPSE), Lisbon, Portugal, IEEE Computer Society Press (September 2005) 103–112 [59]

433. Ratzinger, J., Fischer, M., Gall, H.: Improving evolvability through refactoring. In: Proc. Int'l Workshop on Mining Software Repositories (MSR), New York, NY, USA, ACM Press (2005) 1–5 [59]

434. Raymond, E.S.: The cathedral and the bazaar: musings on Linux and open source by an accidental revolutionary. Revised edn. O'Reilly & Associates, Inc. (2001) [269]

435. Reddy, Y.R., Ghosh, S., France, R.B., Straw, G., Bieman, J.M., McEachen, N., Song, E., Georg, G.: Directives for composing aspect-oriented design class models. Trans. Aspect-Oriented Software Development (2006) 75–105 [259, 260]

436. Reiss, S.P.: Constraining software evolution. In: Proc. Int'l Conf. Software Maintenance (ICSM), IEEE Computer Society Press (2002) 162–171 [174]

437. Rieger, M., Ducasse, S., Lanza, M.: Insights into system-wide code duplication. In: Proc. Working Conf. Reverse Engineering (WCRE), IEEE Computer Society Press (2004) 100–109 [32]

438. Rieger, M.: Effective Clone Detection Without Language Barriers. Dissertation, University of Bern, Switzerland (2005) [30]

439. Riel, A.J.: Object-Oriented Design Heuristics. Addison-Wesley, Boston MA (April 1996) [57, 102]

440. Roberts, D., Brant, J., Johnson, R.E.: A refactoring tool for Smalltalk. Theory and Practice of Object Systems **3**(4) (1997) 253–263 [93]

441. Roberts, D.B.: Practical Analysis for Refactoring. PhD thesis, University of Illinois at Urbana-Champaign (1999) [94, 95]

442. Robillard, M.P., Murphy, G.C.: Concern graphs: Finding and describing concerns using structural program dependencies. In: Proc. Int'l Conf. Software Engineering (ICSE), ACM Press (2002) 406–416 [213, 216]

443. Robles, G., Amor, J.J., Gonzalez-Barahona, J.M., Herraiz, I.: Evolution and growth in large libre software projects. In: Proc. Int'l Workshop on Principles of Software Evolution (IWPSE), Lisbon, IEEE Computer Society Press (September 2005) 165–174 [270]

444. Rosenblum, D.S., Weyuker, E.J.: Using coverage information to predict the cost-effectiveness of regression testing strategies. IEEE Trans. Software Engineering **23**(3) (1997) 146–156 [7, 200]

445. Rothermel, G., Harrold, M.J.: Empirical studies of a safe regression test selection technique. IEEE Trans. Software Engineering **24**(6) (1998) 401–419 [200, 202]

446. Royce, W.W.: Managing the development of large software systems: concepts and techniques. In: Proc. IEEE WESTCON, IEEE Computer Society Press (August 1970) Reprinted in Proc. Int'l Conf. Software Engineering (ICSE) 1989, ACM Press, pp. 328-338. [1]

447. Runeson, P., Andersson, C., Höst, M.: Test processes in software product evolution: a qualitative survey on the state of practice. Software Maintenance and Evolution: Research and Practice **15**(1) (2003) 41–59 [174]

448. Saff, D., Ernst, M.D.: An experimental evaluation of continuous testing during development. In: Proc. ACM/SIGSOFT Int'l Symp. Software Testing and Analysis (ISSTA), ACM (2004) 76–85 [201]

449. Sahraoui, H.A., Lounis, H., Melo, W., Mili, H.: A concept formation based approach to object identification in procedural code. Automated Software Engineering 6(4) (1999) 387–410 [109]

450. Scacchi, W., Feller, J., Fitzgerald, B., Hissam, S., Lakhani, K.: Understanding free/open source software development processes. Software Process: Improvement and Practice 11(2) (March/April 2006) 95–105 [286, 287]

451. Schärli, N., Ducasse, S., Nierstrasz, O., Black, A.: Traits: Composable units of behavior. In: Proc. European Conf. Object-Oriented Programming (ECOOP). Volume 2743 of Lecture Notes in Computer Science., Springer-Verlag (July 2003) 248–274 [9]

452. Schleimer, S., Wilkerson, D.S., Aiken, A.: Winnowing: local algorithms for document fingerprinting. In: Proc. ACM SIGMOD Conf. (2003) 76–85 [29, 34]

453. Schmidt, D.C.: Model-driven engineering. IEEE Computer 39(2) (2006) 25–31 [199]

454. Schneider, A.: JUnit best practices. Java World 12 (2000) [184]

455. Schröter, A., Zimmermann, T., Zeller, A.: Predicting component failures at design time. In: Proc. Int'l Symp. Empirical Software Engineering. (September 2006) 18–27 [70, 77, 79]

456. Schürr, A., Winter, A., Zündorf, A.: The PROGRES approach: Language and environment. In Ehrig, H., Engels, G., Kreowski, H.J., Rozenberg, G., eds.: Handbook of Graph Grammars and Computing by Graph Transformation: Applications, Languages, and Tools. Volume 3. World Scientific (1999) 487–550 [150]

457. Seacord, R.C., Plakosh, D., Lewis, G.A.: Modernizing Legacy Systems: Software Technologies, Engineering Processes, and Business Practices. 1st edn. Addison-Wesley Professional (2003) [7, 292]

458. Serrano, M.A., Carver, D.L., de Oca, C.M.: Reengineering legacy systems for distributed environments. Systems and Software 64(1) (2002) 37–55 [109]

459. Shaw, M., Garlan, D.: Software Architecture – Perspectives on an Emerging Discipline. Prentice Hall, Upper Saddle River, NJ, USA (1996) [297]

460. Shepherd, D., Pollock, L., Tourwé, T.: Using language clues to discover crosscutting concerns. In: Proc. workshop on Modeling and Analysis of Concerns in Software (MACS), New York, NY, USA, ACM Press (2005) 1–6 [211]

461. Smith, N., Capiluppi, A., Ramil, J.F.: A study of open source software evolution data using qualitative simulation. Software Process: Improvement and Practice 10(3) (July/September 2005) 287–300 [8, 279, 280]

462. Smith, N., Capiluppi, A., Ramil, J.F.: Agent-based simulation of open source evolution. Software Process: Improvement and Practice 11(4) (July/August 2006) 423–434 [279, 280, 281, 287]

463. Sneed, H., Sneed, S.: Creating web services from legacy host programs. In: Proc. Workshop on Website Evolution (WSE), Los Alamitos, CA, USA, IEEE Computer Society Press (2003) 59–65 [139]

464. Sneed, H.M.: Encapsulation of legacy software: A technique for reusing legacy software components. Annals of Software Engineering 9(1-4) (2000) 293–313 [122]

465. Sneed, H.M.: Integrating legacy software into a service oriented architecture. In: Proc. European Conf. Software Maintenance and Reengineering (CSMR), Los Alamitos, CA, USA, IEEE Computer Society Press (2006) 3–14 [109, 168]

466. Sneed, H.: Estimating the costs of software maintenance tasks. In: Proc. Int'l Conf. Software Maintenance (ICSM), IEEE Computer Society Press (1995) 168–181 [7]

467. SOA, S.A.: Simple blog about service oriented architecture (SOA), its tooling and delivery or realisation.
http://soa-testing.blogspot.com (January 20 2007) [200]

468. Sommerville, I.: Software Engineering. 6th edn. Addison-Wesley (2001) [266]
469. Sourceforge: Emma.
    http://emma.sourcefourge.net (January 20 2007) [192]
470. Sourceforge: Jester.
    http://jester.sourcefourge.net (January 20 2007) [192]
471. Spanoudakis, G., Zisman, A.: Inconsistency management in software engineering: Survey and open research issues. In: Handbook of Software Engineering and Knowledge Engineering. World scientific (2001) 329–380 [10, 300]
472. Sprott, D., Wilkes, L.: Understanding service-oriented architecture. CBDI Forum (January 2004) [140]
473. Srivastava, A., Thiagarajan, J., Schertz, C.: Efficient integration testing using dependency analysis. Technical Report MSR-TR-2005-94, Microsoft Research (2005) [79]
474. Stahl, T., Völter, M.: Model Driven Software Development: Technology, Engineering, Management. John Wiley & Sons (2006) [8]
475. Stevens, P., Pooley, R.: System reengineering patterns. In: Proc. Foundations of Software Engineering Conf. (FSE), ACM-SIGSOFT (1998) 17–23 [98, 102]
476. Stewart, K.J., Darcy, D.P., Daniel, S.L.: Opportunities and challenges applying functional data analysis to the study of open source software evolution. Statistical Science 21(2) (September 06 2006) 167–178 [272, 274]
477. Stoerzer, M., Graf, J.: Using pointcut delta analysis to support evolution of aspect-oriented software. In: Proc. Int'l Conf. Software Maintenance (ICSM), IEEE Computer Society Press (2005) 653–656 [228, 230]
478. Stroulia, E., El-Ramly, M., Iglinski, P., Sorenson, P.: User interface reverse engineering in support of interface migration to the web. Automated Software Engineering 10(3) (2003) 271–301 [108]
479. Subramanyam, R., Krishnan, M.: Empirical analysis of CK metrics for object-oriented design complexity: Implications for software defects. IEEE Trans. Software Engineering 29(4) (2003) 297–310 [73, 74]
480. Subversion: Subversion.
    http://subversion.tigris.org (2006) [40]
481. Succi, G., Paulson, J.W., Eberlein, A.: Preliminary results from an empirical study on the growth of open source and commercial software products. In: Proc. Int'l Workshop on Economics-Driven Software Engineering Research, Toronto, Canada (14–15 May 2001) [8]
482. Sullivan, K., Griswold, W., Song, Y., Chai, Y., Shonle, M., Tewari, N., Rajan, H.: On the criteria to be used in decomposing systems into aspects. In: Proc. European Software Engineering Conf. and Foundations of Software Engineering (ESEC/FSE), ACM Press (2005) [228, 230]
483. Sun Microsystems: The SOA platform guide: Evaluate, extend, embrace. White Paper (February 2006) [140]
484. SWI-Prolog: Swi-prolog.
    http://www.swiprolog.org/ (2006) [258]
485. Synytskyy, N., Cordy, J.R., Dean, T.: Resolution of static clones in dynamic web pages. In: Proc. Workshop on Website Evolution (WSE). (2003) 49–56 [27]
486. Szyperski, C.: Component Software: Beyond Object-Oriented Programming. ACM Addison-Wesley (1998) [9]
487. Taentzer, G.: AGG.
    http://tfs.cs.tu-berlin.de/agg/index.html (2007) [150, 258]
488. Taentzer, G.: Tiger EMF Transformation.
    http://tfs.cs.tu-berlin.de/emftrans (2007) [158]

489. Tairas, R., Gray, J., Baxter, I.: Visualization of clone detection results. In: Proc. OOPSLA workshop on Eclipse technology eXchange. (2006) 50–54 [33, 34]

490. Tarr, P., Ossher, H., Harrison, W., Sutton, S.M.: N degrees of separation: multi-dimensional separation of concerns. In: Proc. Int'l Conf. Software Engineering (ICSE), IEEE Computer Society Press (1999) 107–119 [203, 216, 234, 299]

491. Taylor, R.N., Medvidovic, N., Anderson, K.M., Whitehead, E.J., Robbins, J.E., Nies, K.A., Oreizy, P., Dubrow, D.L.: A component- and message-based architectural style for GUI software. IEEE Trans. Software Engineering **22**(6) (1996) 390–406 [236]

492. Tekinerdogan, B., Aksit, M.: Deriving design aspects from canonical models. In Demeyer, S., Bosch, J., eds.: Workshop Reader of the 12th European Conf. Object-Oriented Programming (ECOOP). Lecture Notes in Computer Science, Springer-Verlag (1998) 410–413 [213]

493. Terekhov, A.A., Verhoef, C.: The realities of language conversions. IEEE Software **17**(6) (2000) 111–124 [108]

494. The Eclipse Foundation: Eclipse.
http://www.eclipse.org/ (2007) [165]

495. The Eclipse Foundation: Eclipse modeling framework.
http://www.eclipse.org/emf/ (2007) [167]

496. The JBoss Community: Drools 3.0.
http://labs.jboss.com/jbossrules/ (2007) [258]

497. Thiran, P., Hainaut, J.L., Houben, G.J., Benslimane, D.: Wrapper-based evolution of legacy information systems. ACM Trans. Software Engineering and Methodology **15**(4) (October 2006) 329–359 [123]

498. Tibermacine, C., Fleurquin, R., Sadou, S.: Preserving architectural choices throughout the component-based software development process. In: Proc. IEEE/IFIP Working Conf. Software Architecture (WICSA). (2005) 121–130 [241]

499. Tichelaar, S.: Modeling Object-Oriented Software for Reverse Engineering and Refactoring. PhD thesis, University of Bern (2001) [93, 94]

500. Tilley, S.R., Smith, D.B.: Perspectives on legacy system reengineering. Technical report, Software Engineering Institute, Carnegie Mellon University (1995) [107]

501. Tip, F., Kiezun, A., Baumer, D.: Refactoring for generalization using type constraints. In: Proc. ACM SIGPLAN Conf. Object-Oriented Programming, Systems, Languages and Applications (OOPSLA), New York, NY, USA, ACM Press (2003) 13–26 [94]

502. Tip, F., Snelting, G., Johnson, R., eds. In Tip, F., Snelting, G., Johnson, R., eds.: Schloss Dagstuhl: Program Analysis for Object-Oriented Evolution. (February 2003) http://www.dagstuhl.de/de/programm/kalender/semhp/?semid=-2003091. [93]

503. Tonella, P., Ceccato, M.: Aspect mining through the formal concept analysis of execution traces. In: Proc. Working Conf. Reverse Engineering (WCRE), Washington, DC, USA, IEEE Computer Society Press (2004) 112–121 [109]

504. Toomim, M., Begel, A., Graham, S.: Managing duplicated code with linked editing. In: Proc. IEEE Symp. Visual Languages: Human Centric Computing, IEEE Computer Society Press (2004) 173–180 [26]

505. Tourwé, T., Brichau, J., Gybels, K.: On the existence of the AOSD-evolution paradox. In Bergmans, L., Brichau, J., Tarr, P., Ernst, E., eds.: SPLAT: Software engineering Properties of Languages for Aspect Technologies. (March 2003) [226, 245, 261]

506. Tourwé, T., Mens, K.: Mining aspectual views using formal concept analysis. In: Proc. Workshop Source Code Analysis and Manipulation (SCAM), IEEE Computer Society Press (September 2004) 97–106 [109]

507. Tsai, W.T., Paul, R., Song, W., Cao, Z.: Coyote: An XML-based framework for web services testing. In: Proc. IEEE Int'l Symp. High Assurance Systems Engineering (HASE), IEEE Computer Society Press (2002) 173–174 [200]

508. Tu, Q.: On navigation and analysis of software architecture evolution. Master's thesis, University of Waterloo (1992) [34]

509. Tu, Q., Godfrey, M.W.: An integrated approach for studying architectural evolution. In: Int'l Workshop on Program Comprehension (IWPC), IEEE Computer Society Press (June 2002) 127–136 [35]

510. Cubranic, D., Murphy, G.C., Singer, J., Booth, K.S.: Learning from project history: a case study for software development. In: Proc. ACM Conf. on Computer supported cooperative work (CSCW), New York, NY, USA, ACM Press (2004) 82–91 [43]

511. Cubranic, D., Murphy, G.C., Singer, J., Booth, K.S.: Hipikat: A project memory for software development. IEEE Trans. Software Engineering **31**(6) (2005) 446–465 [43, 44]

512. Ueda, Y., Kamiya, T., Kusumoto, S., Inoue, K.: Gemini: Maintenance support environment based on code clone analysis. In: Proc. IEEE Symp. Software Metrics, IEEE Computer Society Press (2002) 67–76 [31]

513. van den Brand, M., Heering, J., Klint, P., Olivier, P.: Compiling language definitions: the ASF+SDF compiler. ACM Trans. Programming Languages and Systems **24**(4) (July 2002) 334–368 [164]

514. van den Brand, M., Klint, P.: ASF+SDF Meta-Environment User Manual. (2005) [129]

515. van den Brand, M., van Deursen, A., Heering, J., de Jong, H., de Jonge, M.T.K., Klint, P., Moonen, L., Olivier, P., Scheerder, J., Vinju, J., Visser, E., Visser, J.: The ASF+SDF Meta-Environment: A component-based language development environment. In Wilhelm, R., ed.: Proc. Int'l Conf. Compiler Construction (CC). Volume 2027 of Lecture Notes in Computer Science., Springer-Verlag (2001) 365–370 [129]

516. van Deursen, A.: Program comprehension risks and benefits in extreme programming. In: Proc. Working Conf. Reverse Engineering (WCRE), IEEE Computer Society Press (2001) 176–185 [174]

517. van Deursen, A., Kuipers, T.: Identifying objects using cluster and concept analysis. In: Proc. Int'l Conf. Software Engineering (ICSE), Los Alamitos, CA, USA, IEEE Computer Society Press (1999) 246–255 [109]

518. van Deursen, A., Moonen, L., van den Bergh, A., Kok, G.: Refactoring test code. In Marchesi, M., ed.: Proc. Int'l Conf. eXtreme Programming and Flexible Processes in Software Engineering (XP). (2001) [183, 186, 191]

519. Van Eetvelde, N., Janssens, D.: Extending graph transformation for refactoring. In: Proc. Int'l Conf. Graph Transformation (ICGT). Volume 3256 of Lecture Notes In Computer Science., Springer-Verlag (2004) 399–415 [94]

520. van Glabbeek, R.: The linear time – branching time spectrum I. The semantics of concrete, sequential processes. In J.A. Bergstra, A.P..S.S., ed.: Handbook of Process Algebra, Elsevier Science (2001) 3–99 [256]

521. Van Rompaey, B., Du Bois, B., Demeyer, S.: Characterizing the relative significance of a test smell. In: Proc. Int'l Conf. Software Maintenance (ICSM), IEEE Computer Society Press (2006) 391–400 [184]

522. Van Rysselberghe, F.: Lessons Learned Studying Historic Change Operations. PhD thesis, University of Antwerp (September 2007) [95]

523. van Rysselberghe F., M.R., Demeyer, S.: Detecting move operations in versioning information. In: Proc. European Conf. Software Maintenance and Reengineering (CSMR), IEEE Computer Society Press (2006) 271–278 [95]

524. Van Rysselberghe, F., Demeyer, S.: Reconstruction of successful software evolution using clone detection. In: Proc. Int'l Workshop on Principles of Software Evolution (IW-PSE). (2003) 126–130 [35]

525. Van Rysselberghe, F., Demeyer, S.: Evaluating clone detection techniques from a refactoring perspective. In: Proc. Int'l Conf. Automated Software Engineering (ASE). (2004) [30]

526. Vestal, S.: Fixed-priority sensitivity analysis for linear compute time models. IEEE Trans. Software Engineering **20**(4) (1994) [239]

527. Visaggio, G.: Ageing of a data-intensive legacy system: symptoms and remedies. Software Maintenance and Evolution: Research and Practice **13**(5) (2001) 281–308 [110]

528. Voinea, L., Telea, A.: CVSgrab: Mining the history of large software projects. In: Eurographics / IEEE VGTC Symp. Visualization (EuroVis), Lisbon, Portugal, IEEE VGTC,EG,, Eurographics (2006) 187–194 [51]

529. Voinea, L., Telea, A., van Wijk, J.J.: CVSscan: visualization of code evolution. In: Proc. ACM Symp. Software Visualization, New York, NY, USA, ACM Press (2005) 47–56 [51]

530. von Mayrhauser, A., Vans, A.M.: Program comprehension during software maintenance and evolution. IEEE Computer **28**(8) (August 1995) 44–55 [177]

531. Wahler, V., Seipel, D., von Gudenberg, J.W., Fischer, G.: Clone detection in source code by frequent itemset techniques. In: Proc. Workshop Source Code Analysis and Manipulation (SCAM). (2004) 128–135 [28]

532. Walenstein, A., Jyoti, N., Li, J., Yang, Y., Lakhotia, A.: Problems creating task-relevant clone detection reference data. In: Proc. Working Conf. Reverse Engineering (WCRE), IEEE Computer Society Press (2003) 285–294 [17]

533. Walenstein, A., Lakhotia, A., Koschke, R.: 2nd int'l workshop on detection of software clones: workshop report. SIGSOFT Software Engineering Notes **29**(2) (2004) 1–5 [36]

534. Warren, I.: The Renaissance of Legacy Systems: Method Support for Software-System Evolution. Springer-Verlag, Secaucus, NJ, USA (1999) [109]

535. Waters, R.C.: Program translation via abstraction and reimplementation. IEEE Trans. Software Engineering **14**(8) (1988) 1207–1228 [108]

536. Wattenberg, M.: Map of the market.
http://www.bewitched.com/ (1998) [70]

537. Wattenberg, M.: Arc diagrams: Visualizing structure in strings. In: Proc. InfoVis, IEEE Computer Society Press (2002) 10–17 [33]

538. Weiser, M.: Program slicing. IEEE Trans. Software Engineering **10**(4) (July 1984) 352–357 [138, 218]

539. Weyuker, E.J.: Component-based software engineering: Putting the pieces together. Addison-Wesley (2001) 499–512 [200]

540. Whittaker, J.: Markov Chain Techniques for Software Testing and Reliability Analysis. PhD thesis, Department of Computer Science, University of Tenn (1992) [73]

541. Wiederhold, G.: Modeling and system maintenance. In: Proc. Int'l Conf. Object-Oriented and Entity-Relationship Modeling, Berlin (1995) [107]

542. Wiki, C.: Refactor broken unit tests.
http://c2.com/cgi/wiki?RefactorBrokenUnitTests (January 20 2007) [184]

543. Wilkes, L., Veryard, R.: Service-oriented architecture: Considerations for agile systems. CBDI Forum (April 2004) [140, 143]

544. World Wide Web Consortium (W3C): Web services glossary.
http://www.w3.org/TR/ws-gloss/ (February 2004) [305]

545. Wu, B., Lawless, D., Bisbal, J., Grimson, J., Wad, V., O'Sullivan, D., Richardson, R.: Legacy system migration: A legacy data migration engine. In Czechoslovak Computer Experts, ed.: Proc. Int'l Database Conf. (DATASEM), Brno, Czech Republic (1997) 129–138 [111]

546. Wu, B., Lawless, D., Bisbal, J., Richardson, R., Grimson, J., Wade, V., O'Sullivan, D.: The butterfly methodology: A gateway-free approach for migrating legacy information systems. In: Proc. IEEE Conf. Engineering of Complex Computer Systems, Italy (September 1997) [107]

547. Wu, J.: Open Source Software Evolution and Its Dynamics. PhD thesis, University of Waterloo, Ontario, Canada (2006) [275]

548. Wu, J., Spitzer, C.W., Hassan, A.E., Holt, R.C.: Evolution spectrographs: Visualizing punctuated change in software evolution. In: Proc. Int'l Workshop on Principles of Software Evolution (IWPSE), Kyoto, Japan, IEEE Computer Society Press (September 2004) 57–66 [66, 275, 276]

549. Xie, T., Zhao, J.: A framework and tool supports for generating test inputs of AspectJ programs. In: Proc. Int'l Conf. Aspect-Oriented Software Development (AOSD). (2006) 190–201 [223]

550. Xie, Y., Engler, D.: Using redundancies to find errors. In: Proc. Foundations of Software Engineering Conf. (FSE), ACM Press (2002) 51–60 [16]

551. Xie, Y., Engler, D.: Using redundancies to find errors. IEEE Trans. Software Engineering **29**(10) (October 2003) 915–928 [16]

552. Xing, Z., Stroulia, E.: Refactoring detection based on UMLDiff change-facts queries. In: Proc. Working Conf. Reverse Engineering (WCRE), IEEE Computer Society Press (2003) 263–274 [35]

553. Xing, Z., Stroulia, E.: Analyzing the evolutionary history of the logical design of object-oriented software. IEEE Trans. Software Engineering **31**(10) (October 2005) 850–868 [35]

554. Xing, Z., Stroulia, E.: Refactoring practice: How it is and how it should be supported – an Eclipse case study. In: Proc. Int'l Conf. Software Maintenance (ICSM), IEEE Computer Society Press (2006) 458–468 [95]

555. Xu, D., Xu, W.: State-based incremental testing of aspect-oriented programs. In: Proc. Int'l Conf. Aspect-Oriented Software Development (AOSD), ACM Press (2006) 180–189 [223]

556. Yan, H., Garlan, D., Schmerl, B., Aldrich, J., Kazman, R.: Discotect: A system for discovering architectures from running systems. In: Proc. Int'l Conf. Software Engineering (ICSE), Edinburgh, Scotland (23-28 May 2004) [235, 236]

557. Yang, W.: Identifying syntactic differences between two programs. Software – Practice and Experience **21**(7) (July 1991) 739–755 [28]

558. Yasumatsu, K., Doi, N.: SPiCE: A system for translating Smalltalk programs into a C environment. IEEE Trans. Software Engineering **21**(11) (1995) 902–912 [108]

559. Yau, S.S., Colofello, J.S., MacGregor, T.: Ripple effect analysis of software maintenance. In: Proc. Int'l Computer Software and Applications Conf. (COMPSAC), IEEE Computer Society Press (1978) 60–65 [2, 6]

560. Yeh, A.S., Harris, D.R., Reubenstein, H.B.: Recovering abstract data types and object instances from a conventional procedural language. In: Proc. Working Conf. Reverse Engineering (WCRE), Washington, DC, USA, IEEE Computer Society (1995) 227 [109]

561. Ying, A.T.T., Murphy, G.C., Ng, R., Chu-Carroll, M.C.: Predicting source code changes by mining change history. IEEE Trans. Software Engineering **30**(9) (September 2004) 574–586 [59]

562. Zaidman, A., Van Rompaey, B., Demeyer, S., Van Deursen, A.: Mining Software Repositories to Study Co-Evolution of Production and Test Code. Proceedings of the 1st International Conference on Software Testing, Verification, and Validation (ICST), IEEE Computer Society (2008) [201]

563. Zhang, C., Jacobsen, H.: Extended aspect mining tool.
http://www.eecg.utoronto.ca/~czhang/amtex (August 2002) [213]

564. Zhang, C., Jacobsen, H.A.: PRISM is research in aspect mining. In: Proc. ACM SIG-PLAN Conf. Object-Oriented Programming, Systems, Languages and Applications (OOPSLA), ACM Press (2004) 20–21 [213]

565. Zhang, Z., Yang, H., Chu, W.C.: Extracting reusable object-oriented legacy code segments with combined formal concept analysis and slicing techniques for service integration. In: Proc. Int'l Conf. Software Quality (QSIC), Washington, DC, USA, IEEE Computer Society Press (2006) 385–392 [168]

566. Zimmermann, T., Weißgerber, P.: Preprocessing CVS data for fine-grained analysis. In: Proc. Int'l Workshop on Mining Software Repositories (MSR), Los Alamitos CA, IEEE Computer Society Press (2004) 2–6 [40, 53]

567. Zimmermann, T., Weißgerber, P., Diehl, S., Zeller, A.: Mining version histories to guide software changes. In: Proc. Int'l Conf. Software Engineering (ICSE), Los Alamitos CA, IEEE Computer Society Press (2004) 563–572 [59]

568. Zou, L., Godfrey, M.: Detecting merging and splitting using origin analysis. In: Proc. Working Conf. Reverse Engineering (WCRE), IEEE Computer Society Press (2003) 146–154 [16, 35]

569. Zou, Y., Kontogiannis, K.: A framework for migrating procedural code to object-oriented platforms. In: Proc. IEEE Asia-Pacific Software Engineering Conf. (APSEC), Los Alamitos, CA, USA, IEEE Computer Society Press (2001) 408–418 [109]

570. Zowghi, D., Gervasi, V.: On the interplay between consistency, completeness and correctness in requirements evolution. Information and Software Technology **45**(14) (2003) 993–1009 [8]

571. Zowghi, D., Offen, R.: A logical framework for modeling and reasoning about the evolution of requirements. In: Proc. IEEE Int'l Symp. Requirements Engineering, IEEE Computer Society Press (1997) 247–259 [8]

Index